CASES ON
CRIMINAL LAW

CASES
ON
CRIMINAL LAW

BY

RUPERT CROSS, F.B.A., D.C.L.

SOLICITOR

Vinerian Professor of English Law in the University of Oxford and Fellow of All Souls College, Oxford

AND

P. ASTERLEY JONES, LL.B.

SOLICITOR

Principal Lecturer in Law at the City of Birmingham Polytechnic

FIFTH EDITION

LONDON

BUTTERWORTHS

1973

ENGLAND: BUTTERWORTH & CO. (PUBLISHERS) LTD.
LONDON: 88 KINGSWAY, WC2B 6AB

AUSTRALIA: BUTTERWORTHS PTY. LTD.
SYDNEY: 586 PACIFIC HIGHWAY, CHATSWOOD, NSW 2067
MELBOURNE: 343 LITTLE COLLINS STREET, 3000
BRISBANE: 240 QUEEN STREET, 4000

CANADA: BUTTERWORTH & CO. (CANADA) LTD.
TORONTO: 14 CURITY AVENUE, 374

NEW ZEALAND: BUTTERWORTHS OF NEW ZEALAND LTD.
WELLINGTON: 26/28 WARING TAYLOR STREET, 1

SOUTH AFRICA: BUTTERWORTH & CO. (SOUTH AFRICA) (PTY.) LTD.
DURBAN: 152/154 GALE STREET

First Edition 1949
Second Edition May 1953
Third Edition June 1962
Fourth Edition September 1968
Fifth Edition May 1973

ISBN Casebound: 0 406 57023 X
Limp: 0 406 57024 8

Printed in Great Britain by
Cox & Wyman Ltd.
London, Fakenham and Reading

PREFACE

We have inserted thirty-six new cases and deleted thirty-one old ones. Many of the deletions were due to the need to prevent excessive expansion of the book. One of the effects has been the elimination of the sections on treason, criminal libel and perjury; no doubt this will be regretted by some teachers, but the three subjects can hardly be said to bristle with contemporary academic controversy and the principal users of any case-book are presumably students who like, or have to affect to like, such controversy. It is for their sakes that we have retained the occasional comment and reference to the law of other countries. For the sake of all those who wish to make intelligent use of the book we have, wherever it seemed necessary, included, either in the text or in a footnote, an extract from the statutory provision with which the case is concerned.

The judgments in all cases have been copied from the reports mentioned at the beginning of the case and we would like to thank the proprietors of these reports for kind permission to publish the extracts.

R. v. *Feely,* [1973] 1 All E.R., was reported in time for inclusion in an addendum, but there are four recent decisions of the court of Appeal of great interest to law students in which leave to appeal to the House of Lords has been granted, and we have been unable to do more with regard to these than mention them in footnotes. The decisions are *R.* v. *Kamara,* [1972] 3 All E.R. 999; *R.* v *Lowe,* [1973] 1 All E. R. 805; *R.* v. *Turner* (1973) *Times,* 30th March and *R.* v. *Smith* (1973) *Times,* 31st March.

R.C.
P.A.J.

31*st March,* 1973

TABLE OF CONTENTS

SECTION 1. CRIMINAL LIABILITY—*cont.*

SECTION 2. COMPLICITY

SECTION 3. ATTEMPTS

SECTION 3. ATTEMPTS—*cont.*

SECTION 4. HOMICIDE

SECTION 5. ASSAULTS AND WOUNDING

SECTION 5. ASSAULTS AND WOUNDING—*cont.* PAGE

SECTION 6. BIGAMY

SECTION 7. OFFENCES AGAINST THE THEFT ACT, 1968

SECTION 8. PUBLIC ORDER

SECTION 8. PUBLIC ORDER—*cont.*

SECTION 9. PUBLIC MISCHIEF AND CONSPIRACY

SECTION 10. FORGERY

SECTION 11. SENTENCING

ADDENDUM

TABLE OF STATUTES

References in this Table to *Statutes* are to Halsbury's Statutes of England (Third Edition) showing the volume and page at which the annotated text of the Act will be found. Page references printed in bold type indicate where the Act is set out in part or in full.

TABLE OF CASES

In the following Table references are given where applicable to the English and Empire Digest where a digest of the case will be found. The numbers in bold type indicate where a case is set out in the text.

C

G

H

SECTION 1
CRIMINAL LIABILITY

WOOLMINGTON v. DIRECTOR OF PUBLIC PROSECUTIONS

[1935] A. C. 462

Subject to the exceptional case of the defence of insanity,[1] *and to certain statutory exceptions*[2]*, the onus of proving beyond reasonable doubt that the accused not only committed the guilty act, but also did so with the guilty mind requisite to constitute the crime charged, rests upon the prosecution throughout a criminal charge, and never shifts to the defence; in particular, the guilty mind will not of necessity be presumed from the fact that the accused committed the guilty act.*

Facts.

Woolmington was charged with the murder of his wife. He did not deny that he had shot her, but he stated that the gun had gone off accidentally while he was endeavouring to induce her to return to live with him by threatening to shoot himself.

Swift, J., directed the jury that, once it is shown that death was caused by the act of the accused, the law presumes malice until the contrary is proved, and the jury returned a verdict of guilty.

---

[1] *M'Naghten's Case* (1843), 10 Cl. & Fin. 200; p. 60 *infra*.

[2] If clause 8 of the draft bill attached to the 11th Report of the Criminal Law Revision Committee (Cmnd. 4991, 1972) is adopted, there will be no exceptions unless created by subsequent enactments, or by existing statutory provisions such as s. 113(1) of the Food and Drugs Act, 1955 allowing for third party procedure under which it is a defence for the defendant to prove that another person (the manufacturer of food sold by the defendant, for instance) was really responsible for the offence. See further comment on *Warner* v. *Metropolitan Police Commissioner* and *Sweet* v. *Parsley* at p. 59, *infra*.

Woolmington appealed against his conviction to the Court of Criminal Appeal, and that court affirmed the conviction and dismissed the appeal on the ground that the direction to the jury was supported by authority.

Woolmington appealed to the House of Lords, who allowed the appeal and quashed the conviction after an exhaustive review of the authorities which had been said to support the summing up.

Extracts from Speeches of the House of Lords.

VISCOUNT SANKEY, L.C.—

" . . . if it is proved that the conscious act of the prisoner killed a man and nothing else appears in the case, there is evidence upon which the jury may, not must, find him guilty of murder. It is difficult to conceive so bare and meagre a case, but that does not mean that the onus is not still on the prosecution.

If at any period of a trial it was permissible for the judge to rule that the prosecution had established its case and that the onus was shifted on the prisoner to prove that he was not guilty and that unless he discharged that onus the prosecution was entitled to succeed, it would be enabling the judge in such a case to say that the jury must in law find the prisoner guilty and so make the judge decide the case and not the jury, which is not the common law. . . . Just as there is evidence on behalf of the prosecution so there may be evidence on behalf of the prisoner which may cause a doubt as to his guilt. In either case, he is entitled to the benefit of the doubt. But while the prosecution must prove the guilt of the prisoner, there is no such burden laid on the prisoner to prove his innocence and it is sufficient for him to raise a doubt as to his guilt ; he is not bound to satisfy the jury of his innocence. . . .

Throughout the web of the English Criminal Law one golden thread is always to be seen, that it is the duty of the prosecution to prove the prisoner's guilt subject to what I have already said as to the defence of insanity[1] and subject also to any statutory exception[2]. If, at the end of and on the whole of the case, there is a reasonable doubt, created by the evidence given by either the prosecu-

[1] His Lordship had already treated *M'Naghten's Case* (1843), 10 Cl. & Fin. 200, p. 60, *infra,* as exceptional so far as the onus of proof is concerned, [1935] A. C. 462, at p. 475.

[2] See note 2, p. 1.

tion or the prisoner, as to whether the prisoner killed the deceased with a malicious intention, the prosecution has not made out the case and the prisoner is entitled to an acquittal. No matter what the charge or where the trial, the principle that the prosecution must prove the guilt of the prisoner is part of the common law of England and no attempt to whittle it down can be entertained. When dealing with a murder case the Crown must prove (a) death as the result of a voluntary act of the accused and (b) malice of the accused. It may prove malice either expressly or by implication. For malice may be implied where death occurs as the result of a voluntary act of the accused which is (i) intentional and (ii) unprovoked. When evidence of death and malice has been given (this is a question for the jury) the accused is entitled to show, by evidence or by examination of the circumstances adduced by the Crown that the act on his part which caused death was either unintentional or provoked. If the jury are either satisfied with his explanation or, upon a review of all the evidence, are left in reasonable doubt whether, even if his explanation be not accepted, the act was unintentional or provoked, the prisoner is entitled to be acquitted [*sic*].[1] It is not the law of England to say, as was said in the summing up in the present case ; 'if the Crown satisfy you that this woman died at the prisoner's hands then he has to show that there are circumstances to be found in the evidence which has been given from the witness-box in this case which alleviate the crime so that it is only manslaughter or which excuse the homicide altogether by showing it was a pure accident.' . . ."

APPEAL ALLOWED AND CONVICTION QUASHED.

R. v. STEANE[2]
[1947] K. B. 997

Where the essence of a statutory offence is the existence of a specific intent the burden of proving it rests on the Crown, and in any case it will not necessarily be sufficient to rely on the

---

[1] As was pointed out in *Mancini* v. *Director of Public Prosecutions*, [1942] A. C. 1, at p. 13 (p. 195, *infra*), the sentence should have concluded not with the word "acquitted" but with the words "the prisoner is entitled to the benefit of the doubt." This is because when there is provocation, a verdict of manslaughter instead of murder may be returned but the prisoner is not entitled to be acquitted.

[2] *Cf. R.* v. *Ahlers*, p. 8 *infra*.

presumption that a man intends the natural consequences of his acts, while in particular such a presumption cannot be relied upon when the accused is subject to the power of an enemy.

Facts.

Steane was charged under Reg. 2 (a)[1] of the Defence (General) Regulations, 1939, with "doing acts likely to assist the enemy, with intent to assist the enemy." He had been employed as a film actor in Germany for some time before the outbreak of the war of 1939–45, and he was then residing in Germany with his wife and children.

Shortly after the outbreak of the war, he had an interview with representatives of the German government at which he was knocked down and told to say "Heil Hitler!" In consequence of threats subsequently made against himself, his wife and children, he broadcast news for the Germans between January and April, 1940. Subsequently, and after further threats were made against himself and his family, he returned to work for his former employer, and assisted in the preparation of films until 1945.

He swore that, throughout, he had no intention or idea of assisting the enemy, and that his sole object had been to save his wife and children from trouble.

HENN-COLLINS, J., in effect directed the jury that, if they were satisfied that the accused had done acts which were likely to assist the enemy, the intent to do so might be presumed, and Steane was convicted.

He appealed to the Court of Criminal Appeal against his conviction, which was quashed on the ground of misdirection of the jury.

Extracts from the Judgment of the Court of Criminal Appeal.

LORD GODDARD, C.J.—

"... While no doubt the motive of a man's act and his intention in doing the act are, in law, different things, it is, none the less, true that in many offences a specific intention is a necessary ingredient and the jury have to be satisfied that a particular act was done with that specific

[1] Since revoked.

intent, although the natural consequences of the act might, if nothing else were proved, be said to show the intent for which it was done. To take a simple illustration, a man is charged with wounding with intent to do grievous bodily harm. It is proved that he did severely wound the prosecutor. Nevertheless, unless the Crown can prove that the intent was to do the prosecutor grievous bodily harm, he cannot be convicted of that felony. It is always open to the jury to negative by their verdict the intent and to convict only of the misdemeanour of unlawful wounding. . . . No doubt, if the prosecution prove an act the natural consequence of which would be a certain result and no evidence or explanation is given, then a jury may, on a proper direction, find that the prisoner is guilty of doing the act with the intent alleged, but if on the totality of the evidence there is room for more than one view as to the intent of the prisoner, the jury should be directed that it is for the prosecution to prove the intent to the jury's satisfaction, and if, on a review of the whole evidence, they either think that the intent did not exist or they are left in doubt as to the intent, the prisoner is entitled to be acquitted. . . .

In this case the court cannot but feel that some confusion arose with regard to the question of intent by so much being said in the case with regard to the subject of duress. Duress is a matter of defence where a prisoner is forced by fear of violence or imprisonment to do an act which in itself is criminal. . . . There is very little learning to be found in any of the books or cases on the subject of duress and it is by no means certain how far the doctrine extends, though we have the authority both of Hale and of Fitzjames Stephen, that while it does not apply to treason, murder and some other felonies, it does apply to misdemeanours; and offences against these regulations are misdemeanours. But here again, before any question of duress arises, a jury must be satisfied that the prisoner had the intention which is laid in the indictment. Duress is a matter of defence and the onus of proving it is on the accused.[1] As we have already said, where an intent is charged on the indictment, it is for the prosecution to prove it, so the onus is the other way.

Now, another matter which is ofconsiderable importance in this case, but does not seem to have been brought directly to the attention of the jury, is that very different considerations may apply where the accused at the time he did the

---

[1] But see next case and *R.* v. *Hudson and Taylor*, p. 106, *infra*.

acts is in subjection to an enemy power and where he is not . . . if invasion had unhappily taken place, British subjects who might have been set to work by the enemy digging trenches would undoubtedly be doing actslikely to assist the enemy. It would be unnecessary surely in their cases to consider any of the niceties of the law relating to duress, because no jury would find that merely by doing this work they were intending to assist the enemy."

APPEAL ALLOWED AND CONVICTION QUASHED.

R. v. GILL
[1963] 2 All E.R. 688

The burden of adducing evidence of duress is borne by the accused; but the ultimate burden of disproving it is borne by the prosecution.

Facts

Gill was convicted of conspiracy and larceny. So far as the charge of larceny was concerned his defence was that, having entered into a conspiracy to steal a lorry and its load from his employers, he repented and told his fellow conspirators that he would not go through with the conspiracy. The fellow conspirators then threatened him with physical violence, producing a crow bar and a bottle of petrol. The accused thereupon drove the lorry into a lay-by on the M.1 having, after the threats, gone to collect it from his employers' yard. The trial judge used language which, taken by itself, might have led the jury to suppose that the ultimate burden of proving duress was borne by the accused; but the Court of Criminal Appeal held on the accused's appeal against the conviction on the larceny count, that, read as a whole, the trial judge's summing-up did not amount to a misdirection with regard to the burden of proof.

Extracts from the Judgment of the Court of Criminal Appeal.

EDMUND DAVIES, J.—

"The third and most interesting point taken relates only to the larceny count, it being submitted that the learned deputy-chairman wrongly directed the jury that it was for the appellant to establish that he was acting under duress. The account given by the appellant himself makes it very doubtful whether such a defence was strictly open to him, inasmuch as there was a time after the alleged threats when, having been left outside his employers' yard and having then entered it, he could presumably have raised the alarm and so wrecked the whole criminal enterprise. In *M'Growther's Case*[1] LEE, L.C.J. directed the jury that, to establish a plea of duress, the defendant must have resisted or fled from the wrongdoer if that were possible. Seemingly, the position under American law is the same, as appears from the statement in Professor Rollin Perkins' *Criminal Law* that,

'The excuse (of compulsion) is not available to someone who had an obviously safe avenue of escape before committing the prohibited act.'

The issue of duress was, nevertheless, left to the jury in the present case, and that may well have been the prudent course. Having been left, did the burden rest on the Crown conclusively to destroy this defence, in the same way as it is required to destroy such other defences as provocation or self-defence? For the latter view, reliance was placed on the judgment of Lord GODDARD, C.J., in *R.* v. *Steane*[2] in the course of which he said:

'. . . before any question of duress arises, a jury must be satisfied that the prisoner had the intention which is laid in the indictment. Duress is a matter of defence and the onus of proving it is on the accused. As we have already said, where intent is charged in the indictment, it is for the prosecution to prove it, so the onus is the other way.'

On the other hand, in *R.* v. *Purdy*[3] where a British prisoner of war was charged with treason, OLIVER, J., directing the jury on the defence of duress, said:

'If you believe, or if you think that it might be true, that he only did that because he had the fear of death upon him, then you will acquit him on that charge, because to act in matters of this sort under threat of death is excusable.'

Similarly, in *R.* v. *Shiartos*[4] where duress was relied on by an accused charged with arson, LAWTON, J., directed the jury that: 'If, in all the circumstances of this case, you are satisfied that what he did he did at pistol point and in fear

---

[1] (1746), 18 State Tr. 391.
[2] [1947] K. B. 997, at p. 1005; [1947] 1 All E.R. 813, at p. 817; p. 3 *supra*.
[3] (1946), 10 J.C.L. 182, at p. 186.
[4] (1961), unreported September 19th, Central Criminal Court.

of his life, he is entitled to be acquitted. If, although you are not satisfied, you think it might well be that he was forced at pistol point to do what he had to do, then again you should acquit him, because the prosecution would not have made you feel sure that what he did he did maliciously.'

In our judgment, the law on this matter is to be found correctly stated in Dr. Glanville Williams' *Criminal Law* (2nd Edn.), p. 762, para. 247, in this way: '. . . although it is convenient to call duress a "defence", this does not mean that the ultimate (persuasive) burden of proving it is on the accused . . . But the accused must raise the defence by sufficient evidence to go to the jury; in other words, the evidential burden is on him.'

The Crown are not called on to anticipate such a defence and destroy it in advance. The accused, either by the cross-examination of the prosecution witnesses or by evidence called on his behalf, or by a combination of the two, must place before the court such material as makes duress a live issue and proper to be left to the jury. But, once he has succeeded in doing this, it is then for the Crown to destroy that defence in such a manner as to leave in the jury's minds no reasonable doubt that the accused cannot be absolved on the grounds of the alleged compulsion. It is true that this approach appears to conflict with the literal reading of the passage from Lord GODDARD, C.J.'s judgment in *R.* v. *Steane*. It is to be observed, however, that that passage was *obiter*, in that the real decision there was that it was for the Crown to prove the specific intent laid and that, in the particular circumstances of that case, an inference could not be drawn that the appellant intended the natural consequences of his act. We agree with Dr. Glanville Williams that the *dictum* must be read as relating only to what the author calls the 'evidential' burden cast on the accused, and not to the ultimate (or 'persuasive') burden placed on the Crown of destroying the defence of duress where it has been substantially raised."

APPEAL DISMISSED.

R. v. AHLERS
[1915] 1 K. B. 616

A person cannot be convicted of treason by adhering to the King's enemies if he had not got the purpose and intention of doing so.

Facts.

The accused, a British subject, was German consul at Sunderland in August, 1914. A state of war was declared to exist between Great Britain and Germany on the 4th of August 1914. On the 5th, the accused gave money and information to German subjects of military age who were living in England, to facilitate their return to Germany. He was charged with treason by adhering to the King's enemies in consequence. At the trial, his principal defence was that he did not know that war had been declared, and the trial judge directed the jury fully on this point. There was also evidence that the accused believed that he was obliged by international law to assist the return of enemy subjects shortly after the outbreak of war, but the trial judge gave no direction to the jury with regard to this. The accused was convicted but he successfully appealed to the Court of Criminal Appeal on the ground that the jury should have been directed on the second point.

Extract from the Judgment of the Court of Criminal Appeal.

LORD READING, C.J.—

"... It cannot be doubted that his intention and purpose in doing the acts were material to the issue which was then before the jury. Unless the jury were satisfied that his intentions and purpose in acting as he did were evil, not to use the more stately language both of the statute and of the indictment, and that he was intending to aid and comfort the King's enemies and did these acts with that object, they could not find him guilty of the act charged. He was charged in the words of the indictment with 'contriving and with all his strength intending to aid and assist the enemies of our Lord the King against our said Lord the King and his subjects heretofore during the said war . . . and with force of arms unlawfully maliciously and traitorously was adhering to aiding and comforting the German Emperor against our Lord the King.' The defence put forward on his behalf at the trial was that, acting in his capacity of a Consul, and with the belief that he had, his object was to assist German subjects to return to their own country, and that his intention was not in any way to injure this country's interests, but merely to carry out his duty and help these German subjects to return to their own country.

It is not for this Court to pronounce an opinion as to which of those two views was correct. The learned judge dealt most carefully with the facts in summing up the case to the jury, and certainly treated not unkindly the evidence given by the prisoner, but, unfortunately, his attention was centred in the main upon the prisoner's contention that he did not know that war had commenced at the time of doing the acts on August 5, and the learned judge did not put to the jury the alternative views as to his purpose and intention to which we have called attention. It is worthy of observation that the learned judge summed up in this way out of consideration for the prisoner because, in the learned judge's view, the one branch of the defence put forward on behalf of the prisoner was inconsistent with and would prejudice the other, which he thought from the course taken by the defence was the one mainly relied upon. We cannot, however, find that the jury ever had it brought to their minds that it was possible, if they chose to adopt the view, that the prisoner was not actuated by the intention and had not the purpose of aiding and comforting the King's enemies. Neither can we say that the jury could not possibly have come to a conclusion favourable to the appellant if those two alternative views had been put before them. . . ."

CONVICTION QUASHED.

SHERRAS v. DE RUTZEN
[1895] 1 Q. B. 918

Even in the case of a modern statutory crime the accused will normally be entitled to be acquitted if he did not know of the facts which the prosecution must prove in order to convict him of the offence charged.

Facts.

The appellant, a licensed victualler, was convicted before a magistrate of supplying liquor to a constable on duty, without the authority of his superior officer, contrary to s. 16 (2) of the Licensing Act, 1872.[1] The constable was served by the appellant's daughter in his presence, and no questions were asked as to whether he was on duty, because he had removed his armlet which, to the knowledge of the

---

[1] Re-enacted by s. 178 (*b*) of the Licensing Act, 1964.

appellant, was worn by constables in the locality of his public house, when they were on duty. The magistrate found as a fact that the appellant did not know the constable to be on duty.

The appellant's conviction was confirmed by Quarter Sessions, and a case was stated for the opinion of the Divisional Court, who were of opinion that the conviction should be quashed.

Extracts from the Judgment of the Divisional Court.

DAY, J.—

"... An argument has been based on the appearance of the word 'knowingly' in sub-s. 1 of s. 16, and its omission in sub-s. 2. In my opinion the only effect of this is to shift the burden of proof. In cases under sub-s. 1 it is for the prosecution to prove the knowledge, while in cases under sub-s. 2 the defendant has to prove that he did not know. That is the only inference I draw from the insertion of the word 'knowingly' in the one sub-section and its omission in the other.

It appears to me that it would be straining the law to say that this publican, acting as he did in the *bona fide* belief that the constable was off duty, and having reasonable grounds for that belief, was nevertheless guilty of an offence against the section, for which he was liable both to a penalty and to have his licence indorsed."

WRIGHT, J.—

"... There is a presumption that *mens rea*, an evil intention, or a knowledge of the wrongfulness of the act, is an essential ingredient in every offence; but that presumption is liable to be displaced either by the words of the statute creating the offence or by the subject-matter with which it deals, and both must be considered: *Nichols* v. *Hall.*[1] One of the most remarkable exceptions was in the case of bigamy. It was held by all the judges, on the statute 1 Jac. 1, c. 11, that a man was rightly convicted of bigamy who had married after an invalid Scotch divorce, which had been obtained in good faith, and the validity of which he had no reason to doubt: *Lolley's* Case.[2] Another exception, apparently grounded on the language of a statute, is *Prince's* Case,[3] where it was held by fifteen judges against one that

[1] (1873), L. R. 8 C.P. 322.
[2] (1812), Russ. & Ry. 237.
[3] (1875), L. R. 2 C.C.R. 154; p. 20 *infra*.

a man was guilty of abduction of a girl under sixteen, although he believed, in good faith and on reasonable grounds, that she was over that age. Apart from isolated and extreme cases of this kind, the principal classes of exceptions may perhaps be reduced to three. One is a class of acts which, in the language of LUSH, J. in *Davies* v. *Harvey*,[1] are not criminal in any real sense, but are acts which in the public interest are prohibited under a penalty. Several such instances are to be found in the decisions on the Revenue Statutes, *e.g.*, *Attorney General* v. *Lockwood*,[2] where the innocent possession of liquorice by a beer retailer was held an offence. So under the Adulteration Acts, *R.* v. *Woodrow*[3] as to innocent possession of adulterated tobacco; *Fitzpatrick* v. *Kelly*[4] and *Roberts* v. *Egerton*[5] as to the sale of adulterated food. So under the Game Acts, as to the innocent possession of game by a carrier: *R.* v. *Marsh*.[6] So as to the liability of a guardian of the poor, whose partner, unknown to him, supplied goods for the poor: *Davies* v. *Harvey*.[1] To the same head may be referred *R.* v. *Bishop*,[7] where a person was held rightly convicted of receiving lunatics in an unlicensed house, although the jury found that he honestly and on reasonable grounds believed that they were not lunatics. Another class comprehends some, and perhaps all, public nuisances: *R.* v. *Stephens*[8] where the employer was held liable on indictment for a nuisance caused by workmen without his knowledge and contrary to his orders; and so in *R.* v. *Medley*[9] and *Barnes* v. *Akroyd*.[10] Lastly, there may be cases in which, although the proceeding is criminal in form, it is really only a summary mode of enforcing a civil right: see *per* WILLIAMS and WILLES JJ. in *Morden* v. *Porter*,[11] as to unintentional trespass in pursuit of game; *Lee* v. *Simpson*,[12] as to unconscious dramatic piracy; and *Hargreaves* v. *Diddams*,[13] as to a *bona fide* belief in a legally

---

[1] (1874), L. R. 9 Q. B. 433.
[2] (1842), 9 M. & W. 378.
[3] (1846), 15 M. & W. 404.
[4] (1873), L. R. 8 Q. B. 337.
[5] (1874), L. R. 9 Q. B. 494.
[6] (1824), 2 B. & C. 717.
[7] (1880), 5 Q. B. D. 259.
[8] (1866), L. R. I Q. B. 702.
[9] (1834), 6 C. & P. 292.
[10] (1872), L. R. 7 Q. B. 474.
[11] (1860), 7 C. B. (N. S.) 641.
[12] (1847), 3 C. B. 871.
[13] (1875), L. R. 10 Q. B. 582.

impossible right to fish. But, except in such cases as these, there must in general be guilty knowledge on the part of the defendant, or of some one whom he has put in his place to act for him, generally, or in the particular matter, in order to constitute an offence. It is plain that if guilty knowledge is not necessary, no care on the part of the publican could save him from a conviction under s. 16, sub-s. 2, since it would be as easy for the constable to deny that he was on duty when asked, or to produce a forged permission from his superior officer, as to remove his armlet before entering the public-house. I am, therefore, of opinion that this conviction ought to be quashed."

CONVICTION QUASHED.

CUNDY v. LE COCQ

(1884), 13 Q. B. D. 207

The prohibition in s. 13 *of the Licensing Act,* 1872 (*re-enacted by s.* 172 (3) *of the Licensing Act,* 1964) *against a publican selling liquor to a drunken person is absolute.*

Facts.

The appellant, a licensed victualler, was convicted of unlawfully selling liquor to a drunken person, contrary to s. 13 of the Licensing Act, 1872. The magistrate found that the person to whom the liquor was supplied was drunk, but that the appellant was not aware of this fact, and the appellant unsuccessfully appealed to the Divisional Court by way of case stated.

Extract from the Judgments of the Divisional Court.

STEPHEN, J.—

" . . . I am of opinion that the words of the section amount to an absolute prohibition of the sale of liquor to a drunken person, and that the existence of a *bona fide* mistake as to the condition of the person served is not an answer to the charge, but is a matter only for mitigation of the penalties that may be imposed. I am led to that conclusion both by the general scope of the Act, which is for the repression of drunkenness, and from a comparison of the various sections under the head 'offences against public order'. Some of these contain the word 'knowingly', as for instance s. 14, which deals with keeping a disorderly house, and s. 16, which deals with the penalty for harbouring a constable.

Knowledge in these and other cases is an element in the offence; but the clause we are considering says nothing about the knowledge of the state of the person served. I believe the reason for making this prohibition absolute was that there must be a great temptation to a publican to sell liquor without regard to the sobriety of the customer, and it was thought right to put upon the publican the responsibility of determining whether his customer is sober. Against this view we have had quoted the maxim that in every criminal offence there must be a guilty mind; but I do not think that maxim has so wide an application as it is sometimes considered to have. In old time, and as applicable to the common law or to earlier statutes, the maxim may have been of general application; but a difference has arisen owing to the greater precision of modern statutes. It is impossible now, as illustrated by the cases of *R.* v. *Prince*[1] and *R.* v. *Bishop*,[2] to apply the maxim generally to all statutes, and the substance of all the reported cases is that it is necessary to look at the object of each Act that is under consideration to see whether and how far knowledge is of the essence of the offence created. Here, as I have already pointed out, the object of this part of the Act is to prevent the sale of intoxicating liquor to drunken persons, and it is perfectly natural to carry that out by throwing on the publican the responsibility of determining whether the person supplied comes within that category.

I think, therefore, the conviction was right and must be affirmed."

APPEAL DISMISSED.

ALPHACELL, LTD. v. WOODWARD

[1972] 2 All E.R. 475

The offence of causing poisonous, noxious or polluting matter to enter a stream created by s. 2(1) *of the Rivers (Prevention of Pollution) Act,* 1951 *is absolute.*

Facts.

Alphacell, Ltd. prepared manilla fibres for paper on premises adjoining a river. The water in which the fibres were washed was polluted and, in order to prevent it from flowing into the river, Alphacell, Ltd. installed pumps in

---

[1] (1875), L. R. 2 C. C. R. 154; p. 20 *infra*.
[2] (1880), 5 Q. B. D. 259.

the cleansing tank. On one occasion these pumps, designed to work automatically, did not do so owing to the fact that the rose was blocked by brambles. Alphacell, Ltd. were charged with causing polluted matter to enter the river contrary to s. 2 of the Rivers (Prevention of Pollution) Act, 1951.[1] They were convicted by the Magistrates although there was no finding that they knew of the defect in the pumps or that they were negligent. Alphacell, Ltd. unsuccessfully appealed to a Divisional Court and to the House of Lords.

Extracts from the speeches of the House of Lords.

LORD SALMON.—

" The appellants contend that even if they caused the pollution still they should succeed since they did not cause it intentionally or knowingly or negligently. Section 2(1)(*a*) of the Rivers (Prevention of Pollution) Act, 1951 is undoubtedly a penal section. It follows that if it is capable of two or more meanings then the meaning most favourable to the subject should be adopted. Accordingly, so the argument runs, the words ' intentionally ' or ' knowingly ' or ' negligently ' should be read into the section immediately before the word ' causes '. I do not agree. It is of the utmost public importance that our rivers should not be polluted. The risk of pollution, particularly from the vast and increasing number of riparian industries, is very great. The offences created by the 1951 Act seem to me to be prototypes of offences which 'are not criminal in any real sense, but are acts which in the public interest are prohibited under a penalty ': *Sherras* v. *De Rutzen*,[2] *per* WRIGHT, J., referred to with approval by my noble and learned friends, Lord REID and Lord DIPLOCK, in *Sweet* v. *Parsley*.[3] I can see no valid reason for reading the word, 'intentionally ', ' knowingly ' or ' negligently ' into s. 2(1)(*a*) and a number of cogent reasons for not doing so. In the case of a minor pollution such as the present, when the justices find that there is no wrongful intention or negligence on the part of the defendant, a comparatively nominal fine will no doubt be imposed. This may be regarded as a not

---

[1] " A person commits an offence if he causes or knowingly permits to enter a stream any poisonous, noxious or polluting matter."

[2] [1895] 1 Q.B. 918 at p. 922; [1895–99] All E.R. Rep. 1167 at p. 1169; p. 10, *supra*.

[3] [1970] A.C. 132 at pp. 149, 162; [1969] 1 All E.R. 347 at pp. 350, 360; p. 52, *infra*.

unfair hazard of carrying on a business which may cause pollution on the banks of a river. The present appellants were fined £20 and ordered to pay in all £24 costs. I should be surprised if the costs of pursuing this appeal to this House were incurred to the purpose of saving these appellants £43.

If this appeal succeeded and it were held to be the law that no conviction could be obtained under the 1951 Act unless the prosecution could discharge the often impossible onus of proving that the pollution was caused intentionally or negligently, a great deal of pollution would go unpunished and undeterred to the relief of many riparian factory owners. As a result, many rivers which are now filthy would become filthier still and many rivers which are now clean would lose their cleanliness. The legislature no doubt recognised that as a matter of public policy this would be most unfortunate. Hence s. 2(1)(*a*) which encourages riparian factory owners not only to take reasonable steps to prevent pollution but to do everything possible to ensure that they do not cause it.

I do not consider that the appellants can derive any comfort (as they seek to do) from the inclusion in s. 2(1)(*a*) of the words 'knowingly permits'. . . . The inclusion of the word 'knowingly' before 'permits' is probably otiose and, if anything, is against the appellants, since it contrasts with the omission of the word 'knowingly' before the word 'causes'."

APPEAL DISMISSED.

LIM CHIN AIK v. R.
[1963] 1 All E.R. 223

Before a regulation is construed so as to impose strict liability, it is generally necessary inter alia *for the court to be satisfied that the imposition of strict liability will assist the enforcement of the regulation.*

Facts.

The appellant was charged with entering and remaining in Singapore as a prohibited person contrary to the Singapore Immigration Ordinance. The evidence was that an order had been made prohibiting his entry into Singapore, and that he entered Singapore after the order had been made. There was, however, no evidence that the order had been served on the appellant, or that it had been published, or that he was aware of its existence. The trial judge and the Court of Appeal of Singapore nonetheless convicted the appellant of the offence. The appellant successfully appealed to the Privy Council.

Extracts from the Advice of the Judicial Committee of the Privy Council.

LORD EVERSHED.—

"Where the subject-matter of the statute is the regulation for the public welfare of a particular activity—statutes regulating the sale of food and drink are to be found among the earliest examples—it can be and frequently has been inferred that the legislature intended that such activities should be carried out under conditions of strict liability. The presumption is that the statute or statutory instrument can be effectively enforced only if those in charge of the relevant activities are made responsible for seeing that they are complied with. When such a presumption is to be inferred, it displaces the ordinary presumption of *mens rea*. Thus sellers of meat may be made responsible for seeing that the meat is fit for human consumption and it is no answer for them to say that they were not aware that it was polluted. If that were a satisfactory answer, then as KENNEDY, L.J., pointed out in *Hobbs* v. *Winchester Corporation*[1] the distribution of bad meat (and its far-reaching consequences) would not be effectively prevented. So a publican may be made responsible for observing the condition of his customers, *Cundy* v. *Le Cocq*.[2]

But it is not enough in their Lordships' opinion merely to label the statute as one dealing with a grave social evil and from that to infer that strict liability was intended. It is pertinent also to inquire whether putting the defendant under strict liability will assist in the enforcement of the regulations. That means that there must be something he can do, directly or indirectly, by supervision or inspection, by improvement of his business methods or by exhorting those whom he may be expected to influence or control, which will promote the observance of the regulations. Unless this is so, there is no reason in penalising him, and it cannot be inferred that the legislature imposed strict liability merely

---

[1] [1910] 2 K.B. 471, at pp. 482–485.
[2] (1884), 13 Q.B.D. 207; p. 13 *supra*.

in order to find a luckless victim. This principle has been expressed and applied in *Reynolds* v. *G. H. Austin & Sons, Ltd.*[1] and *James & Sons, Ltd.* v. *Smee, Green* v. *Burnett.*[2] Their Lordships prefer it to the alternative view that strict liability follows simply from the nature of the subject-matter and that persons whose conduct is beyond any sort of criticism can be dealt with by the imposition of a nominal penalty. This latter view can perhaps be supported to some extent by the dicta of KENNEDY, L.J., in *Hobbs* v. *Winchester Corporation* and of DONOVAN, J., in *R.* v. *St. Margaret's Trust, Ltd.*[3] But though a nominal penalty may be appropriate in an individual case where exceptional lenience is called for, their Lordships cannot, with respect, suppose that it is envisaged by the legislature as a way of dealing with offenders generally. Where it can be shown that the imposition of strict liability would result in the prosecution and conviction of a class of persons whose conduct could not in any way affect the observance of the law, their Lordships consider that, even where the statute is dealing with a grave social evil, strict liability is not likely to be intended."

APPEAL ALLOWED.

R. v. HIBBERT

(1869), L. R. 1 C. C. R. 184

A person cannot be convicted of taking a girl out of the possession and against the will of her father contrary to s. 55 *of the Offences against the Person Act,* 1861, (*substantially re-enacted by s.* 20 *of the Sexual Offences Act,* 1956) *in the absence of evidence that he knew or had reason to believe that she had a father.*

Facts.

The accused met a girl called Elizabeth Ann Oldham in the street. He took her to another place where he seduced her and then took her back to the place where he had met her. The girl was fourteen years old and the accused made no inquiry as to whether she had a father.

---

[1] [1951] 2 K. B. 135; [1951] 1 All E. R. 606.
[2] [1955] 1 Q. B. 78; [1954] 3 All E. R. 273.
[3] [1958] 2 All E. R. 289, at p. 293;

He was charged with and found guilty of an offence under s. 55 of the Offences against the Person Act, 1861, but a case was reserved for the opinion of the Court for Crown Cases Reserved who quashed the conviction.

Extract from the Judgments of the Court for Crown Cases Reserved.

BOVILL, C. J.—

" . . . In the present case there is no statement of any finding of fact that the prisoner knew or had reason to believe that the girl was under the lawful care or charge of her father, mother, or of any other person. Still less is there any statement that the prisoner knew that she was under the care of her father as charged in this indictment. In some cases, as, for instance, if the girl were a girl of the town, there would be a probability that the person taking her away had no reason to believe that he was taking her out of the possession of her father or other person. In other cases, again, the surrounding circumstances might be such as to satisfy a jury that he had knowledge that he was taking the girl from the possession of those who lawfully had charge of her. In the absence, however, of any finding of fact on this point the conviction cannot be supported. The decision at which we have arrived is quite in accordance with *R.* v. *Green,*[1] where the facts resembled those of the present case. MARTIN, B., there said, 'There must be a taking out of the possession of the father; here the prisoners picked up the girl in the streets, and for anything that appeared, they might not have known that the girl had a father. The essence of the offence was the taking the girl out of the possession of the father. The girl was not taken out of the possession of any one. . . . The act of the prisoners was scandalous, but it was not any legal offence.' Under these circumstances, therefore, the conviction must be quashed."

CONVICTION QUASHED.

---

[1] (1862), 3 F. & F. 274.

R. v. PRINCE

(1875), L. R. 2 C. C. R. 154

A reasonable belief that the girl is over sixteen is no defence to a charge under s. 55 *of the Offences against the Person Act,* 1861 (*substantially re-enacted by s.* 20 *of the Sexual Offences Act,* 1956).

Facts.

Prince was charged with having unlawfully taken an unmarried girl under the age of sixteen out of the possession and against the will of her father contrary to s. 55 of the Offences against the Person Act, 1861.

It was proved that he took a girl named Annie Phillips out of the possession and without the consent of her father, but that he believed her on reasonable grounds to be of the age of eighteen.

On these facts, a case was reserved for the opinion of the Court for Crown Cases Reserved, and Prince was convicted, sentence being deferred pending the statement of the opinion of the Court for Crown Cases Reserved as to the correctness of the conviction.

By a majority of fifteen to one, the Court was of opinion that Prince's conviction was correct.

Extracts from Judgments of the Court for Crown Cases Reserved.

BLACKBURN, J.—

" . . . we are of opinion that the intention of the legislature sufficiently appears to have been to punish the abduction, unless the girl, in fact, was of such an age as to make her consent an excuse, irrespective of whether he knew her to be too young to give an effectual consent, and to fix that age at sixteen. The section in question is one of a series of enactments, beginning with s. 48, and ending with s. 55, forming a code for the protection of women, and the guardians of young women.[1] . . .

---

[1] The code, with different age limits, is now contained in the Sexual Offences Act, 1956.

Sect. 50 enacts, that whosoever shall 'unlawfully and carnally know and abuse any girl under the age of ten years,' shall be guilty of felony. Sect. 51, whoever shall 'unlawfully and carnally know and abuse any girl being above the age of ten years, and under the age of twelve years,' shall be guilty of a misdemeanour.

It seems impossible to suppose that the intention of the legislature in those two sections could have been to make the crime depend upon the knowledge of the prisoner of the girl's actual age. It would produce the monstrous result that a man who had carnal connection with a girl, in reality not quite ten years old, but whom he on reasonable grounds believed to be a little more than ten, was to escape altogether. He could not, in that view of the statute, be convicted of the felony, for he did not know her to be under ten. He could not be convicted of the misdemeanour, because she was in fact not above the age of ten.[1] It seems to us that the intention of the legislature was to punish those who had connection with young girls, though with their consent, unless the girl was in fact old enough to give a valid consent. The man who has connection with a child, relying on her consent, does it at his peril, if she is below the statutable age.

The 55th section, on which the present case arises, uses precisely the same words as those in ss. 50 and 51, and must be construed in the same way. . . ."

BRAMWELL, B.—

" . . . the question is, has the prisoner taken an unmarried girl under the age of sixteen out of the possession of and against the will of her father? In fact, he has; but it is said not within the meaning of the statute, and that that must be read as though the word 'knowingly,' or some equivalent word, was in; and the reason given is, that as a rule the *mens rea* is necessary to make any act a crime or offence, and that if the facts necessary to constitute an offence are not known to the alleged offender, there can be no *mens rea* . . . what the statute contemplates, and what I say is wrong, is the taking of a female of such tender years that she is properly called a *girl*, can be said to be in another's

---

[1] This point owes its validity to the fact that offences under s. 50 and s. 51 of the Act of 1861 were defined exclusively. S. 6 of the Sexual Offences Act, 1956 (as amended by the Criminal Law Act, 1967) punishes intercourse with girls under 16 and thus overlaps with s. 5, punishing intercourse with girls under 13.

possession, and in that other's *care or charge*. No argument is necessary to prove this; it is enough to state the case. The legislature has enacted that if anyone does this wrong act, he does it at the risk of her turning out to be under sixteen. This opinion gives full scope to the doctrine of the *mens rea*. If the taker believed he had the father's consent, though wrongly, he would have no *mens rea*; so if he did not know she was in anyone's possession, nor in the care or charge of anyone.[1] In those cases he would not know he was doing the *act* forbidden by the statute—an act which, if he knew she was in possession and in care or charge of anyone, he would know was a crime or not, according as she was under sixteen or not. He would not know he was doing an act wrong in itself, whatever was his intention, if done without lawful cause.

In addition to these considerations, one may add that the Statute does use the word 'unlawfully,' and does not use the words 'knowingly' or 'not believing to the contrary.' If the question was whether his act was unlawful, there would be no difficulty, as it clearly was not lawful.

This view of the section, to my mind, is much strengthened by a reference to other sections of the same statute. Sect. 50 makes it a felony to unlawfully and carnally know a girl under the age of ten. Sect. 51 enacts when she is above ten and under twelve to unlawfully and carnally know her is a misdemeanour. Can it be supposed that in the former case a person indicted might claim to be acquitted on the ground that he had believed the girl was over ten though under twelve, and so that he had only committed a misdemeanour; or that he believed her over twelve, and so had committed no offence at all; or that in a case under s. 51 he could claim to be acquitted, because he believed her over twelve. In both cases the act is intrinsically wrong; for the statute says if 'unlawfully' done.[2] The act done with a *mens rea* is unlawfully and carnally knowing the girl, and the man doing that act does it at the risk of the child being under the statutory age. It would be mischievous to hold otherwise. So s. 56, by which, whoever shall take away any child under fourteen with intent to deprive parent or guardian of the possession of the child, or with intent to steal any article upon such child, shall be guilty of felony. Could a prisoner say, 'I did take away the child to steal its clothes, but I

[1] See *R.* v. *Hibbert*, p. 18, *supra*.

[2] For the present position see footnote to Blackburn, J.'s judgment on the same point.

believed it to be over fourteen?' If not, then neither could he say, 'I did take the child with intent to deprive the parent of its possession, but I believed it over fourteen.' Because if words to that effect cannot be introduced into the statute where the intent is to steal the clothes, neither can they where the intent is to take the child out of the possession of the parent. But if those words cannot be introduced in s. 56, why can they be in s. 55 ?

The same principle applies in other cases. A man was held liable for assaulting a police officer in the execution of his duty, though he did not know he was a police officer.[1] Why ? because the act was wrong in itself. So, also, in the case of burglary, could a person charged claim an acquittal on the ground that he believed it was past six when he entered, or in housebreaking, that he did not know the place broken into was a house ?[2] . . ."

DENMAN, J.—

" . . . In the present case the jury find that the defendant believed the girl to be eighteen years of age; even if she had been of that age, she would have been in the lawful care and charge of her father, as her guardian by nature: see Co. Litt. 88, b, n. 12, 19th ed., recognized in *R.* v. *Howes.*[3] Her father had a right to her personal custody up to the age of twenty-one, and to appoint a guardian by deed or will, whose right to her personal custody would have extended up to the same age. The belief that she was eighteen would be no justification to the defendant for taking her out of his possession, and against his will. By taking her, even with her own consent, he must at least have been guilty of aiding and abetting her in doing an unlawful act, viz. in escaping against the will of her natural guardian from his lawful care and charge. This, in my opinion, leaves him wholly without lawful excuse or justification for the act he did, even though he believed that the girl was eighteen, and therefore unable to allege that what he has done was not unlawfully done, within the meaning of the clause. In other words, having knowingly done a wrongful act, viz. in taking the girl away from the lawful possession

---

[1] 10 Cox C. C. 362. See also *Kenlin* v. *Gardiner*, [1967] 2 Q. B. 510; [1966] 3 All E. R. 931; p. 254 *infra*.

[2] Under the Theft Act, 1968, burglary can be committed in any building at any time, so the old distinction between burglary and housebreaking is obsolete.

[3] (1860), 3 E. & E. 332.

of her father against his will, and in violation of his rights as guardian by nature, he cannot be heard to say that he thought the girl was of an age beyond that limited by the statute for the offence charged against him. He had wrongfully done the very thing contemplated by the legislature: he had wrongfully and knowingly violated the father's rights against the father's will. And he cannot set up a legal defence by merely proving that he thought he was committing a different kind of wrong from that which in fact he was committing."

CONVICTION AFFIRMED.

Comment on R. v. Hibbert and R. v. Prince

One way in which the student may approach the artificial task of reconciling these two cases is to imagine that the accused was being questioned in the presence of the other parties. If Hibbert had been asked whether he intended to take Elizabeth Ann Oldham out of the possession of her father, Mr. Oldham, he could truthfully have said " No ", and might have been able to add " I have never seen, or thought about him before ". On the other hand, if Prince had been asked whether he intended to take Annie Phillips out of the possession of Mr. Phillips, he would have been constrained to say " Yes ", as he was, at all material times, aware that the girl had a father. The artificiality of the distinction is shown by the fact that if, in either case, the accused had been asked whether he intended to take a girl under 16 away from her father, the answer would have been in the negative, although for different reasons. Such artificiality appears to be inevitable once the Courts depart from the ordinary doctrine of *mens rea*.

R. v. MAUGHAN

(1934), 24 Cr. App. Rep. 130

A reasonable belief that the girl was over sixteen is no defence to a charge of indecent assault on her by a man under 24, *although it is a defence to a charge of unlawful carnal knowledge*[1] *and the facts relied on in support of the charge*

[1] See now Sexual Offences Act, 1956, s. 6(3), "a man is not guilty of an offence under this section (unlawful sexual intercourse with a girl not under the age of thirteen but under the age of sixteen) because he has unlawful sexual intercourse with a girl under the age of sixteen if he is under the age of twenty-four and has not previously been charged with a like offence and he believes her to be of the age of sixteen or over and has reasonable cause for the belief."

of indecent assault are the same as those supporting the charges of unlawful carnal knowledge.

Facts.

Maughan was charged on an indictment containing six counts. Three charged unlawful carnal knowledge of a girl between the ages of thirteen and sixteen, and the remaining three counts charged indecent assaults on the same girl on the same facts. Maughan was twenty-two years of age, and the judge directed the jury to acquit him on the charges of unlawful carnal knowledge if they came to the conclusion that he believed, on reasonable grounds, that the girl was over sixteen. The judge also directed the jury that such belief was no defence to the charges of indecent assault.

Maughan was acquitted of the unlawful carnal knowledge, but convicted of indecent assault. He unsuccessfully appealed to the Court of Criminal Appeal.

Extracts from the Judgment of the Court of Criminal Appeal.

AVORY, J.—

"Mr. Moore (Counsel for the appellant) has invited the court to say that the Judge was wrong in his direction to the jury and that he ought to have left the case to the jury to say whether the appellant had reasonable cause to believe that the girl was over sixteen, and that if the appellant had that belief, it would be an answer to the charge of indecent assault.

The argument which has been put forward by Mr. Moore cannot be given effect to in view of the decision of this court in *Forde* (17 Cr. App. Rep. 99; [1923] 2 K.B. 400), a case in which the very point in question here was raised. In that case the appellant, who was under twenty-three years of age, was charged both with carnal knowledge and with indecent assault, and the prosecution admitted that the only indecent assault alleged was the act of carnal knowledge. The Recorder of London granted a certificate of appeal to this court upon the ground that the alleged indecent assault 'consisted solely of the act of carnal knowledge of a girl under sixteen by a man under twenty-three who had, in law and in fact, a complete defence to such act of carnal knowledge.'

It is not necessary to read any part of the judgment,

except one passage (17 Cr. App. Rep. at p. 103;[1923] 2 K.B. at p. 404) in which it was said: 'The result of this legislation is that a boy who is tempted and induced to have carnal knowledge of a girl who misrepresents herself to be over sixteen, and who appears to be so, has no possible answer if he is charged with indecent assault and not with the full offence.' It was hoped at the time when that judgment was delivered that the legislation would take notice of the apparent absurdity resulting from this state of legislation and that it would be amended. That course has not been taken and we can see no reason for adopting any different view in this case from that adopted in *Forde* (*supra*).

If any further authority were necessary in answer to the argument put forward by Mr. Moore, it would be found in *Prince* (1875), L.R. 2 C.C.R. 154.[1] In that case a man was charged with abducting a girl under sixteen years of age and the same suggested defence was put forward—that he did not know she was under sixteen, and that he *bona fide* believed she was sixteen or over, yet the court held that, the act having been absolutely prohibited by statute, the man who did the act took the risk of offending against the statute. So here the legislature says that it shall be an offence for a man to commit an act which amounts to an indecent assault on a girl under sixteen years of age whether she consents or not.

We think, therefore, that no effect can be given to the argument of Mr. Moore in this case and that the appeal must be dismissed."

APPEAL DISMISSED.

R. v. TOLSON

(1889), 23 Q. B. D. 168

A reasonable belief in the death of the first spouse is a defence to a charge of bigamy, although he or she has not been continuously absent from the accused for seven years.

Facts.

Mrs. Tolson was charged with bigamy contrary to s. 57 of the Offences against the Person Act, 1861, under which " whosoever, being married, shall marry any other person

---

[1] Page 20 *supra*.

during the life of the former husband or wife shall be guilty of felony. . . . Provided that nothing in this section shall extend to any person marrying a second time whose husband or wife shall have been continually absent from such person for the space of seven years last past and shall not have been known by such person to have been living within that time or shall extend to any person who, at the time of such second marriage, shall have been divorced from the bond of the first marriage, or to any person whose former marriage shall have been declared void by the sentence of any court of competent jurisdiction."

Mrs. Tolson was married to Mr. Tolson on the 11th of September, 1880, and was deserted by her husband on the 13th of December, 1881. As a result of enquiries made on her behalf by her father, she was led to believe that her husband had been drowned on his way to America, and, on the 10th of January, 1887, she went through a second ceremony of marriage. Mr. Tolson returned from America at the end of 1887.

In response to a question put to them by STEPHEN, J., who was the trial judge, the jury found that, at the time she went through the second ceremony of marriage, Mrs. Tolson believed in good faith, and upon reasonable grounds, that her first husband was dead.

As there had been conflicting decisions of Courts of first instance on the point, STEPHEN, J., directed the jury that this was no defence to the charge, in order that he might reserve the case for the opinion of the Court for Crown Cases Reserved on the point of law involved. Mrs. Tolson was accordingly found guilty, and sentenced to a day's imprisonment.

The Court for Crown Cases Reserved, of which STEPHEN, J., was a member in accordance with a practice which was then common, quashed the conviction by a majority of nine to five judges.

Extracts from Judgments of the Court for Crown Cases Reserved.

CAVE, J.—

" . . . At common law an honest and reasonable belief in the existence of circumstances, which, if true, would make the act for which a prisoner is indicted an innocent act has always been held to be a good defence. This doctrine is embodied in the somewhat uncouth maxim '*actus non facit reum, nisi mens sit rea*'. Honest and reasonable mistake stands in fact on the same footing as absence of the reasoning faculty, as in infancy, or perversion of that faculty, as in lunacy. Instances of the existence of this common law doctrine will readily occur to the mind. So far as I am aware it has never been suggested that these exceptions do not equally apply in the case of statutory offences unless they are excluded expressly or by necessary implication. . . . It is argued, however, that, assuming the general exception to be as stated, yet the language of the Act (24 & 25 Vict. c. 100, s. 57), is such that that exception is necessarily excluded in this case. Now it is undoubtedly within the competence of the legislature to enact that a man shall be branded as a felon and punished for doing an act which he honestly and reasonably believes to be lawful and right; just as the legislature may enact that a child or a lunatic shall be punished criminally for an act which he has been led to commit by the immaturity or perversion of his reasoning faculty. But such a result seems so revolting to the moral sense that we ought to require the clearest and most indisputable evidence that such is the meaning of the Act. It is said that this inference necessarily arises from the language of the section in question, and particularly of the proviso. The section (omitting immaterial parts) is in these words: 'Whosoever being married shall marry any other person during the life of the former husband or wife shall be guilty of felony: provided that nothing in this section contained shall extend to any person marrying a second time whose husband or wife shall have been continually absent from such person for the space of seven years then last past and shall not have been known by such person to be living within that time.' It is argued that the first part is expressed absolutely; but, surely, it is not contended that the language admits of no exception, and therefore that a lunatic who, under the influence of a delusion, marries again, must be convicted; and, if an exception is to be admitted where the reasoning faculty is perverted by disease, why is not an exception equally to be admitted where the reasoning faculty, although honestly and reasonably exercised, is deceived? But it is said that the proviso is inconsistent with the exception contended for; and, undoubtedly, if the proviso covers less ground or only the same ground as the exception, it follows that the legislature has expressed an intention that the exception shall not operate until after seven years from the disappearance of the first husband. But if, on the other hand, the proviso covers more ground than the general exception, surely it is no argument to say that the legislature must have intended that the more limited defence shall not operate within the seven years because it has provided that a less limited defence shall only come into operation at the expiration of those years.

What must the accused prove to bring herself within the general exception ? She must prove facts from which the jury may reasonably infer that she honestly and on reasonable grounds believed her first husband to be dead before she married again. What must she prove to bring herself within the proviso ? Simply that her husband has been continually absent for seven years; and, if she can do that, it will be no answer to prove that she had no reasonable grounds for believing him to be dead or that she did not honestly believe it. Unless the prosecution can prove that she knew her husband to be living within the seven years she must be acquitted. The honesty or reasonableness of her belief is no longer in issue. Even if it could be proved that she believed him to be alive all the time, as distinct from knowing him to be so, the prosecution must fail. The proviso, therefore, is far wider than the general exception, and the intention of the legislature, that a wider and more easily established defence should be open after seven years from the disappearance of the husband, is not necessarily inconsistent with the intention that a different defence, less extensive and more difficult of proof, should be open within the seven years. . . ."

STEPHEN, J.—

" . . . My view of the subject is based upon a particular application of the doctrine usually, though I think not happily, described by the phrase '*non est reus, nisi mens sit rea.*' Though this phrase is in common use, I think it most unfortunate, and not only likely to mislead, but actually misleading, on the following grounds. It naturally suggests that, apart from all particular definitions of crimes, such a thing exists as a '*mens rea,*' or 'guilty mind', which is always expressly or by implication involved in every definition. This is obviously not the case, for the mental elements of different crimes differ widely. '*Mens rea*' means in the case of murder, malice aforethought; in the case of theft, an intention to steal; in the case of rape, an intention to have forcible connection with a woman without her consent; and in the case of receiving stolen goods, knowledge that the goods were stolen. In some cases it denotes mere inattention. For instance, in the case of manslaughter by negligence it may mean forgetting to notice a signal. It appears confusing to call so many dissimilar states of mind by one name. It seems contradictory indeed to describe a mere absence of mind as a '*mens rea,*' or guilty mind. The expression again is likely to and often does mislead. To an unlegal mind it suggests that by the law of England no act is a crime which is done from laudable motives, in other words, that immorality is essential to crime. . . .

The principle involved appears to me, when fully considered, to amount to no more than this. The full definition of every crime contains expressly or by implication a proposition as to a state of mind. Therefore, if the mental element of any conduct alleged to be a crime is proved to have been absent in any given case, the crime so defined is not committed; or, again, if a crime is fully defined, nothing amounts to that crime which does not satisfy that definition. Crimes are in the present day much more accurately defined by statute or otherwise than they formerly were. The mental element of most crimes is marked by one of the words 'maliciously,' 'fraudulently,' 'negligently,' or 'knowingly,' but it is the general—I might, I think, say, the invariable—practice of the legislature to leave unexpressed some of the mental elements of crime. In all cases whatever, competent age, sanity, and some degree of freedom from some kinds of coercion are assumed to be essential to criminality, but I do not believe they are ever introduced into any statute by which any particular crime is defined.

The meanings of the words 'malice,' 'negligence,' and 'fraud' in relation to particular crimes has been ascertained by numerous cases. Malice means one thing in relation to murder, another in relation to the Malicious Mischief Act, and a third in relation to libel, and so of fraud and negligence.

With regard to knowledge of fact, the law, perhaps, is not quite so clear, but it may, I think, be maintained that in every case knowledge of fact is to some extent an element of criminality as much as competent age and sanity. To take an extreme illustration, can any one doubt that a man who, though he might be perfectly sane, committed what would otherwise be a crime in a state of somnambulism, would be entitled to be acquitted? And why is this? Simply because he would not know what he was doing. A multitude of illustrations of the same sort might be given. I will mention one or two glaring ones. *Levett's Case*[1] decides that a man who, making a thrust with a sword at a place where, upon reasonable grounds, he supposed a burglar to be, killed a person who was not a burglar, was held not to be a felon, though he might be (it was not decided that he was) guilty of killing *per infortunium*, or possibly, *se defendendo*, which then involved certain forfeitures. In other words, he was in the same situation as far as regarded the homicide as if he had killed a burglar. In the decision of the judges in *M'Naghten's Case*[2] it is stated that if under an insane delusion one man killed another, and if the delusion was such that it would, if true, justify or excuse the killing, the homicide would be justified or excused. This could hardly be if the same were not law as to a sane mistake. . . .

It is said, first, that the words of 24 & 25 Vict. c. 100, s. 57, are absolute, and that the exceptions which that section contains are the only ones which are intended to be admitted, and this it is said is confirmed by the express proviso in the section—an indication which is thought to negative any tacit exception. It is also supposed that the case of *R.* v. *Prince*,[3] decided on s. 55, confirms this view. I will begin by saying how far I agree with these views. First, I agree that the case turns exclusively upon the construction of s. 57 of 24 & 25 Vict. c. 100. . . . Of course, it would be competent to the legislature to define a crime in such a way as to make the existence of any state of mind immaterial. The question is solely whether it has actually done so in this case.

In the first place I will observe upon the absolute character of the section. It appears to me to resemble most of the enactments contained in the Consolidation Acts of 1861, in passing over the general mental elements of crime which are presupposed in every case. Age, sanity, and more or less freedom from compulsion, are always presumed, and I think it would be impossible to quote any statute which in any case specifies these elements of criminality in the definition of any crime. It will be found that either by using the words wilfully and maliciously, or by specifying some special intent as an element of particular crimes,

---

[1] (1639), 1 Hale P. C. 474.
[2] (1843), 10 Cl. & Fin. 200; p. 60, *infra*.
[3] (1875), L. R. 2 C. C. R. 154; p. 20, *supra*.

knowledge of fact is implicitly made part of the statutory definition of most modern definitions of crimes, but there are some cases in which this cannot be said. Such are s. 55, on which *R.* v. *Prince*[1] was decided, s. 56, which punishes the stealing of 'any child under the age of fourteen years,' s. 49, as to procuring the defilement of any 'woman or girl under the age of twenty-one,' in each of which the same question might arise as in *R.* v. *Prince*;[1] to these I may add some of the provisions of the Criminal Law Amendment Act of 1885. Reasonable belief that a girl is sixteen or upwards is a defence to the charge of an offence under ss. 5, 6 and 7 but this is not provided for as to an offence against s. 4, which is meant to protect girls under thirteen.

It seems to me that as to the construction of all these sections the case of *R.* v. *Prince*[1] is a direct authority. It was the case of a man who abducted a girl under sixteen, believing, on good grounds, that she was above that age. Lord ESHER, then BRETT, J., was against the conviction. His judgment establishes at much length, and, as it appears to me, unanswerably, the principle above explained, which he states as follows: 'That a mistake of facts on reasonable grounds, to the extent that, if the facts were as believed, the acts of the prisoner would make him guilty of no offence at all, is an excuse, and that such an excuse is implied in every criminal charge and every criminal enactment in England.'

Lord BLACKBURN, with whom nine other judges agreed, and Lord BRAMWELL, with whom seven others agreed, do not appear to me to have dissented from this principle, speaking generally; but they held that it did not apply fully to each part of every section to which I have referred. Some of the prohibited acts they thought the legislature intended to be done at the peril of the person who did them, but not all.

The judgment delivered by Lord BLACKBURN proceeds upon the principle that the intention of the legislature in s. 55 was 'to punish the abduction unless the girl was of such an age as to make her consent an excuse.'

Lord BRAMWELL's judgment proceeds upon this principle; 'The legislature has enacted that if any one does this wrong act he does it at the risk of her turning out to be under sixteen. This opinion gives full scope to the doctrine of the *mens rea*. If the taker believed he had her father's consent, though wrongly, he would have no *mens rea*; so if he did

---

[1] (1875), L. R. 2 C.C.R. 154; p. 20, *supra*.

not know she was in any one's possession nor in the care or charge of anyone. In those cases he would not know he was doing the act forbidden by the statute.'

All the judges therefore in *R.* v. *Prince*[1] agreed on the general principle, though they all, except Lord ESHER, considered that the object of the legislature being to prevent a scandalous and wicked invasion of parental rights (whether it was to be regarded as illegal apart from the statute or not) it was to be supposed that they intended that the wrongdoer should act at his peril.

As another illustration of the same principle, I may refer to *R.* v. *Bishop*.[2] The defendant in that case was tried before me for receiving more than two lunatics into a house not duly licensed, upon an indictment on 8 & 9 Vict. c. 100, s. 44. It was proved that the defendant did receive more than two persons, whom the jury found to be lunatics, into her house, believing honestly, and on reasonable grounds, that they were not lunatics. I held that this was immaterial, having regard to the scope of the Act, and the object for which it was apparently passed, and this Court upheld that ruling.

The application of this to the present case appears to me to be as follows. The general principle is clearly in favour of the prisoners, but how does the intention of the legislature appear to have been against them ? It could not be the object of parliament to treat the marriage of widows as an act to be if possible prevented as presumably immoral. The conduct of the women convicted[3] was not in the smallest degree immoral, it was perfectly natural and legitimate. Assuming the facts to be as they supposed, the infliction of more than a nominal punishment on them would have been a scandal. Why, then, should the legislature be held to have wished to subject them to punishment at all. . .

It is argued that the proviso that a re-marriage after seven years' separation shall not be punishable, operates as a tacit exclusion of all other exceptions to the penal part of the section. It appears to me that it only supplies a rule of evidence which is useful in many cases, in the absence of explicit proof of death. But it seems to me to shew not that belief in the death of one married person excuses the marriage of the other only after seven years' separation, but that mere separation for that period has the effect which reasonable

---

[1] (1875), L. R. 2 C. C. R. 154; p. 20 *supra*.
[2] (1880), 5 Q. B. D. 259.
[3] Another case involving the identical point had also been reserved.

belief of death caused by other evidence would have at any time. It would to my mind be monstrous to say that seven years' separation should have a greater effect in excusing a bigamous marriage than positive evidence of death, sufficient for the purpose of recovering a policy of assurance or obtaining probate of a will, would have . . . or in others which might be even stronger."

CONVICTION QUASHED.

R. v. GOULD

[1968] 1 All E.R. 849

A reasonable belief that the first marriage has been dissolved is a defence to a charge of bigamy.

Facts.

On being charged with bigamy, the appellant pleaded guilty but, when his counsel, who was late, arrived in court, he wished to change the plea in order to argue that an honest and reasonable belief that he had been divorced provided the accused with a defence. The trial judge held that this would not be a defence on the authority of *R.* v. *Wheat and Stocks.*[1]

Gould successfully appealed to the Criminal Division of the Court of Appeal.

Extracts from the Judgment of the Court of Appeal (Criminal Division).

DIPLOCK, L.J.—

" The offence of bigamy is a statutory offence. Our task is, therefore, to construe s. 57 of the Act of 1861 which is in the following terms:

' Whosoever, being married, shall marry any other person during the life of the former husband or wife, whether the second marriage shall have taken place in England or Ireland or elsewhere, shall be guilty of felony, . . . Provided, that nothing in this section contained shall extend to any second marriage contracted elsewhere than in England or Ireland by

---

[1] [1921] 2 K. B. 119.

any other than a subject of Her Majesty, or to any person marrying a second time whose husband or wife shall have been continually absent from such person for the space of seven years then last past, and shall not have been known by such person to be living within that time, or shall extend to any person who, at the time of such second marriage, shall have been divorced from the bond of the first marriage, or to any person whose former marriage shall have been declared void by the sentence of any court of competent jurisdiction.'

The enacting words, which are absolute in their terms, set out the three elements in the offence: (a) a married person; (b) going through the form or ceremony of marriage with another person; (c) during the life of his or her spouse. The circumstances referred to in the first two parts of the proviso relate to element (b) and element (c) respectively and are true exceptions, that is to say, but for the proviso they would fall within the enacting words which precede it, but the second two parts which refer to cases where the former marriage has been dissolved or declared void at the time of the second marriage are not exceptions. They subtract nothing from and add nothing to the enacting words, for a person whose former marriage has been dissolved or avoided is no longer a married person and element (a) in the offence is absent. . . .

In *R.* v. *Wheat, R.* v. *Stocks*[1] the accused's mistaken belief related to element (a). He claimed to have had at the time of his second marriage ceremony an honest and reasonable belief that his former marriage had been dissolved. The Court of Criminal Appeal consisting of five judges, held that this belief, had it been proved, would have been no defence. They sought to distinguish *R.* v. *Tolson*[2] on the ground that that decision turned on the presence of the exception relating to seven years absence as indicating that an honest belief in the death of the former spouse before the seven years had elapsed was a defence, which, but for the exception, it would not have been. This, however, is almost exactly the converse of the reasoning of the judges in *R.* v. *Tolson*[2] . . .

In *Thomas* v. *R.*[3] the defendant's mistake of fact related to element (a). His former marriage was to a woman who had herself been previously married. At the time of his second marriage he believed honestly and on reasonable grounds that his first wife's decree nisi had not been made absolute at the date when he married her. Had his belief

[1] [1921] 2 K.B. 119; [1921] All E.R. Rep. 602.
[2] (1889), 23 Q.B.D. 168; [1886–90] All E.R. Rep. 26; p. 26, *supra*.
[3] (1937), 59 C.L.R. 279.

been correct, his first marriage would have been void *ab initio* not merely voidable; but what is important is that his mistake of fact was whether or not the court had made a decree dissolving the previous marriage of his first wife. All members of the High Court regarded the case as indistinguishable in principle from *R.* v. *Wheat, R.* v. *Stocks*[1]. The majority (LATHAM, C. J., and DIXON, J., with whom RICH, J., agreed) considered *R.* v. *Wheat, R.* v. *Stocks*[1] to be inconsistent with *R.* v. *Tolson*[2]. LATHAM, C.J., said so in terms[3]. DIXON, J., after discussing two suggested grounds of distinction says this:[4]

'The truth appears to be that a reluctance on the part of courts has repeatedly appeared to allow a prisoner to avail himself of a defence depending on his own state of knowledge and belief. The reluctance is due in great measure, if not entirely, to a mistrust of the tribunal of fact—the jury. Through a feeling that, if the law allows such a defence to be submitted to the jury, prisoners may too readily escape by deposing to conditions of mind and describing sources of information, matters upon which their evidence cannot be adequately tested and contradicted, judges have been misled into a failure steadily to adhere to principle. It is not difficult to understand such tendencies, but a lack of confidence in the ability of a tribunal correctly to estimate evidence of states of mind and the like can never be sufficient ground for excluding from inquiry the most fundamental element in a rational and humane criminal code . . .'

In *R.* v. *King*, [1964] 1 Q.B. 285; [1963] 3 All E.R. 561 the Court of Criminal Appeal in England followed the decision of the High Court of Australia. The mistake of fact there was that at the time of his former marriage the defendant's own previous marriage to another person had not been dissolved. Had this been so the former marriage would have been void *ab initio* and his second marriage in respect of which he was charged with bigamy would not have been bigamous. In this respect the case was on all fours with *Thomas* v. *R.* ((1937), 59 C.L.R. 279). The Court of Criminal Appeal, however, expressed the view not only that their own decision did not conflict with the decision in *Wheat's* case, but that the Australian High Court themselves

[1] [1921] 2 K.B. 119; [1921] All E.R. Rep. 602.
[2] (1889), 23 Q.B.D. 168; [1886–90] All E.R. Rep. 26.
[3] (1937), 59 C.L.R. at p. 292.
[4] (1937), 59 C.L.R. at p. 309.

felt that *Thomas* v. *R.* was clearly distinguishable from *Wheat's* case. With great respect, this latter view must have been formed *per incuriam*. . . .

Once it is accepted, as it has been in *King's* case, that the offence is not an absolute one and that honest and reasonable belief in a fact affecting the matrimonial status of the defendant which, if true, would make his second marriage lawful and innocent can constitute a defence, there can in our view be no possible ground in justice or in reason for drawing a distinction between facts the result of which would be that he was innocent because he did not come within the enacting words at all, and facts the result of which would be that he was excluded from the enacting words by the proviso. Given that the belief is formed honestly and on reasonable grounds, there can be no difference on grounds of moral blameworthiness or of public policy between a mistaken belief that a decree absolute has been granted as in *Wheat's* case and one that it has not as in *King's*. Indeed, it needs little ingenuity to postulate circumstances in which the existence of a decree absolute would make the defendant's first purported marriage void *ab initio* as the absence of a decree absolute would have done in *King's* case and *Thomas* v. *R.* To draw such fine distinctions would we think, in the words of DIXON, J., ((1937), 59 C.L.R. 279, at p. 311) '. . . lead to consequences which would not only be contrary to principle but which would be discreditable to our system of criminal law.'

We think that *Wheat's* case was wrongly decided. We agree with the High Court of Australia that it conflicts with *Tolson's* case. In this respect we respectfully differ from the opinion expressed by the Court of Criminal Appeal in *King's* case, but our decision is in conformity with the result arrived at in *King's* case and those parts of the reasoning which led to that result.

The prosecution accept that the appellant at the time of the second marriage did honestly believe that his former marriage had been dissolved and that he had reasonable ground for that belief."

APPEAL ALLOWED.

HARDING v. PRICE

[1948] 1 K. B. 695

Where a statute requires a positive act to be done on the occurrence of a specified event, a person ought not to be convicted of failing to do the act if he was unaware of the occurrence of the event.

Facts.

The appellant was convicted by the magistrates of having failed to report an accident contrary to s. 22(2) of the Road Traffic Act, 1930, which re-enacted a similar provision in the Motor Car Act, 1903, with the difference that the word knowingly is omitted from the definition of the offence.[1]

The vehicle which he was driving was a mechanical horse with a trailer attached to it, and it collided with a stationary car. The magistrates found as a fact that, owing to the noise made by the vehicle which he was driving, the appellant was unaware that an accident had occurred and, on being requested to do so by the appellant, they stated a case for the opinion of the Divisional Court who quashed the conviction.

Extracts from Judgments of the Divisional Court.

LORD GODDARD, C.J.—

" . . . I venture to repeat what I said in *Brend* v. *Wood*[2] ; 'it is of the utmost importance for the protection of the liberty of the subject that a court should always bear in mind that, unless a statute either clearly or by necessary implication rules out *mens rea* as a constituent part of a crime, the court should not find a man guilty of an offence against the criminal law unless he has a guilty mind.' In these days when offences are multiplied by various regulations and orders to an extent which makes it difficult for the most law-abiding subjects in some way or at some time to avoid offending against the law, it is more important than ever to adhere to this principle. The presumption is always liable to be displaced either by the words of the statute, or by the subject matter with which it deals; *per* R. S. WRIGHT, J., in *Sherras* v. *De Rutzen* [3] . . .

[1] See now Road Traffic Act, 1972, s. 25.

[2] (1946), 62 T. L. R. 462, at p. 463.

[3] [1895] 1 Q. B. 918, at p. 921; p. 10, *supra*.

If, apart from authority, one seeks to find a principle applicable to this matter it may be thus stated: if a statute contains an absolute prohibition against the doing of some act, as a general rule *mens rea* is not a constituent of the offence; but there is all the difference between prohibiting an act and imposing a duty to do something on the happening of a certain event. Unless a man knows that the event has happened, how can he carry out the duty imposed? If the duty be to report, he cannot report something of which he has no knowledge. . . . Any other view would lead to calling on a man to do the impossible.

I should, however, add that the authorities show that, even where the statute imposes what is apparently an absolute prohibition, an absence of guilty knowledge may in some cases be a defence; *Sherras* v. *De Rutzen*[1] is one instance, *R.* v. *Sleep*[2] and *Hearne* v. *Garton and Stone*[3] are others. Such cases depend on the wording and purpose of the particular statute, and it is unnecessary to consider them in detail.

In deciding whether *mens rea* is excluded as a necessary constituent of a crime, it is, in my opinion, always necessary to consider whether the offence consists in doing a prohibited act or in failing to perform a duty which only arises if a particular state of affairs exists. It must not be thought that this decision provides an easy defence to motorists, who fail to report an accident. The number of cases in which a motor car driver is ignorant that he has been involved in an accident must be small; where he in fact has no knowledge, it may well be, though I do not mean it was so in the present case, that the appropriate charge would be driving without proper care and attention. . . ."

CONVICTION QUASHED.

GRAYS HAULAGE CO., LTD. v. ARNOLD

[1966] 1 All E.R. 896

A person is not guilty of permitting unless he either has actual knowledge of the relevant facts or else shuts his eyes to the obvious.

---

1 [1895] 1Q.B.918; p. 10, *supra*.
2 (1861), 30 L. J. (M. C.) 170.
3 (1859), 2 E. & E. 66.

Facts.

The appellants were charged with permitting one of their drivers to drive for continuous periods amounting in the aggregate to more than eleven hours in twenty-four, contrary to s. 73(1) (ii) of the Road Traffic Act, 1960. It was not disputed that the driver had driven for continuous periods of more than eleven hours, but the appellants contended that they had no knowledge of this fact. The justices nonetheless convicted them on the footing that they could have taken more precautions to prevent the driving for excessive periods. A case was stated for the opinion of the Divisional Court who were of opinion that no offence had been committed by the appellants.

Extracts from the Judgments of the Divisional Court.

LORD PARKER, C.J.—

"The prosecution case was that the appellants were guilty of permitting in that they had failed to take certain steps which they might have taken which would or might have prevented the driver from acting as he did. Those that were referred to, which admittedly the appellants had not carried out, were the supply of staff at their yard to check the coming in of the vehicle, devices on the vehicle, an arrangement whereby the driver could telephone to them during the journey by reverse charges, and matters of that sort. The justices, in convicting the appellants said: 'We were of opinion that the appellants had failed to take adequate steps to prevent their driver driving for continuous periods amounting as alleged', and accordingly convicted them.

In my judgment, there is a tendency today to impute knowledge in circumstances which really do not justify knowledge being imputed. It is of the very essence of the offence of permitting someone to do something that there should be knowledge. The case that is always referred to in this connexion is *James & Sons, Ltd.* v. *Smee, Green* v. *Burnett*,[1] where in giving judgment, I pointed out that knowledge is really of two kinds, actual knowledge, and knowledge which arises either from shutting one's eyes to the obvious, or, what is very much the same thing but put in another way, failing to do something or doing something not caring whether contravention takes place or not. Here, there is no question of actual knowledge at all, nor is it a

[1] [1955] 1 Q. B. 78; [1954] 3 All E. R. 273.

case where there is a shutting of eyes to the obvious as, for instance, refraining from looking at the records which had to be kept of hours of work showing that the driver was not complying with the statute. This, of course, goes very much further, because it is said that the mere fact that they did not take steps which would have prevented the driver from doing this, amounts to a permitting. A similar case, *Fransman* v. *Sexton*,[1] came before this court recently on July 8, 1965. In that case I tried to limit the tendency that there is today for extending imputing knowledge in this way. The justices there had said that knowledge could be imputed when a man fails 'to take adequate steps to prevent defects occurring by an adequate system of maintenance of vehicles'. I said:

'For myself I very much doubt whether those words really do properly define what I may call the third category of knowledge (it is really part of the second category of knowledge). If they are meaning merely this, that knowledge was being imputed to the appellant because in fact he had failed to discover the defect and might have taken steps which would have revealed a defect, then in my judgment the test is completely wrong. Knowledge is not imputed by mere negligence but by something more than negligence, something which one can describe as reckless, sending out a car not caring what happens.'

So here, it seems to me, there was no knowledge and no *prima facie* evidence that the appellants had actual knowledge or knowledge of circumstances which fixed them, as it were, with a suspicion or knowledge of circumstances so that it could be said that they had shut their eyes to the obvious, or had allowed something to go on, not caring whether an offence was committed or not."

APPEAL ALLOWED.

R. v. SPURGE

[1961] 2 All E.R. 688

A defect in the vehicle unknown to the accused and not attributable to any fault on his part is a defence to a charge of dangerous driving.

Facts.

Spurge was charged with dangerous driving. There was no doubt that he was driving in a manner which was

[1] [1965] Crim. L. R. 556.

objectively dangerous, but he alleged that his car got out of control owing to a defective brake. He was convicted and his conviction was affirmed by the Court of Criminal Appeal because there was evidence that he knew of a tendency of the car to move to the right when the brakes were applied. The possibility of a defence based on defective brakes was, however, recognised by the Court of Criminal Appeal.

Extracts from the Judgment of the Court of Criminal Appeal.

SALMON, J.—

"This case . . . raises a point hitherto undecided, namely, whether a mechanical defect can ever be relied on as a defence to a charge of driving in a manner dangerous to the public, and, if so, what are the circumstances in which a mechanical defect can be so relied on.

The Road Traffic Act, 1930, s.11(1)[1], provides:

'If any person drives a motor vehicle on a road recklessly, or at a speed or in a manner which is dangerous to the public, having regard to all the circumstances of the case, including the nature, condition, and use of the road, and the amount of traffic which is actually at the time, or which might reasonably be expected to be, on the road . . . .'

he commits an offence. If, on a prosecution under this section, the Crown proves that a motor vehicle driven by an accused in fact endangers the public, that is strong evidence and, indeed, in any but the most exceptional circumstances, is likely to be regarded by the jury as conclusive evidence that the accused was driving in a manner dangerous to the public. If, however, a motor car endangers the public solely by reason of some sudden overwhelming misfortune suffered by the man at the wheel for which he is in no way to blame—if, for example, he suddenly has an epileptic fit or passes into a coma, or is attacked by a swarm of bees or stunned by a blow on the head from a stone, then he is not guilty of driving in a manner dangerous to the public (*Hill* v. *Baxter*).[2] It would be otherwise if he had felt an illness coming on but had still continued to drive, for that would have been a manifestly dangerous thing to do. It is true that in the examples given above it may be said that in a sense the man at the wheel was not driving at all, and therefore not driving dangerously. Indeed, that was the view

---

[1] Re-enacted by s. 2 of The Road Traffic Act, 1972.

[2] [1958] 1 Q. B. 277; [1958] 1 All E. R. 193.

expressed by the Divisional Court in *Hill* v. *Baxter,* a view with which this court entirely concurs. But it is also true that the sudden mischance suffered by the man at the wheel totally prevented him from controlling the movements of the motor car, and that no fault of his in any way contributed to the danger. On that ground also, it seems to this court that even if the man at the wheel could in any sense be said to be driving, he would not be guilty of driving in a manner dangerous to the public. There does not seem to this court to be any real distinction between a man being suddenly deprived of all control of a motor car by some sudden affliction of his person and being so deprived by some defect suddenly manifesting itself in the motor car. In both cases the motor car is suddenly out of control of its driver through no fault of his.

. . . This court desires to emphasise that cases in which a mechanical defect can successfully be relied on as a defence to a charge of dangerous driving must be rare indeed. This defence has no application where the defect is known to the driver or should have been discovered by him had he exercised reasonable prudence . . . The court will consider no such special defence unless and until it is put forward by the accused. Once, however, it has been put forward it must be considered with the rest of the evidence in the case. If the accused's explanation leaves a real doubt in the mind of the jury, then the accused is entitled to be acquitted. If the jury rejects the accused's explanation, the jury should convict. It has been suggested by counsel for the Crown that the onus of establishing any defence based on mechanical defect must be on the accused because necessarily the facts relating to it are peculiarly within his own knowledge. The facts, however, relating to a defence of provocation or self-defence in a charge of murder are often peculiarly within the knowledge of the accused since often the only persons present at the time of the killing are the accused and the deceased. Yet once there is any evidence to support these defences, the onus of disproving them undoubtedly rests on the prosecution (*Woolmington* v. *Director of Public Prosecutions*).[1] There is no rule of law that where the facts are peculiarly within the knowledge of the accused, the burden of establishing any defencebased on these facts shifts to the accused."

APPEAL DISMISSED.

---

[1] [1935] A.C. 462; [1935] All E.R. Rep. 1; p. 1, *supra.*

R. v. EVANS

[1962] 3 All E.R. 1086

A person is guilty of dangerous driving if, through the slightest negligence, he adopts a manner of driving which the jury thinks was dangerous.

Facts.

Evans was charged with causing death by dangerous driving. He was driving on an open road about twenty feet wide when he increased speed in order to overtake a car in front of him. While on the wrong side of the road he had a head-on collision with an oncoming car which he had not seen owing to a dip in the road which he knew was there. The judge directed the jury that Evans was guilty of dangerous driving if they would have considered his driving to be dangerous had they been bystanders observing it, and had the dangerous driving been caused by the slightest negligence on the part of the accused.

Evans was convicted and unsuccessfully appealed to the Court of Criminal Appeal.

Extracts from the Judgment of the Court of Criminal Appeal.

FENTON ATKINSON, J.—

" . . . The main criticism arises on a passage in the summing-up itself. I think that, for completeness, this should be read:

'Members of the jury, there is no legal definition of driving to the danger of the public, and there cannot be any legal definition. It has sometimes been said that a very good test is for the jury to make up their minds on the evidence what actually happened, and in their minds' eye to put themselves down at the scene of the accident, and to ask themselves this question, " Had we seen this should we have said without any doubt, that was a dangerous piece of driving? " If the answer to the question is " Yes ", then the man is guilty, and if the answer to the question is, " Oh, no ", or " We cannot be sure about it ", then he is not guilty.'

So far counsel makes no criticism whatever of that direction. The learned judge went on:

'You see, members of the jury, you are the public, and it is for you to set the standards. You, no doubt all of you, use the roads and no doubt a good many of you drive motor cars (so far no criticism) and you have got to make up your minds here whether or not what (the appellant) did was dangerous to the public, that is dangerous to other road users. If it was, then even although the dangerous driving was caused by slight negligence, the slightest negligence on his part, he is guilty of the offence of driving to the danger of the public. That is the law, members of the jury, and you must take the law from me . . .'

It is quite clear from the reported cases that, if a man in fact adopts a manner of driving which the jury think was dangerous to other road users in all the circumstances, then on the issue of guilt it matters not whether he was deliberately reckless, careless, momentarily inattentive or even doing his incompetent best. It is highly relevant if it ever comes to sentence, and equally relevant in the mind of any person who has to consider whether a prosecution is justified or not."

APPEAL DISMISSED

R. v. GOSNEY

[1971] 3 All E.R. 220

The offence of driving in a manner dangerous to the public is not absolute.

Facts.

Mrs. Gosney was stopped by the police when driving in the wrong direction down a dual carriageway. She had turned right into the road with which she was unfamiliar, and she contended that there was nothing to indicate that the turn was prohibited. The trial judge would not allow her to adduce evidence in support of her contention because he took the view that driving in a manner dangerous to the public was an absolute offence. Mrs. Gosney was convicted, but she successfully appealed to the Court of Appeal.

Extracts from the Judgment of the Court of Appeal.

MEGAW, L. J.—

"The deputy chairman appears to have accepted that on that [the respondent's] view of the law a driver would be guilty of dangerous driving even if the fact were that he had been positively directed, by a road sign which had been turned the wrong way round, to travel in the wrong direction. It would mean (to use as an illustration the facts of an actual case in which some years ago one member of this court was concerned as counsel, in the civil jurisdiction) that a driver would be guilty of dangerous driving where, as a result of an obstruction in the highway, he had been affirmatively directed by a police officer to travel on the wrong carriageway and there, without any lack of care on his part, collided with a car travelling in the opposite direction, the police having omitted to stop or warn traffic coming from that direction.

It may well be thought that, if that is indeed the law, while it may lead towards certainty, it offends the sense of justice. The deputy chairman dealt with that aspect by saying: 'The practical answer is that there would be no prosecution.' That is not much comfort to the accused if a prosecution is brought and he is precluded from proving the facts by cross-examination or direct evidence. By way of background, it may also be said that in an enactment designed primarily to promote safe and careful driving it is unlikely that Parliament intended to subject to the risk of conviction a driver who is doing nothing contrary to the standard of a competent and careful driver.

As has been said, the deputy chairman's ruling excluding the evidence was founded on what was said in *R.* v. *Ball, R.* v. *Loughlin* . . .[1] In that case these words were used:[2]

'It has been held time and again that an offence under this section is an absolute offence . . . it is a liability on the driver which he cannot get rid of, and if the result of his driving produced what the jury consider to be a dangerous situation, a dangerous manoeuvre, then even though he had been completely blameless, he can be held liable.'

A little later this was said:[3]

'The case of *Evans*[4] now sets out quite clearly that the test is a purely objective one and it matters not why the dangerous situation was caused or the dangerous manoeuvre executed.'

With very great respect, we disagree with both those passages. We do not think that they represent correctly the law as it had been previously stated in the authorities. We do not accept that the offence of dangerous driving is 'an

---

[1] [1966], 50 Cr. App. Rep. 266.
[2] (1966), 50 Cr. App. Rep. at p. 270.
[3] (1966), 50 Cr. App. Rep. at p. 270.
[4] *R.* v. *Evans*, [1963] 1 Q.B. 412; [1962] 3 All E.R. 1086; p. 44, *supra*.

absolute offence '. We do not accept that a driver who has been completely blameless can be held guilty. We do not accept that ' it matters not why the dangerous situation was caused . . .'

The well-known passage in the judgment of the Court of Criminal Appeal in *R.* v. *Evans*,[1] so indicates by, for example, its reference to 'even doing his incompetent best . . .'

We would state briefly what in our judgment the law was and is on this question of fault in the offence of driving in a dangerous manner. It is not an absolute offence. In order to justify a conviction there must be, not only a situation which, viewed objectively, was dangerous, but there must also have been some fault on the part of the driver, causing that situation. ' Fault ' certainly does not necessarily involve deliberate misconduct or recklessness or intention to drive in a manner inconsistent with proper standards of driving. Nor does fault necessarily involve moral blame. Thus there is fault if an inexperienced or a naturally poor driver, while straining every nerve to do the right thing, falls below the standard of a competent and careful driver. Fault involves a failure; a falling below the care or skill of a competent and experienced driver, in relation to the manner of the driving and to the relevant circumstances of the case. A fault in that sense, even though it might be slight, even though it be a momentary lapse, even though normally no danger would have arisen from it, is sufficient."

APPEAL ALLOWED.

WARNER v. METROPOLITAN POLICE COMMISSIONER

[1968] 2 All E.R. 356

Although the offence created by s. 1 *of the Drugs (Prevention of Misuse) Act,* 1964, *was absolute, a person in control of a package did not have possession of its contents within the meaning of the section unless he was aware of their general nature; but it was unnecessary for the prosecution to show that the accused knew that the contents consisted of prohibited drugs.*[2]

---

[1] [1963] 1 Q.B. at p. 418; [1962] 3 All E.R. at p. 1088.

[2] The past tense is used in the headnote and statement of facts because the Act of 1964 is repealed by the Misuse of Drugs Act, 1971 (see comment on p. 58, *infra*), although, at the time of going to press that Act has not yet been brought into force.

Facts.

Warner sold scent as a sideline to his normal occupation of floor-layer. He was stopped by the police when driving a lorry containing boxes, one of which was found to contain twenty thousand tablets of amphetamine sulphate, a substance the possession of which was, subject to irrelevant exceptions, prohibited by the Drugs (Prevention of Misuse) Act, 1964. Warner was charged with being in possession of the tablets contrary to the provisions of the statute. His defence was that he believed the box in question to contain scent as did another box which he picked up together with it from a café.

The jury were directed that it was sufficient for the prosecution to prove that the accused was in control of the box containing the tablets and that his ignorance of the nature of the contents of the box was no defence. Warner was convicted and appealed unsuccessfully to the Court of Appeal. His appeal to the House of Lords was also dismissed on the ground that there had been no miscarriage of justice, but a majority of three to two was of opinion that the direction to the jury had been incorrect as a person cannot possess the contents of a package without at least being aware of their general nature.

Extracts from the speeches of the House of Lords.

LORD REID.—

> " There is no doubt that for centuries *mens rea* has been an essential element in every common law crime or offence. Equally there is no doubt that Parliament, being sovereign, can create absolute offences if so minded; but we were referred to no instance where Parliament in giving statutory form to an old common law crime has or has been held to have excluded the necessity to prove *mens rea*. There are a number of statutes going back for over a century where Parliament in creating a new offence has transferred the onus of proof so that, once the facts necessary to constitute the crime have been proved, the accused will be held to be guilty unless he can prove that he had no *mens rea*. We were not referred, however, to any except quite recent cases in which it was held that it was no defence to a charge of a serious and truly criminal statutory offence to prove absence of *mens rea*.
>
> On the other hand there is a long line of cases in which it

has been held with regard to less serious offences that absence of *mens rea* was no defence. Typical examples are offences under public health, licensing and industrial legislation. If a person sets up as say a butcher, a publican, or a manufacturer and exposes unsound meat for sale, or sells drink to a drunk man or certain parts of his factory are unsafe, it is no defence that he could not by the exercise of reasonable care have known or discovered that the meat was unsound, or that the man was drunk or that his premises were unsafe. He must take the risk and when it is found that the statutory prohibition or requirement has been infringed he must pay the penalty. This may well seem unjust, but it is a comparatively minor injustice and there is good reason for it as affording some protection to his customers or servants or to the public at large. . . .

In a very recent case *R.* v. *Gould*[1] the Court of Appeal refused to follow *R.* v. *Wheat, R.* v. *Stocks*,[2] and, in my view rightly, cited with approval a judgment[3] of DIXON, J., than whom there is no greater authority on questions of legal principle: . . .

The only thing that makes me hesitate about this case is the severity of the penalty and the fact that this would be regarded as a truly criminal and disgraceful offence, so that a stigma would attach to a person convicted of it. Applicants for employment, permits or other advantages are often asked whether they have been convicted of any offence. Admission of a conviction of an ordinary offence of this class ought not to be too seriously regarded—and the conviction might be of the man's company and not of the man himself. A man who had, however, to admit a conviction with regard to dangerous drugs might be at a grave disadvantage, and this might not be removed by an explanation that he had only suffered a small penalty. He might even be dismissed by his employer. This makes me hesitate to impute to Parliament an intention to deprive persons accused of these offences of the defence that they had no *mens rea*. I would think it difficult to convince Parliament that there was any real need to convict a man who could prove that he had neither knowledge of what was being done nor any grounds for suspecting that there was anything wrong.

I dissent emphatically from the view that Parliament can be supposed to have been of the opinion that it could be

---

[1] [1968] 2 Q.B. 65; [1968] 1 All E.R. 849; p. 34, *supra*.
[2] [1921] 2 K.B. 119; [1921] All E.R. Rep. 602.
[3] *Thomas* v. *R.* (1937), 59 C.L.R. 279.

left to the discretion of the police not to prosecute, or that if there was a prosecution justice would be served by only a nominal penalty being imposed. . . .

The object of this legislation is to penalise possession of certain drugs. So if *mens rea* has not been excluded what would be required would be the knowledge of the accused that he had prohibited drugs in his possession. It would be no defence, though it would be a mitigation, that he did not intend that they should be used improperly. And it is a commonplace that, if the accused had a suspicion but deliberately shut his eyes, the court or jury is well entitled to hold him guilty. Further, it would be pedantic to hold that it must be shown that the accused knew precisely which drug he had in his possession. Ignorance of the law is no defence and in fact virtually everyone knows that there are prohibited drugs. So it would be quite sufficient to prove facts from which it could properly be inferred that the accused knew that he had a prohibited drug in his possession. That would not lead to an unreasonable result. In a case like this Parliament, if consulted, might think it right to transfer the onus of proof so that an accused would have to prove that he neither knew nor had any reason to suspect that he had a prohibited drug in his possession; I am unable to find sufficient grounds for imputing to Parliament an intention to deprive the accused of all rights to show that he had no knowledge or reason to suspect that any prohibited drug was on his premises or in a container which was in his possession."

LORD PEARCE.—

"My Lords, the illicit drug traffic is a very serious evil. Parliament intended by the Act of 1964 to prevent it so far as possible by penalising the unauthorised possession of certain drugs. There are three methods, broadly speaking, by which Parliament may have intended to achieve its purpose. The first (for which the appellant contends) is this. Parliament, it is said, intended that the word ' possession' should connote some knowledge of the thing possessed and of its quality. It also intended that a defendant should only be convicted if he had a guilty mind. The extent of the knowledge and the exact nature of the guilty mind are problems which obviously overlap. The second possible view (for which the Crown contend) is that Parliament intended that the defendant, even if innocent of any knowledge of the nature of the drug or any guilty knowledge, must be convicted when once it was shown that he had to his knowledge physical control of a thing which (whether he knows it or not) is or contains unlawful drugs. Thirdly, Parliament may have intended what was described as a 'half-way house' in the full and able argument by counsel on both sides. Each acknowledged its possibility and certain obvious advantages, but neither felt able to give it any very solid support. By this method the mere physical possession of drugs would be enough to throw on a defendant the onus of establishing his innocence, and unless he did so (on a balance of probabilities) he would be convicted. The Explosive Substances Act, 1883, produces this fair and sensible result but it does so by express words ('Unless he can show that he had it in his possession for a lawful object') . . .

Unfortunately I do not find the half-way house reconcilable with the speech of Viscount SANKEY, L.C., in *Woolmington* v. *Director of Public Prosecutions*.[1] Reluctantly, therefore, I am compelled to the decision that it is not maintainable. Ultimately the burden of proof is always on the prosecution, unless it has been shifted by any statutory provision. If, therefore, there is initially in the crime an element of knowledge or guilty mind, the jury must at the end of the case acquit, if they are left in doubt . . .

Lord PARKER, C.J., in *Lockyer* v. *Gibb*[2] was right (and this is conceded by both sides) in taking the view that a person did not have possession of something which has been 'slipped into his bag' without his knowledge. One may, therefore, exclude from the 'possession' intended by the Act of 1964 the physical control of articles which have been 'planted' on him without his knowledge; but how much further is one to go? If one goes to the extreme length of requiring the prosecution to prove that 'possession' implies a full knowledge of the name and nature of the drug concerned, the efficacy of the Act is seriously impaired, since many drug pedlars may in truth be unaware of this. I think that the term 'possession' is satisfied by a knowledge only of the existence of the thing itself and not its qualities, and that ignorance or mistake as to its qualities is not an excuse. This would comply with the general understanding of the word 'possess'. Though I reasonably believe the tablets which I possess to be aspirin, yet if they turn out to be heroin I am in possession of heroin tablets. This would be so I think even if I believed them to be sweets. It would be otherwise if

---

[1] [1935] A.C. 462 at p. 481; [1935] 1 All E.R. Rep. 1 at p. 8.
[2] [1967] 2 Q.B. 243; [1966] 2 All E.R. 653.

I believed them to be something of a wholly different nature. At this point a question of degree arises as to when a difference in qualities amounts to a difference in kind. That is a matter for a jury who would probably decide it sensibly in favour of the genuinely innocent but against the guilty."

APPEAL DISMISSED.

SWEET v. PARSLEY

[1969] 1 All E.R. 347

The offence created by s. 5(b) *of the Dangerous Drugs Act,* 1965 *of being, as occupier, concerned in the management of premises used for the purpose of smoking cannabis was not absolute.*

Facts.

Miss Sweet was the sublessee of a farmhouse. She let the rooms in the house, but retained possession of one room which she occasionally used when visiting the house in order to collect the rents. Cigarette ends containing cannabis were found in the kitchen and boxes of cannabis and L.S.D. were hidden in the garden, but there was no evidence that Miss Sweet knew that cannabis was being smoked on the premises. She was nonetheless charged with being concerned in the management of premises used for the purpose of smoking cannabis contrary to s. 5(*b*) of the Dangerous Drugs Act, 1965.[1]

Miss Sweet unsuccessfully appealed to a Divisional Court, but her appeal to the House of Lords succeeded.

Extracts from the speeches of the House of Lords.

LORD PEARCE.—

"... Before the court will dispense with the necessity for *mens rea* it has to be satisfied that Parliament so intended. The mere absence of the word 'knowingly' is not enough. But the nature of the crime, the punishment, the absence of

[1] "If a person (a) being the occupier of any premises, permits those premises to be used for the purpose of smoking cannabis or cannabis resin, or of dealing in cannabis or cannabis resin (whether by sale or otherwise); or (b) is concerned in the management of any premises used for any such purpose as aforesaid; he shall be guilty of an offence against this Act." (For the position under the Misuse of Drugs Act, 1971, see p. 58, *infra*.)

social obloquy, the particular mischief and the field of activity in which it occurs, and the wording of the particular section and its context, may show that Parliament intended that the act should be prevented by punishment regardless of intent or knowledge.

Viewing the matter on these principles, it is not possible to accept the respondent's contention. Even granted that this were in the public health class of case, such as, for instance, are offences created to ensure that food shall be clean, it would be quite unreasonable. It is one thing to make a man absolutely responsible for all his own acts and even vicariously liable for his servants if he engages in a certain type of activity. But it is quite another matter to make him liable for persons over whom he has no control. The innocent hotel-keeper, the lady who keeps lodgings or takes paying guests, the manager of a cinema, the warden of a hostel, the matron of a hospital, the housemaster and matron of a boarding school, all these, it is conceded, are on the respondent's argument liable to conviction the moment that irresponsible occupants smoke cannabis cigarettes . . .

If, therefore, the words creating the offence are as wide in their application as the respondent contends, Parliament cannot have intended an offence to which absence of knowledge or *mens rea* is no defence.

Parliament might, of course, have taken what was conceded in argument to be a fair and sensible course. It could have said, in appropriate words, that a person is to be liable unless he proves that he had no knowledge or guilty mind. Admittedly, if the prosecution have to prove a defendant's knowledge beyond reasonable doubt, it may be easy for the guilty to escape. But it would be very much harder for the guilty to escape if the burden of disproving *mens rea* or knowledge is thrown on the defendant. And if that were done, innocent people could satisfy a jury of their innocence on a balance of probabilities. It has been said that a jury might be confused by the different nature of the onus of satisfying ' beyond reasonable doubt ' which the prosecution have to discharge and the onus ' on a balance of probabilities ' which lies on a defendant in proving that he had no knowledge or guilt. I do not believe that this would be so in this kind of case. Most people can easily understand rules that express in greater detail that which their own hearts and minds already feel to be fair and sensible. What they find hard to understand is rules that go ' against the grain ' of their own common sense . . .

If it were possible in some so-called absolute offences to take this sensible half-way house, I think that the courts should do so. This has been referred to in *Warner's* case.[1] I see no difficulty in it apart from the opinion of Lord SANKEY, L.C., in *Woolmington* v. *Director of Public Prosecutions*.[2] But so long as the full width of that opinion is maintained, I see difficulty. There are many cases where the width of that opinion has caused awkward problems. But before reducing that width, your Lordships would obviously have to consider all the aspects of so far-reaching a problem. In the present case, counsel for the appellant was wisely loth to involve herself in this when she had easier and surer paths to pursue.

The Australian High Court, founding on CAVE, J.,[3] and WILLS, J.,[4] in *R.* v. *Tolson*,[5] have evolved a defence of reasonable mistake of fact and the burden of proving this on a balance of probabilities rests on the defendant . . .

Being concerned in the management of premises used for the purpose of smoking cannabis necessarily imports some knowledge of the use of the premises for the purpose. Admittedly the appellant had no knowledge.

I appreciate that this limitation will, as the respondent contends, rob s. 5(*b*) of the Act of 1965 of much of its force. If a wider application or efficiency were desired, it could be achieved by a change of onus and a consideration of what exactly *is* being required of landladies and the like. They cannot reasonably be branded with guilt whenever there happens to be on their premises someone who without their knowledge or assent smokes cannabis."

LORD DIPLOCK.—

"The expression 'absolute offence' used in the first question is an imprecise phrase currently used to describe an act for which the doer is subject to criminal sanctions, even though when he did it he had no *mens rea*; but *mens rea* itself also lacks precision and calls for closer analysis than is involved in its mere translation into English by WRIGHT, J., in *Sherras* v. *De Rutzen*[6] as 'evil intention, or a knowledge of

---

[1] [1969] 2 A.C. 256; [1968] 2 All E.R. 356; p. 47, *supra*.
[2] [1935] A.C. 462; [1935] All E.R. Rep. 1; p. 10, *supra*.
[3] (1889), 23 Q.B.D. at p. 181; [1886–90] All E.R. Rep. at p. 34.
[4] (1889), 23 Q.B.D. at p. 175; [1886–90] All E.R. Rep. at pp. 30, 31.
[5] (1889), 23 Q.B.D. 168; [1886–90] All E.R. Rep. 26; p. 26, *supra*.
[6] [1895] 1 Q.B. 918 at p. 921; [1895–99] All E.R. Rep. 1167 at p. 1169; p. 10, *supra*.

the wrongfulness of the act '—a definition which suggests a single mental element common to all criminal offences and appears to omit thoughtlessness which, at any rate if it amounted to a reckless disregard of the nature or consequences of an act, was a sufficient mental element in some offences at common law. A more helpful exposition of the nature of *mens rea* in both common law and statutory offences is to be found in the judgment of STEPHEN, J., in *R.* v. *Tolson*:[1]

' The full definition of every crime contains expressly or by implication a proposition as to a state of mind. Therefore, if the mental element of any conduct alleged to be a crime is proved to have been absent in any given case, the crime so defined has not been committed; or, again, if a crime is fully defined, nothing amounts to that crime which does not satisfy that definition.'

Where the crime consists of doing an act which is prohibited by statute, the proposition as to the state of mind of the doer which is contained in the full definition of the crime must be ascertained from the words and subject-matter of the statute. The proposition, as Stephen, J., pointed out,[2] may be stated explicitly by the use of such qualifying adverbs as ' maliciously ', ' fraudulently ', ' negligently ' or ' knowingly '—expressions which in relation to different kinds of conduct may call for judicial exegesis. And even without such adverbs the words descriptive of the prohibited act may themselves connote the presence of a particular mental element. Thus, where the prohibited conduct consists in permitting a particular thing to be done the word ' permit ' connotes at least knowledge or reasonable grounds for suspicion on the part of the permittor that the thing will be done and an unwillingness to use means available to him to prevent it and, to take a recent example, to have in one's ' possession ' a prohibited substance connotes some degree of awareness of that which was within the possessor's physical control (*Warner* v. *Metropolitan Police Comr.*[3])

But only too frequently the actual words used by Parliament to define the prohibited conduct are in themselves descriptive only of a physical act and bear no connotation as to any particular state of mind on the part of the person who does the act. Nevertheless, the mere fact that Parliament

[1] (1889), 23 Q.B.D. 168 at p. 187; [1886–90] All E.R. Rep. 26 at p. 37.
[2] (1889), 23 Q.B.D. at p. 187; [1886–90] All E.R. Rep. at p. 37.
[3] [1969] 2 A.C. 256; [1968] 2 All E.R. 356.

has made the conduct a criminal offence gives rise to *some* implication about the mental element of the conduct proscribed . . .

But where the subject-matter of a statute is the regulation of a particular activity involving potential danger to public health, safety or morals, in which citizens have a choice whether they participate or not, the court may feel driven to infer an intention of Parliament to impose, by penal sanctions, a higher duty of care on those who choose to participate and to place on them an obligation to take whatever measures may be necessary to prevent the prohibited act, without regard to those considerations of cost or business practicability which play a part in the determination of what would be required of them in order to fulfil the ordinary common law duty of care. But such an inference is not lightly to be drawn, nor is there any room for it unless there is something that the person on whom the obligation is imposed can do directly or indirectly, but supervision or inspection, by improvement of his business methods or by exhorting those whom he may be expected to influence or control, which will promote the observance of the obligation. (See *Lim Chin Aik* v. *R.*[1]).

The numerous decisions in the English courts since *R.* v. *Tolson*[2] in which this later inference has been drawn rightly or, as I think, often wrongly, are not easy to reconcile with others where the court has failed to draw the inference, nor are they always limited to penal provisions designed to regulate the conduct of persons who choose to participate in a particular activity as distinct from those of general application to the conduct of ordinary citizens in the course of their everyday life. It may well be that, had the significance of *R.* v. *Tolson*[2] been appreciated here, as it was in the High Court of Australia, our courts, too, would have been less ready to infer an intention of Parliament to create offences for which honest and reasonable mistake was no excuse. Its importance as a guide to the construction of penal provisions in statutes of general applications was recognized by DIXON, J., in *Maher* v. *Musson*,[3] and by the majority of the High Court of Australia in *Thomas* v. *R.*[4] It is now regularly adopted in Australia as a general principle of construction of statutory provisions of this kind.

---

[1] [1963] A.C. 160 at p. 174; [1963] 1 All E.R. 223 at p. 228; p. 16, *supra*.
[2] (1889), 23 Q.B.D. 168; [1886–90] All E.R. Rep. 26; p. 26, *supra*.
[3] (1934), 52 C.L.R. 100 at p. 104.
[4] (1937), 59 C.L.R. 279.

By contrast, in England the principle laid down in *R.* v. *Tolson*[1] has been overlooked until recently (see *R.* v. *Gould*[2]) partly because the *ratio decidendi* was misunderstood by the Court of Criminal Appeal in *R.* v. *Wheat, R.* v. *Stocks,*[3] and partly, I suspect, because the reference in *R.* v. *Tolson*[4] to the mistaken belief as being a ' defence ' to the charge of bigamy was thought to run counter to the decision of your Lordships' House in *Woolmington* v. *Director of Public Prosecutions.*[5] That expression might have to be expanded in the light of what was said in *Woolmington's* case,[5] though I doubt whether a jury would find the expansion much more informative than describing the existence of the mistaken belief as a defence to which they should give effect unless they felt sure either that the accused did not honestly hold it or, if he did, that he had no reasonable grounds for doing so.

Woolmington's case[5] affirmed the principle that the onus lies on the prosecution in a criminal trial to prove all the elements of the offence with which the accused is charged. It does not purport to lay down how that onus can be discharged as respects any particular elements of the offence. This, under our system of criminal procedure, is left to the common sense of the jury. *Woolmington's* case[5] did not decide anything so irrational as that the prosecution must call evidence to prove the absence of any mistaken belief by the accused in the existence of facts which, if true, would make the act innocent, any more than it decided that the prosecution must call evidence to prove the absence of any claim of right in a charge of larceny. The jury is entitled to presume that the accused acted with knowledge of the facts, unless there is some evidence to the contrary originating from the accused who alone can know on what belief he acted and on what ground the belief if mistaken was held. What *Woolmington's* case[5] did decide is that, where there is any such evidence, the jury, after considering it and also any relevant evidence called by the prosecution on the issue of the existence of the alleged mistaken belief, should acquit the accused unless they feel sure that he did not hold the belief or that there were no reasonable grounds on which he could have done so. This, as I understand it, is the approach of DIXON, J., to the onus of proof of honest and reasonable

---

[1] [1889] 23 Q.B.D. 168; [1886–9] All E.R. Rep. 26. p. 26 *supra.*
[2] [1968] 2 Q.B. 65; [1968] 1 All E.R. 849; p. 34, *supra.*
[3] [1921] 2 K.B. 119; [1921] All E.R. Rep. 602.
[4] (1889), 23 Q.B.D. 168; [1886–90] All E.R. Rep. 26.
[5] [1935] A.C. 462; [1935] All E.R. Rep. 1.

mistaken belief as he expressed it in *Proudman* v. *Dayman*.[1] Unlike the position where a statute expressly places the onus of proving lack of guilty knowledge on the accused, the accused does not have to prove the existence of mistaken belief on the balance of probabilities; he has to raise a reasonable doubt as to its non-existence.

It has been objected that the requirement laid down in *R.* v. *Tolson*[2] and the *Bank of New South Wales* v. *Piper*[3] that the mistaken belief should be based on reasonable grounds introduces an objective mental element into *mens rea*. This may be so, but there is nothing novel in this. The test of the mental element of provocation which distinguishes manslaughter from murder has always been at common law and now is by statute the objective one of the way in which a reasonable man would react to provocation. There is nothing unreasonable in requiring a citizen to take reasonable care to ascertain the facts relevant to his avoiding doing a prohibited act . . .

In my opinion, in the compound phrase ' is concerned in the management of premises used for the purpose of smoking cannabis ', etc., the purpose described must be the purpose of the person concerned in the management of the premises. But at its highest against the appellant, the words of the paragraph are ambiguous as to whose is the relevant purpose. That ambiguity in a penal statute which, on the alternative construction that it would be sufficient if the purpose to use the premises for smoking cannabis were that of anyone who in fact smoked cannabis, would render her liable, despite lack of any knowledge or acquiescence on her part, should be unhesitatingly resolved in her favour."

APPEAL ALLOWED.

Comment on Warner v. Metropolitan Police Commissioner and Sweet v. Parsley

The statutory provisions on which these two cases turned are repealed by the Misuse of Drugs Act, 1971. Section 28(2) provides that, on a prosecution, inter alia, for possession of a controlled drug,

> ". . . it shall be a defence for the accused to prove that he neither knew nor suspected nor had reason to suspect the existence of some fact alleged by the prosecution which it is

---

[1] (1941), 67 C.L.R. 536 at p. 541.
[2] (1889), 23 Q.B.D. 168; [1886–90] All E.R. Rep. 26.
[3] [1897] A.C. 383.

necessary for the prosecution to prove if he is to be convicted of the offence charged."[1]

The effect of s. 8 is to place it beyond doubt that guilty knowledge is necessary to constitute the offence with which Miss Sweet was charged. When the Act of 1971 is fully in force, the *rationes decidendi* of the above two cases will therefore be of little importance. We have, however, included extracts from the speeches in the House of Lords because of their importance in relation to strict liability generally. The majority of these speeches confirm the modern trend of the decisions against strict liability although *Alphacell, Ltd.* v. *Woodward*,[2] decided after *Sweet* v. *Parsley* shows that the House of Lords is prepared to construe a statute in such a way as to impose strict liability. If the proposals contained in the Law Commission's published working paper no. 31[3] are adopted, it will be necessary for the prosecution to prove negligence even in the case of a statutory offence such as that with which *Alphacell, Ltd.* v. *Woodward* was concerned, although negligence will be presumed in the absence of evidence to the contrary, *i.e.* the accused will bear the burden of adducing evidence of due care.

Section 28 of the Misuse of Drugs Act, 1971 seems to produce the " half-way house " canvassed by Lord PEARCE in *Warner's* case for there is little doubt that the section would be so construed as to place the burden of proving ignorance, lack of suspicion, or reason to suspect on the accused[4]. There is even less doubt that the accused would be held to have discharged the burden by proof on a preponderance of probability, but the fact would remain that, once possession was proved, the onus of establishing his innocence would rest on the accused. In this respect the English statutory solution of some of the problems of strict liability tends to be less favourable to the accused than the Australian solution as explained by Lord DIPLOCK in *Sweet* v. *Parsley*[5]. The Australian solution, as thus explained, is embodied

---

[1] Under s. 28(3) it is necessary for the accused to prove not merely that he was unaware or did not suspect or have reason to suspect that the controlled drug he possessed was that alleged by the prosecution; he must show further either that he did not know or suspect or have reason to suspect that it was a controlled drug at all, or else that he believed it to be a controlled drug which he was entitled to possess.

[2] P. 14, *supra*.

[3] See Cross and Jones, *Introduction to Criminal Law*, 7th Edn., 73.

[4] *Jayasena* v. *R.*, [1970] A.C. 618; [1970] 1 All E.R. 219.

[5] The Australian decisions are sometimes construed in such a way as to place the burden of proving reasonable mistake, as opposed to the burden of adducing evidence of it, on the accused. The statement with regard to the burden of proof by DIXON, J., in *Proudman* v. *Dayman* ((1941), 67 C.L.R. 536 at p. 541) is cast in indefinite terms.

in clause 8(1) of the draft bill attached to the 11th report of the Criminal Law Revision Committee published in 1972, cmnd. 4991. The clause reads as follows:

> " Where by virtue of any rule of law or existing enactment there falls on the accused in any [criminal] proceedings any burden of proof with respect to a matter relevant to his guilt or innocence, then, subject to subsection (4) below[1]—
>
> (*a*) unless there is sufficient evidence to raise an issue with respect to that matter, that matter shall be taken as proved against him; but
>
> (*b*) if there is sufficient evidence to raise an issue with respect to that matter, the court or jury, in determining whether he is guilty of the offence charged, shall decide by reference to the whole of the evidence whether the prosecution has proved that matter against the accused, drawing such inferences from the evidence as appear proper in the circumstances."

If adopted, the effect of the clause would be to place the ultimate burden of disproving all common law defences (including insanity) on the prosecution as well as the burden of disproving statutory defences unless the operation of the clause is expressly excluded. So far as common law defences (apart from insanity) are concerned, the clause would give statutory effect to the decision in *Woolmington* v. *Director of Public Prosecutions*[2]. Lord PEARCE'S speech in *Sweet* v. *Parsley* gives no indication of the nature of the " awkward problems " to which the breadth of the decision in *Woolmington*'s case gives rise. Subject to these, whatever they may be, it is to be hoped that clause 8 will be adopted for the solution on the lines of s. 28 of the Misuse of Drugs Act, 1971 is open to the grave objection that a jury might have to convict a man of a serious offence although they thought it as likely as not that the accused was unaware of such essential facts as the nature of the tablets in his possession.

M'NAGHTEN'S CASE

(1843), 10 Cl. & F. 200

In order to be exempt from criminal responsibility on the ground of insanity, the accused must prove that, owing to a defect of reason, due to a disease of the mind, he did not know the nature and quality of his act, or, if he did know this, that he did not know that he was doing wrong.

---

[1] This deals with third party procedure; see note 2, p. 1, *supra*.
[2] P. 1, *supra*.

Facts.

M'Naghten was indicted for murder and acquitted on the ground of insanity. In consequence debates took place in the House of Lords, and it was decided to take the opinion of the judges as to the nature and extent of the unsoundness of mind which would excuse the commission of a felony of this sort. Five questions were put to the judges in the terms set out in the following extract from their opinions.

Extract from opinion of the judges.

LORD CHIEF JUSTICE TINDAL.—

" . . . The first question proposed by your Lordships is this : 'What is the law respecting alleged crimes committed by persons afflicted with insane delusion in respect of one or more particular subjects or persons: as, for instance, where at the time of the commission of the alleged crime the accused knew he was acting contrary to law, but did the act complained of with a view, under the influence of insane delusion, of redressing or revenging some supposed grievance or injury, or of producing some supposed public benefit ?'

In answer to which question, assuming that your Lordships' inquiries are confined to those persons who labour under such partial delusions only, and are not in other respects insane, we are of opinion that, notwithstanding the party accused did the act complained of with a view, under the influence of insane delusion, of redressing or revenging some supposed grievance or injury, or of producing some public benefit, he is nevertheless punishable according to the nature of the crime committed, if he knew at the time of committing such crime that he was acting contrary to law; by which expression we understand your Lordships to mean the law of the land.

Your Lordships are pleased to inquire of us, secondly, 'What are the proper questions to be submitted to the jury where a person alleged to be afflicted with insane delusion respecting one or more particular subjects or persons, is charged with the commission of a crime (murder, for example), and insanity is set up as a defence ?' And, thirdly, 'In what terms ought the question to be left to the jury as to the prisoner's state of mind at the time when the act was committed ?' And as these two questions appear to us to be more conveniently answered together, we have to submit our opinion to be, that the jurors ought to be told in all cases that every man is to be presumed to be sane, and to possess a sufficient degree of reason to be responsible for his crimes, until the contrary be proved to their satisfaction;[1] and that to establish a defence on the ground of insanity, it must be clearly proved that, at the time of the committing of the act, the party accused was labouring under such a defect of reason, from disease of the mind, as not to know the nature and quality of the act he was doing; or, if he did know it, that he did not know he was doing what was wrong. The mode of putting the latter part of the question to the jury on these occasions has generally been, whether the accused at the time of doing the act knew the difference between right and wrong: which mode, though rarely, if ever, leading to any mistake with the jury, is not, as we conceive, so accurate when put generally and in the abstract, as when put with reference to the party's knowledge of right and wrong in respect to the very act with which he is charged. If the question were to be put as to the knowledge of the accused solely and exclusively with reference to the law of the land, it might tend to confound the jury, by inducing them to believe that an actual knowledge of the law of the land was essential in order to lead to a conviction; whereas the law is administered upon the principle that everyone must be taken conclusively to know it, without proof that he does know it. If the accused was conscious that the act was one which he ought not to do, and if that act was at the same time contrary to the law of the land, he is punishable; and the usual course therefore has been to leave the question to the jury, whether the party accused has a sufficient degree of reason to know that he was doing an act that was wrong: and this course we think is correct, accompanied with such observations and explanations as the circumstances of each particular case may require.

The fourth question which your Lordships have proposed to us is this :—' If a person under an insane delusion as to existing facts, commits an offence in consequence thereof, is he thereby excused ? ' To which question the answer must of course depend on the nature of the delusion: but, making the same assumption as we did before, namely, that he labours under such partial delusion only, and is not in other respects insane, we think he must be considered in the same situation as to responsibility as if the facts with respect to which the delusion exists were real. For example,

[1] See note 2, p. 1, *supra*.

if under the influence of his delusion he supposes another man to be in the act of attempting to take away his life, and he kills that man, as he supposes, in self-defence, he would be exempt from punishment. If his delusion was that the deceased had inflicted a serious injury to his character and fortune, and he killed him in revenge for such supposed injury, he would be liable to punishment.

The question lastly proposed by your Lordships is :—'Can a medical man conversant with the disease of insanity, who never saw the prisoner previously to the trial, but who was present during the whole trial and the examination of all the witnesses, be asked his opinion as to the state of the prisoner's mind at the time of the commission of the alleged crime, or his opinion whether the prisoner was conscious at the time of doing the act that he was acting contrary to law, or whether he was labouring under any and what delusion at the time ?' In answer thereto, we state to your Lordships, that we think the medical man, under the circumstances supposed, cannot in strictness be asked his opinion in the terms above stated, because each of those questions involves the determination of the truth of the facts deposed to, which it is for the jury to decide, and the questions are not mere questions upon a matter of science, in which case such evidence is admissible. But where the facts are admitted or not disputed, and the question becomes substantially one of science only, it may be convenient to allow the question to be put in that general form, though the same cannot be insisted on as a matter of right."

R. v. CLARKE
[1972] 1 All E.R. 219

A diabetic's temporary fit of absentmindedness due to sugar deficiency is not a defect of reason within the meaning of the M'Naghten rules.

Facts.

Mrs. Clarke was charged with theft. While shopping in a supermarket, she had removed goods for which she had not paid from the market's basket to her own. Her defence was that she had no intention to steal, having acted in a moment of absent-mindedness caused by a diabetic depression brought on by sugar deficiency. She called a psychiatrist who spoke of her condition as a 'mental illness'. The Recorder said that he would treat the defence as one of insanity whereupon Mrs. Clarke pleaded guilty on legal advice. She appealed to the Court of Appeal who quashed the conviction.

Extracts from the Judgment of the Court of Appeal.

ACKNER, J.—

" It may be that on the evidence in this case the assistant recorder was entitled to the view that the appellant suffered from a disease of the mind but we express no concluded view on that. However, in our judgment the evidence fell very far short either of showing that she suffered from a defect of reason or that the consequences of that defect in reason, if any, were that she was unable to know the nature and quality of the act she was doing. The *M'Naghten* rules relate to accused persons who by reason of a disease of the mind are deprived of the power of reasoning. They do not apply and never have applied to those who retain the power of reasoning but who in moments of confusion or absent-mindedness fail to use their powers to the full. The picture painted by the evidence was wholly consistent with this being a woman who retained her ordinary powers of reason but who was momentarily absent-minded or confused and acted as she did by failing to concentrate properly on what she was doing and by failing adequately to use her mental powers.

Because the assistant recorder ruled that the defence put forward had to be put forward as a defence of insanity, although the medical evidence was to the effect that it was absurd to call anyone in the appellant's condition insane, defending counsel felt constrained to advise the appellant to alter her plea from not guilty to guilty so as to avoid the disastrous consequences of her defence, as wrongly defined by the assistant recorder, succeeding."

CONVICTION QUASHED.

R. v. WINDLE

[1952] 2 Q. B. 826

The trial judge may withdraw a plea of insanity from the jury where there is no evidence that the accused did not know that what he was doing was legally wrong.

Facts.

Windle was charged with murdering his wife with whom

he had led an unhappy life for some time, on account of the fact that she was probably certifiably insane, and constantly complained of her unhappiness. Windle was accustomed to discuss his domestic troubles with his workmates, one of whom said " give her a dozen aspirins ", in order to stop further conversation on the subject. Shortly afterwards, Windle gave his wife a hundred aspirins, and she died in consequence of the dose. He admitted that he had administered it, and said that he supposed that he would hang for it. There was some evidence that he was suffering from a form of communicated insanity, but DELVIN, J., before whom the case was tried, refused to leave the question of insanity to the jury.

Windle appealed against conviction to the Court of Criminal Appeal who held that the course adopted by DEVLIN, J., was correct.

Extracts from the Judgment of the Court of Criminal Appeal.

LORD GODDARD, C. J.—

" . . . If the only question in this case had been whether the appellant was suffering from a disease of the mind, I should say that that was a question which must have been left to the jury. That, however, is not the question.

As I endeavoured to point out in giving the judgment of the court in *R.* v. *Rivett*,[1] in all cases of this kind, the real test is responsibility. A man may be suffering from a defect of reason, but if he knows that what he is doing is ' wrong ' and by ' wrong ' is meant contrary to law, he is responsible. . . .

In the opinion of the court there is no doubt that in the M'Naghten rules ' wrong ' means contrary to law and not ' wrong ' according to the opinion of one man or of a number of people on the question whether a particular act might or might not be justified. In the present case, it could not be challenged that the appellant knew that what he was doing was contrary to law. . . .

In these circumstances what evidence was there to leave to the jury which could suggest that the appellant was entitled to a verdict of guilty but insane—that is, that he was guilty of the act, but that when he committed it he was

---

[1] (1950), 34 Cr. App. Rep. 87.

insane so as not to be responsible according to law? If there was no such evidence, the judge was entitled to withdraw the case from the jury and was, I think, right in doing so."

APPEAL DISMISSED.

SODEMAN v. R.

[1936] 2 All E. R. 1138

(1) *The Courts will not add to the law as to insanity laid down in M'Naghten's case*[1] *a rule to the effect that where a man knew that he was doing wrong, but was forced to do the act charged by an irresistible impulse induced by disease of the mind he is entitled to a verdict of guilty but insane.*[2] (2) *The burden which rests upon the defence to establish a plea of insanity in a criminal case is similar to that which rests upon the parties in civil proceedings.*[3]

Facts.

Sodeman was charged with murder in Victoria. He took a girl for a ride on a bicycle, and strangled her. His defence was that he was insane at the time. Medical evidence was given on his behalf, and none was called by the prosecution. He was convicted, and his conviction was affirmed by the Supreme Court of Victoria. He unsuccessfully petitioned both the High Court of Australia and the Privy Council for special leave to appeal.

Extract from advice of the Privy Council.

VISCOUNT HAILSHAM, L.C.—

"There are two principal grounds in the petition for special leave to appeal. First, it is suggested by the petitioner that the rules in *M'Naghten's case*[4] are no longer to be treated as an exhaustive statement of the law with regard to

---

[1] (1843), 10 Cl. & F. 200; p. 60, *supra*.

[2] A person labouring under an uncontrollable impulse may now succeed on a plea of diminished responsibility and thus be entitled to a verdict of manslaughter instead of murder under s. 2 of the Homicide Act, 1957 (see *R.* v. *Byrne*, p. 72, *infra*).

[3] There will be no burden of proof as distinct from a burden of producing evidence on the accused in an insanity case if clause 8 of the bill attached to the Eleventh Report of the Criminal Law Revision Committee is adjusted.

[4] (1843), 10 Cl. & F. 200; p. 60, *supra*.

insanity, and that there is to be engrafted upon those rules another rule that where a man knows that he is doing what is wrong, none the less he may be held to be insane if he is caused to do the act by an irresistible impulse produced by disease. It is admitted by Mr. Pritt [counsel for Sodeman] that, so far as this country is concerned, the more recent cases, finishing with *R.* v. *Flavell*[1], excludes that addition to the law in *M'Naghten's case*[2], but it is argued that, since there have been earlier decisions which suggest that such a rule exists, this is a good opportunity for establishing the law beyond doubt. Their Lordships do not think that the argument is a sound one. If they are to take a different view of the law from that which prevailed in *R.* v. *Flavell*[1] and *R.* v. *Kopsch*[3] the effect will be that different standards of law will prevail in England and in the Dominions. The adoption of such a view obviously cannot alter the authorities laid down by the English Court of Criminal Appeal, and their Lordships do not think that the ground suggested is one for granting special leave to appeal in a criminal case. The other point is that the trial judge in directing the jury as to the burden of proof, having stated that it was for the Crown to establish its case beyond reasonable doubt, went on to say that the burden of proof in a case of insanity rested upon the accused, and the suggestion made by the petitioner was that the jury may have been misled by the judge's language into the impression that the burden of proof resting upon an accused to prove insanity is as heavy as the burden of proof resting upon the prosecution to prove the facts which they have to establish. In fact there is no doubt that the burden of proof for the defence is not so onerous. It has not been very definitely defined. The Canadian case of *R.* v. *Clark*[4] was referred to, but even there the judges were not able to find a very satisfactory definition, but it is certainly plain that the burden in cases in which an accused has to prove insanity may fairly be stated as not being higher than the burden which rests upon a plaintiff or defendant in civil proceedings."

PETITION DISMISSED.

---

[1] (1926), 19 Cr. App. Rep. 141.
[2] (1843), 10 Cl. & F. 200: p. 60, *supra*.
[3] (1925), 19 Cr. App. Rep. 50.
[4] (1921), 61 S. C. R. 608.

ATTORNEY-GENERAL FOR THE STATE OF SOUTH AUSTRALIA v. BROWN

[1960] A. C. 432

The law does not recognise irresistible impulse as a symptom from which the jury may, without evidence, infer insanity within the M'Naghten rules.

Facts.

Brown shot and killed his employer without motive or provocation. His defence to a charge of murder was insanity. There was medical evidence that he was a schizoid personality and the submission made on his behalf was that he did not know that he was doing wrong. Brown said that he felt he could not help doing what he did, but admitted that he would not have shot at the deceased if a policeman had been present. The trial judge directed the jury that, if the true explanation of the accused's conduct was that he was unable to control his impulse to kill his employer, he had no defence to the charge. Brown was convicted and unsuccessfully appealed to the full court of South Australia. He succeeded on an appeal to the High Court of Australia on the ground that the jury should have been directed to consider whether his inability to control his impulse to kill the deceased prevented him from knowing that what he was doing was wrong. The Attorney-General for South Australia successfully appealed to the Privy Council.

Extracts from the advice of the Privy Council read by:

LORD TUCKER—

" At various times in the past attempts have been made to temper the supposed harshness or unscientific nature of the M'Naghten rules. These attempts were supported by the high authority of Sir James Fitzjames Stephen, but in the end the rules remain in full force and their harshness has in this country been to some extent alleviated by the recent legislative enactment affording the defence of diminished responsibility. While the High Court, of course, fully recognise the binding force of the M'Naghten rules, their Lordships think that the directions which they have indicated as appropriate for use by trial judges would in effect make a very considerable inroad into those rules as hitherto interpreted. Moreover, unless the law is presumed to take cognisance of irresistible impulse as a symptom of legal insanity, whence does the judge derive his knowledge of these matters, it not being permissible for him to make use of what he may have learned from evidence given in other cases?

Their Lordships must not, of course, be understood to suggest that in a case where evidence has been given (and it is difficult to imagine a case where such evidence would be other than medical evidence) that irresistible impulse is a symptom of the particular disease of the mind from which a prisoner is said to be suffering and as to its effect on his ability to know the nature and quality of his act or that his act is wrong it would not be the duty of the judge to deal with the matter in the same way as any other relevant evidence given at the trial.

Sodeman v. *The King*[1] is an Australian example of such a case. The actual decision in that case related to the burden of proof in cases where the defence of insanity is raised and to the sufficiency of the trial judge's direction thereon, but in the course of the judgments references were made to 'irresistible impulse' and its possible bearing on the defence raised by the medical evidence in that case to the effect that if a man has an obsession and if he gives way to that obsession and does the thing which is always before his mind as the thing he wants to do, then in doing it he does not know the quality of his act, he does not know what he is doing, and does not know whether it is right or wrong. (*Vide* the judgment of LATHAM, C.J.[2]) The learned Chief Justice used these words:[3] 'But, on the other hand, it should be remembered that, as already stated, the law recognises that mental disease manifested in, for example, what is called 'uncontrollable impulse', may also be manifested in lack of knowledge, or incapacity to have knowledge, of the nature and quality of an act or of its character as a wrong act. Such an impulse may be evidence of this very lack or incapacity. *Indeed, that was the effect of the medical opinions given in evidence in this case, and this aspect of the case was definitely put to the jury by the judge.*'

This passage must be read in the light of the concluding sentence now italicised. So read, their Lordships would not

---

[1] (1936), 55 C. L. R. 192; affirmed, [1936] W. N. 190; [1936] 2 All E. R 1138, P. C.; p. 66, *supra*.

[2] (1936), 55 C. L. R. 192, at p. 203.

[3] *Ibid.*, at p. 205.

question it. But if the word ' recognises ' in the first sentence is construed to mean that the words which follow are matters of law which must or may be accepted and acted upon by juries without evidence it would not in their Lordships' opinion be an accurate statement of the law. The word ' recognises ' would seem to have been used in contrast to the rejection of irresistible impulse *per se* and means no more than that the law will not refuse to listen to evidence to the effect stated whereas it will refuse to listen to evidence of irresistible impulse *per se*.

The presumption that the law takes note of such matters without evidence is implicit in the language of the High Court's judgment in the present case. It is this that their Lordships with great respect feel unable to accept."

APPEAL ALLOWED.[1]

Comment on A.-G. for South Australia v. Brown and the defence of insanity in some other parts of the British Commonwealth

Before *Brown's* case the Australian courts had approached the M'Naghten rules in a different way from the English courts. According to the Australian courts " wrong " in the rules means "morally wrong", and "know" means "rationally appreciate ". Hence someone suffering from seriously impaired self control could be said to come within the rules because he would be unable to reason about what he was doing with a moderate degree of composure.[2] From the point of view of the Australian courts a classic summing-up is that of DIXON, J., in *R.* v. *Porter*:[3]

" The question is whether he was able to appreciate the wrongness of the particular act he was doing at the particular time. Could this man be said to know in this sense whether his act was wrong if through a disease or defect or disorder of the mind he would not think rationally of the reasons which to ordinary people make that act right or wrong? If through the disordered condition of the mind he could not reason about the matter with a moderate degree of sense and composure it may be said that he could not know that what he was doing was wrong."

This is very like letting the so-called plea of irresistible

---

[1] There is no equivalent to the Homicide Act, 1957, in South Australia The Judicial Committee considered that Brown might well have been entitled to a verdict of manslaughter on the grounds of diminished responsibility in this country.

[2] See the judgment of DIXON, C.J., in *Stapleton* v. *R.* (1952), 86 C. L. R. 358.

[3] (1933), 55 C. L. R. 182, at p. 189,

impulse in at the back door, but the approach was formerly favoured by Sir James Stephen in England. He said, " The absence of the power of self control would involve an incapacity to know right from wrong."[1] Stephen's view failed to gain favour in England, but it is doubtful whether *Brown's* case means the end of it in Australia for all that the decision requires is that there should be medical evidence bearing on the accused's impaired self control through disease of the mind[2] and its effect on his knowledge that his conduct was wrong. The Privy Council made no pronouncement on the meaning of " wrong".

Section 16 of the Canadian Criminal Code comes near to a statutory formulation of the M'Naghten rules, but in several other parts of the Commonwealth, allowance is made in the Criminal Code or by special statute for a broader interpretation of the word " wrong " than " contrary to law " and for a person whose self control is impaired owing to a disease of the mind.

Section 16 of the Canadian Criminal Code of 1955 declares that a person is insane for the purpose of the Code " when he is in a state of natural imbecility or has a disease of the mind to an extent that renders him incapable of appreciating the nature and quality of an act or omission or of knowing that an act or omission is wrong."

Under the Criminal Justice Act (Northern Ireland) 1966, an insane person may not be convicted, but is detained under the Northern Irish Mental Health Act. An " insane person " is " a person who suffers from mental abnormality which prevents him (a) from appreciating what he is doing; or (b) from appreciating that what he is doing is either wrong or contrary to law; or (c) from controlling his own conduct."

Section 27 of the Queensland Criminal Code[3] provides that:

" A person is not criminally responsible for an act or omission if at the time of doing the act or making the omission he is in such a state of mental disease or natural mental infirmity as to deprive him of capacity to understand what he is doing, or of capacity to control his actions, or of capacity to know that he ought not to do the act or make the omission."

Section 16 of the Tasmanian Code reads as follows:

" (1) A person is not criminally responsible for an act done or an omission made by him—(i) when afflicted with mental

---

1 *History of Criminal Law* Vol. 2, p. 171.

2 For the interpretation of this expression see note 5, p. 83, *infra*.

3 Queensland and Western Australia have similar criminal codes. Tasmania has a different one, while the general part of the criminal law of New South Wales, Victoria and South Australia is mainly governed by the common law.

disease to such an extent as to render him incapable of—(a) understanding the physical character of such act or omission, or (b) knowing that such act or omission was one which he ought not to do or make; or (ii) when such act or omission was done or made under an impulse which, by reason of mental disease, he was in substance deprived of any power to resist.

(2) The fact that a person was at the time at which he is alleged to have done an act or made an omission, incapable of controlling his conduct generally, is relevant to the question whether he did such act or made such omission under an impulse which by reason of mental disease he was in substance deprived of any power to resist."

Section 23(2) of the New Zealand Crimes Act 1961 provides that:

" No person shall be convicted of an offence by reason of an act done or an omission by him when labouring under natural imbecility or disease of the mind to such an extent as to render such person incapable of understanding the nature and quality of the act or omission or (b) of knowing that the act or omission was morally wrong having regard to the commonly accepted standards of right and wrong."[1]

R. v. BYRNE

[1960] 2 Q. B. 396

The fact that the accused's powers of self control were seriously impaired is evidence that he was suffering from diminished responsibility within the meaning of s. 2 (1) *of the Homicide Act*, 1957.[2]

Facts.

Byrne strangled a girl and mutilated her dead body. He was a sexual psychopath and there was evidence that he found it difficult, if not impossible, to control himself at the material time. The trial judge directed the jury that, even if this was the case, it was insufficient to establish the plea of diminished responsibility. Byrne was convicted of

---

[1] The whole question of the defence of mental abnormality in English law is under consideration by a committee presided over by Lord Butler.

[2] " Where a person kills, or is a party to the killing of another, he shall not be convicted of murder if he was suffering from such abnormality of mind (whether arising from a condition of arrested or retarded development of mind or any inherent causes or induced by disease or injury) as substantially impaired his mental responsibility for his acts and omissions in doing or being a party to the killing."

murder and successfully appealed to the Court of Criminal Appeal who substituted a verdict of manslaughter, but did not alter the sentence of imprisonment for life.

Extracts from the Judgment of the Court of Criminal Appeal.

LORD PARKER, C.J.—

" 'Abnormality of mind', which has to be contrasted with the time-honoured expression in the M'Naghten rules 'defect of reason', means a state of mind so different from that of ordinary human beings that the reasonable man would term it abnormal. It appears to us to be wide enough to cover the mind's activities in all its aspects, not only the perception of physical acts and matters, and the ability to form a rational judgment as to whether an act is right or wrong, but also the ability to exercise will power to control physical acts in accordance with that rational judgment. The expression 'mental responsibility for his acts' points to a consideration of the extent to which the accused's mind is answerable for his physical acts which must include a consideration of the extent of his ability to exercise will power to control his physical acts.

Whether the accused was at the time of the killing suffering from any 'abnormality of mind' in the broad sense which we have indicated above is a question for the jury. On this question medical evidence is no doubt of importance, but the jury are entitled to take into consideration all the evidence, including the acts or statements of the accused and his demeanour. They are not bound to accept the medical evidence if there is other material before them which, in their good judgment, conflicts with it and outweighs it.

The aetiology of the abnormality of mind (namely, whether it arose from a condition of arrested or retarded development of mind or any inherent causes, or was induced by disease or injury) does, however, seem to be a matter to be determined on expert evidence.

Assuming that the jury are satisfied on the balance of probabilities that the accused was suffering from 'abnormality of mind' from one of the causes specified in the parenthesis of the subsection, the crucial question nevertheless arises: was the abnormality such as substantially impaired his mental responsibility for his acts in doing or being a party to the killing? This is a question of degree and essentially one for the jury. Medical evidence is, of course, relevant, but the question involves a decision not merely as to whether there was some impairment of the mental responsibility of the accused for his acts but whether such impairment can properly be called ' substantial ', a matter upon which juries may quite legitimately differ from doctors.

Furthermore, in a case where the abnormality of mind is one which affects the accused's self-control the step between ' he did not resist his impulse ' and ' he could not resist his impulse ' is, as the evidence in this case shows, one which is incapable of scientific proof. *A fortiori* there is no scientific measurement of the degree of difficulty which an abnormal person finds in controlling his impulses. These problems which in the present state of medical knowledge are scientifically insoluble, the jury can only approach in a broad, common-sense way. This court has repeatedly approved directions to the jury which have followed directions given in Scots cases where the doctrine of diminished responsibility forms part of the common law. We need not repeat them. They are quoted in *R.* v. *Spriggs*.[1] They indicate that such abnormality as ' substantially impairs his mental responsibility ' involves a mental state which in popular language (not that of the M'Naghten rules) a jury would regard as amounting to partial insanity or being on the border-line of insanity.

It appears to us that the judge's direction to the jury that the defence under section 2 of the Act was not available even though they found the facts set out in Nos. 2 and 3 of the judge's summary,[2] amounted to a direction that difficulty or even inability of an accused person to exercise will power to control his physical acts could not amount to such abnormality of mind as substantially impairs his mental responsibility. For the reasons which we have already expressed we think that this construction of the Act is wrong. Inability to exercise will power to control physical acts, provided that it is due to abnormality of mind from one of the causes specified in the parenthesis in the subsection is, in our view, sufficient to entitle the accused to the benefit of the section; difficulty in controlling his physical acts depending on the degree of difficulty, may be. It is for the jury to decide on the whole of the evidence whether such inability

[1] [1958] 1 All E. R. 300. See comment on p. 75, *post*.

[2] These were that Byrne found it difficult or impossible to resist putting his perverted desires into practice and that the act of killing was done under such an impulse or urge.

or difficulty has, not as a matter of scientific certainty but on the balance of probabilities, been established, and in the case of difficulty whether the difficulty is so great as to amount in their view to a substantial impairment of the accused's mental responsibility for his acts. The direction in the present case thus withdrew from the jury the essential determination of fact which it was their province to decide."

APPEAL ALLOWED.

Comment on R. v. Byrne

The Scots cases mentioned in the judgment of Lord GODDARD C.J. in *R.* v. *Spriggs* were *H.M. Advocate* v. *Braithwaite*,[1] *H.M. Advocate* v. *Savage*[2] and *Muir* v. *H.M. Advocate*.[3] The following is an extract from the charge to the jury by Lord COOPER, Lord Justice-Clerk in *H.M. Advocate* v. *Braithwaite*:

" Now I have got to give you the most accurate instruction I can on this delicate question. The Solicitor-General read to you a passage from the charge of the Lord Justice-Clerk in the case of *H.M. Advocate* v. *Savage*,[2] and I am going to read a sentence or two again, because it seems to me to give as explicit and clear a statement of the sort of thing which you have to look for as I can find. He says; ' It is very difficult to put it in a phrase ' and I respectfully agree, ' but it has been put in this way; that there must be aberration or weakness of mind; that there must be some form of mental unsoundness; there must be a state of mind which is bordering on, though not amounting to, insanity; that there must be a mind so affected that responsibility is diminished from full responsibility to partial responsibility—in other words, the prisoner in question must be only partially accountable for his actions.' And then he adds: ' And I think one can see running through the cases that there is implied . . . . that there must be some form of mental disease '. The matter has been put in different words by other judges. I notice in a later case[3] that the condition was referred to for short as ' partial insanity '; and that this was explained as meaning ' that weakness or great peculiarity of mind which the law has recognised as possibly differentiating a case of murder from one of culpable homicide.'[4] And finally to give you one last test, the question as put by the late Lord CLYDE in the same case, quoting from a charge to a jury by Lord MONCRIEFF, was stated thus ([1933] S.C.(J) 46 at p. 48): ' Was he, owing to his mental

[1] 1945 S.C. (J.) 55.
[2] 1932 S.C. (J.) 49, at p. 51.
[3] 1933 S.C. (J.) 46, at p. 49.
[4] The Scots equivalent to manslaughter.

state, of such inferior responsibility that his act should have attributed to it the quality not of murder but of culpable homocide?' You will see, ladies and gentlemen, the stress that has been laid in all these formulations upon weakness of intellect, aberration of mind, mental unsoundness, partial insanity, great peculiarity of mind, and the like. I am emphasising that just now because I shall have to refer to it when I come to say a word about the evidence we have heard today from Dr. Harrowes; but meantime, with those passages in your mind, I can only say to you that this is the sort of thing you have got to look for in the evidence in support of this defence. If you can find enough to justify such a conclusion, your verdict should be one of culpable homicide only. If on the other hand you cannot find enough in the evidence to justify such a conclusion then I have to tell you that so far as this issue is concerned, you must steel yourselves to do your full duty by returning a verdict of guilty of murder."

On the question of the propriety of directing juries to consider whether someone pleading diminished responsibility was, at the material time, on the border-line of insanity, the following statement by Lord TUCKER in the Privy Council in *Rose* v. *R.*,[1] should be borne in mind:

"There may be cases in which the abnormality of mind relied on cannot readily be related to any of the generally recognised types of insanity. If, however, insanity is to be taken into consideration, as undoubtedly will usually be the case, the word must be used in its broad, popular sense. It cannot too often be emphasised that there is no formula that can be safely used in every case—the direction to the jury must always be related to the particular evidence that has been given, and there may be cases where the words 'border-line' and 'insanity' may not be helpful."

The following extract from the Queensland Criminal Code, closely geared to the provisions of that Code about insanity which have already been quoted, may be thought to contrast favourably with s. 2 of the Homicide Act 1957, set out in note 1 on p. 72 *supra*.

Section 305 (A) of the Queensland Criminal Code: "When a person who unlawfully kills another under circumstances which, but for the provisions of this section, would constitute wilful murder or murder, is, at the time of doing the act or making the omission which causes death, in such a state of abnormality of mind (whether arising from a condition of arrested or retarded

---

[1] [1961] A. C. 496, at pp. 507, 508; [1961] 1 All E. R. 859, at pp. 863–864.

development of mind or induced by disease or injury) as substantially to impair his capacity to understand what he is doing, or his capacity to control his actions, or his capacity to know that he ought not to do the act or make the omission, he is guilty of manslaughter only."

R. v. CHARLSON
[1955] 1 All E.R. 859

Automatism is a defence to a charge of unlawfully and maliciously causing grievous bodily harm as well as to charges of causing grievous bodily harm with intent.

Facts.

Without any apparent motive the accused hit his son aged ten over the head with a mallet and threw him out of the window. There was evidence that the accused may have been suffering from a cerebral tumour which would cause acts of impulsive violence. The accused was charged with causing grievous bodily harm to his son with intent to murder or with intent to do grievous bodily harm. The accused was also charged with unlawfully and maliciously causing grievous bodily harm contrary to s. 20 of the Offences against the Person Act, 1861.

Extracts from the Summing up.[1]

BARRY, J.—

" No plea of insanity is raised in this case. If the facts warrant it, it is always open to an accused person to say: 'I was guilty of the offence with which I am charged, but at the time when I committed the offence I was insane, and therefore I should not be punished for what I did.' That is a defence which has to be raised by the accused, and in this case it has not been raised. Indeed, you have heard from the medical officer at Her Majesty's prison in Manchester that this man is sane and is not suffering from a disease of the mind.

. . . Lastly, there is the third charge of inflicting grievous bodily harm. In relation to that charge the prosecution need not prove a definite intent. They do have to prove, however, that the grievous bodily harm was caused by

[1] See the comment of Lord DENNING in *Bratty* v. *A.-G.* for Northern Ireland, p. 81, *post*.

the accused unlawfully and maliciously. This means that there must be a conscious act on the part of the accused. Malice does not necessarily involve the existence of some hostility to the person injured. It does, however, mean that the act must be done consciously. In order to commit an unlawful and malicious act, the accused must know what he is doing and must realise that he has no lawful justification for his act.

These are charges of criminal offences, and the first two are charges of criminal offences of the utmost gravity. In order to commit them an accused must have a guilty mind. For example, an act which otherwise might be an assault would not be an assault if it was done purely accidentally.

You or I in a public street might suddenly put up our hands to stop our hat being blown off, and might hit a passer-by on the nose without knowing he was there. If we had consciously put out our hands, whatever the motive, and hit the passer-by on the nose, it would be an assault, for it would have been a conscious act. If it is purely accidental, no assault is committed; for the element of consciousness is not present.

Similarly in the case of certain diseases, a person suffering from the disease may be deprived of the control of his actions. A man in the throes of an epileptic fit does not know what he is doing. If a friend bends over to assist him, and in the midst of his fit the epileptic grips that friend by the throat, not knowing what he is doing, and in so doing throttles the friend and causes his death, no offence has been committed against the criminal law; because the actions of an epileptic are automatic and unconscious, and his will or consciousness is not applied to what he is doing. He is not in conscious control of his actions, and I do not propose to worry you, or take up your time, by reminding you of the details of the evidence.

. . . . . No specific intention need be proved by the prosecution before the accused can be found guilty of the third charge of inflicting grievous bodily harm. You must, however, be satisfied that he was acting consciously and that he knew what he was doing when he inflicted those blows. If he did, however much his mind was disturbed, and whatever mitigating circumstances there may be, he would be guilty of this offence. If the accused knew that he was striking his son, and if the accused realised that he had no legal excuse for striking him, as clearly he had not, and realised that he was in fact striking his son and did that act consciously and of the accused's own volition, then he would be guilty of inflicting grievous bodily harm. Therefore in considering this third charge you have to ask yourself 'was the accused knowingly striking his son, or was he acting as an automaton without any control or knowledge of the act which he was committing?' "

VERDICT NOT GUILTY

R. v. KEMP

[1956] 3 All E.R. 249[1]

A defect of reason due to arteriosclerosis is a defect of reason due to disease of the mind within the M'Naghten rules.

Facts.

The accused was charged with causing grievous bodily harm to his wife. It was common ground that he hit her over the head with a hammer without any apparent motive, and that at the time he was unaware of the nature and quality of his act. There was evidence that the accused was suffering from arteriosclerosis which interfered with the flow of blood to his brain. The sole issue was whether the accused was suffering from a disease of the mind in which case the proper verdict would have been "guilty but insane" (now not guilty on the ground of insanity) or whether the disease was not a disease of the mind in which case the proper verdict would be a complete acquittal.

Extracts from the Judgment Given before Directing the Jury.

DEVLIN, J.—

" It is not merely a question of his striking his wife when in some mental derangement, not appreciating that what he was doing was wrong, but in the view of all three doctors it is a case in which the accused was not conscious that he picked up the hammer or that he was striking his wife with it. In those circumstances if the presumption that a man is sane continues to govern the case and if the jury accept the evidence to which I have referred, they would have to return a verdict of not guilty on the basis that the

[1] *Cf. R.* v. *Clarke*, p. 63, *supra*.

man was not responsible for his acts and did not know what he was doing and therefore could not have had the necessary guilty intent. That, indeed, was what happened in *R.* v. *Charlson*[1] where the facts were somewhat similar.

. . . . here the doctors are not so agreed and the whole question that I have to determine, which was not considered in that case, is what is meant by ' disease of the mind ' within the meaning of the M'Naghten rules?

. . . . . The prime thing is to determine what is admitted in the present case, namely, whether or not there is a defect of reasoning, and in my judgment the words ' from disease of the mind' are not to be construed as if they were put in for the purposes of distinguishing between diseases of the mind and diseases of the body, diseases which had mental or physical origin, but they were put in primarily for the purpose of limiting the effect of the words ' defect of reason '. A defect of reason is by itself normally enough to make the act irrational and therefore to deny responsibility in law, but it was not intended by that rule that it should apply to defects of reason which were caused simply by brutish stupidity without rational power. It was not intended that the law should say of a person: 'Although with a healthy mind he nevertheless had been brought up in such a way that he had never learned to exercise his reason, and therefore he is suffering from a defect of reason '. The main object, in my judgment, was that it should be decided whether there was a defect of reason which had been caused by a disease affecting the mind; if it were so decided, then there would be insanity within the meaning of the rule in *M'Naghten's* case[2]. The hardening of the arteries is a disease which is shown on the evidence to be capable of affecting the mind in such a way as to cause a defect, temporarily or permanently, of its reasoning and understanding, and is thus a disease of the mind within the meaning of the rule."

GUILTY BUT INSANE[3]

---

[1] [1955] 1 All E. R. 859; p. 77, *supra.*
[2] (1843), 10 Cl. & Fin. 200; p. 60, *supra.*
[3] The verdict would now be an acquittal on the ground of insanity under the Criminal Procedure (Insanity) Act, 1964.

BRATTY v. ATTORNEY-GENERAL FOR NORTHERN IRELAND

[1961] 3 All E. R. 523

(1) *Where the only cause alleged for an involuntary act is a defect of reason due to disease of the mind the judge need not direct the jury on the issue of automatism in addition to that of insanity.* (2) *The burden of disproving automatism which is not due to insanity is borne by the prosecution.*

Facts

Bratty was charged with the murder of a girl. It was not disputed that he had strangled her, but he said that a feeling of blackness came over him when he was with the girl and there was some evidence that he was suffering from psychomotor epilepsy. Bratty's counsel asked, *inter alia*, for an acquittal on the ground of automatism or a verdict of " guilty but insane ". The trial judge directed the jury fully on the issue of insanity, but he did not say that, even if the jury should conclude that Bratty was not insane within the meaning of the M'Naghten rules, they might yet return a verdict of " not guilty " on the ground of automatism due to some cause other than insanity. Bratty was convicted and he unsuccessfully appealed first to the Northern Irish Court of Criminal Appeal and thence to the House of Lords.

Extracts from the speeches in the House of Lords.

LORD DENNING.—

" My Lords, in *Woolmington* v. *Director of Public Prosecutions*[1] Viscount SANKEY, L.C., said: ' When dealing with a murder case the Crown must prove (a) death as the result of a voluntary act of the accused and (b) malice of the accused.' The requirement that it should be a voluntary act is essential, not only in a murder case, but also in every criminal case. No act is punishable if it is done involuntarily: and an involuntary act in this context—some people nowadays prefer to speak of it as ' automatism '—means an act which is done by the muscles without any control by the mind such as a spasm, a reflex action or a convulsion; or an

---

[1] [1935] A.C. 462 [1935] All E.R. Rep. 1; p. 1, *supra*.

act done by a person who is not conscious of what he is doing such as an act done whilst suffering from concussion or whilst sleepwalking. The point was well put by STEPHEN, J., in 1889: '. . . can anyone doubt that a man who, though he might be perfectly sane, committed what would otherwise be a crime in a state of somnambulism, would be entitled to be acquitted? And why is this? Simply because he would not know what he was doing'; see *R.* v. *Tolson.*[1] The term 'involuntary act' is, however, capable of wider connotations: and to prevent confusion it is to be observed that in the criminal law an act is not to be regarded as an involuntary act simply because the doer does not remember it. When a man is charged with dangerous driving, it is no defence for him to say 'I don't know what happened. I cannot remember a thing': see *Hill* v. *Baxter.*[2] Loss of memory afterwards is never a defence in itself, so long as he was conscious at the time; see *Russell* v. *H.M. Advocate*;[3] *R.* v. *Podola.*[4] Nor is an act to be regarded as an involuntary act simply because the doer could not control his impulse to do it. When a man is charged with murder, and it appears that he knew what he was doing, but that he could not resist it, then his assertion 'I couldn't help myself' is no defence in itself: see *A.-G. for South Australia* v. *Brown*:[5] though it may go towards a defence of diminished responsibility, in places where that defence is available, see *R.* v. *Byrne*:[6] but it does not render his act involuntary so as to entitle him to an unqualified acquittal. Nor is an act to be regarded as an involuntary act simply because it is unintentional or its consequences are unforeseen. When a man is charged with dangerous driving, it is no defence for him to say, however truly, 'I did not mean to drive dangerously'. There is said to be an absolute prohibition against that offence, whether he had a guilty mind or not (see *Hill* v. *Baxter*[7] *per* Lord GODDARD, C.J.) but even though it is absolutely prohibited, nevertheless he has a defence if he can show that it was an involuntary act in the sense that he was unconscious at the time and did not know what he was doing (see *H.M. Advocate* v. *Ritchie,*[8] *R.* v.

---

1 (1889), 23 Q.B.D. 168 at p. 187; p. 26, *supra.*
2 [1958] 1 Q.B. 277; [1958] 1 All E.R. 193.
3 1946 S.C. (J.) 37.
4 [1960] 1 Q.B. 325; [1959] 3 All E.R. 418.
5 [1960] A.C. 432, p. 68, *supra*; [1960] 1 All E.R. 734.
6 [1960] 2 Q.B. 396; p. 72, *supra*; [1960] 3 All E.R. 1.
7 [1958] 1 Q.B. 277 at p. 282; [1958] 1 All E.R. 193 at p. 195; but see now *R.* v. *Gosney*, p. 45, *supra.*
8 1926 S. C. (J.) 45.

Minor[1] and *Cooper* v. *McKenna, Ex parte Cooper*[2]).

Another thing to be observed is that it is not every involuntary act which leads to a complete acquittal. Take first an involuntary act which proceeds from a state of drunkenness. If the drunken man is so drunk that he does not know what he is doing, he has a defence to any charge, such as murder or wounding with intent, in which a specific intent is essential, but he is still liable to be convicted of manslaughter or unlawful wounding for which no specific intent is necessary; see *Beard's* case.[3] Again, if the involuntary act proceeds from a disease of the mind, it gives rise to a defence of insanity, but not to a defence of automatism. Suppose a crime is committed by a man in a state of automatism or clouded consciousness due to a recurrent disease of the mind. Such an act is no doubt involuntary, but it does not give rise to an unqualified acquittal, for that would mean that he would be let at large to do it again. The only proper verdict is one which ensures that the person who suffers from the disease is kept secure in a hospital so as not to be a danger to himself or others. That is, a verdict of guilty but insane . . .
. . . The major mental diseases, which the doctors call psychoses, such as schizophrenia, are clearly diseases of the mind. But in *R.* v. *Charlson*,[4] BARRY J. seems to have assumed that other diseases such as epilepsy or cerebral tumour are not diseases of the mind, even when they are such as to manifest themselves in violence. I do not agree with this. It seems to me that any mental disorder which has manifested itself in violence and is prone to recur is a disease of the mind. At any rate it is the sort of disease for which a person should be detained in hospital rather than be given an unqualified acquittal.[5]

---

1 (1955), 15 W.W.R. (N. S.) 433.

2 [1960] Qd. R. 406.

3 *Director of Public Prosecutions* v. *Beard*, [1920] A.C. 479 at pp. 494, 498, 504, p. 87, *supra*; [1920] All E. R. Rep. 21 at pp. 25, 27, 30.

4 [1955] 1 All E.R. 859; p. 77, *supra*.

5 In the course of his summing-up in *R.* v. *Porter* (1933), 55 C. L. R. 182, at pp. 188–189 DIXON J. said: "Mere excitability of a normal man, passion, even stupidity, obtuseness, lack of self-control, impulsiveness are quite different things from what I have attempted to describe as a state of disease or disorder or mental disturbance arising from some infirmity, temporary or of long standing. . . . That does not mean that there must be some physical deterioration of the cells of the brain some actual change in the material, physical constitution of the mind, as disease ordinarily means when you are dealing with other organs of the body where you can see and feel and appreciate structural changes in fibre tissue and the like."

It is to be noticed that in *R.* v. *Charlson* and *R.* v. *Kemp*[1] the defence raised only automatism, not insanity.

In the present case the defence raised both automatism and insanity. And herein lies the difficulty because of the burden of proof. If the accused says he did not know what he was doing, then, so far as the defence of automatism is concerned, the Crown must prove that the act was a voluntary act; see *Woolmington's* case.[2] But so far as the defence of insanity is concerned, the defence must prove that the act was an involuntary act due to disease of the mind; see *M'Naghten's* case.[3] This apparent incongruity was noticed by Sir Owen Dixon, Chief Justice of the High Court of Australia, in an address which is to be found in 31 *Australian Law Journal* 255 and it needs to be resolved. The defence here say: Even though we have not proved that the act was involuntary, yet the Crown have not proved that it was a voluntary act: and that point at least should have been put to the jury.

My Lords, I think that the difficulty is to be resolved by remembering that, whilst the *ultimate* burden rests on the Crown of proving every element essential in the crime, nevertheless in order to prove that the act was a voluntary act, the Crown is entitled to rely on the *presumption* that every man has sufficient mental capacity to be responsible for his crimes: and that if the defence wish to displace that presumption they must give some evidence from which the contrary may reasonably be inferred. . . .

All the doctors agreed that psychomotor epilepsy, if it exists, is a defect of reason due to disease of the mind: and the judge accepted this view. No other cause was canvassed.

In those circumstances, I am clearly of opinion that, if the act of the appellant was an involuntary act, as the defence suggested, the evidence attributed it solely to a disease of the mind and the only defence open was the defence of insanity. There was no evidence of automatism apart from insanity. There was, therefore, no need for the judge to put it to the jury. And when the jury rejected the defence of insanity, they rejected the only defence disclosed by the evidence."

APPEAL DISMISSED.

---

[1] [1957] 1 Q. B. 399; [1956] 3 All E. R. 249.
[2] [1935] A.C. 462 at p. 482; p. 1, *supra*; [1935] All E.R. Rep. 1 at p. 8.
[3] (1843), 10 Cl. & Fin. 200 at p. 210; p. 60, *supra*.

R. v. DOHERTY
(1887), 16 Cox C. C. 306

On a charge of murder, the accused's intoxication may be taken into account in determining whether he had the intention to kill or cause grievous bodily harm.

Facts.

The accused was charged with murder. The evidence was that he shot and killed the deceased whom he had asked to dinner after he had had words with him concerning a bet with a third party. The accused left the room in which he had been talking to the deceased and fetched a revolver which he fired. The accused relied on drunkenness as a defence, and a verdict of manslaughter was returned after the evidence had been reviewed by STEPHEN, J., in his summing-up.

Extracts from the summing-up of:—

STEPHEN, J.—

" It is my duty first, gentlemen, to lay down the law for your instruction with regard to what constitutes the crime of murder. Murder is unlawful homicide with malice aforethought. Manslaughter is unlawful homicide without malice aforethought. First, as to the term 'aforethought,' its meaning has been laid down clearly by HOLT, C. J., who, in *R.* v. *Mawgridge*[1] says: 'He that doth a cruel act voluntarily, doth it of malice prepensed,' which is the same as aforethought. 'Aforethought,' therefore, does not necessarily imply premeditation, but it implies intention which must necessarily precede the act intended. What, then, is the intention necessary to constitute murder? Several intentions would have this effect; but I need mention only two in this case, namely, an intention to kill and an intention to do grievous bodily harm. If the act which caused death, the firing of the pistol, was done with either of these intentions, Doherty's crime was murder. But it is difficult to see how a man can fire a loaded pistol at another without intending to do him grievous bodily harm, so that if you think that Doherty fired the pistol at the deceased's body, intending to hit him, but taking his chance where he

---

[1] (1706), Kel. 119.

hit him, that would be murder, though he did not intend to kill. If, on the other hand, you think that he fired it vaguely, without any special intent at all, and by so doing caused his death, that would be manslaughter. The general rule as to intention is that a man intends the natural consequences of his act. As a rule the use of a knife to stab or of a pistol to shoot shows an intention to do grievous bodily harm, but this is not a necessary inference. In drawing it you should consider for one thing the question whether the prisoner is drunk or sober. It is almost trivial for me to observe that a man is not excused from crime by reason of his drunkenness. If it were so, you might as well at once shut up the criminal courts, because drink is the occasion of a large proportion of the crime which is committed; but, although you cannot take drunkenness as any excuse for crime, yet when the crime is such that the intention of the party committing it is one of its constituent elements, you may look at the fact that a man was in drink in considering whether he formed the intention necessary to constitute the crime. If a sober man takes a pistol, or a knife, and strikes or shoots at some-one else, the inference is that he intended to strike or shoot him with the object of doing him grievous bodily harm. If, however, a man acting in that way was drunk, you have to consider the effect of his drunkenness upon his intention. In such cases a distinction of vital importance occurs to which it is necessary to point. A drunken man may form an intention to kill another, or to do grievous bodily harm to him, or he may not: but if he did form that intention, although a drunken intention, he is just as much guilty of murder as if he had been sober. . . . Manslaughter by negligence occurs when a person is doing anything dangerous in itself, or has charge of anything dangerous in itself, and conducts himself in regard to it in such a careless manner that the jury feel that he is guilty of culpable negligence, and ought to be punished. As to what act of negligence is culpable, you, gentlemen, have a discretion, and you ought to exercise it as well as you can. I will illustrate my meaning. Supposing a man performed a surgical operation, whether from losing his head, or from forgetfulness, or from some other reason, omitted to do something he ought to have done, or did something he ought not to have done, in such a case there would be negligence. But if there was only the kind of forgetfulness which is common to everybody, or if there was a slight want of skill, any injury which resulted might furnish a ground for claiming civil damages, but it would be wrong to proceed against a man criminally in respect of such injury. But if a surgeon was engaged in attending a woman during her confinement, and went to the engagement drunk, and through his drunkenness neglected his duty, and the woman's life was in consequence sacrificed, there would be culpable negligence of a grave kind. It is not given to everyone to be a skilful surgeon, but it is given to everyone to keep sober when such a duty has to be performed. To find culpable negligence in the present case you must assume that the prisoner went into his bedroom, brought out the loaded revolver, and so handled it as in some manner to fire the two shots without intending to fire at all. If, gentlemen, you convict the prisoner of manslaughter, I must ask you to be good enough to say whether you mean manslaughter by violence wilfully inflicted, or by culpable negligence, for, of course, it will make a considerable difference in the punishment. . . ."

VERDICT, GUILTY OF MANSLAUGHTER BY UNLAWFUL VIOLENCE.[1]

DIRECTOR OF PUBLIC PROSECUTIONS v. BEARD

[1920] A. C. 479

Evidence of drunkenness which rendered the accused incapable of forming the specific intent[2] essential to constitute the crime charged ought to be taken into consideration with the other facts proved in order to determine whether he had the intent, but, on a plea of drunkenness, where insanity is not pleaded, the jury should not be asked to consider whether if the accused knew what he was doing, he also knew that he was doing wrong.

Facts.

Beard was charged with the murder of a girl of thirteen He ravished her, and, in furtherance of the rape, he placed

---

[1] The practice of asking the jury to note the grounds for their verdict once given, was deprecated by the Court of Criminal Appeal in *R.* v. *Larkin*, p. 209, *infra*, but in *R.* v. *Matheson*, [1958] 2 All E. R. 87, the same court held that a jury might in appropriate circumstances be asked to indicate whether they returned a verdict of manslaughter on the ground of diminished responsibility or provocation.

[2] In this case "specific intent" is used to mean the intent necessary to constitute the crime charged. Contrast its use in the sense of purpose in the decision in *R.* v. *Steane*, p. 3, *supra*.

his hand over her mouth and his thumb upon her throat, in consequence of which she was suffocated. His defence was that he was drunk.

At the trial before BAILHACHE, J., the jury were directed, *inter alia*, that they must consider whether the accused knew that he was doing wrong. Beard was convicted of murder, and appealed to the Court of Criminal Appeal.

The Court of Criminal Appeal substituted a verdict of manslaughter on the ground that, on the authority of *R.* v. *Meade*[1], the jury should have been asked whether the accused knew that what he did was dangerous.

The prosecution appealed to the House of Lords, but it was intimated that the capital sentence would not be carried out, even if the appeal were successful, as, in fact, it was.

Extracts from Judgments of the House of Lords.

LORD BIRKENHEAD, L.C.—

" . . . In the Court of Criminal Appeal, two separate and independent points of misdirection were raised on behalf of the prisoner :—

(1) That the learned judge should have told the jury that if they were of opinion that the violent act which was the immediate cause of death was not intentional but was an accidental consequence of placing his hand over the mouth of the deceased so as to prevent her screaming, they could and should return a verdict of manslaughter, and

(2) That the learned judge wrongly directed the jury as to the defence of drunkenness, and gave a direction which was not in accordance with the decisions in *Meade's Case*[1] and was applicable only to the defence of insanity.

The first objection failed, the Court being of opinion (apart from the defence of drunkenness) that the evidence established that the prisoner killed the child by an act of violence done in the course or in the furtherance of the crime of rape, a felony involving violence. The Court held that by the law of England such an act was murder. No attempt has been made in your Lordships' House to displace this view of the law and there can be no doubt as to its soundness.[2]

With regard to the second objection the Court of Criminal Appeal, holding itself bound, by previous decisions

---

[1] [1909] 1 K. B. 895.

[2] But the law has now been changed by s. 1 of the Homicide Act, 1957.

of its own, to the view that *R.* v. *Meade*[1] laid down a general code, came to the conclusion that the learned judge had given a direction which was calculated to mislead the jury by imposing a test applicable only to the defence of insanity instead of the test, imagined to be generally laid down in *Meade's Case*, for application to the defence of drunkenness. The Court was not satisfied that the verdict would have been the same if the proper direction had been given, and substituted a verdict of manslaughter for that of murder. . . .

It becomes necessary . . . to consider the state of the law before *Meade's Case* and to examine the authority of this decision.

Under the law of England as it prevailed until early in the nineteenth century voluntary drunkenness was never an excuse for criminal misconduct; and indeed the classic authorities broadly assert that voluntary drunkenness must be considered rather an aggravation than a defence. . . .

Judicial decisions extending over a period of nearly one hundred years make it plain that the rigidity of this rule was gradually relaxed in the nineteenth century, though this mitigation cannot for a long time be affiliated upon a single or very intelligible principle. . . .

The conclusions to be drawn from these cases may be stated under three heads :—

1. That insanity, whether produced by drunkenness or otherwise, is a defence to the crime charged. The distinction between the defence of insanity in the true sense caused by excessive drinking, and the defence of drunkenness which produces a condition such that the drunken man's mind becomes incapable of forming a specific intention, has been preserved throughout the cases. The insane person cannot be convicted of a crime: *Felstead* v. *R.*;[2] but, upon a verdict of insanity, is ordered to be detained during His Majesty's pleasure. The law takes no note of the cause of the insanity. If actual insanity in fact supervenes, as the result of alcoholic excess, it furnishes as complete an answer to a criminal charge as insanity induced by any other cause. . . .

2. That evidence of drunkenness which renders the accused incapable of forming the specific intent essential to constitute the crime should be taken into consideration with the other facts proved in order to determine whether or not he had this intent.[3]

---

[1] [1909] 1 K.B. 895.
[2] [1914] A. C. 534.
[3] See criticism of this proposition in *Broadhurst* v. *R.*, p. 96, *infra*.

3. That evidence of drunkenness falling short of a proved incapacity in the accused to form the intent necessary to constitute the crime, and merely establishing that his mind was affected by drink so that he more readily gave way to some violent passion, does not rebut the presumption that a man intends the natural consequences of his acts.[1]

I now come to *R.* v. *Meade.*[2] The prisoner was charged with murder. He brutally ill-treated the deceased woman during the night of her death; broke a broomstick over her, and struck her a violent blow with his fist, rupturing an intestine and causing her death. The defence was that he was drunk and did not intend to cause death or grievous bodily harm, and consequently that the verdict should be manslaughter. Lord COLERIDGE, J., directed the jury in the following terms: 'In the first place, every one is presumed to know the consequences of his acts. If he is insane, that knowledge is not presumed. Insanity is not pleaded here, but where it is part of the essence of a crime that a motive, a particular motive' (meaning intent), 'shall exist in the mind of the man who does the act, the law declares this—that if the mind at that time is so obscured by drink, if the reason is dethroned and the man is incapable therefore of forming that intent, it justifies the reduction of the charge from murder to manslaughter.' The objection raised in the Court of Criminal Appeal was that the summing up led the jury to believe that to justify a verdict of manslaughter they must find that the prisoner was insane or in a state resembling insanity, whereas the direction should have been that if there was absence of intention in fact it was manslaughter.

DARLING, J., in delivering the judgment of the Court reviewed many of the authorities that were cited to your Lordships, and came to the conclusion that the judges by these decisions had attempted to express the doctrine that, where intent is of the essence of the crime charged, the intent may be disproved by showing that the prisoner was in a condition of drunkenness which made him incapable of forming the intent. The learned judge said: 'We desire to state the rule in the following terms: A man is taken to intend the natural consequences of his acts. This presumption may be rebutted—(1) in the case of a sober man, in many ways; (2) it may also be rebutted in the case of a man who is drunk, by showing his mind to have been so affected by the drink

[1] See *Broadhurst* v. *R.*, p. 96, *infra*, on the use of the word "proved" in this context. [1909] 1 K. B. 895, at pp. 896-899.

[2] [1909] 1 K.B. 895.

he had taken that he was incapable of knowing that what he was doing was dangerous—*i.e.*, likely to inflict serious injury. If this be proved, the presumption that he intended to do grievous bodily harm is rebutted.' The learned judge then expressed the conclusion of the Court that on a true construction, the language used by Lord COLERIDGE, J., did not differ from this rule. The language of the Court of Criminal Appeal contains a proposition of law which, regarded as a rule of general application, would mean that a person charged with a crime of violence may show, in order to rebut the presumption that he intended the natural consequences of his acts, that he was so drunk that he was incapable of knowing what he was doing was dangerous. The Court of Criminal Appeal in the present case, notwithstanding the opinion it had expressed that an act of violence done in furtherance of rape was murder, held that it was bound to follow this decision, and that the jury should have been directed to consider whether Beard, at the time of placing his hand on the child as described, was incapable of knowing that what he was doing was dangerous—that is, likely to cause serious injury.

. . . The difficulty has arisen largely because the Court of Criminal Appeal used language which has been construed as suggesting that the test of the condition of mind of the prisoner is not whether he was incapable of forming the intent but whether he was incapable of foreseeing or measuring the consequences of the act. In this respect the so-called rule differs from the direction of Lord COLERIDGE, J., which is more strictly in accordance with the earlier authorities.

Consideration of the judgment, and particularly of DARLING, J.'s observations that the Court did not wish to extend the ambit of its decision beyond that laid down in the older cases, makes it clear that it was not intended to lay down a rule which should be applied to such a case as the present. In *Meade's Case*[1] the crime charged was that death arose from violence done with intent to cause grievous bodily harm. In this case the death arose from a violent act done in furtherance of what was in itself a felony of violence. In *Meade's Case*,[1] therefore, it was essential to prove the specific intent; in Beard's case it was only necessary to prove that the violent act causing death was done in furtherance of the felony of rape.[2]

---

[1] [1909] 1 K. B. 895.

[2] This would now be insufficient to procure a conviction for murder on account of s. 1 of the Homicide Act, 1957.

I do not think that the proposition of law deduced from these earlier cases is an exceptional rule applicable only to cases in which it is necessary to prove a specific intent in order to constitute the graver crime—*e.g.*, wounding with intent to do grievous bodily harm or with intent to kill. It is true that in such cases the specific intent must be proved to constitute the particular crime, but this is, on ultimate analysis, only in accordance with the ordinary law applicable to crime, for, speaking generally (and apart from certain special offences), a person cannot be convicted of a crime unless the *mens* was *rea*. Drunkenness rendering a person incapable of the intent would be an answer, as it is for example in a charge of attempted suicide. In *R.* v. *Moore*[1] drunkenness was held to negative the intent in such a case, and JERVIS, C.J., said: 'If the prisoner was so drunk as not to know what she was about, how can you say that she intended to destroy herself?'

My Lords, drunkenness in this case could be no defence unless it could be established that Beard at the time of committing the rape was so drunk that he was incapable of forming the intent to commit it, which was not in fact, and manifestly, having regard to the evidence, could not be contended. For in the present case the death resulted from two acts or from a succession of acts, the rape and the act of violence causing suffocation. These acts cannot be regarded separately and independently of each other. The capacity of the mind of the prisoner to form the felonious intent which murder involves is in other words to be explored in relation to the ravishment; and not in relation merely to the violent acts which gave effect to the ravishment. . . .

Neither should the learned judge in my opinion have introduced the question whether 'the prisoner knew that he was doing wrong' in a defence of drunkenness, where insanity was not pleaded. It is a dangerous and confusing question to put to a jury, for a drunken man's judgment upon such a question is very likely to be impaired, and it might well be perplexing to a jury to determine whether, if he knew what he was doing, he knew also that he was doing wrong. The general proposition that drunkenness is no excuse for crime may be seriously affected in its operation if such a question is to be a test by which the jury may determine whether the verdict should be murder or manslaughter. It is noteworthy that, notwithstanding that the judges ever

[1] (1852), 3 Car. & Kir. 319.

since *M'Naghten's Case*[1] in 1843 have had these questions in mind as the test of insanity, there is no single case, known to me, where drunkenness has been the defence, in which the judge has directed the jury to consider whether the prisoner knew that he was doing wrong. Whenever this question has been put the defence has been that there existed insanity caused by drink. I look upon the direction of BAILHACHE, J., as an innovation which is not supported by authority and which should not be repeated or imitated. But while I think that the summing up was in some respects unhappily conceived, I am not prepared, reading it as a whole, to hold in this case that it amounted to, or should be treated as, a misdirection. The defence which is founded upon insanity is one thing. The defence which is founded upon drunkenness is another. The relevant considerations are not identical. It is inconvenient to use the same language in charging juries in relation to different defences. But the portions of the summing up which I have criticised were in fact unduly favourable to the prisoner. He cannot complain of them unless they so confused the jury as to prevent them from properly appreciating the true issue, and I am not prepared to lay it down—though I have felt some doubt upon the point—that the actual direction given to the jury by BAILHACHE, J., disabled them from reaching a true conclusion upon the matters which required decision. . . ."

APPEAL ALLOWED.

ATTORNEY-GENERAL FOR NORTHERN IRELAND v. GALLAGHER

[1961] 3 All E. R. 299

When a disease of the mind is aggravated by self-induced intoxication, regard may be had to the accused's state of mind before the intoxication in determining whether the M'Naghten rules apply to the case.

Facts.

Gallagher was charged with the murder of his wife. He was probably a psychopath, suffering from a disease of the mind which was liable to be exaggerated by drink. Gallagher formed the intention of killing his wife and, in

[1] (1843), 10 Cl. & F. 200; p. 60, *supra*.

furtherance of that intention, bought a knife and a bottle of whisky. On the same day he killed his wife with the knife and consumed a considerable quantity of the whisky. He pleaded insanity and drunkenness of such a degree that he was incapable of forming the intent necessary for murder. The summing-up contained a suggestion that, in considering the defence of insanity, the jury should pay attention to the accused's state of mind before he consumed the whisky and Gallagher was convicted. He successfully appealed to the Northern Irish Court of Criminal Appeal by which he was acquitted. The court took the view that the summing-up was wrong in so far as it suggested that, in considering the applicability of the M'Naghten rules, regard might be had to any period of time before the homicidal act. The Attorney-General for Northern Ireland successfully appealed to the House of Lords.

Extracts from the speeches in the House of Lords.

LORD DENNING.—

" My Lords, this case differs from all others in the books in that the respondent, whilst sane and sober, before he took to the drink, had already made up his mind to kill his wife. This seems to me to be far worse—and far more deserving of condemnation—than the case of a man who, before getting drunk, has no intention to kill, but afterwards in his cups, whilst drunk, kills another by an act which he would not dream of doing when sober. Yet, by the law of England, in this latter case his drunkenness is no defence even though it has distorted his reason and his will-power. So why should it be a defence in the present case? And is it made any better by saying that the man is a psychopath? The answer to the question is, I think, that the case falls to be decided by the general principle of English law that, subject to very limited exceptions, drunkenness is no defence to a criminal charge nor is a defect of reason produced by drunkenness. . .

The general principle which I have enunciated is subject to two exceptions: (i) If a man is charged with an offence in which a specific intention is essential (as in murder, though not in manslaughter), then evidence of drunkenness, which renders him incapable of forming that intent, is an answer; see *Beard's* case.[1] This degree of drunkenness is reached

---

[1] [1920] A. C. 479 at pp. 501, 504; [1920] All E. R. Rep. 21 at pp. 28, 30.

when the man is rendered so stupid by drink that he does not know what he is doing (see *R.* v. *Moore*[1]) as where, at a christening, a drunken nurse put the baby behind a large fire, taking it for a log of wood (18 *Gentleman's Magazine*, 1748, p. 570); and where a drunken man thought his friend (lying in his bed) was a theatrical dummy placed there and stabbed him to death (*The Times*, 13th January, 1951). In each of those cases it would not be murder. But it would be manslaughter. (ii) If a man by drinking brings on a distinct disease of the mind such as delirium tremens, so that he is temporarily insane within the M'Naghten rules,[2] that is to say, he does not at the time know what he is doing or that it is wrong, then he has a defence on the ground of insanity; see *R.* v. *Davis*[3] and *Beard's* case.[4]

Does the present case come within the general principle or the exceptions to it? It certainly does not come within the first exception. The respondent was not incapable of forming an intent to kill. Quite the contrary. He knew full well what he was doing. He formed an intent to kill, he carried out his intention and he remembered afterwards what he had done. And the jury, properly directed on the point, have found as much, for they found him guilty of murder. Then does the case come within the second exception? It does not to my mind; for the simple reason that he was not suffering from a disease of the mind brought on by drink. He was suffering from a different disease altogether. . . .

My Lords, I think the law on this point should take a clear stand. If a man, whilst sane and sober, forms an intention to kill and makes preparation for it, knowing it is a wrong thing to do, and then gets himself drunk so as to give himself Dutch courage to do the killing, and whilst drunk carries out his intention, he cannot rely on this self-induced drunkenness as a defence to a charge of murder, nor even as reducing it to manslaughter. He cannot say that he got himself into such a stupid state that he was incapable of an intent to kill. So, also, when he is a psychopath, he cannot by drinking rely on his self-induced defect of reason as a defence of insanity. The wickedness of his mind before he got drunk is enough to condemn him, coupled with the act which he intended to do and did do. A psychopath who goes out intending to kill, knowing it is wrong, and does kill,

---

[1] (1852), 3 Car. & Kir. 319.
[2] (1843), 10 Cl. & Fin. 200.
[3] (1881), 14 Cox, C. C. 563.
[4] [1920] .A C. 479 at pp. 500, 501; [1920] All E. R. Rep. 21 at pp. 28, 29.

cannot escape the consequences by making himself drunk before doing it. That is, I believe, the direction which the Lord Chief Justice gave to the jury and which the Court of Criminal Appeal found to be wrong. I think that it was right, and for this reason I would allow the appeal."

APPEAL ALLOWED.[1]

BROADHURST v. R.

[1964] 1 All E.R. 111

Dicta *of Lord Birkenhead in* Director of Public Prosecutions *v.* Beard[2] *basing the defence of drunkenness on incapacity to form the intent may require reconsideration, and* dicta *suggesting that the burden of establishing the defence of drunkenness is borne by the accused are wrong.*

Facts.

The accused was convicted by a Maltese court of causing grievous bodily harm from which death ensued, contrary to the Criminal Code of Malta. The Judicial Committee of the Privy Council advised that his appeal should be allowed on the ground that the judge had gone too far in expressing his views with regard to the evidence. The accused raised the defence of drunkenness to a charge of wilful homicide of his wife, and, for present purposes, the case is only important because of the observations of the Judicial Committee on the subject of drunkenness. Section

---

[1] The approach of the other Lords of Appeal was slightly different from that of Lord DENNING for they appear to have considered that the summing-up as a whole directed the jury to consider whether the accused knew the nature and quality of his act at the time he did it. The reference to the position before the whisky was opened may have been designed to direct the jury to examine the question whether the accused could be said to have been suffering, at the time of the homicide, from a disease of the mind induced by drink in which case the M'Naghten rules could have been applied.

Section 6 of the Criminal Justice Act (Northern Ireland), 1966 provides that the insane person whose mental abnormality was of a temporary nature and attributable solely to his own voluntary conduct in taking intoxicating liquor or drugs shall on a charge of murder be convicted of manslaughter unless, immediately before he took the intoxicating liquor or drugs, he had formed the intention to kill or cause serious bodily harm, in which case his crime will continue to be murder.

[2] [1920] A. C. 479; p. 87, *supra*.

35(4) of the Criminal Code of Malta provides that: " Intoxication shall be taken into account for the purpose of determining whether the person charged had formed any intention, specific or otherwise, in the absence of which he would not be guilty of the offence."

Extracts from the Advice of the Judicial Committee.

LORD DEVLIN.—

" Their lordships have already referred to s. 35 of the Code which, it was said, embodies the law of England. Under sub-s. (4) it would appear that drunkenness is to be taken into account for the purpose of determining whether the person charged had in fact formed any intention necessary to constitute the crime. The corresponding proposition laid down in *Director of Public Prosecutions* v. *Beard* is that evidence of drunkenness which renders the accused *incapable* of forming the specific intent essential to constitute the crime should be taken into consideration with the other facts proved in order to determine whether or not he had this intent. There is no mention in the Code of incapacity. The proposition stated in *Director of Public Prosecutions* v. *Beard* is not altogether easy to grasp. If an accused is rendered incapable of forming an intent, whatever the other facts in the case may be, he cannot have formed it; and it would not, therefore, be sensible to take the incapacity into consideration together with the other facts in order to determine whether he had the necessary intent. It may be that the wording of s. 35(4) of the Code is designed to avoid this logical difficulty and that there is no substantial difference between the two propositions. Or it may be that the law as laid down in *Director of Public Prosecutions* v. *Beard* must now be interpreted in the light of later decisions on the proof of guilty intent. But superficially at any rate s. 35(4) of the Code and *Director of Public Prosecutions* v. *Beard* approach differently the problem of proving intent. One way of approaching the problem is to say that it is always for the Crown to prove that the accused actually had the intent necessary to constitute the crime: and that that proof may emerge from evidence or statements made by the accused about his own state of mind or may be made by way of inference from the totality of the circumstances. *Prima facie* intoxication is one circumstance to be taken into account and on this view all that s. 35(4) is doing is to make it plain that intoxication is not to be excluded. On the other hand, the sort of approach that is contemplated in *Director of Public Prosecutions* v. *Beard* is that there must be proof (or at least some suggestion) of incapacity in order to rebut the presumption that a man intends the natural consequences of his acts.

In his directions to the jury in this matter the learned Chief Justice adopted the language of *Director of Public Prosecutions* v. *Beard* and talked throughout of incapacity. At first sight this might seem to make it necessary for their lordships to explore further the difficulties which they have just indicated; but on the particular facts of this case their lordships find it unnecessary to do so. This is not a case in which there is direct evidence about the accused's state of mind and the effect of drink on it. There is evidence about what the accused did in fact, but what he intended to do is a matter for inference. In a case in which the intent of an accused is to be ascertained solely by inference, nothing short of incapacity need be considered. If an accused cannot himself give evidence about his state of mind, he cannot say what intent he in fact formed or did not form; and it is, therefore, only if there is material to suggest that by reason of intoxication he could not have formed a guilty intent that the inference which would otherwise naturally be drawn from the circumstances can be questioned. No valid criticism can, therefore, be based on the fact that the learned Chief Justice throughout referred to incapacity as the test. . . . . The other passage which is complained of is as follows: ' Evidence of drunkenness falling short of a proved incapacity in the accused to form the intent necessary to constitute the crime, and merely establishing that his mind was affected by drink so that he more readily gave way to some violent passion does not rebut the presumption that a man intends the natural consequences of his acts.'

Objection is taken to the word ' proved '. In putting the matter in this way the learned Chief Justice was following verbatim the words used by Lord BIRKENHEAD, L.C., in *Director of Public Prosecutions* v. *Beard*. But much has been said judicially since 1920 about proof of intent, notably in *Woolmington* v. *Director of Public Prosecutions*.[1] Before the Board the Crown conceded that it is not for an accused to prove incapacity affecting the intent and that, if there is material suggesting intoxication, the jury should be directed to take it into account and to determine whether it is weighty

---

[1] [1935] All E. R. Rep. 1; p. 1, *supra*.

enough to leave them with a reasonable doubt about the accused's guilty intent. Their lordships approve this concession. The dictum of Lord BIRKENHEAD cannot be treated as laying down the law on burden of proof, and it is therefore unwise to use the dictum in a direction to a jury."

APPEAL ALLOWED.

R. v. LIPMAN

[1970] 1 Q.B. 152

(1) *For the purposes of criminal responsibility there is no distinction between the effect of drink voluntarily taken and of drugs voluntarily consumed;* (2) *the fact that the accused was unaware of what he was doing owing to the influence of drugs voluntarily consumed is no defence to a charge of involuntary manslaughter by means of an unlawful act.*

Facts.

Lipman was charged with the murder of a girl. It was not disputed that he had gone with her to her rooms, and that she had met her death in consequence of severe blows over the head and of asphyxia due to having had about eight inches of sheet thrust into her mouth. Lipman's defence was that he and the girl had gone together on a 'trip' involving the consumption of LSD and that, in the course of that trip, he had the illusion that he had got to the centre of the earth where he was attacked by snakes.

As to manslaughter, the trial judge directed the jury to consider whether (1) the accused must have realised, before he took the LSD, that the acts subsequently performed by him were dangerous; (2) the accused was aware that the consumption of the LSD involved the risk of harm to others; and (3) the accused was grossly negligent and reckless in taking the LSD. The jury returned a verdict of manslaughter under heads (1) and (3).

Lipman unsuccessfully appealed to the Court of Appeal against conviction and sentence.

Extracts from the Judgment of the Court of Appeal.

WIDGERY, L. J.—

" For the purposes of criminal responsibility we see no

reason to distinguish between the effect of drugs voluntarily taken and drunkenness voluntarily induced. As to the latter there is a great deal of authority. First of all, in *Director of Public Prosecutions* v. *Beard*[1] there appears the following oft quoted passage from the speech of Lord BIRKENHEAD, L.C.[2]:

"... where a specific intent is an essential element in the offence, evidence of a state of drunkenness rendering the accused incapable of forming such an intent should be taken into consideration in order to determine whether he had in fact formed the intent necessary to constitute the particular crime. If he was so drunk that he was incapable of forming the intent required he could not be convicted of a crime which was committed only if the intent was proved."

More recently, in two further cases in the House of Lords, the same principle is to be found. The first is *Bratty* v. *Attorney-General for Northern Ireland*[3]. I quote from the speech of Lord Denning where he said[4]:

"... If the drunken man is so drunk that he does not know what he is doing, he has a defence to any charge, such as murder or wounding with intent, in which a specific intent is essential, but he is still liable to be convicted of manslaughter or unlawful wounding for which no specific intent is necessary, see *Beard's* case ."

The other case is *Attorney-General for Northern Ireland* v. *Gallagher*,[5]. . . Those authorities show quite clearly in our opinion that it was well established that no specific intent was necessary to support a conviction for manslaughter based upon a killing in the course of an unlawful act and that accordingly, self-induced drunkenness was no defence to such a charge. In a case of manslaughter by neglect, however, it has been recognised that some mental element must be established, and for this I turn to *Andrews* v. *Director of Public Prosecutions*[6].

It is to be observed that in that case there are two references to *mens rea*; and the next case in which a similar reference is made is *R.* v. *Church*[7]. That seems to be the first case in which a reference to *mens rea* occurs when the killing

---

[1] [1920] A.C. 479, p. 87, *supra*.
[2] At p. 499.
[3] [1963] A.C. 386, p. 81, *supra*.
[4] At p. 410.
[5] [1963] A.C. 349, p. 93, *supra*.
[6] [1937] A.C. 576; [1937] 2 All E.R. 552; p. 224, *infra*.
[7] [1966] 1 Q.B. 59; [1965] 2 All E.R. 72, p. 214, *infra*.

was the result of an allegedly unlawful act, and the crucial passage appears in the judgment of Edmund DAVIES, J.[1]:

'. . . it appears to this court that the passage of years has achieved a transformation in this branch of the law and, even in relation to manslaughter, a degree of *mens rea* has become recognised as essential. To define it is a difficult task, and in *Andrews* v. *Director of Public Prosecutions*,[2] Lord ATKIN spoke[3] of the " element of ' unlawfulness ' which is the elusive factor ". Stressing that we are here leaving entirely out of account those ingredients of homicide which might justify a verdict of manslaughter on the grounds of (a) criminal negligence, or (b) provocation, or (c) diminished responsibility, the conclusion of this court is that an unlawful act causing the death of another cannot, simply because it is an unlawful act, render a manslaughter verdict inevitable. For such a verdict inexorably to follow, the unlawful act must be such as all sober and reasonable people would inevitably recognise must subject the other person to, at least, the risk of some harm resulting therefrom, albeit not serious harm.'

That passage forms the basis of the defendant's submission before us, namely, that by 1965, the date of *R.* v. *Church*, it had become recognised that guilt of manslaughter derived from the prisoner's having intended or foreseen that some harm should befall the victim as a result of his action. It is accepted in this argument that, at that time, the so-called objective test was applied to the state of the prisoner's mind, so that the issue was concluded against him if ordinary sober and reasonable people would recognise that harm was likely to be caused. But it is nevertheless maintained that the theoretical basis of guilt was the prisoner's supposed intent or foresight.

The final step in the argument is that s. 8 of the Criminal Justice Act, 1967, has replaced the objective test by a subjective one, so that the jury are now required to consider the actual state of the prisoner's own mind at the relevant time. Section 8 is in these terms:

' A court or jury, in determining whether a person has committed an offence,—(a) shall not be bound in law to infer that he intended or foresaw a result of his actions by reason only of its being a natural and probable consequence of those actions; but (b) shall decide whether he did intend or foresee

[1] At p. 69.
[2] [1937] A.C. 576.
[3] *Ibid.*, at p. 581.

that result by reference to all the evidence, drawing such inferences from the evidence as appear proper in the circumstances.'

If the defendant's argument be sound, it follows that we have come a long way since *Beard's* case,[1] and that events have moved very fast. In our judgment, there is a flaw in the defendant's argument; and the flaw lies in the assumption that *R.* v. *Church*[2] introduced a new element of intent or foreseeability into this type of manslaughter. All that the judgment in *Church's* case says in terms is that whereas, formerly, a killing by any unlawful act amounted to manslaughter, this consequence does not now inexorably follow unless the unlawful act is one in which ordinary sober and responsible people would recognise the existence of risk.

The development recognised by *R.* v. *Church* relates to the type of act from which a charge of manslaughter may result, not in the intention (real or assumed) of the prisoner. It is perhaps unfortunate that a reference to *mens rea*, which had been found unhelpful by Lord ATKIN (in *Andrews* v. *Director of Public Prosecutions*, [1937] A. C. 576, 583), was repeated in *R.* v. *Church*,[3] and to give it the effect now contended for would be contrary to *Beard's* case,[4] and the other authorities which we have cited . . . Even if intent has to be proved to constitute the unlawful act, no specific further intent is required to turn that act into manslaughter. Manslaughter remains a most difficult offence to define because it arises in so many different ways and, as the mental element (if any) required to establish it varies so widely, any general reference to *mens rea* is apt to mislead.

We can dispose of the present application by reiterating that when the killing results from an unlawful act of the prisoner no specific intent has to be proved to convict of manslaughter, and self-induced intoxication is accordingly no defence. Since in the present case the acts complained of were obviously likely to cause harm to the victim (and did, in fact, kill her) no acquittal was possible and the verdict of manslaughter, at the least, was inevitable . . .

APPEAL DISMISSED.

---

[1] [1920] A.C. 479.
[2] [1966] 1 Q.B. 59; [1965] 2 All E.R. 72.
[3] [1966] 1 Q.B. 59; [1965] 2 All E.R. 72.
[4] [1920] A.C. 479.

Comment on Director of Public Prosecutions v. Beard, Attorney-General for Northern Ireland v. Gallagher, and R. v. Lipman.

Beard's case.—

Lord BIRKENHEAD's statement of the conclusions to be drawn from the early authorities on drunkenness, and particularly the conclusion that " evidence of drunkenness which renders the accused incapable of forming the specific intent essential to constitute the crime should be taken into consideration with the other facts proved in order to determine whether or not he had this intent ", is to the same effect as s. 28 of the Queensland Code which reads as follows:

" When an intention to cause a specific result is an element of an offence, intoxication, whether complete or partial, and whether intentional or unintentional, may be regarded for the purpose of ascertaining whether such an intention in fact existed."

Section 17 of the Tasmanian Code, enacted four years after Lord BIRKENHEAD's speech is even more reminiscent of the terms of part of that speech. After providing that the rules governing insanity shall apply to a person suffering from a disease of the mind caused by intoxication, s. 17 continues:

" (2) Evidence of such intoxication as would render the accused incapable of forming the specific intent essential to constitute the offence with which he is charged shall be taken into consideration with the other evidence in order to determine whether or not he had that intent.

(3) Evidence of intoxication not amounting to any such incapacity as aforesaid shall not rebut the presumption that a person intends the natural and probable consequences of his act."

Broadhurst v. *R.* has been included on account of the criticism of two passages in Lord BIRKENHEAD'S speech in *Beard's* case. Further criticism can be based on the fact that the drawback of any statement of the law based on the requirement of " specific intent " is the ambiguity of that phrase. It is sometimes used to mean the intent which must be specified in the indictment, as an intent to cause grievous bodily harm or resist arrest must be specified on charges of wounding or causing grievous bodily harm with intent contrary to s. 18 of the Offences against the Person Act 1861. Sometimes " specific intent " is used as a synonym for further intent as the further intent to steal must be proved in addition to the intentional trespass in burglary; on other occasions " specific intent " seems to be used in the sense of direct as opposed to oblique intent, i.e. the aim to produce a particular result as distinct from knowledge that such a result is likely or even certain (see the explanation of *R.* v. *Steane* (p. 3, *ante*) in *Director of Public Prosecutions* v. *Smith* at p. 189, *post*). The only result of the use of the phrase in the Commonwealth Codes has been futile controversy on such questions as whether rape is a crime in relation to which a " specific intent " must be proved.

Gallagher's case.—

Lord DENNING's restriction of the defence of drunkenness to cases in which a specific intent must be proved or in which drink causes a disease of the mind, seems to be inconsistent with the later part of Lord BIRKENHEAD's speech in *Beard's* case in which he treats the law with regard to drunkenness as an application of the ordinary requirement of *mens rea*. On this view, though drunkenness should not be a defence when liability is based on negligence as it is in manslaughter, it should, if of the requisite degree, be a defence when liability is based on recklessness or malice, and the Courts of New South Wales, a jurisdiction in which the defence of drunkenness is governed by the common law, have reached this conclusion (*R.* v. *Stones*, [1956] S.R.(N.S.W.) 25). Such a conclusion conflicts with Lord DENNING's statement in *Bratty* v. *A.-G. for Northern Ireland* (at p. 81, *ante*.) that drunkenness can never be a defence to unlawful and malicious wounding contrary to s. 20 of the Offences against the Person Act, 1861.

R. v. *Lipman*.

In *R.* v. *Haywood*[1] CROCKETT, J., sitting in the Supreme Court of Victoria, declined to follow *R.* v. *Lipman* and the dicta in the House of Lords upon which that decision was based. Australian courts are not bound to follow decisions of the English Court of Appeal or dicta in the House of Lords, but the dissent of CROCKETT, J., is nonetheless interesting.

Haywood was a boy of fifteen who, after consuming some valium tablets, broke into a house where he drank whisky. He found a rifle and ammunition in the house and fired some shots into the street outside. One of these shots killed a woman and Haywood was charged with her murder. His defence amounted to a plea of automatism due to the consumption of valium and whisky. Before the judge summed up to the jury, counsel for the Crown submitted, on the authority of *R.* v. *Lipman*, that the verdict must be one of manslaughter at least, an acquittal being impossible in law. CROCKETT, J., held against the submission and said that he would direct the jury that they must acquit Haywood unless satisfied that he was not acting in a state of automatism.

---

[1] [1971] V.R. 755.

After citing the observation of WIDGERY, L.J., in *R.* v. *Lipman* that the authorities show quite clearly that it was well established that no specific intention was necessary to support a conviction for manslaughter based on a killing in the course of an unlawful act and that accordingly self-induced drunkenness was no defence to such a charge, CROCKETT, J., continued:

" It seems to me, if I might say so with respect, that that observation fails to take account of the fact that in some offences, such as murder, the question of the mental state of the accused person has to be considered in respect of no less than two of the elements of the crime charged.

One of the elements is that the act done must be with the intent to kill or cause grievous bodily harm. The passage to which I have just referred, I think, makes it clear enough that if that intent is unable to be established beyond reasonable doubt by the Crown, then a jury is unable to find the person charged guilty of murder, and that is so even if the inability to establish the existence of such an intent flows from an impairment of the accused's state of mind that is attributable to an intake of a drug, be it alcohol or some other form of drug. Moreover, it is of no relevance that the intake is due to some act of self-induction. But there still remains what to my mind is the necessity to have regard to the mental element or the mental state of the accused person in respect of the first and foremost element of the crime of murder namely, that the act which caused the death must be a conscious voluntary and deliberate act. . . . It seems to me that, in order to determine the voluntariness or otherwise of the act, the state of mind of the accused must be looked at. And it is in this particular connection that the cases to which reference has already been made do not appear to give specific attention.

It is also true enough that it is now well settled that in the absence of a specific intention to kill or cause grievous bodily harm, if the act in question that causes death is an unlawful one, then the correct verdict is manslaughter if the jury are satisfied by the application of an objective test that a reasonable person in the accused's situation would realise that the act would expose the deceased to an appreciable danger of some really serious injury.[1] . . . But this, I think, does not remove the difficulty of considering the state of mind of the accused person in limine as it were so as to determine whether the initial action which is that which causes

[1] According to *R.* v. *Church*, [1966] 1 Q.B. 59; [1965] 2 All E.R. 72, the act must be one from which there is at least the risk of some harm resulting, albeit not serious harm. The recent Australian cases tend to define the unlawful act which will support a verdict of manslaughter in narrower terms, such as those used by CROCKETT, J.

the death of the deceased could be characterised as a conscious deliberate and voluntary act. . . .

It may be said that a reasonable rationalisation is that, being a drug addict, the appellant in *Lipman's* case was well aware that a result or possible result of his self-induced state of hallucination following upon the intake of the drug LSD would be that he would involve himself in dangerous acts from any one of which injury or death might possibly result, and that the voluntary act in those circumstances of taking the drug itself constitutes the act of a voluntary nature upon which can be erected the other elements to support a verdict of manslaughter. Indeed a somewhat analogous analysis might be thought to have been suggested by the facts of *Gallagher's* case. I find it difficult myself to rationalise the authorities on this basis. Furthermore I do not think that the Court of Appeal itself was of the view that any such rationalisation was being undertaken by it."

Lord Denning's dictum in *Bratty's* case, upon which the decision in *R.* v. *Lipman* in part depended, that an involuntary act which proceeds from drunkenness cannot lead to a complete acquittal, is of course based on public policy. It may be said that acquittals of serious crimes such as manslaughter and unlawful wounding on the ground of self-induced incapacity due to drink or drugs would outrage public opinion. But some people may think that it would be better to create an independent crime of causing bodily harm while incapacitated by drink or drugs voluntarily consumed.

R. v. HUDSON AND R. v. TAYLOR[1]

[1971] 2 All E.R. 244

Duress by threats is a defence to all crimes with the possible exceptions of treason and murder, and it is a question of fact whether the threats were effective at the time the alleged crime was committed.

Facts.

Miss Hudson and Miss Taylor gave false evidence at a criminal trial, and they were charged with perjury. Their defence was that a man who was present at the trial at which the false evidence was given had together with others threatened to cut them up unless they gave it. The recorder held that duress was no defence because the accused had not

[1] See also *R.* v. *Gill*, p. 6, *supra*.

been subject to the threat of immediate physical violence when they gave the false evidence. The accused were convicted, but successfully appealed to the Court of Appeal.

Extracts from the Judgment of the Court of Appeal.

WIDGERY, L. J.—

" Despite the concern expressed in 2 Stephen's History of the Criminal Law in England,[1] that it would be—

'. . . a much greater misfortune for society at large if criminals could confer impunity upon their agents by threatening them with death or violence if they refused to execute their commands . . .'

it is clearly established that duress provides a defence in all offences including perjury (except possibly treason or murder as a principal)[2] if the will of the accused has been overborne by threats of death or serious personal injury so that the commission of the alleged offence was no longer the voluntary act of the accused. This appeal raises two main questions: first, as to the nature of the necessary threat and, in particular, whether it must be ' present and immediate '; secondly, as to the extent to which a right to plead duress may be lost if the accused has failed to take steps to remove the threat as, for example, by seeking police protection.

It is essential to the defence of duress that the threat shall be effective at the moment when the crime is committed. The threat must be a ' present ' threat in the sense that it is effective to neutralise the will of the accused at that time. Hence an accused who joins a rebellion under the compulsion of threats cannot plead duress if he remains with the rebels after the threats have lost their effect and his own will has had a chance to re-assert itself (*McCrowther's* case[3] and *A.-G.* v. *Whelan*[4]). Similarly a threat of future violence may be so remote as to be insufficient to overpower the will at the moment when the offence was committed, or the accused may have elected to commit the offence in order to rid himself of a threat hanging over him and not because he was driven to act by immediate and unavoidable pressure. In none of these cases is the defence of duress available

---

[1] Vol. 2, p. 107.
[2] On this possibility see 30 Camb. L.J. 202.
[3] (1746) Fost. 13.
[4] [1934] I.R. 518.

because a person cannot justify the commission of a crime merely to secure his own peace of mind.

When, however, there is no opportunity for delaying tactics, and the person threatened must make up his mind whether he is to commit the criminal act or not, the existence at that moment of threats sufficient to destroy his will ought to provide him with a defence even though the threatened injury may not follow instantly, but after an interval. This principle is illustrated by *Subramaniam* v. *R.*,[1] when the appellant was charged in Malaya with unlawful possession of ammunition and was held by the Privy Council to have a defence of duress, fit to go to the jury, on his plea that he had been compelled by terrorists to accept the ammunition and feared for his safety if the terrorists returned.

In the present case the threats of Farrell were likely to be no less compelling, because their execution could not be effected in the court room, if they could be carried out in the streets of Salford the same night. Insofar, therefore, as the recorder ruled as a matter of law that the threats were not sufficiently present and immediate to support the defence of duress we think that he was in error. He should have left the jury to decide whether the threats had overborne the will of the appellants at the time when they gave the false evidence.

Counsel for the Crown, however, contends that the recorder's ruling can be supported on another ground, namely, that the appellants should have taken steps to neutralise the threats by seeking police protection either when they came to court to give evidence, or beforehand. He submits on grounds of public policy that an accused should not be able to plead duress if he had the opportunity to ask for protection from the police before committing the offence and failed to do so. The argument does not distinguish cases in which the police would be able to provide effective protection, from those when they would not, and it would, in effect, restrict the defence of duress to cases where the person threatened had been kept in custody by the maker of the threats, or where the time interval between the making of the threats and the commission of the offence had made recourse to the police impossible. We recognise the need to keep the defence of duress within reasonable bounds but cannot accept so severe a restriction on it. The duty, of the person threatened, to take steps to remove the threat does not seem to have arisen in an English case but in a full review of

[1] [1956] 1 W.L.R. 965.

the defence of duress in the Supreme Court of Victoria (*R.* v. *Hurley*, *R.* v. *Murray*[1]), a condition of raising the defence was said to be that the accused 'had no means, with safety to himself, of preventing the execution of the threat'.

In the opinion of this court it is always open to the Crown to prove that the accused failed to avail himself of some opportunity which was reasonably open to him to render the threat ineffective, and that on this being established the threat in question can no longer be relied on by the defence. In deciding whether such an opportunity was reasonably open to the accused the jury should have regard to his age and circumstances, and to any risks to him which may be involved in the course of action relied on."

APPEAL ALLOWED.

R. v. DUDLEY AND STEPHENS

(1884), 14 Q. B. D. 273

A man who, in order to escape death from hunger, kills another for the purpose of eating his flesh, is guilty of murder although, at the time of the act, he is in such circumstances that he believes, and has reasonable grounds for believing, that it affords the only chance of saving his life.

Facts.

Dudley and Stephens were charged at the Devon Assizes with the murder of a boy, and the following is the effect of the special verdict which was found by the jury at the trial before HUDDLESTON, B. The prisoners, the deceased and a fourth person were shipwrecked, and cast adrift in an open boat a thousand miles from land. After eighteen days, by which time they had been without food for seven days, and without water for five days, the prisoners decided to kill the deceased in order that they might eat his body. On the 20th day, Dudley, with the assent of Stephens (the fourth man refusing to assent), knifed the deceased who, on account of his youth, was in a weaker state than any other member of the party, and who in no way assented to his death. The three survivors lived on the flesh of the deceased for a further four days, after which they were picked up by a passing ship.

[1] [1967] V.R. 526.

At the time the boy was killed, there was no reasonable prospect of relief, and there was every probability that, unless the prisoners ate the deceased, or one of the other members of the party, they would have died of starvation.

On these findings, HUDDLESTON, B., adjourned the case for argument before five judges at the Royal Courts of Justice where the accused were held guilty of murder.

Extracts from the Judgment of the Five Judges read by:

LORD COLERIDGE, C.J.—

" . . . it appears sufficiently that the prisoners were subject to terrible temptation, to sufferings which might break down the bodily power of the strongest man, and try the conscience of the best. Other details yet more harrowing, facts still more loathsome and appalling, were presented to the jury, and are to be found recorded in my learned Brother's notes. But nevertheless this is clear, that the prisoners put to death a weak and unoffending boy upon the chance of preserving their own lives by feeding upon his flesh and blood after he was killed, and with the certainty of depriving *him* of any possible chance of survival. . . .

There remains to be considered the real question in the case—whether killing under the circumstances set forth in the verdict be or be not murder. The contention that it could be anything else was, to the minds of us all, both new and strange, and we stopped the Attorney-General in his negative argument in order that we might hear what could be said in support of a proposition which appeared to us to be at once dangerous, immoral, and opposed to all legal principle and analogy. All, no doubt, that can be said has been urged before us, and we are now to consider and determine what it amounts to. First it is said that it follows from various definitions of murder in books of authority, which definitions imply, if they do not state, the doctrine, that in order to save your own life you may lawfully take away the life of another, when that other is neither attempting nor threatening yours, nor is guilty of any illegal act whatever towards you or any one else. But if these definitions be looked at they will not be found to sustain this contention. . . . Decided cases there are none. . . . The American case cited by my Brother Stephen in his Digest, from Wharton on Homicide, in which it was decided, correctly indeed, that sailors had no right to throw passengers overboard to save themselves, but on the somewhat strange ground that the proper mode of determining who was to be sacrificed was to vote upon the subject by ballot, can hardly, as my Brother Stephen says, be an authority satisfactory to a court in this country . . .

Now, except for the purpose of testing how far the conservation of a man's own life is in all cases and under all circumstances, an absolute, unqualified, and paramount duty, we exclude from our consideration all the incidents of war. We are dealing with a case of private homicide, not one imposed upon men in the service of their Sovereign and in the defence of their country. Now it is admitted that the deliberate killing of this unoffending and unresisting boy was clearly murder, unless the killing can be justified by some well-recognised excuse admitted by the law. It is further admitted that there was in this case no such excuse, unless the killing was justified by what has been called ' necessity '. But the temptation to the act which existed here was not what the law has ever called necessity. Nor is this to be regretted. Though law and morality are not the same, and many things may be immoral which are not necessarily illegal, yet the absolute divorce of law from morality would be of fatal consequence; and such divorce would follow if the temptation to murder in this case were to be held by law an absolute defence of it. It is not so. To preserve one's life is generally speaking a duty, but it may be the plainest and the highest duty to sacrifice it. War is full of instances in which it is a man's duty not to live, but to die. The duty, in case of shipwreck, of a captain to his crew, of the crew to the passengers, of soldiers to women and children, as in the noble case of the *Birkenhead* ; these duties impose on men the moral necessity, not of the preservation, but of the sacrifice of their lives for others, from which in no country, least of all, it is to be hoped, in England, will men ever shrink, as indeed, they have not shrunk. . . . It would be a very easy and cheap display of commonplace learning to quote from Greek and Latin authors, from Horace, from Juvenal, from Cicero, from Euripides, passage after passage, in which the duty of dying for others has been laid down in glowing and emphatic language as resulting from the principles of heathen ethics; it is enough in a Christian country to remind ourselves of the Great Example whom we profess to follow. . . .

It must not be supposed that in refusing to admit temptation to be an excuse for crime it is forgotten how terrible the temptation was; how awful the suffering; how hard in such trials to keep the judgment straight and the conduct pure. We are often compelled to set up standards we cannot reach ourselves, and to lay down rules which we could not ourselves satisfy.[1] But a man has no right to declare temptation to be an excuse, though he might himself have yielded to it, nor allow compassion for the criminal to change or weaken in any manner the legal definition of the crime. It is therefore our duty to declare that the prisoners' act in this case was wilful murder, that the facts as stated in the verdict are no legal justification of the homicide ; and to say that in our unanimous opinion the prisoners are upon this special verdict guilty of murder."[2]

THE PRISONERS WERE SENTENCED TO DEATH, BUT THEIR SENTENCE WAS COMMUTED TO SIX MONTHS' IMPRISONMENT.

Comment on R. v. Dudley and Stephens.

The American case mentioned in Lord COLERIDGE'S judgment in *R.* v. *Dudley and Stephens* is *U.S.* v. *Holmes* (26 Fed. Cas. 360.) After a shipwreck in 1842, a number of members of the crew and passengers were adrift in an open boat which was too full to remain afloat. Holmes was a member of the crew, and, acting under orders, he threw some of the passengers overboard. He was charged with manslaughter and convicted. The sentence was six months hard labour and a fine of twenty dollars. Points made by the judge were (1) provided enough members of the crew were left to navigate the boat, the crew should perish first because of the duty of protection owed to passengers, and (b) subject to the above point, lots should have been drawn. It is not without significance that the charge was only one of manslaughter for it is arguable that, at the very least, this is the proper verdict on facts such as those of *R.* v. *Dudley and Stephens*.

---

[1] This is particularly so in the law of homicide. *Cf.* the rule that duress may not be a defence to murder and the fact that someone whose murder charge is reduced to manslaughter on account of provocation is often severely punished although, *ex hypothesi*, the provocation might have caused a reasonable man, *i.e.* an average man, to do what the accused did.

[2] GROVE, J., who was one of the judges in the above case, pointed out (14 Q. B. D. 287) that, if the defence of necessity were allowed to prevail on such facts, it would mean that one of the three survivors might be killed by the others, of whom the stronger might kill the weaker, with the result that three lives might ultimately be taken in order to save one. STEPHEN, J., who was not one of the judges in the above case, subsequently indicated his approval of the actual decision, although he disagreed with some of the arguments advanced by Lord COLERIDGE in his judgment (*Digest of Criminal Law*, 9th Edn., p. 10, n. 2).

Section 25 of the Queensland Code reads as follows:

"Subject to the express provisions of this Code relating to acts done upon compulsion or provocation or in self-defence, a person is not criminally responsible for an act or omission done or made under such circumstances of sudden or extraordinary emergency that an ordinary person possessing ordinary powers of self-control could not reasonably be expected to act otherwise."

The emergency in *R.* v. *Dudley and Stephens* was certainly "extraordinary" although there is room for argument whether it was "sudden" within the meaning of the above provision. However, s. 25 does show that under some legal systems, extreme necessity may be a defence, even to a charge of intentional killing. The provision would certainly apply to the case of two shipwrecked mariners who arrived simultaneously at a plank large enough for only one. If the stronger pushed the weaker off the plank with the result that he was drowned, he would have a defence in Queensland but not, on the literal construction of Lord COLERIDGE's words, in England.

MOUSELL BROTHERS, LTD. v. LONDON AND NORTH WESTERN RAIL. CO.

[1917] 2 K. B. 836

A statute may be so construed as to render a master or principal criminally liable for the acts of his servant or agent.

Facts.

Mousell Bros., Ltd. were charged before the magistrates with having given a false account of goods consigned for carriage with intent to avoid payment of tolls, contrary to ss. 98–9 of the Railways Clauses Consolidation Act, 1845. It was proved that they were the owners of the goods in question and that a false account of them had been prepared by one of the company's servants on the instructions of another servant whom the magistrates found to have had the intention to avoid payment of tolls, and, on this evidence, the magistrates convicted the company at whose request a case was stated for the opinion of the Divisional Court who affirmed the conviction.

Extracts from Judgments of the Divisional Court.

ATKIN, J.—

" . . . I think that the authorities . . . make it plain that while *prima facie* a principal is not to be made criminally responsible for the acts of his servants, yet the Legislature may prohibit an act or enforce a duty in such words as to make the prohibition or the duty absolute; in which case the principal is liable if the act is in fact done by his servants. To ascertain whether a particular Act of Parliament has that effect or not regard must be had to the object of the statute, the words used, the nature of the duty laid down, the person upon whom it is imposed, the person by whom it would in ordinary circumstances be performed, and the person upon whom the penalty is imposed. If authority for this is necessary it will be found in the judgment of BOWEN, L. J., in *R.* v. *Tyler.*[1] Now in this case the duty is imposed upon 'every person being the owner or having the care of any goods' to 'give to the collector of tolls . . . an exact account.' . . . the duty which is imposed upon an owner or a person having care of the carriage or goods was a duty which even in 1845 would ordinarily be performed by a servant of the owner or the person having care. The account would in those days, as it certainly would in these days, be prepared by some clerk, servant, or manager. When a penalty is imposed for the breach of the duty, it is reasonable to infer that the penalty is imposed for a default of the person by whom the duty would ordinarily be performed. If the servant is to prepare the account, then it is the fault of the servant in not preparing the account that makes the owner liable to the penalty. This is borne out by s. 99, which imposes the penalty for breach of the duties imposed by s. 98—namely, for failure to give the account or for giving a false account. It is true it proceeds to provide a penalty for other offences, such as unloading and withholding a way-bill or bill of lading. I see no difficulty in the fact that an intent to avoid payment is necessary to constitute the offence. That is an intent which the servant might well have, inasmuch as he is the person who has to deal with the particular matter. The penalty is imposed upon the owner for the act of the servant if the servant commits the default provided for in the statute in the state of mind provided for by the statute. Once it is decided that this is one of those cases where a principal may be held liable criminally for the act of his

[1] [1891] 2 Q. B. 588, at p. 592.

servant, there is no difficulty in holding that a corporation may be the principal. No *mens rea* being necessary to make the principal liable, a corporation is in exactly the same position as a principal who is not a corporation. . . ."

APPEAL DISMISSED AND CONVICTION AFFIRMED.

VANE v. YIANNOPOULLOS

[1964] 3 All E.R. 820

A restaurateur is not vicariously liable for knowingly supplying liquor to a customer to whom he is not permitted to supply it, when he retains control of his business and has no guilty knowledge himself.

Facts.

The respondent was the holder of a restaurant licence under which he was not permitted to supply liquor to customers who did not consume a meal. He instructed his waitress not to supply liquor to customers who did not eat meals and on the occasion in question had withdrawn to the basement. The waitress knowingly supplied liquor to customers who did not consume a meal. The Divisional Court held that the respondent was not guilty of an offence under s. 22(1)(a) of the Licensing Act, 1961 which punishes the holder of a justices' on-licence who 'knowingly sells or supplies intoxicating liquor to persons to whom he is not permitted by the conditions of the licence to sell or supply' it (see now s. 161(1) of the Licensing Act, 1964). The appellant unsuccessfully appealed to the House of Lords. The House of Lords decided in favour of the respondent on the construction of the relevant legislation and reservations were expressed about the validity of the principle of delegation under which the delegator may be held guilty of licensing offences in the absence of guilty knowledge or connivance on his part.

Extract from the Speeches of the House of Lords.

LORD REID.—

" The appellant maintains that under this section there is vicarious responsibility, so that the licence holder must be held guilty if a servant employed to sell liquor sells knowingly to a person to whom the licence holder is not permitted to sell, and that it is no defence that the accused had forbidden the servant so to sell and did not know of or connive at the sale. The appellant does not dispute that it is the general rule in criminal cases that an accused person cannot be convicted unless he has *mens rea;* but he maintains that the authorities have established a principle of interpretation of the provisions of the Licensing Acts that, where a licence holder is prohibited from doing or suffering certain things, vicarious responsibility must be inferred, so that the knowledge of the servant must be imputed to the licence holder whatever be the terms of the section under which he is prosecuted. His counsel frankly agreed that, but for this principle, a man charged with knowingly selling could not be convicted unless it was shown that he knew what his servant was doing or at least connived or shut his eyes to facts indicating that the servant was doing wrong or disobeying his orders.

. . . . . There are four cases since 1903 where the word 'knowingly' did occur in the relevant section, but they do not support the contention of the appellant in this case. There the courts adopted a construction which on any view I find it hard to justify. They drew a distinction between acts done by a servant without the knowledge of the licence holder while the licence holder was on the premises and giving general supervision to his business, and acts done without the knowledge of the licence holder but with the knowledge of a person whom the licence holder had left in charge of the premises. In the latter case they held that the knowledge of the person left in charge must be imputed to the licence holder. If that distinction is valid then I agree with the Divisional Court that, on the facts of this case, there was not that 'delegation' by the accused necessary to make him answerable for the servant having acted against the orders of the accused.

Counsel for the appellant strenuously argued that this distinction is illogical and not warranted by any statutory provision. He maintained that if a licence holder entrusts to his wine waiter the duty of selling intoxicating liquor that is sufficient delegation and that, if the wine waiter disobeys his orders and sells to persons to whom he ought not to sell, there is nothing to justify the licence holder being acquitted, if he happens to have been in some other part of the premises, but held vicariously liable if he happens to have gone out leaving the wine waiter in charge. If this were a new distinction recently introduced by the courts I would think it necessary to consider whether a provision that the licence holder shall not knowingly sell can ever make him vicariously liable by reason of the knowledge of some other person; but this distinction has now been recognised and acted on by the courts for over half a century[1]. It may have been unwarranted in the first instance, but I would think it now too late to upset so long-standing a practice."

APPEAL DISMISSED.[2]

BARKER v. LEVINSON

[1950] 2 All E.R. 825

A master is not liable for criminal acts committed by his servant in the course of his employment if they are outside the general scope of that employment.

Facts.

Levinson was an estate agent who employed P to negotiate a tenancy. P took a premium contrary to the absolute prohibition imposed by s. 2 of the Landlord and Tenant (Rent Control) Act, 1949. The justices found that Levinson was not guilty of any contravention of the statute, and the Divisional Court held on a case stated that they were right.

Extracts from the Judgment of the Divisional Court.

LORD GODDARD, C.J.—

" The principle underlying the cases which deal with the criminal responsibility of a master for the act of his servant can be stated in this way. The master is responsible for a

---

[1] The distinction will disappear if proposition 4(2) of the Law Commission's published Working Paper No. 43 is adopted. Subject to express provision to the contrary, the licensee will only be liable if he is at fault.

[2] The Court of Appeal, Criminal Division has since accepted the principle of delegation as part of the current law (*R.* v. *Winson*, [1968] 1 All E.R. 197 in which leave to appeal to the House of Lords was granted but not acted upon. Leave to appeal to the House of Lords from the Divisional Court has been granted in *Howker* v. *Robinson*, [1972] 2 All E.R. 786, a case in which the principle of delegation was applied where a licensee retained control of one bar but delegated complete control of another bar to his servant who knowingly sold drinks to a boy under eighteen, an offence for which the servant as well as the licensee may be prosecuted (Licensing Act, 1964, s. 169(1)), contrast the provision with which *Vane* v. *Yiannopoulos* was concerned under which the licensee alone is liable.

criminal act of the servant if the act is done within the general scope of the servant's employment. In other words, if a master chooses to delegate the conduct of his business to a servant, then, if the servant, in the course of conducting the business, does an act which is absolutely prohibited, the master is liable, which is really only another way of saying that the act done must be within the general scope of the servant's employment.

. . . . . If, in the case now before us, the respondent had put Purkis into the position of being a general agent in respect of the flats and had left the management to him, and Purkis had done an illegal act, it may be that the respondent would have been liable. The case stated, however, shows no such finding by the justices. Purkis had no authority to negotiate the terms. He had no authority to take a premium, and what he did was an illegal act which his master had in no way, either expressly or impliedly, authorised him to do, and which, moreover the master had no means of preventing."

APPEAL DISMISSED.

R. v. I.C.R. HAULAGE, LTD.[1]

[1944] K.B. 551

A corporation may be indicted for a conspiracy to defraud.

Facts.

The appellant company and nine individuals were charged at the Kent Assizes with conspiring to defraud the purchaser of hard core by overcharging him, one of the other conspirators being the managing director of the appellant company.

Counsel for the appellant company moved to quash the indictment and the motion was refused by the Commissioner of Assize. The company was convicted together with some of the accused individuals, and the company unsuccessfully appealed to the Court of Criminal Appeal. The case is only reported on the question whether the Commissioner was right in rejecting the motion to quash the indictment.

---

[1] Corporate liability is considered in the Law Commission's published Working Paper No. 44 which appeared after the 7th edition of Cross & Jones' *Introduction to Criminal Law* had been published.

Extracts from the Judgment of the Court of Criminal Appeal read by:

STABLE, J.—

" . . . Counsel for the company contended that the true principle was that an indictment against a limited company for any offence involving as an essential ingredient *mens rea* in the restricted sense of a dishonest or criminal mind, must be bad for the reason that a company, not being a natural person, cannot have a mind honest or otherwise, and that, consequently, though under certain circumstances it is civilly liable for the fraud of its officers, agents or servants, it is immune from criminal process. Counsel for the Crown contended that a limited company, like any other entity recognised by the law, can as a general rule be indicted for its criminal acts which from the very necessity of the case must be performed by human agency and which in given circumstances become the acts of the company, and that for this purpose there was no distinction between an intention or other function of the mind and any other form of activity.

The offences for which a limited company cannot be indicted are, it was argued, exceptions to the general rule arising from the limitations which must inevitably attach to an artificial entity, such as a company. Included in these exceptions are the cases in which, from its very nature, the offence cannot be committed by a corporation, as, for example, perjury,[1] an offence which cannot be vicariously committed, or bigamy, an offence which a limited company, not being a natural person, cannot commit vicariously or otherwise. A further exception, but for a different reason, comprises offences of which murder is an example, where the only punishment the court can impose is corporal, the basis on which this exception rests being that the court will not stultify itself by embarking on a trial in which, if a verdict of guilty is returned, no effective order by way of sentence can be made. In our judgment these contentions of the Crown are substantially sound, and the existence of these exceptions, and it may be that there are others, is by no means inconsistent with the general rule. . . .

In *Chuter* v. *Freeth and Pocock, Ltd.*[2] . . . a limited

---

[1] It has been suggested that a company which authorises the swearing of a false affidavit may be guilty of perjury ; Stephen's *Digest of Criminal Law*, 9th Edn. Illustration 3, pp. 4–5.

[2] [1911] 2 K. B. 832.

company was charged before a magistrate under s. 20, sub-s. 6, of the Sale of Food and Drugs Act, 1899, with giving a purchaser of food a false warranty. The section contains a proviso to the effect that it is a defence to a charge under the section if the person charged proves that when he gave the warranty he believed that it was true. The magistrate, although of opinion that the evidence established the giving of a knowingly false warranty by the company's servant, dismissed the charge against the company on substantially the grounds contended for by the company in this case. The case came before a Divisional Court by way of case stated where it was decided that the magistrate had taken too narrow a view of the law. Lord ALVERSTONE, C.J., in giving the judgment of the court in which PICKFORD, J. and LUSH, J., concurred, said[1]: 'There is no reason why a warranty should not be given by a corporation. It can give a warranty through its agents, and through its agents it can believe or not believe, as the case may be, that the statements in the warranty are true.' This passage in our judgment, is directly in point on the question we have to decide. . . .

The authority latest in date which was cited in support of the company's contention was *R.* v. *Cory Brothers & Co. Ltd.*,[2] where FINLAY, J., on motion quashed an indictment against a limited company containing two counts, the first for manslaughter, which is a felony, and the second for an offence under s. 31 of the Offences against the Person Act, 1861, a statutory misdemeanour punishable with penal servitude. Both these offences can be punished on conviction with the infliction of a fine, the felony under s. 5 of the Offences against the Person Act, 1861, and the misdemeanour by common law. It appears from the report that the substantial argument addressed to the Court was that s. 33 of the Criminal Justice Act, 1925, had enlarged the category of offences for which a corporation could be indicted, a contention which, as we think rightly, the learned judge rejected holding that the section merely dealt with procedure. The learned judge advanced no reasons of his own for quashing the whole indictment, simply expressing the view that he felt compelled by the authorities to which his attention had been called to decide as he did. It is sufficient, in our judgment, to say that, inasmuch as that case was decided before the decision in *Director of Public Prosecutions* v. *Kent and Sussex*

[1] *Ibid.*, at p. 846.
[2] [1927] 1 K. B. 810.

Contractors, Ltd.,[1] and that *Chuter* v. *Freeth and Pocock, Ltd.*[2] was not cited at all, if the matter came before the court today, the result might well be different. As was pointed out by HALLETT, J., in the *Kent and Sussex Contractors'* case,[3] this is a branch of the law to which the attitude of the courts has in the passage of time undergone a process of development. . . .

In our judgment, both on principle and in accordance with the balance of authority, the present indictment was properly laid against the company, and the learned commissioner rightly refused to quash. We are not deciding that in every case where an agent of a limited company acting in its business commits a crime the company is automatically to be held criminally responsible. Our decision only goes to the invalidity of the indictment on the face of it, an objection which is taken before any evidence is led and irrespective of the facts of the particular case. Where in any particular case there is evidence to go to a jury that the criminal act of an agent, including his state of mind, intention, knowledge or belief is the act of the company, and, in cases where the presiding judge so rules, whether the jury are satisfied that it has been proved, must depend on the nature of the charge, the relative position of the officer or agent, and the other relevant facts and circumstances of the case. It was because we were satisfied on the hearing of this appeal that the facts proved were amply sufficient to justify a finding that the acts of the managing director were the acts of the company and the fraud of that person was the fraud of the company, that we upheld the conviction against the company. . . ."

APPEAL DISMISSED.

JOHN HENSHALL (QUARRIES), LTD. v. HARVEY

[1965] 1 All E.R. 725

In order that a limited company may be convicted of aiding and abetting the commission of an offence it is essential that a responsible official of the company be aware of the facts constituting the offence.

---

[1] [1944] K. B. 146.
[2] [1911] 2 K. B. 832.
[3] At p. 157.

Facts.

The appellants were convicted of aiding and abetting one H to drive a lorry with an excessive load on a road. The appellants' weighbridge manager, B, inadvertently allowed H to drive away from the appellants' premises with a lorry containing a load in excess of that permitted. The appellants successfully appealed against conviction to the Divisional Court.

Extracts from the Judgment of the Divisional Court.

LORD PARKER, C.J.—

" In my judgment, while sympathising with the justices in this rather difficult area of the law, they were wrong in convicting the appellants. Quite shortly, my reasons are as follows: there is absolutely no doubt that in the case of absolute offences as they are sometimes called, a master whether an individual or a company, is criminally liable for the acts of any servant acting within the scope of his authority. That has been held in many cases; I need only mention two, *Mousell Brothers, Ltd.* v. *London and North Western Rail. Co.*[1] and *Police Commissioners* v. *Cartman.*[2] It is, however, quite clear that when one is dealing with aiding and abetting, as has been often said, the master must know of the facts out of which the offence arises, albeit he does not know that an offence is committed. In the case of *National Coal Board* v. *Gamble,*[3] Lord GODDARD, C.J., quoting from *Ackroyds Air Travel, Ltd.* v. *Director of Public Prosecutions*[4] said:

' I stated the law with regard to aiding and abetting in this way:

" . . . a person could only be convicted . . . as an aider and abettor if he knew all the circumstances which constituted the offence. Whether he realised that those circumstances constituted an offence was immaterial. If he knew all the circumstances and those circumstances constituted the offence . . . that was enough to convict him of being an aider and abettor." ' Accordingly, in the case of a master who is an individual, he must have actual knowledge of the circumstances which constitute the offence. The

1 [1917] 2 K. B. 836; p. 113, *supra.*
2 [1896] 1 Q. B. 655.
3 [1959] 1 Q. B. 11; [1958] 3 All E. R. 203; p. 144, *infra.*
4 [1950] 1 All E. R. 933.

same position arises in the many offences of permitting somebody to do something unlawful, or indeed when any knowledge is necessary. In *Vane* v. *Yiannopoullos*[1] the House of Lords recently held, and in so holding followed a long line of authority, that as an individual master does not know what is in the mind of his servant he must, for the purpose of knowingly committing an offence, be shown to have actual knowledge of it. There is possibly one exception to that, where he shuts his eyes and is regardless of whether a servant does perform his duty or not. It seems perfectly clear, without going through the authorities, that if in this case the appellants had been an individual master they would not have been fixed with knowledge of the actions of Mr. Burrell. It is quite clear however that Mr. Price the appellants' manager, did not actually know, and from the findings in the case it is clear that they in no way shut their eyes to what Mr. Burrell was doing, but took particular care to see that he performed his duty properly. In this case by an oversight he failed to do so.

. . . . . there is fundamentally no difference between a master who is an individual and a master who is a limited company, save that in the case of a limited company their knowledge must be the knowledge of those whom, in the case of *H. L. Bolton (Engineering) Co., Ltd.* v. *T. J. Graham & Sons, Ltd.*,[2] DENNING, L.J., referred to as the brains of the company. There is no doubt that there are many cases where somebody who is in the position of the brains—maybe a director, the managing director, the secretary or a responsible officer of the company—has knowledge, his knowledge has been held to be the knowledge of the company. It seems to me that that is a long way away from saying that a company is fixed with the knowledge of any servant. Again, to adopt the simile of DENNING, L.J., the knowledge of the hands as opposed to the brain, is not imputed to the company merely because it is the servant's duty to perform that particular task.

For those reasons, which I have endeavoured to state shortly, I think that the justices came to a wrong conclusion in law. I should have added this, that as is shown by *Vane's* case in the House of Lords, there can be cases in which a master is fixed with the knowledge of his servant, where there has been what is referred to as true delegation. If a

---

[1] [1965] A. C. 486; [1964] 3 All E. R. 820; p. 115 *supra*.
[2] [1957] 1 Q. B. 159; [1956] 3 All E. R. 624.

master completely hands over the effective management of a business to somebody else, then as it is often said he cannot get out of his responsibility by such delegation."[1]

APPEAL ALLOWED.

TESCO SUPERMARKETS, LTD. v. NATTRASS

[1971] 2 All E.R. 127

A shop manager employed by a limited company is 'another person' within the meaning of s. 24(1) *of the Trade Descriptions Act,* 1968, *and he will not necessarily be identified with the company for the purposes of corporate liability.*

Facts.

Tesco Supermarkets, Ltd. were charged with giving an indication that goods were offered for sale at a price less than that at which they were in fact offered contrary to s. 11(2) of the Trade Descriptions Act, 1968.[2] A poster in one of the company's shops managed by a Mr. Clement stated that Radiant Washing Powder was being sold at 2s. 11d. a packet instead of the normal 3s. 11d. It was the practice in the shop to remove all stock priced at the normal price while the reduced offer was operative. On the occasion in question, however, there being no stock marked with the reduced price, a Miss Rogers, a shop girl, put out stock marked with the normal price. Had C. known of the facts, he would either have withdrawn the poster, or else sold the goods at the reduced price. The company relied on s. 24(1) of the act which reads as follows:

> "In any proceedings for an offence under this Act it shall, subject to subsection (2) of this section, be a defence for the person charged to prove (a) that the commission of the offence was due to a mistake or to reliance on information supplied to him or to the act or default of another person, an accident or some other cause beyond his control; and (b) that he took all

---

[1] See note 2, p. 117, *supra*.

[2] "If any person offering to supply any goods gives, by whatever means, any indication likely to be taken as an indication that the goods are being offered at a price less than that at which they are in fact being offered he shall, subject to the provisions of this Act, be guilty of an offence."

reasonable precautions and exercised all due diligence to avoid the commission of such an offence by himself or any person under his control."

Section 24(2) provides for the giving of notice of intention to rely on s. 24(1) and the company gave such notice alleging that the commission of the offence was due to the act or default of C. and there was no finding that they had failed to use due diligence in supervising him.

The Magistrates nonetheless convicted the company because they were not satisfied that C. was "another person" within the meaning of s. 24 (1)(*a*). The conviction was affirmed by a Divisional Court because, although C. was "another person" within the meaning of s. 24(1)(*a*), the provisions of s. 24(1)(*b*) had not been satisfied because C. was a servant of the company.

The company successfully appealed to the House of Lords.

Extracts from the speeches of the House of Lords.

LORD REID.—

"Over a century ago the courts invented the idea of an absolute offence. The accepted doctrines of the common law put them in a difficulty. There was a presumption that when Parliament makes the commission of certain acts an offence it intends that *mens rea* shall be a constituent of that offence whether or not there is any reference to the knowledge or state of mind of the accused. And it was and is held to be an invariable rule that where *mens rea* is a constituent of any offence the burden of proving *mens rea* is on the prosecution. Some day this House may have to re-examine that rule, but that is another matter. For the protection of purchasers or consumers Parliament in many cases made it an offence for a trader to do certain things. Normally those things were done on his behalf by his servants and cases arose where the doing of the forbidden thing was solely the fault of a servant, the master having done all he could to prevent it and being entirely ignorant of its having been done. The just course would have been to hold that, once the facts constituting the offence had been proved, *mens rea* would be presumed unless the accused proved that he was blameless. The courts could not, or thought they could not, take that course. But they could and did hold in many such cases on a construction of the statutory provision that Parliament must be deemed to have intended to depart from the general rule and to make the offence absolute in the sense that *mens rea* was not to be a constituent of the offence.

This has led to great difficulties. If the offence is not held to be absolute the requirement that the prosecutor must prove *mens rea* makes it impossible to enforce the enactment in very many cases. If the offence is held to be absolute that leads to the conviction of persons who are entirely blameless: an injustice which brings the law into dispute. So Parliament has found it necessary to devise a method of avoiding this difficulty. But instead of passing a general enactment that it shall always be a defence for the accused to prove that he was no party to the offence and has done all he could to prevent it, Parliament has chosen to deal with the problem piecemeal and has in an increasing number of cases enacted in various forms with regard to particular offences that it shall be a defence to prove various exculpatory circumstances . . .

But in several cases the courts, for reasons which it is not easy to discover, have given a restricted meaning to such provisions. It has been held that such provisions afford a defence if the master proves that the servant at fault was the person who himself did the prohibited act, but that they afford no defence if the servant at fault was one who failed in his duty of supervision to see that his subordinates did not commit the prohibited act. Why Parliament should be thought to have intended this distinction or how as a matter of construction these provisions can reasonably be held to have that meaning is not apparent.

In some of these cases the employer charged with the offence was a limited company. But in others the employer was an individual and still it was held that he, though personally blameless, could not rely on these provisions if the fault which led to the commission of the offence was the fault of a servant in failing to carry out his duty to instruct or supervise his subordinates. Where a limited company is the employer difficult questions do arise in a wide variety of circumstances in deciding which of its officers or servants is to be identified with the company so that his guilt is the guilt of the company.

I must start by considering the nature of the personality which by a fiction the law attributes to a corporation. A living person has a mind which can have knowledge or intention or be negligent and he has hands to carry out his intentions. A corporation has none of these; it must act through living persons, though not always one or the same person. Then the person who acts is not speaking or acting for the company. He is acting as the company and his mind which directs his acts is the mind of the company. There is no question of the company being vicariously liable. He is not acting as a servant, representative, agent or delegate. He is an embodiment of the company or, one could say, he hears and speaks through the persona of the company, within his appropriate sphere, and his mind is the mind of the company. If it is a guilty mind then that guilt is the guilt of the company. It must be a question of law whether, once the facts have been ascertained, a person in doing particular things is to be regarded as the company or merely as the company's servant or agent. In that case any liability of the company can only be a statutory or vicarious liability . . .

In some cases the phrase alter ego has been used. I think it is misleading. When dealing with a company the word alter is I think misleading. The person who speaks and acts as the company is not alter. He is identified with the company. And when dealing with an individual no other individual can be his alter ego. The other individual can be a servant, agent, delegate or representative but I know of neither principle nor authority which warrants the confusion (in the literal or original sense) of two separate individuals . . .

I think that the true view is that the judge must direct the jury that if they find certain facts proved then as a matter of law they must find that the criminal act of the officer, servant or agent including his state of mind, intention, knowledge or belief is the act of the company. I have already dealt with the considerations to be applied in deciding when such a person can and when he cannot be identified with the company. I do not see how the nature of the charge can make any difference. If the guilty man was in law identifiable with the company then whether his offence was serious or venial his act was the act of the company but if he was not so identifiable then no act of his, serious or otherwise, was the act of the company itself . . .

It is sometimes argued—it was argued in the present case—that making an employer criminally responsible, even when he has done all that he could to prevent an offence, affords some additional protection to the public because this will induce him to do more. But if he has done all he can how can he do more?"

APPEAL ALLOWED.

SECTION 2
COMPLICITY

Preliminary note.

Terminology.

The student should bear in mind that, apart from *R.* v. *Brindley* and *R.* v. *Long,* all the cases in this section were decided before the Criminal Law Act, 1967 came into force. That Act abolished the distinction between felonies and misdemeanours. A fairly precise terminology had formerly been in use with regard to the different parties to a felony. The actual offender was a " principal in the first degree "; he was the one who actually did the criminal act, although allowance had to be made for the possibility of joint principals to cover cases in which the act was performed by both of them whether by agreement or otherwise, and of innocent agency, where the person who did the criminal act under the instigation of the principal offender was himself not committing any crime. All other parties to a felony were secondary parties, and it was a debatable point whether they could be liable where there was no principal in the first degree. The possible secondary parties were, " principals in the second degree ", *i.e.* those present at and assisting in the commission of the felony by, for example, keeping watch, or handing the lethal weapon to a murderer; " accessories before the fact ", *i.e.* successful instigators who were not actually present at and encouraging the commission of the felony; and " accessories after the fact ", *i.e.* those who assisted the felon after he had committed the crime. The liability of those who assist those who have committed arrestable offences is defined by s. 4 of the Criminal Law Act, 1967 with which *R.* v. *Brindley* and *R.* v. *Long* is concerned. The Act has not affected the substantive law with regard to the liability of the remaining secondary parties to a felony. They are liable to be tried, convicted and punished as the principal offender. The extent to which the old terminology will survive is perhaps debatable. In the case of a misdemeanour, those who would if the crime were a felony have been principals in the second degree, or accessories before the fact were said to be guilty of " aiding and abetting ". Strictly speaking, this term was only appropriate to those who would have been principals in the second degree in the case of a felony; those who would, in the case of a felony, have been accessories before the fact, were guilty of "counselling or procuring" the commission of the misdemeanour. "Aiding and abetting" is, moreover, sometimes used to cover the activities of a principal offender in cases in which there are more than one.

The Law Commission.

Since the publication of the seventh edition of Cross and Jones's *Introduction to Criminal Law*, the Law Commission's published Working Paper No. 43 has appeared. It makes tentative suggestions for reform of the law relating to complicity and liability for the acts of others. References to some of these suggestions are made in footnotes at appropriate points. Unfortunately the paper does not consider the possibility of divorcing the liability of those who aid in the commission of crimes from the notion that they must be considered as parties to the crime.[1]

R. v. SWINDALL AND OSBORNE

(1846), 2 Car. & Kir. 230

(1) *The contributory negligence of the deceased is no defence to a charge of manslaughter.* (2) *If two drivers encourage each other to drive their respective vehicles at a furious speed, they may each be convicted as principal to the crime of manslaughter although it is not clear which vehicle ran the deceased down.*

Facts.

The accused were charged on an indictment containing several counts alleging that they had aided each other to commit manslaughter. They were each driving furiously along a road and encouraging each other to do so. The vehicle of one of them ran down and killed the deceased. The accused were convicted as principals on all counts.

Extracts from the summing-up to the jury.

POLLOCK, C.B.—

"The prisoners are charged with contributing to the death of the deceased, by their negligence and improper conduct, and, if they did so, it matters not whether he was deaf, or drunk, or negligent, or in part contributed to his

[1] See Cross and Jones, *Introduction to Criminal Law*, 116, and the article in 85 Law Quarterly Review 252 there cited.

own death; for in this consists a great distinction between civil and criminal proceedings. If two coaches run against each other, and the drivers of both are to blame, neither of them has any remedy against the other for damages[1]. So, in order that one ship-owner may recover against another for any damage done, he must be free from blame: he cannot recover from the other if he has contributed to his own injury, however slight the contribution may be.[1] But, in the case of loss of life, the law takes a totally different view—the converse of that proposition is true; for there each party is responsible for any blame that may ensue, however large the share may be; and so highly does the law value human life, that it admits of no justification wherever life has been lost, and the carelessness or negligence of any one person has contributed to the death of another person. Generally, it may be laid down, that, where one by his negligence has contributed to the death of another, he is responsible; therefore, you are to say, by your verdict, whether you are of opinion that the deceased came to his death in consequence of the negligence of one or both of the prisoners. A distinction has been taken between the prisoners: it is said that the one who went first is responsible, but that the second is not. If it is necessary that both should have run over the deceased, the case is not without evidence that both did so. But it appears to me that the law, as stated by Mr. Greaves, is perfectly correct. Where two coaches, totally independent of each other, are proceeding in the ordinary way along a road, one after the other, and the driver of the first is guilty of negligence, the driver of the second, who had not the same means of pulling up, may not be responsible. But when two persons are driving together, encouraging each other to drive at a dangerous pace, then, whether the injury is done by the one driving the first or the second carriage, I am of opinion that in point of law the other shares the guilt."

VERDICT, GUILTY.

---

[1] This statement of the law is not correct to-day.

MOHAN v. R.

[1967] 2 All E.R. 58

Two persons may be convicted of aiding and abetting each other to commit a crime though there was no agreement between them.

Facts.

The two appellants were charged and convicted of the murder of one Mootoo. The evidence was that one of them quarrelled with Mootoo and chased him towards his house. The other appellant then appeared, and Mootoo suffered wounds at the hands of each appellant. It was not clear which of the two inflicted the fatal wound. There was no evidence of any prearranged plan between the appellants, but the Judicial Committee of the Privy Council recommended that their convictions should be affirmed.

Extracts from the Advice of the Judicial Committee.

LORD PEARSON.—

" It is impossible on the facts of this case to contend that the fatal blow was outside the scope of the common intention. The two appellants were attacking the same man at the same time with similar weapons and with the common intention that he should suffer grievous bodily harm. Each of the appellants was present and aiding and abetting the other of them in the wounding of Mootoo.

That is the feature which distinguishes this case from cases in which one of the accused was not present or not participating in the attack or not using any dangerous weapon, but may be held liable as a conspirator or an accessory before the fact or by virtue of a common design, if it can be shown that he was party to a prearranged plan in pursuance of which the fatal blow was struck. In this case one of the appellants struck the fatal blow, and the other of them was present aiding and abetting him. In such a case the prosecution do not have to prove that the accused were acting in pursuance of a prearranged plan.

In *R.* v. *Kupferberg*[1] the accused had in an earlier trial been acquitted on a charge of conspiracy, and in a later trial

---

[1] (1918), 34 T. L. R. 587.

he was charged and convicted of aiding and abetting. LAWRENCE, J., in giving the judgment of the Court of Criminal Appeal, said that:

'Mr. Purchase had also contended that the acquittal on the count charging conspiracy, which was framed on the same clause of the regulations as the charge of aiding and abetting of which the appellant had been found guilty, entitled the appellant to plead autrefois acquit. That was not so, because conspiracy was not the same as aiding and abetting. The two offences had different ingredients: previous agreement was necessary in the one, but not in the other.' "

APPEAL DISMISSED.

R. v. ANDERSON AND MORRIS

[1966] 2 All E.R. 644

Where two persons embark on a joint enterprise, each is liable criminally for acts done in pursuance of the joint enterprise, including unusual consequences arising from the execution of the joint enterprise; but if one of them goes beyond what has been tacitly agreed as part of the joint enterprise the other is not liable for the consequence of the unauthorised act.

Facts.

Anderson and Morris agreed to attack one Welch. There was evidence that Anderson had a knife with him and stabbed Welch to death with it. The jury were directed that, if they were satisfied that Anderson and Morris had a common design to attack Welch, although they were not satisfied that Morris intended to kill Welch or cause him grievous bodily harm, they might convict Anderson of murder and Morris of manslaughter. Anderson was convicted of murder, and a new trial was ordered by the Court of Criminal Appeal because of the adduction of fresh evidence before that Court. Morris was convicted of manslaughter, and he successfully appealed to the Court of Criminal Appeal on the ground that the jury had been misdirected in his case.

Extracts from the Judgment of the Court of Criminal Appeal.

LORD PARKER, C.J.—

"Counsel for the applicant Morris . . . (puts) . . . the principle of law to be invoked in this form: that where two persons embark on a joint enterprise each is liable for the acts done in pursuance of that joint enterprise, that that includes liability for unusual consequences if they arise from the execution of the agreed joint enterprise but (and this is the crux of the matter) that if one of the adventurers goes beyond what has been tacitly agreed as part of the common enterprise, his co-adventurer is not liable for the consequences of that unauthorised act. Finally, he says it is for the jury in every case to decide whether what was done was part of the joint enterprise, or went beyond it and was in fact an act unauthorised by that joint enterprise. In support of that, he refers to a number of authorities to which this court finds it unnecessary to refer in detail . . . In *R.* v. *Smith*[1] the co-adventurer who in fact killed was known by the accused to have a knife, and it was clear on the facts of that case that the common design involved an attack on a man, in that case a barman, in which the use of the knife would not be outside the scope of the concerted action. Reference was there made to the fact that the case might have been different if in fact the man using the knife had used a revolver, a weapon which he had, unknown to Smith. . . . Counsel for the Crown, on the other hand, while recognising that he cannot go beyond this long string of decided cases, has said that they are really all part and parcel of a much wider principle which he would put in this form, that if two or more persons engage in an unlawful act and one suddenly develops an intention to kill whereby death results, not only is he guilty of murder, but all those who have engaged in the unlawful act are guilty of manslaughter. He recognises that the present trend of authority is against that proposition, but he goes back to *R.* v. *Salisbury*[2] in 1553. In that case a master had lain in wait to attack a man, and his servants who had no idea of what his, the master's idea was, joined in the attack, whereby the man was killed. It was held there that those servants were themselves guilty of manslaughter. The court is by no means clear on the facts as reported that that case is really

---

[1] [1963] 3 All E. R. 597.

[2] (1553), 1 Plowd. 100; see p. 182 *infra*.

on all fours, but it is in the opinion of the court quite clear that that principle is wholly out of touch with the position today. It seems to this court that to say that adventurers are guilty of manslaughter when one of them has departed completely from the concerted action of the common design and has suddenly formed an intent to kill and has used a weapon and acted in a way which no party to that common design could suspect is something which would revolt the conscience of people today. Counsel for the Crown in his attractive argument points to the fact that it would seem to be illogical that, whereas if two people had formed a common design to do an unlawful act and death resulted by an unforeseen consequence, they should be held, as they would undoubtedly be held, guilty of manslaughter; yet if one of them in those circumstances had in a moment of passion decided to kill, the other would be acquitted altogether. The law, of course, is not completely logical, but there is nothing really illogical in such a result, in that it could well be said as a matter of common-sense that in the latter circumstances the death resulted or was caused by the sudden action of the adventurer who decided to kill and killed. Considered as a matter of causation, there may well be an overwhelming supervening event which is of such a character that it will relegate into history matters which would otherwise be looked on as causative factors. Looked at in that way, there is really nothing illogical in the result to which counsel for the Crown points."

APPEAL ALLOWED.

R. v. TYRRELL

[1894] 1 Q.B. 710

A girl under sixteen cannot be convicted of aiding and abetting or inciting a man to have unlawful intercourse with her.

Facts.

The accused, a girl under sixteen, was charged on an indictment containing two counts. The first count alleged that she aided and abetted a youth to have intercourse with her, and the second account alleged that she had incited him to do so. There was evidence that she had done each of these things, and the trial judge recorded a conviction after taking the verdict of the jury, but reserved a case for the opinion of the Court for Crown Cases Reserved.

Extract from the opinions of the Court for Crown Cases Reserved.

LORD COLERIDGE, C.J.—

"The Criminal Law Amendment Act, 1885 was passed for the purpose of protecting women and girls against themselves. At the time it was passed there was a discussion as to what point should be fixed as the age of consent. That discussion ended in a compromise, and the age of consent was fixed at sixteen. With the object of protecting women and girls against themselves the Act of Parliament has made illicit connection with a girl under that age unlawful; if a man wishes to have such illicit connection he must wait until the girl is sixteen, otherwise he breaks the law; but it is impossible to say that the Act, which is absolutely silent about aiding or abetting, or soliciting or inciting, can have intended that the girls for whose protection it was passed should be punishable under it for offences committed upon themselves."

CONVICTION QUASHED.

R. v. TYLER AND PRICE

(1838), 8 C. & P. 616

(1) *A person cannot be convicted as aiding and abetting the commission of an offence where the criminal act is done by a person who is insane because no crime is committed by the latter.*

(2) *A person may be convicted as a principal offender if he encourages or assists in the commission of criminal acts by an insane person.*

Facts.

Tyler and Price were tried on an indictment containing two counts. The first charged them with aiding and abetting one Thom (since deceased) in the murder of a constable, Nicholas Meares, and the second charged them with the murder of the constable as principals in the first degree.

It appeared that Thom, who described himself as the

saviour of the world, had created a number of disturbances in the neighbourhood of Canterbury, and that a warrant had been issued for his arrest. Thom assembled a number of people, including the accused, for the purpose of preventing his apprehension, and he shot the constable who was sent with others to arrest him. Acting on the orders of Thom, who was subsequently shot himself, the accused threw the body of the constable, while he was still alive, into a ditch.

Extracts from the summing-up of :

LORD DENMAN, C.J.—

" In order to make out that part of the charge which imputes to Thom the act of murder, and that these persons were guilty of aiding and abetting him to commit the murder, it would be necessary to shew that Thom was a person capable of committing that murder. In order to make out the malicious intention imputed in the indictment to the act of Thom, he must be shewn to have been of sound mind at the time when he committed it, for it is a maxim of law, that persons not of sound mind cannot be held responsible for their acts. It seems to me, therefore, that if it appears in evidence that Thom was not, at the time of committing the act, of sound mind, you must acquit the prisoners upon the first count of the indictment, for there will be no foundation on which the accessory crime can rest . . . if Thom was now on his trial, it could hardly be said, from the evidence, that he could be called on to answer for his criminal acts ; that, therefore, simplifies the question you will have to decide, and confines it to the second count of the indictment. There these persons are themselves charged with having committed the offence; and if they were aware of the malignant purpose entertained by Thom, and shared in that purpose with him, and were present aiding and abetting, and assisting him in the commission of acts fatal to life, in the course of accomplishing this purpose, then no doubt they are guilty as principals on this second count. . . . If any man is found aiding another, of whose ill intentions he is thoroughly apprised, he is responsible. It will be for you to say whether, from what was done by these men both before and after the killing of Nicholas Meares, they did not intend this general resistance to the law . . . You will, therefore, say whether these two men were so far cognisant of an illegal purpose in Thom, and joined in his acts, that they are guilty of the murder which the hand of Thom committed. You will say whether they were abetting Thom in the blow he gave the deceased; for if they were, the blow of Thom was the blow of them all, and they are answerable for it. If you think that they kept together with the knowledge of any general purpose of resistance to the law, then they are guilty. . . . You will, therefore, . . . say whether you find that Thom was a dangerous and mischievous person; that these two prisoners knew he was so, and yet kept with him, aiding and abetting him by their presence, and concurring in his acts: and if you do so, you will find them guilty, for they are then liable as principals for what was done by his hand."

VERDICT—NOT GUILTY ON THE FIRST COUNT, BUT GUILTY ON THE SECOND COUNT.

R. v. BOURNE

(1952), 36 Cr. App. Rep. 125

A husband who compels his wife to commit buggery per vaginam *with a dog can be convicted as principal in the second degree although the wife is entitled to be acquitted with the result that there is no principal in the first degree.*

Facts.

Bourne was charged, *inter alia,* with aiding and abetting his wife to commit buggery with a dog. There was evidence that he had, on two occasions, compelled his wife to submit herself to intercourse *per vaginam* with a dog. Bourne was convicted and appealed unsuccessfully to the Court of Criminal Appeal.

Extracts from the judgment of the Court of Criminal Appeal

LORD GODDARD, L.C.J.—

" . . . in fact we have allowed Mr. Green to argue this case on the footing that the wife would have been entitled to be acquitted on the ground of duress. The learned judge left no question to the jury on duress, but the jury have found that she did not consent. Assuming that she could have set up duress, what does that mean? It means that she admits that she has committed the crime but prays to be excused from punishment for the consequences of the crime by reason of the duress, and no doubt in those circumstances the law would allow a verdict of Not Guilty to be entered. . . . There may be certain doctrines with regard to murder which do not apply to other cases, but I am willing to assume for the purpose of this case, and I think my brethren are too, that if this woman had been charged herself with committing the offence, she could have set up the plea of duress, not as showing that no offence had been committed, but as showing that she had no *mens rea* because her will was overborne by threats of imprisonment or violence so that she would be excused from punishment. But the offence of buggery whether with man or beast does not depend upon consent; it depends on the act, and if an act of buggery is committed, the felony is committed.

A point is raised here that the appellant was charged with being not merely an accessory before the fact but with being an aider and abettor. So he was, because the charge is: 'you being present aided and abetted, counselled and procured.' The only questions that were left to the jury by the learned judge, and he was not asked to leave any more, were these: (1) 'Did the prisoner on a day in or about the month of September, 1949, in the County of Stafford cause his wife Adelaide Bourne to have carnal knowledge of a dog?' and the jury have found that he did. (2) 'Are you satisfied that she did not consent to having such carnal knowledge?' The answer of the jury was: 'Yes, we are satisfied she did not consent.' Then the same two questions were asked with regard to the other day on which an offence was alleged to have been committed.

In the opinion of the court, there is no doubt that the appellant was properly indicted for being a principal in the second degree to the commission of the crime of buggery. That is all that it is necessary to show. The evidence was, and the jury by their verdict have shown they accepted it, that he caused his wife to have connection with a dog, and if he caused his wife to have connection with a dog he is guilty, whether you call him an aider and abettor or an accessory, as a principal in the second degree. For that reason, this appeal fails and is dismissed."

APPEAL DISMISSED.

Comment on R. v. Tyler and Price and R. v. Bourne

At first sight Lord DENMAN's statement that, if Thom was of unsound mind at the material time, there was no foundation on which the accessory crime could rest, appears to be quite inconsistent with the conclusion that Bourne could be convicted as a principal in the second degree although, had she been tried, Mrs. Bourne would have been acquitted. As a matter of substantive law, the statement and the conclusion can be reconciled on the ground that there is a difference between the defences of insanity and duress. In the case of insanity, it is established that the accused did not know the nature and quality of his act, or, if he did know this much, he did not know that he was doing wrong. In the case of duress, on the other hand, the accused admits that he knew what he was doing and that it was wrong, but claims that he acted as he did in order to avoid threats. Duress is thus a plea in confession and avoidance, and the person responsible for the threats can be said to have aided and abetted the accused because he caused the accused knowingly to commit wrongful acts.

In most cases of duress, it is possible to hold that the person acting under it was an innocent agent and thus to hold that the person responsible for the duress was a principal in the first degree. Perhaps this could have been done in Bourne's case, but there may have been a difficulty on account of the fact that a man cannot commit the particular form of buggery which was in question in *R.* v. *Bourne*. To illustrate from the crime of bigamy: A., a bachelor, compels a married woman to go through a form of marriage with him. If duress is a defence to bigamy, the woman must be acquitted, but A. cannot be convicted as a principal offender because bigamy can only be committed by a married person.

Even if *R.* v. *Bourne* and *R.* v. *Tyler and Price* can be reconciled on the lines suggested above, there may yet be difficulty in cases in which the secondary party is, by definition, incapable of committing the crime charged. To illustrate again from bigamy: A., a bachelor, persuades B., a married woman to go through a ceremony of marriage with him. B.'s husband has been absent for more than seven years and B. does not know that he is alive. A. knows that B.'s husband is alive. B. must be acquitted, A. cannot be convicted as a principal offender and, on the view taken by Lord DENMAN in *R.* v. *Tyler and Price*, he cannot be convicted of aiding and abetting bigamy. If he were so convicted, there would be no means of reconciling the case with *R.* v. *Tyler and Price*. This type of problem does not appear to be touched upon by the Law Commission's published Working Paper No. 43 on complicity.

R. v. CONEY

(1882), 8 Q. B. D. 534

(1) *Consent does not prevent an assault from being criminal if unlawful violence is used.*[1]

(2) *Mere presence at the commission of a crime did not render a person liable as a principal in the second degree if the crime was a felony, or for aiding and abetting in the case of a misdemeanour.*

Facts.

Two persons fought with bare fists in a ring in the presence of a crowd including the prisoners who were charged with aiding and abetting the fight. There was no evidence that they said or did anything to assist or encourage the pugilists, but the Chairman of the Berkshire Quarter Sessions directed the jury that mere presence at an unlawful fight was, if unexplained, conclusive proof of aiding and abetting. The prisoners were accordingly convicted, but the Chairman stated a case for the opinion of the Court for Crown Cases Reserved. This court quashed the conviction by a majority of 8 to 3 judges.

Extracts from the Judgments of the Court for Crown Cases Reserved.

CAVE, J.—

" . . . For the defence it was first contended that inasmuch as Burke and Mitchell had agreed to fight there was no assault. I am, however, of opinion that this is not so. With regard to an action for an assault, in the case of *Boulter* v *Clark*[2] it was held by PARKER, C.B., that it was no defence to allege that the plaintiff and defendant fought together by consent, the fighting itself being unlawful, and in *Matthew* v. *Ollerton*[3] it was held that if one license another to beat him, such licence is no defence, because it is against the peace. . . . It was next contended that the chairman was wrong in directing the jury in the words of LITTLEDALE, J.,

---

[1] On this point this case should be compared with *R.* v. *Donovan* p. 238, *infra*.

[2] (1747), Bull. N. P. 16.

[3] (1693), Comb. 218.

in *R.* v. *Murphy*[1] that if the prisoners were not merely casually passing by, but stayed at the place, they encouraged it by their presence, although they did not say or do anything.

Now it is a general rule in the case of principals in the second degree that there must be participation in the act, and that, although a man is present whilst a felony is being committed, if he takes no part in it, and does not act in concert with those who commit it, he will not be a principal in the second degree merely because he does not endeavour to prevent the felony, or apprehend the felon. . . .

Where presence may be entirely accidental, it is not even evidence of aiding and abetting. Where presence is *prima facie* not accidental it is evidence, but no more than evidence, for the jury. . . .

In *R.* v. *Young*,[2] the prisoners were indicted for the murder of Mirfin, who was killed in a duel by one Eliot. In summing up, VAUGHAN, J., said, 'There is no difficulty as to the law upon this subject. Principals in the first degree are those by whom the death wound is inflicted. Principals in the second degree, those who are present at the time it is given, aiding and abetting, comforting and assisting the persons actually engaged in the contest—mere presence alone will not be sufficient to make a party an aider and abettor, but it is essential that he should by his countenance and conduct in the proceeding, being present, aid and assist the principals. If either of the prisoners sustained the principal by his advice or presence, or if you think he went down for the purpose of encouraging and forwarding the unlawful conflict, although he did not do or say anything ; yet, if he was present and was assisting and encouraging when the pistol was fired, he will be guilty of the offence imputed by the indictment.'[3] In that direction I entirely concur, but I believe if a similar direction had been given in the present case the prisoners would have been acquitted. . . ."

STEPHEN, J.—

" . . . The principle as to consent seems to me to be this : when one person is indicted for inflicting personal injury upon another, the consent of the person who sustains the injury is no defence to the person who inflicts the injury,

---

[1] (1833), 6 C. & P. 103.
[2] (1838), 8 C. & P. 644.
[3] Cf. *Wilcox* v. *Jeffery*, [1951] 1 All E. R. 464, p. 142, *infra*.

if the injury is of such a nature, or is inflicted under such circumstances, that its infliction is injurious to the public as well as to the person injured. But the injuries given and received in prize-fights are injurious to the public, both because it is against the public interest that the lives and the health of the combatants should be endangered by blows, and because prize-fights are disorderly exhibitions, mischievous on many obvious grounds. Therefore the consent of the parties to the blows which they mutually receive does not prevent those blows from being assaults . . .

In all cases the question whether consent does or does not take from the application of force to another its illegal character, is a question of degree depending upon circumstances. . . ."

CONVICTION QUASHED.

WILCOX v. JEFFERY

[1951] 1 All E. R. 464

A person who is present encouraging the commission of a crime aids and abets it.

Facts.

Wilcox was charged with aiding and abetting Hawkins, a citizen of the United States, to commit an offence against the Aliens Order, 1920. Hawkins was a professional saxophonist who had been given leave to land in this country on condition he took no employment. Wilcox was aware of this condition but nevertheless accompanied Hawkins to a concert at which he played the saxophone. Wilcox applauded the performance and wrote a laudatory review of it. The Magistrates convicted Wilcox but stated a case for the opinion of the Divisional Court who were of opinion that the conviction was right.

Extracts from the judgments of the Divisional Court.

LORD GODDARD, C.J.—

" Reliance is placed by the prosecution on *R.* v. *Coney*[1] which dealt with a prize fight. This case relates to a jazz band concert, but the particular nature of the entertainment provided, whether by fighting with bare fists or playing on saxophones, does not seem to me to make any difference to the question which we have to decide. The fact is that a man is charged with aiding and abetting an illegal act, and I can find no authority for saying that it matters what that illegal act is, provided that the aider and abettor knows the facts sufficiently well to know that they would constitute an offence in the principal. In *R.* v. *Coney*[1] the prize fight took place in the neighbourhood of Ascot, and four or five men were convicted of aiding and abetting the fight. The conviction was quashed on the ground that the chairman had not given a correct direction to the jury when he told them that, as the prisoners were physically present at the fight, they must be held to have aided and abetted. That direction, the court held, was wrong, it being too wide. The matter was very concisely put by CAVE, J., whose judgment was fully concurred in by that great master of the criminal law, STEPHEN, J. CAVE, J., said (8 Q. B. D. at p. 540): 'Where presence may be entirely accidental, it is not even evidence of aiding and abetting. Where presence is *prima facie* not accidental it is evidence, but no more than evidence, for the jury.'

There was not accidental presence in this case. The appellant paid to go to the concert and he went there because he wanted to report it. He must, therefore, be held to have been present, taking part, concurring, or encouraging, whichever word you like to use for expressing this conception. It was an illegal act on the part of Hawkins to play the saxophone or any other instrument at this concert. The appellant clearly knew that it was an unlawful act for him to play. He had gone there to hear him, and his presence and his payment to go there was an encouragement. He went there to make use of the performance, because he went there, as the magistrate finds and was justified in finding, to get 'copy' for his newspaper. It might have been entirely different, as I say, if he had gone there and protested, saying: 'The musicians' union do not like you foreigners coming here and playing and you ought to get off the stage.' If he had booed, it might have been some evidence that he was not aiding and abetting. If he had gone as a member of a *clique* to try to drown the noise of the saxophone, he might very likely be found not guilty of aiding and abetting. In this case it seems clear that he was there, not only to approve and encourage what was done, but to take advantage of it by getting 'copy' for his paper. In those circumstances there was evidence on which the magistrate could find

---

[1] P. 140, *supra*.

that the appellant aided and abetted, and for these reasons I am of opinion that the appeal fails."

CONVICTION AFFIRMED.

Comment on Wilcox v. Jeffery.

The Law Commission's Working Paper No. 43, published after the appearance of the seventh edition of Cross and Jones's *Introduction to Criminal Law*, contains the suggestion that *Wilcox* v. *Jeffery* might justify the conviction of those attending an obscene performance of aiding and abetting it. On the assumption that such a result would be undesirable, proposition 8 reads:

"A person does not become an accessory to an offence if the offence is so defined as that his conduct in it is inevitably incidental to its commission and such conduct is not expressly penalised".

If the proposition were adopted, *Wilcox* v. *Jeffery* itself would be unaffected because Hawkins's offence was not so defined as that Wilcox's conduct in it was inevitable to its commission. Another case which would not be affected is *R.* v. *Tyrrell*[1] because the girl's conduct in the man's offence, though inevitable to the commission of that offence, was not expressly penalised.

NATIONAL COAL BOARD v. GAMBLE

[1959] 1 Q. B. 11

Someone who knowingly assists another to commit a crime aids and abets him to do so, although he does nothing to encourage the commission of the crime.

Facts.

Mallender, a servant of a firm of hauliers, drove a lorry to one of the Board's quarries in order to take delivery of a quantity of coal which the Board had contracted to supply to an electricity authority. After the lorry had been loaded, it was weighed on a weighbridge and Haslam, a servant of the Board, informed Mallender that the lorry was four tons over weight. Mallender said that he would take the risk, and Haslam allowed him to drive away after handing over the weight ticket. He need not have done so because the property in the coal had not previously passed to the electricity authority. The Board was charged and convicted

---

[1] P. 134, *supra*.

before the Magistrates with aiding and abetting Mallender to commit an offence against the Motor Vehicles (Construction and Use) Regulations, 1955. The Magistrates stated a case for the opinion of the Divisional Court where their decision was affirmed by a majority.

Extracts from the judgments of the Divisional Court.

DEVLIN, J.—

" A person who supplies the instrument for a crime or anything essential to its commission aids in the commission of it; and if he does so knowingly and with intent to aid, he abets it as well and is therefore guilty of aiding and abetting. I use the word ' supplies ' to comprehend giving, lending, selling or any other transfer of the right of property. In a sense a man who gives up to a criminal a weapon which the latter has a right to demand from him aids in the commission of the crime as much as if he sold or lent the article. But this has never been held to be aiding in law; see *R.* v. *Lomas*[1] and *R.* v. *Bullock*.[2] The reason, I think, is that in the former case there is in law a positive act and in the latter only a negative one. In the transfer of property there must be either a physical delivery or a positive act of assent to a taking. But a man who hands over to another his own property on demand, although he may physically be performing a positive act, in law is only refraining from detinue. Thus in law the former act is one of assistance voluntarily given and the latter is only a failure to prevent the commission of the crime by means of a forcible detention, which would not even be justified except in the case of felony. Another way of putting the point is to say that aiding and abetting is a crime that requires proof of *mens rea*, that is to say, of intention to aid as well as of knowledge of the circumstances, and that proof of the intent involves proof of a positive act of assistance voluntarily done.

These considerations make it necessary to determine at what point the property in the coal passed from the board and what the board's state of knowledge was at that time. If the property had passed before the board knew of the proposed crime, there was nothing they could legally do to prevent the driver of the lorry from taking the overloaded lorry out onto the road. If it had not, then they sold the

---

[1] (1913), 110 L. T. 239.
[2] [1955] 1 All E. R. 15; [1955] 1 W. L. R. 1.

coal with knowledge that an offence was going to be committed.

The board called no evidence,[1] so that a good deal was left to inference; but the conclusions of fact reached by the magistrates have not been seriously disputed. . . .

I think that the delivery of the coal was not completed until after the ascertained weight had been assented to and some act was done signifying assent and passing the property. The property passed when Haslam asked Mallender whether he intended to take the load and Mallender said he would risk it and when the mutual assent was, as it were, sealed by the delivery and acceptance of the weighbridge ticket. Haslam could therefore after he knew of the overload have refused to transfer the property in the coal.

This is the conclusion to which the justices came. Mr. Thompson [counsel for the appellant] submits on behalf of the board that it does not justify a verdict of guilty of aiding and abetting. He submits, first, that even if knowledge of the illegal purpose had been acquired before delivery began, it would not be sufficient for the verdict; and secondly, that if he is wrong about that, the knowledge was acquired too late, and the board was not guilty of aiding and abetting simply because Haslam failed to stop the process of delivery after it had been initiated.

On his first point Mr. Thompson submits that the furnishing of an article essential to the crime with knowledge of the use to which it is to be put does not of itself constitute aiding and abetting; there must be proved in addition a purpose or motive of the defendant to further the crime or encourage the criminal. Otherwise, he submits, there is no *mens rea*.

I have already said that in my judgment there must be proof of intent to aid. I would agree that proof that the article was knowingly supplied is not conclusive evidence of intent to aid. *R.* v. *Fretwell*[2] is authority for that. *R.* v. *Steane*,[3] in which the defendant was charged with having acted during the war with intent to assist the enemy contrary to the Defence Regulations then in force, makes the same point. But *prima facie*—and *R.* v. *Steane* makes this clear

[1] This probably accounts for the fact that Haslam's knowledge was imputed to the Board in this case although the servant's knowledge was not imputed to the company in *John Henshall (Quarries), Ltd.*, v. *Harvey* p. 121, *supra*.

[2] (1862), Le. & Ca. 161.

[3] [1947] K. B. 997; [1947] 1 All E. R. 813; p. 3, *supra*.

also—a man is presumed to intend the natural and probable consequences of his acts, and the consequence of supplying essential material is that assistance is given to the criminal. It is always open to the defendant, as in *R.* v. *Steane*, to give evidence of his real intention. But in this case the defence called no evidence. The *prima facie* presumption is therefore enough to justify the verdict, unless it is the law that some other mental element besides intent is necessary to the offence.

This is what Mr. Thompson argues, and he describes the additional element as the purpose or motive of encouraging the crime. No doubt evidence of an interest in the crime or of an express purpose to assist it will greatly strengthen the case for the prosecution. But an indifference to the result of the crime does not of itself negative abetting. If one man deliberately sells to another a gun to be used for murdering a third, he may be indifferent about whether the third man lives or dies and interested only in the cash profit to be made out of the sale, but he can still be an aider and abettor. To hold otherwise would be to negative the rule that *mens rea* is a matter of intent only and does not depend on desire or motive.

The authorities, I think, support this conclusion, though none has been cited to us in which the point has been specifically argued and decided."

CONVICTION AFFIRMED.

R. v. BAINBRIDGE

[1960] 1 Q. B. 129

A person was accessory before the fact to a felony if he assisted the felon with knowledge of his intention to commit a felony of the kind actually committed. It was unnecessary for the prosecution to prove that a crime at a particular time and place was contemplated.[1]

Facts.

Bainbridge was convicted as an accessory before the fact to office-breaking. He had purchased oxygen cutting equipment and handed it to some people who used it for the purpose of breaking into and stealing from a bank. He

---

[1] Bainbridge's crime would now be aiding and abetting burglary.

said that he merely suspected that the equipment would be used for some illegal purpose and did not know that it was to be used for breaking into the bank at which the crime was committed. The trial judge directed the jury that it was sufficient for the prosecution to prove that the accused knew that a crime of the type which was in fact committed was intended. Bainbridge unsuccessfully appealed to the Court of Criminal Appeal.

Extracts from the judgment of the Court of Criminal Appeal.

LORD PARKER, C.J.—

" The court fully appreciates that it is not enough that it should be shown that a man knows that some illegal venture is intended. To take this case, it would not be enough if he knew—he says he only suspected—that the equipment was going to be used to dispose of stolen property. That would not be enough. Equally, this court is quite satisfied that it is unnecessary that knowledge of the particular crime which was in fact committed should be shown to his knowledge to have been intended, and by ' particular crime ' I am using the words in the same way in which Mr. Simpson [counsel for the appellant] used them, namely, on a particular date and particular premises.

It is not altogether easy to lay down a precise form of words which will cover every case that can be contemplated but, having considered the cases and the law this court is quite clear that the direction of Judge AARVOLD in this case cannot be criticised. Indeed, it might well have been made with the passage in *Foster's Crown Cases* (3rd ed. (1809), at p. 369) in mind, because there the author says: ' If the principal totally and substantially varieth, if being solicited to commit a felony of one kind he wilfully and knowingly committeth a felony of another, he will stand single in that offence, and the person soliciting will not be involved in his guilt. For on his part it was no more than a fruitless ineffectual temptation,' the converse, of course, being that if the principal does not totally and substantially vary the advice or the help and does not wilfully and knowingly commit a different form of felony altogether, the man who has advised or helped, aided or abetted, will be guilty as an accessory before the fact.

Judge AARVOLD in this case, in the passage to which I have referred, makes it clear that there must be not merely suspicion but knowledge that a crime of the type in question was intended, and that the equipment was bought with that in view. In his reference to the felony of the type intended it was, as he stated, the felony of breaking and entering premises and the stealing of property from those premises. The court can see nothing wrong in that direction."

APPEAL DISMISSED.

THAMBIAH v. R.

[1965] 3 All E.R. 661

A man who helps another to prepare for the commission of a crime in the future may be convicted of aiding and abetting the commission of that crime when it comes to be committed.

Facts.

The appellant was charged and convicted of aiding and abetting another to utter a forged cheque. The appellant had opened a bank account in a false name with the intention of facilitating the uttering of cheques forged by the principal offender. The appellant unsuccessfully appealed to the Privy Council.

Extracts from the Advice of the Privy Council.

LORD PEARCE.—

"The fact that the cheque did not as yet exist, when the account was opened, does not preclude the appellant's actions in opening and maintaining it from constituting an abetting of the fraudulent presentation of the cheque when it had come into existence and been altered by forgery. One man may abet another by helping to set the stage even before the victim has been found. If a man helps another in preparation for crimes of a certain nature with the intention that the other shall commit crimes of that nature he may abet those crimes when they come to be committed. Moreover in the present case at the time when the cheque was fraudulently presented the account still owed not only its origin but also its maintained existence to the appellant.

Nice problems may arise when preparations abetting one kind of crime are followed by the execution of a crime of another kind or when the abetting preparations are merely for some criminal but indefinite purpose."

APPEAL DISMISSED.

FERGUSON v. WEAVING

[1951] 1 K. B. 814

A person cannot be convicted of aiding, abetting, counselling or procuring the commission of an offence if he is personally unaware of the facts constituting it.

Facts.

S. 4 of the Licensing Act, 1921 prohibited the sale or consumption of intoxicants otherwise than during permitted hours. Customers of a public house managed by the appellant were found consuming liquor on the appellant's premises outside permitted hours,[1] and were convicted of an offence under the section. The appellant was charged with counselling or procuring the offence, although there was no evidence that she knew that the liquor was being consumed out of hours, as it was served by waiters employed by her who had failed to collect the customers' glasses in time. A case was stated for the opinion of the Divisional Court who held that the appellant was not guilty of the offence charged.

Extracts from the Judgment of the Divisional Court.

LORD GODDARD, C.J.

" . . . It is well known that the words ' aid and abet ' are apt to describe the action of a person who is present at the time of the commission of an offence and takes some part therein. He is then described as an ' aider and abettor '. The words ' counsel and procure ' are appropriate to a person who, though not present at the commission of the offence, is an accessory before the fact. That all these words may be used together to charge a person who is alleged to have participated in an offence otherwise than as a principal in the first degree was established by *In re Smith.*[2] Whether where the words ' counsel and procure ' alone are used, there must be a proof of something more than would establish a case of being an accessory before the fact is not one which we feel necessary to decide in this case. The main point that was argued is one of general importance with regard to offences under the Licensing Acts, and as we are satisfied

[1] See now Licensing Act, 1964, s. 100.
[2] (1858), 3 H. & N. 227.

that the licensee cannot be convicted as a participant, to use a compendious expression, in the offence charged against the persons who consumed the intoxicating liquor, we give no decision upon it. . . . There can be no doubt that this court has more than once laid it down in clear terms that before a person can be convicted of aiding and abetting the commission of an offence, he must at least know the essential matters which constitute the offence: see, for instance, *Johnson* v. *Youden*.[1] The magistrate in this case has acquitted the licensee of any knowledge of the matters which constituted the principal offence, but it is said that the cases establish that the knowledge of her servants must be imputed to her, and that there are many cases in which a licensee has been convicted although he himself did not know the facts constituting the offence is, of course, beyond question. There are certain offences under the Licensing Acts which arise because the statute imposes an absolute prohibition, for instance, the offence of selling liquor to a drunken person. In *Cundy* v. *Le Cocq*[2] it was held that the prohibition against selling to such a person imposed by s. 13 of the Licensing Act, 1872, now replaced by s. 75 of the Licensing (Consolidation) Act, 1910[3] is absolute and that knowledge of the condition of the person served is not necessary to constitute the offence. On the other hand there are many offences in which it is necessary to show either that the licensee suffered or permitted the offence to take place, or that he knowingly permitted matters which constituted an offence. There is no material difference between permitting or suffering something and knowingly allowing it to take place, for, as was said in *Somerset* v. *Hart*:[4] 'How can a man suffer a thing to be done when he does not know of it?' The difference between an absolute prohibition and a prohibition against permitting or suffering was pointed out by COLLINS, J., in *Somerset* v. *Wade*,[5] where, under other words in the same section as was under consideration in *Cundy* v. *Le Cocq*[2] the licensee was prosecuted, not for selling to a drunken person, but for permitting drunkenness on licensed premises. As it was there proved that the licensee did not know that the person in question was drunk the court held he could not be convicted of permitting drunkenness, though

1 [1950] 1 K. B. 544; [1950] 1 All E. R. 300.
2 (1884), 13 Q. B. D. 207; p. 13, *supra*.
3 See now s. 172(3) of the Licensing Act, 1964.
4 (1884), 12 Q. B. D. 360, 362.
5 [1894] 1 Q. B. 574.

they approved the decision in *Cundy* v. *Le Cocq*[1] because the prohibition against selling to a drunken person is absolute.

We now turn to the cases in which knowledge has been imputed to a licensee because of the knowledge of his manager or servant. It is unnecessary to go through them all because the principle which applies was laid down, not for the first time, in *Linnett* v. *Metropolitan Police Commissioner*.[2] All the cases on the subject were quoted, and, in giving judgment, I said[3]: 'The principle underlying these decisions does not depend upon the legal relationship existing between master and servant or between principal and agent; it depends on the fact that the person who is responsible in law, as, for example, a licensee under the Licensing Acts, has chosen to delegate his duties, powers and authority to another.'

We will assume for the purpose of this case that the licensee had delegated to the waiters the conduct and management of the concert room, and if the Act had made it an offence for a licensee knowingly to permit liquor to be consumed after hours, then the fact that she had delegated the management and control of the concert room to the waiters would have made their knowledge her knowledge.[4] In this case there is no substantive offence in the licensee at all. The substantive offence is committed only by the customers. She can aid and abet the customers if she knows that the customers are committing the offence, but we are not prepared to hold that knowledge can be imputed to her so as to make her, not a principal offender, but an aider and abettor. So to hold would be to establish a new principle in criminal law and one for which there is no authority. If Parliament had desired to make a licensee guilty of an offence by allowing persons to consume liquor after hours it would have been perfectly easy so to provide in the section. But a doctrine of criminal law that a licensee who has knowledge of the facts is liable as a principal in the second degree is no reason for holding that if she herself had no knowledge of the facts but that someone in her employ and to whom she may have entrusted the management of the room did know them, this makes her an aider and abettor. As no duty is imposed on her by the section to prevent the consumption of liquor after hours there was no duty in this

---

[1] (1884), 13 Q. B. D. 207; p. 13, *supra*.
[2] [1946] K.B. 290; [1946] 1 All E.R. 380.
[3] *Ibid.*, at p. 294.
[4] See note 2, p. 117, *supra*.

respect that she could delegate to her employees. While it may be that the waiters could have been prosecuted for aiding and abetting the consumers, as to which we need express no opinion, we are clearly of opinion that the licensee could not be. To hold the contrary would, in our opinion, be an unwarranted extension of the doctrine of vicarious responsibility in criminal law."

CONVICTION QUASHED.

R. v. BRINDLEY AND R. v. LONG

[1971] 2 All E.R. 698

On a charge of impeding the arrest of an offender contrary to s. 4(1) *of the Criminal Law Act,* 1967, *it is not necessary for the prosecution to prove that the accused knew of the identity of the offender.*

Facts.

Two lorries had been stolen, and both Brindley and Long made false statements to the police suggesting that they had not seen the lorries. They were charged with impeding the arrest of the thieves contrary to s. 4(1) of the Criminal Law Act, 1967,[1] and they were convicted notwithstanding their contention that they were unaware of the identity of the thieves. They unsuccessfully appealed to the Court of Appeal.

Extracts from the Judgment of the Court of Appeal.

LYELL, J.—

" First it was argued that the prosecution had to prove that the accused knew who had committed the principal offence and that he did an act relating to that person. In the view of the court there is no foundation for that contention. What has to be proved is as follows: first, it has to be proved that a person has committed an arrestable offence; second, that another person knew or believed that the first person had committed it; third, that the second person did an act with intent to impede the apprehension or prosecution of the first

[1] " Where a person has committed an arrestable offence, any other person who, knowing or believing him to be guilty of the offence or of some other arrestable offence, does without lawful authority or reasonable excuse any act with intent to impede his apprehension or prosecution shall be guilty of an offence."

person; fourth, that the act was done wthout lawful authority or reasonable excuse.

The unsoundness of the applicant Long's contention is perhaps best demonstrated by a simple example. A smash-and-grab raid is carried out in a quiet street and the person or persons committing it run off. Another person sees it. A police car comes by shortly after, the driver sees the broken window, asks the man who has seen the offence committed which way the offenders went and he replies that they went up the street when in fact they went down. That evidence is clearly enough for a jury to convict the bystander of an offence under the section. Anyone who sees a smash-and-grab raid being committed must know that a theft has been committed, and he has seen the person or persons who did it. He sends the police in the wrong direction, so giving the offenders more time to escape. It would then be for the jury to consider whether they are sure he sent the police the wrong way to make it more difficult to catch the thieves and whether there could be any lawful authority or reasonable excuse for his act. It is frivolous to suggest that in such circumstances the by-stander needed to know the identity of the thieves before he could be convicted."

APPEAL DISMISSED

SECTION 3
ATTEMPTS

R. v. COOK
(1964), 48 Cr. App. Rep. 98

It is for the judge to say whether there is evidence that the accused's acts could in law constitute an attempt, but it is for the jury to say whether they do in fact amount to an attempt.

Facts

The accused was convicted *inter alia* of an attempt to take and drive away a motor car. He had jumped into the car admittedly with the intent of driving it away. The judge in effect withdrew the case from the jury, directing that as a matter of law the accused was guilty. The accused unsuccessfully appealed to the Court of Criminal Appeal. That court was of opinion that the judge had been wrong in not leaving the question of whether the accused was in fact guilty of an attempt to the jury, but was also of opinion that the jury could not have failed to convict, had they been properly directed.

Extracts from the Judgment of the Court of Criminal Appeal.

LORD PARKER, C.J.—

"This court is satisfied that, while in every case it is for the judge to rule whether there is any evidence capable of constituting an attempt, it is always for the jury to say whether they accept it as amounting to an attempt. That involves, of course, a careful direction in every case on the general principle with regard to what acts constitute attempts. It may well be that the Deputy-Chairman was misled by para. 4105 in the current (35th) edition of *Archbold's Criminal Pleading etc.* It is unnecessary to read it, but it does suggest, as this court thinks wrongly, that it is for the judge to rule, not merely that there is evidence capable of amounting to an attempt, but whether the *actus reus* concerned is an attempt.

This court has been referred to a number of cases, in all of which save one the court has treated the matter in the way this court suggests is right. Thus in *R.* v. *Landow* (1913), 8 Cr. App. Rep. 218, CHANNELL, J., at p. 222 in giving the judgment of the court of five judges said this: 'On one point we are all agreed; it is on the question of an attempt. Although there was evidence which the jury might have found amounted to an attempt, there was no evidence on which it was necessary that they should take that view; therefore it was a case where it was particularly necessary for the Recorder to explain that which we think an ordinary jury of laymen would not easily understand, the difference between an attempt, a mere intention, and an idle threat. We think that the Recorder did not in fact sufficiently explain this difference to the jury. He was probably misled by the way in which the case was conducted.' . . .

The one case which would appear to suggest the contrary is the case of *R.* v. *Taylor* (1859), 1 F. & F. 511. . . . We think that this case is really, on full consideration, no exception to the rule which has been laid down in all the other cases to which we have been referred. It follows that in the present case the matter ought strictly to have been left to the jury.

Having said that, however, this court is quite clearly of the opinion that on a proper direction the jury could have come only to the same conclusion to which they did. It is unnecessary to go through the many cases which draw a distinction between what one might call an act preparatory and an act constituting an attempt. So far as this case is concerned, we are quite clear that it is impossible to say that the getting into the driving seat and the passenger seat of this vehicle by Howe and the appellant, respectively with the clear intention of taking and driving it away, when the full offence would be constituted in a minute, as the appellant said, did not constitute an attempt.

The nearest authority dealing with the taking and driving away and stealing of a motor-vehicle is an Irish case, *Prendergast* v. *Porter,* [1961] I.R. 440. There a defendant had attempted to start the car with the handle and twice tried to start it with the handle, then sat in the driver's seat but failed to start it. It was argued that all that he had done was to attempt to start it, and that he had never got to the stage of attempting to drive it. The court said that 'although the process of putting a car in motion by driving involves several steps, yet in the ordinary process these steps are so intimately connected as to occupy a matter of seconds and constitute a practically instantaneous succession of semi-automatic movements. In the instant case the defendant attempted to begin this succession and he would have completed the act of driving, had the car started.'

The court is quite clearly of the opinion in the present case that with a proper direction the jury must have come to exactly the same conclusion and accordingly the appeal in regard to this count is dismissed. . . . "

APPEAL ON COUNT FOR TAKING AND DRIVING AWAY DISMISSED.

R. v. ROBINSON

[1915] 2 K. B. 342

A person cannot be convicted of an attempt to obtain money by false pretences when he has not made a pretence to the person from whom it was intended to obtain the money or his agent.

Facts.

Robinson was convicted of attempting to obtain money by false pretences.

The evidence was that he was a jeweller, and that his stock was insured at Lloyd's. He was found tied to a chair in his shop by a policeman who came from the street in response to his call for assistance. He stated that he had been attacked by thieves who had left him tied up on the previous night. The safe in which he placed his jewellery at night was empty. As the police were not satisfied with his story, he was taken to the police station, and the jewellery was found in a recess behind his safe. He later admitted that he had done what he did for the purpose of making a claim against Lloyd's on the insurance policy relating to his jewellery.

He successfully appealed to the Court of Criminal Appeal against his conviction on the ground that it was not warranted by the evidence.

Extract from the Judgment of the Court of Criminal Appeal read by:

LORD READING, C.J.—

" . . . It seems to the Court upon consideration of the authorities that there is no real difficulty in formulating the principle of law which is applicable to cases of this kind. A safe guide is to be found in the statement of the law which is laid down by PARKE, B., in *R.* v. *Eagleton*[1] : 'The mere intention to commit a misdemeanour is not criminal. Some act is required, and we do not think that all acts towards committing a misdemeanour are indictable. Acts remotely leading towards the commission of the offence are not to be considered as attempts to commit it, but acts immediately connected with it are.' The difficulty lies in the application of that principle to the facts of the particular case. In some cases it is a difficult matter to determine whether an act is immediately or remotely connected with the offence of which it is alleged to be an attempt. In other cases the question is easier of solution, as for instance in *R.* v. *Button*.[2] There upon the evidence there was a false pretence made directly to the race authorities with the intent to make them part with the prize, and one which, but for the fact of the fraud being discovered, would necessarily have had that effect. In the present case the real difficulty lies in the fact that there is no evidence of any act done by the appellant in the nature of a false pretence which ever reached the minds of the underwriters, though they were the persons who were to be induced to part with the money. The evidence falls short of any communication of such a pretence to the underwriters or to any agent of theirs. The police were not acting on behalf of the underwriters. In truth what the appellant did was preparation for the commission of a crime, not a step in the commission of it. It consisted in the preparation of evidence which might indirectly induce the underwriters to pay; for if the police had made a report that a burglary had taken place,—and that was presumably what the appellant intended,—it may very well be that the underwriters would have paid without further inquiry. But there must be some act beyond mere preparation if a person is to be charged with an attempt. Applying the rule laid down by PARKE, B., we think that the appellant's act was only remotely connected with the commission of the full offence, and not immediately

---

[1] (1855), Dears. C. C. 515, at p. 538.

[2] [1900] 2 Q. B. 597; p. 159, *infra*.

connected with it. If we were to hold otherwise we should be going further than any case has ever yet gone, and should be opening the door to convictions for acts which are not at present criminal offences. We think the conviction must be quashed, not on the technical ground that no information or evidence as to the property lost was given to the underwriters as required by the policy but upon the broad ground that no communication of any kind of the false pretence was made to them."

APPEAL ALLOWED.[1]

R. v. BUTTON

[1900] 2 Q. B. 597

On a charge of attempting to obtain money by false pretences the accused may be convicted if he does acts sufficiently proximate to the commission of the crime.

Facts.

The appellant was charged with attempting to obtain money by false pretences. He was a good runner, and entered for two races at Lincoln in the name of Sims, a moderate runner. The appellant stated that he had not previously won a race which was untrue. In consequence he received a handicap in each of the races in which he ran and which he won. He did not claim the money prizes because questions were raised as to whether he really was Sims. In his summing up to the jury, the trial judge directed them to acquit if they were of opinion that the whole transaction was entered into by the appellant as a joke. The jury returned a verdict of guilty, and a case was reserved for the opinion of the Court for Crown Cases Reserved who held that the appellant had been rightly convicted.

Extracts from the Judgments of the Court for Crown Cases Reserved.

MATHEW, J.—

". . . It was also contended that his coming in first in the races was owing to his own good running; but it was also

---

[1] Presumably Robinson could now be convicted of an offence under s. 5 (2) of the Criminal Law Act, 1967.

owing, in part at least, to the false pretences, for by means of the false pretences he obtained a longer start than he would have had if his true name and performances had been known. It is also said that some other act had to be done in order to make the offence complete, and that he could not rightly be convicted because it was not shewn that he had applied for the prizes, and that the criminal intention was exhausted. The argument is exceedingly subtle, but unsound. In fact, he was found out before he had the opportunity of applying for the prizes, as no doubt he otherwise would have done. The pretences which the prisoner made were not too remote, and the conviction was good."

WRIGHT, J.—

". . . I am of the same opinion. If nothing more had been shewn than that the defendant had entered for the races in a false name, the case would have been different. If he did not run or claim the prize it would be difficult to say that there was an actual attempt to obtain it. But here in effect he did claim the prize."

CONVICTION AFFIRMED.

HOPE v. BROWN

[1954] 1 All E. R. 330

Giving instructions to a servant to sell meat in excess of the permitted price is mere preparation and not an attempt to sell in excess of the permitted price.

Facts

The accused was charged with an attempt to sell meat at a price in excess of that permitted by legislation which was then in force. He was a butcher and his refrigerator contained packets of meat bearing tickets specifying the contents and correct price. In the drawer there were found duplicate tickets specifying excessive prices and the accused admitted that he had instructed his employee to change the tickets before selling the meat to customers. The Magistrates held that the accused was not guilty and the prosecutor unsuccessfully appealed by way of case stated to the Divisional Court.

Extracts from the Judgments of the Divisional Court.

LORD GODDARD, C.J.—

"In the present case, what remained to be done before there could be an attempt was the affixing to the meat of the false tickets. Until that was done, in my opinion, the matter remained simply what I may call in embryo and in intention. The girl, no doubt, and not the respondent himself, would have affixed the tickets, but that was because she was instructed to do so. Her act would have been the act of the respondent, but until she had affixed the tickets, it seems to me that one cannot say that an offence was committed. The preparation of the false tickets and putting them in the drawer is too remote from the actual transaction which would be necessary to constitute the attempt. It is obvious that there might be a sudden change of heart, or an intervention by the master, or something of that sort, which would have prevented any attempt being made to sell this meat to the customers. The court has always said, in cases where it has been found that there has been an attempt, that the crime would have been committed but for the intervention of someone, but no crime would have been committed in the present case until the meat had been sold to the customer with the false ticket.

Therefore, I think the mere fact that the respondent prepared a false ticket is not enough. No doubt, this charge was preferred because of the decision in *Gardner* v. *Akeroyd*,[1] but that case turned on whether the proprietor of a butcher's business could be made vicariously liable for the act of an assistant in the shop which was preparatory to an illegal sale, but did not amount to an attempt, and we held that the doctrine of vicarious liability could not be so extended. Giving judgment in that case, I said: 'Now, applying the doctrine laid down in *R.* v. *Eagleton*,[2] I should have no hesitation in holding that the servant in this case was guilty of, and could properly have been charged with, an attempt as the facts proved were clearly immediately connected with what would have been a substantive offence had not the enforcement officer intervened before the goods had been actually sold.' But there the false tickets had already been affixed to the meat, while in the present case they had not. For these reasons I think the enforcement officers struck too soon. In my opinion, the justices came to a right decision in point of law and this appeal fails."

APPEAL DISMISSED.

---

[1] [1952] 2 Q. B. 743; [1952] 2 All E. R. 306.
[2] (1855), Dears. C. C. 376.

R. v. MISKELL
[1954] 1 All E. R. 137

All the circumstances of the case must be considered in deciding whether the acts of the accused amount to an attempt to procure another to commit an act of gross indecency.

Facts.

The accused, a British soldier serving abroad, was charged before a Court-Martial with attempting to procure a boy to commit an act of gross indecency. He had met the boy one night when indecent approaches were made and asked the boy to meet him again at a railway station on the following night. The accused met the boy at the station on the following night and suggested that they should go for a walk together. The accused was then arrested and said that he had intended to withdraw any indecent suggestions he may have made. The accused was convicted and unsuccessfully appealed to the Courts-Martial Appeal Court (the Court of Criminal Appeal) on the ground that the invitation to the meeting on the following night and the suggestion of a walk were too remote to constitute an attempt.

Extracts from the Judgment of the Courts-Martial Appeal Court.

HILBERY, J.—

" The law, however, punishes a man, not for a guilty intention, but for the overt act done as part of the carrying out of that intention. The intention of the appellant here was, undoubtedly, to procure an act of gross indecency with the boy. The invitation and the meeting were overt acts. When that invitation and meeting are considered in the light of the circumstances in which the invitation was issued and the meeting took place, it appears to us that those acts cannot be said to be incapable of being attempts to procure the boy to commit an act of gross indecency with the appellant. Once it is decided that they could be so regarded as a matter of law, then the question whether they were an attempt or not becomes one of fact for a jury, or, as in this case, for the court-martial.

In *R.* v. *Cope* Lord TREVETHIN, C.J., said (86 J. P. 78): ' The letters in the present case obviously do not contain an undisguised invitation, nor is a code suggested, but it is said that they do contain terms which would have conveyed the invitation to the mind of their intended recipient as unmistakably as if it had been set out in express terms and that the jury have by convicting found that this is so. . . .' Later on, he said (*ibid.*): 'We think that there was enough [in the letter] to entitle the jury to find that Price would have read into it an invitation to repeat with the appellant the offence which he had committed with Riley, and therefore that the sending of the letters was an attempt to procure Price . . .' That invitation in that letter was no less remote from the procuring than the invitation given by the appellant in this case and the meeting in fulfilment of that invitation, coupled, as it was, with a further invitation to another walk. Here, as in *R.* v. *Cope*, in the circumstances which had occurred, the invitation in question was understood to be an invitation to an act of gross indecency, and the boy's father and the police were informed, and it is not contended that an invitation, however veiled, which in the circumstances is an invitation to commit an act of gross indecency, is not an attempt to procure such an act. For these reasons, the appeal is dismissed."

APPEAL DISMISSED.

R. v. WHITE

[1910] 2 K. B. 124

A person may be convicted of attempted murder by poisoning although the amount of poison he endeavours to administer would, unknown to him, be insufficient for his purpose; and he may be convicted of attempted murder by slow poisoning after he has endeavoured to administer the first dose.

Facts.

The appellant was convicted of attempting to murder his mother. The evidence was that a small quantity of cyanide, insufficient of itself to kill anyone, was found in a glass of lemonade beside the deceased who had died of heart-failure without drinking it. There was evidence that the glass was placed beside the deceased by the appellant and that he believed that the amount of cyanide therein was sufficient to be fatal.

The appellant appealed against conviction to the Court of Criminal Appeal which dismissed the appeal.

Extract from the Judgment of the Court of Criminal Appeal.

BRAY, J.—

" . . . The next point made was that if he put it there with that intent there was no attempt at murder; that the jury must have acted upon a suggestion of the learned judge in his summing up that this was one, the first or some later, of a series of doses which he intended to administer and so cause her death by slow poisoning; and that if they did act on that suggestion there was no attempt at murder, because the act of which he was guilty, namely, the putting the poison in the wine glass, was a completed act and could not be and was not intended by the appellant to have the effect of killing her at once. It could not kill unless it were followed by other acts which he might never have done. There seems no doubt that the learned judge in effect did tell the jury that if this was a case of slow poisoning the appellant would be guilty of the attempt to murder. We are of opinion that this direction was right, and that the completion or attempted completion of one of a series of acts intended by a man to result in killing is an attempt to murder even although this completed act would not, unless followed by the other acts, result in killing. It might be the beginning of the attempt, but would none the less be an attempt. While saying this we must say also that we do not think it likely the jury acted on this suggestion, because there was nothing to shew that the administration of small doses of cyanide of potassium would have a cumulative effect; we think it much more likely, having regard to the statement made by the prisoner to the witness Carden, that the appellant supposed he had put sufficient poison in the glass to kill her. This, of course, would be an attempt to murder. . . ."

APPEAL DISMISSED.

R. v. PERCY DALTON (LONDON) LTD.[1]
(1949), 33 Cr. App. Rep. 102

The accused is not guilty of a criminal attempt if the transaction intended is carried through to completion and does not itself constitute a crime.

Facts.

Percy Dalton (London) Ltd. was charged with selling and two individuals with buying pears at a price in excess of that permitted by the Imported Pears Order, 1946. The pears were sold in boxes stated to contain forty-six pounds or more. If they contained forty-seven pounds fifteen ounces, no offence would have been committed. The prosecution was unable to prove that the boxes contained less than forty-seven pounds fifteen ounces and the jury acquitted the accused of the main offence but convicted them of an attempt to infringe the Order. The accused successfully appealed to the Court of Criminal Appeal.

Extracts from the Judgment of the Court of Criminal Appeal.

BIRKETT, J.—

" Our attention was also drawn to certain cases to which I need make only a very short reference. The first was *R.* v. *Brown* (1889), 24 Q. B. D. 357. That was a case of a person who had pleaded guilty to an indictment ' charging him with having attempted to commit unnatural offences with domestic fowls and was sentenced to a term of imprisonment. After the Judge left the assize town his attention was called to an unreported case which was said to have decided that a duck was not an ' animal ' with the meaning of the Offences against the Person Act, 1861 (24 & 25 Vict., c. 100) s. 61, and he thereupon stated a case requesting the opinion of the Court for Crown Cases Reserved whether the conviction was good.' It was held that the indictment was good and the prisoner was properly convicted. But Lord COLERIDGE, Chief Justice, in giving judgment in that case said (at p. 358),

---

[1] This case was followed in *R.* v. *Smith* (1973), *Times,* March 31st, (no attempt at handling of goods which had ceased to be stolen), in which leave to appeal to the House of Lords was granted.

'In *R.* v. *Collins* (1864) Le. & Ca. 471, the Court held that, where a man put his hand into another's pocket and there was nothing in the pocket which he could steal, he could not be convicted of an attempt to steal. That is a decision with which we are not satisfied. *R.* v. *Dodd* (1877) unrep., proceeded upon the same view, that a person could not be convicted of an attempt to commit an offence which he could not actually commit. Some of the Judges, I know, yielded with great reluctance to the authority of *R.* v. *Collins* (*supra*), and thought that decision was wrong. In this case it would seem on the question of fact that the ground of the decision in *Dodd* (*supra*) fails, because I should suppose it is obvious that as a fact the offence could be committed by the boy.' That case, in our view, is not very helpful, if at all, upon the matter with which the Court is concerned.

Then there was the case of *R.* v. *Williams*, [1893) 1 Q.B. 320. The headnote of that case is: 'Although a boy under 14, who is tried on an indictment under section 4 of the Criminal Law Amendment Act, 1885, charging him with having had carnal knowledge of a girl under 13, is entitled to be acquitted of that offence, he may be convicted of an indecent assault under section 9 of the Act.' That is the purport of the case. It was cited before us because of the difference of opinion which was expressed by the Judges in this way. Lord COLERIDGE said (at p. 321) the boy was proved at the trial 'to be under the age of 14 and, therefore, could not by law be convicted of rape: nor could he, in my opinion, be convicted of attempting to do that which the law says he was physically incapable of doing.' HAWKINS, J., said: 'I do not assent to the notion that the boy cannot be convicted of an attempt to do that which the law says he cannot do.' CAVE. J., said (at p. 322) that he would desire a further discussion on the question before deciding it, but at present he was inclined to agree with the opinion of HAWKINS, J. DAY, J., (at p. 323) agreed with CAVE, J., and COLLINS, J., said that he was of the same opinion. But whatever be the proper answer to that matter, again that case has very little to do with the facts which we have to decide. A further case was cited, *R.* v. *Brown and others*, (1899), 63 J. P. 790, which was a case of a woman taking some material believing it to be noxious though it was in fact innocent, and the charge against her was that she attempted with intent, and it was held there that the conviction was good.

I mention these cases because they were cited before us in argument, but in our view none of them touch the main point in the present case, and none of those decisions is in conflict with the decision to which we have come. We confine ourselves to the facts of this case, which are that the appellant company has been acquitted by the jury of the offences charged in the indictment of selling pears above the maximum price permitted by the Order. All the acts of the company have been considered by the jury in coming to that conclusion; and we feel it impossible to say on the same facts that the company can be convicted of the attempt to sell above the maximum price when the completed transaction was no offence. Steps on the way to the commission of what would be a crime, if the acts were completed, may amount to attempts to commit that crime, to which, unless interrupted, they would have led; but steps on the way to the doing of something, which is thereafter done, and which is no crime, cannot be regarded as attempts to commit a crime."

APPEALS ALLOWED.

R. v. RING, ATKINS AND JACKSON

(1892), 61 L. J. M. C. 116

It is attempted larceny for the accused to put his hand into someone's pocket with intent to steal.

Facts.

The prisoners were charged with attempting to steal from a person unknown, and with assaulting a person unknown with intent to commit felony. They were seen to push and hustle women in a railway station and one of them put his hand in the woman's pocket and withdrew it. There was no evidence that anything was taken from the pocket. The accused were convicted, but the Recorder reserved a case for the opinion of the Court for Crown Cases Reserved who were of opinion that the conviction was correct.

Judgment of the Court for Crown Cases Reserved.

LORD COLERIDGE, C.J.:—

" I am of opinion that the conviction should be affirmed. The case was stated . . . to ascertain whether *R.* v. *Collins*[1] is still law. That case is no longer law. It was overruled by *R.* v. *Brown*,[2] which was decided by five judges; and the

---

[1] (1864), Le. & Ca. 471.
[2] (1889), 24 Q. B. D. 357.

present case is decided by five judges, one of whom was one of the judges in *R.* v. *Brown.* Therefore, nine judges are of opinion that *R.* v. *Collins* is no longer law.

CONVICTION AFFIRMED.[1]

DAVEY v. LEE

[1967] 2 All E.R. 423

The actus reus *necessary to constitute an attempt to commit a crime is complete if the prisoner does an act as a step towards the commission of a specific crime, which is immediately and not merely remotely connected with the commission of it, and the doing of which cannot reasonably be regarded as having any other purpose than the commission of the specific crime.*

Facts.

The accused were charged and convicted of attempting to steal metal from the Electricity Board. They ran away after being detected in endeavouring to break into the property of the Electricity Board near a point at which there was a copper store. They had cut the wire fence and were getting over it. There were other stores and buildings on the property, and it was argued on behalf of the accused that the acts proved against them were not sufficiently proximate to the stealing of the copper. The accused unsuccessfully appealed to Quarter Sessions and then by way of case stated to the Divisional Court.

Extracts from the Judgment of the Divisional Court.

LORD PARKER, C.J.—

" The real point taken by counsel for the appellants is that an intention to steal is not sufficient to constitute an attempt, but that there must be acts which have moved further than being merely preparatory acts. What amounts to an attempt has been described variously in the authorities, and, for my part, I prefer to adopt the definition given in *Stephen's Digest of Criminal Law* (5th Edn., 1894), art. 50, where it says that:

---

[1] Not even referentially is it possible to gather the principle underlying this decision. It is therefore impossible to say how far it goes. The case should be considered in conjunction with *R.* v. *Easom,* p. 271, *infra.*

'An attempt to commit a crime is an act done with intent to commit that crime, and forming part of a series of acts which would constitute its actual commission if it were not interrupted.'

As a general statement that seems to me to be right, though it does not help to define the point of time at which the series of acts begins. That, as *Stephen* said, depends on the facts of each case. A helpful definition is given in para. 4104 in *Archbold's Pleading, Evidence and Practice* (36th Edn.), where it is stated in this form:

'It is submitted that the *actus reus* necessary to constitute an attempt is complete if the prisoner does an act which is a step towards the commission of the specific crime, which is immediately and not merely remotely connected with the commission of it, and the doing of which cannot reasonably be regarded as having any other purpose than the commission of the specific crime.'

It seems to me that the facts of this case fully come within that test, and that the magistrates were undoubtedly right in the view they formed. I would dismiss this appeal."

APPEAL DISMISSED.

JONES v. BROOKS

(1968), 52 Cr.App.Rep. 614

Where the act alleged to constitute an attempt to commit a crime is equivocal, evidence of the accused's intention is admissible in order to explain the object of the act.

Facts.

Two brothers, Brooks, were charged with attempting to take and drive away a motor car. They were seen trying the doors of various cars, and subsequently admitted that they intended to drive home a car into which they could effect an entry. The Magistrates dismissed the charge on the ground that the acts of the accused were equivocal, but they stated a case for the opinion of a Divisional Court which was of opinion that the Magistrates should have convicted.

Extracts from the Opinion of the Divisional Court.

LORD PARKER, C.J.—

" Quite recently this Court in *Davey and Others* v. *Lee*[1], to which the magistrates were referred, adopted and approved the definition which appears in the current (36th) edition of *Archbold* in paragraph 4104 to this effect, that the *actus reus* necessary to constitute an attempt must be immediately, and not merely remotely, connected with the commission of the offence.

Ignoring entirely the expressed intention that these two respondents admitted, it is quite clear that the attempt to open this door was equivocal in the sense that it might have been a step towards the commission of a number of different crimes, not merely taking and driving away, but stealing either the car or some contents of the car, or indeed for the purely innocent purpose of going to sleep in it. If the expressed intention here is to be disregarded entirely, then quite clearly, in my judgment, the justices were right in saying that it had not been shown that the step in attempting to open the door was a step towards the commission of the specific crime of taking and driving away. It was submitted to the justices, and to this Court, that the expressed intention of these respondents does not enter into this matter at all except at a later stage in considering *mens rea*.

I am quite unable to accept that contention. Of course, an expressed intention alone does not amount to an attempt; there must be an *actus reus* which is sufficiently proximate to the expressed intention. But that does not mean to say that the courts should disregard entirely as part of the surrounding circumstances and the evidence in the case the expressed intention of the respondents, both at the time and after the *actus reus*. It seems to me that that intention is relevant when the act concerned is equivocal in order to see towards what the act is directed. Once that is decided, then it still remains for the prosecution to show that the act itself is sufficiently proximate to amount to an attempt to commit the crime which it was the intention of the respondents to commit.

Looked at in this way, I have no doubt that the specific crime being isolated by the expressed intention as one to take and drive away, the insertion of the key into the door and seeking to open the door of the car was an act sufficiently proximate."

---

[1] [1968] 1 Q.B. 306; [1967] 2 All E.R. 423, p. 168, *supra*.

BRIDGE, J.—

"If the argument for the respondents is pressed to its logical conclusion, it would seem to lead to the result that there can never be *actus reus* sufficient to constitute an attempt to commit a crime unless the act itself viewed independently of any other circumstances in the case leads irresistibly to the conclusion that the person accused of the act had a guilty mind."

CASE REMITTED TO MAGISTRATES WITH DIRECTION TO CONVICT.

SECTION 4

HOMICIDE

R. v. SMITH

[1959] 2 Q. B. 35

A wound may be a substantial cause of death although the deceased might not have died had he received proper medical treatment.

Facts.

The accused, a British soldier serving abroad, was charged before a Court-Martial with the murder of a fellow soldier whom he had stabbed in a barrack room fight. The deceased had been dropped twice when being carried to a reception station. He had been wounded in the lung and there was evidence that he might well have survived had he not been given artificial respiration. The accused was convicted and unsuccessfully appealed to the Courts-Martial Appeal Court on the ground, *inter alia*, that the jury had not been properly directed on the question of causation.

Extracts from the Judgment of the Courts-Martial Appeal Court.

LORD PARKER, C.J.—

" It seems to the court that if at the time of death the original wound is still an operating cause and a substantial cause, then the death can properly be said to be the result of the wound, albeit that some other cause of death is also operating. Only if it can be said that the original wounding is merely the setting in which another cause operates can it be said that the death does not result from the wound. Putting it in another way, only if the second cause is so overwhelming as to make the original wound merely part of the history can it be said that the death does not flow from the wound.

There are a number of cases in the law of contract and tort on these matters of causation, and it is always difficult to find a form of words when directing a jury or, as here, a court which will convey in simple language the principle of causation. It seems to the court enough for this purpose to refer to one passage in the judgment of Lord WRIGHT in *The Oropesa*, where he said:[1] ' To break the chain of causation it must be shown that there is something which I will call ultroneous, something unwarrantable, a new cause which disturbs the sequence of events, something which can be described as either unreasonable or extraneous or extrinsic.' To much the same effect was a judgment on the question of causation given by DENNING, L.J., in *Minister of Pensions* v. *Chennell.*[2]

Mr. Bowen [counsel for the accused] placed great reliance on a case decided in this court of *R.* v. *Jordan*, and in particular on a passage in the headnote which says:[3] '. . . that death resulting from any normal treatment employed to deal with a felonious injury may be regarded as caused by the felonious injury, but that the same principle does not apply where the treatment employed is abnormal.' Reading those words into the present case, Mr. Bowen says that the treatment that this unfortunate man received from the moment that he was struck to the time of his death was abnormal. The court is satisfied that *Jordan's* case was a very particular case depending upon its exact facts. It incidentally arose in this court on the grant of an application to call further evidence, and leave having been obtained, two well-known medical experts gave evidence that in their opinion death had not been caused by the stabbing but by the introduction of terramycin after the deceased had shown that he was intolerant to it, and by the intravenous introduction of abnormal quantities of liquid. It also appears that at the time when that was done the stab wound which had penetrated the intestine in two places had mainly healed. In those circumstances the court felt bound to quash the conviction because they could not say that a reasonable jury properly directed would not have been able on that to say that there had been a break in the chain of causation; the court could only uphold the conviction in that case if they

---

1 [1943] P. 32, at p. 39.
2 [1947] K. B. 250; [1946] 2 All E. R. 719.
3 (1956), 40 Cr. App. Rep. 152.

were satisfied that no reasonable jury could have come to that conclusion.

In the present case it is true that the judge-advocate did not in his summing-up go into the refinements of causation. Indeed, in the opinion of this court he was probably wise to refrain from doing so. He did leave the broad question to the court whether they were satisfied that the wound had caused the death in the sense that the death flowed from the wound, albeit that the treatment he received was in the light of after-knowledge a bad thing. In the opinion of this court that was on the facts of the case a perfectly adequate summing-up on causation; I say 'on the facts of the case' because, in the opinion of the court, they can only lead to one conclusion: a man is stabbed in the back, his lung is pierced and haemorrhage results; two hours later he dies of haemorrhage from that wound; in the interval there is no time for a careful examination, and the treatment given turns out in the light of subsequent knowledge to have been inappropriate and, indeed, harmful. In those circumstances no reasonable jury or court could, properly directed, in our view possibly come to any other conclusion than that the death resulted from the original wound. Accordingly, the court dismisses this appeal."

APPEAL DISMISSED.

THABO MELI v. R.
[1954] 1 All E. R. 373

Where several people plan to kill the deceased and in fact kill him, the court will not necessarily divide the transaction into two parts in order to ascertain whether it was the act done with malice aforethought which in fact killed the deceased.[1]

Facts.

The accused were charged and convicted of murder before the High Court of Basutoland. They had planned to kill the deceased in a hut and throw his body over a cliff so as to make it appear that the death was accidental. The accused struck the deceased blows in the hut and threw him over a cliff. There was, however, some evidence that the deceased

---

[1] Compare this case with *R.* v. *Church*, p. 214, *post*.

was not dead when thrown over the cliff but died in consequence of exposure. The accused unsuccessfully appealed to the Privy Council on the ground that the blows inflicted with malice aforethought were not the cause of the death of the deceased and that they lacked malice aforethought when they threw the deceased over the cliff because they believed him to be dead.

Extracts from the advice of the Privy Council.

LORD REID.—

"There is no doubt that the accused set out to do all these acts in order to achieve their plan, and as parts of their plan; and it is much too refined a ground of judgment to say that, because they were under a misapprehension at one stage and thought that their guilty purpose had been achieved before, in fact, it was achieved, therefore they are to escape the penalties of the law. Their Lordships do not think that this is a matter which is susceptible of elaboration. There appears to be no case, either in South Africa or England, or for that matter elsewhere, which resembles the present. Their Lordships can find no difference relevant to the present case between the law of South Africa and the law of England; and they are of opinion that by both laws there can be no separation such as that for which the accused contend. Their crime is not reduced from murder to a lesser crime merely because the accused were under some misapprehension for a time during the completion of their criminal plot.

Their Lordships must, therefore, humbly advise Her Majesty that this appeal should be dismissed."

APPEAL DISMISSED.

R. v. ROSE

(1884), 15 Cox C. C. 540

Homicide is lawful if committed by one who reasonably believes that there is no other means of preventing the commission of a violent crime.

Facts.

The accused was charged with murder. The evidence was that he was living with his mother and father, and that his father, a man of great physical strength, frequently quarrelled with his mother, whom he believed to have been unfaithful. The accused was a boy of 21, and there was no doubt that he would have been worsted in a fight with his father. In the night when the deceased met his death, the accused's mother called out "murder", and there was evidence of a violent quarrel between the accused's father and mother; the father forced the mother to the top of the stairs and threatened to knife her. The accused shot and killed his father, and there was no evidence of the presence of a knife.

Extract from Summing-Up to jury by:—

LOPES, J.—

" Homicide is excusable if a person takes away the life of another in defending himself, if the fatal blow which takes away life is necessary for his preservation. The law says not only in self-defence such as I have described may homicide be excusable, but also it may be excusable if the fatal blow inflicted was necessary for the preservation of life. In the case of parent and child, if the parent has reason to believe that the life of a child is in imminent danger by reason of an assault by another person, and that the only possible, fair, and reasonable means of saving the child's life is by doing something which will cause the death of that person, the law excuses that act. It is the same of a child with regard to a parent; it is the same in the case of a husband and wife. Therefore, I propose to lay the law before you in this form: If you think, having regard to the evidence, and drawing fair and proper inferences from it, that the prisoner at the bar acted without vindictive feeling towards his father when he fired the shot, if you think that at the time he fired that shot he honestly believed, and had reasonable grounds for the belief, that his mother's life was in imminent peril, and that the fatal shot which he fired was absolutely necessary for the preservation of her life, then he ought to be excused, and the law will excuse him, from the consequences of the homicide. If, however, on the other hand, you cannot come to that conclusion, if you think, and think without any reasonable doubt, that it is not a fair inference to be drawn from the evidence, but are clearly of opinion that he acted vindictively, and had not such a belief as I have described to you, or had not reasonable grounds for such a belief, then you must find him guilty of murder."

VERDICT, NOT GUILTY.

PALMER v. R.

[1971] 1 All E.R. 1077

There is no rule of law that, where self-defence is pleaded in answer to a charge of murder, the jury must be directed to convict of manslaughter if, though they think that the accused had reasonable grounds for believing that his life was in danger, he caused the death of the deceased by the use of unreasonable force.

Facts.

Palmer was a member of a party thought to have stolen ganja from a house in Jamaica. The deceased was a member of a party which went in pursuit of Palmer's party. It was not disputed that the deceased was killed by a shot fired from a gun in the possession of one of Palmer's party, but Palmer's defence was that he had not got possession of the gun when the shot was fired. The trial judge took the view that, in addition to putting the defence raised by Palmer to the jury, it was proper to direct the jury with regard to the possibility of an acquittal on the ground of self-defence; but he did not tell the jury that they should return a verdict of manslaughter if of opinion that, though the case was one of self-defence, Palmer had used excessive force in furtherance of self-defence. Palmer was convicted of murder and unsuccessfully appealed to the Court of Criminal Appeal of Jamaica and then to the Privy Council.

Extracts from the advice of the Judicial Committee of the Privy Council.

LORD MORRIS OF BORTH-Y-GEST.—

" It was claimed that support for the contention of the appellant could be found in the judgments of the High Court of Australia in *R.* v. *Howe*[1]—judgments to which their Lordships pay the highest respect . . .

On the assumption that an attack of a violent and felonious nature, or at least of an unlawful nature, was made or threatened so that a person under attack or threat of attack reasonably feared for his life or the safety of his person from

---

[1] (1958) 100 C.L.R. 448.

injury, violation or indecent or insulting usage so that occasion had arisen entitling a person to resort to force to repel force or apprehended force, then Sir Owen DIXON, C.J., stated that the law was as follows:[1]

'Had he used no more force than was proportionate to the danger in which he stood, or reasonably supposed he stood, although he thereby caused the death of his assailant he would not have been guilty either of murder or manslaughter. But assuming that he was not entitled to a complete defence to a charge of murder, for the reason only that the force of violence which he used against his assailant or apprehended assailant went beyond what was needed for his protection or what the circumstances could cause him reasonably to believe to be necessary for his protection, of what crime does he stand guilty? Is the consequence of the failure of his plea of self-defence on the ground that he is guilty of murder or does it operate to reduce the homicide to manslaughter? There is no clear and definite judicial decision providing an answer to this question but it seems reasonable in principle to regard such a homicide as reduced to manslaughter, and that view has the support of not a few judicial statements to be found in the reports . . .'

A wholly different line was taken in *De Freitas* v. *R.*,[2] which was an appeal from the Supreme Court of British Guiana to the Federal Supreme Court. After a review of many authorities the court preferred not to follow the development of the law propounded in *R.* v. *Howe.*[3] They sought to avoid the necessity of requiring a jury to go through a complicated and difficult process. An accused who has done no more than was in the opinion of the jury reasonably necessary in self-defence was entitled to be acquitted. If he has gone further then considerations as to provocation may reduce an offence so that the verdict should be one of manslaughter . . .

But their Lordships consider in agreement with the approach in *De Freitas* v. *R.*[2] that if the prosecution have shown that what was done was not done in self-defence then that issue is eliminated from the case. If the jury consider that an accused acted in self-defence or if the jury are in doubt as to this then they will acquit. The defence of self-defence either succeeds so as to result in an acquittal or it

[1] (1958) 100 C.L.R. at 460, 461.
[2] (1960) 2 W.I.R. 523.
[3] (1958) 100 C.L.R. 448.

is disproved in which case as a defence it is rejected. In a homicide case the circumstances may be such that it will become an issue whether there was provocation so that the verdict might be one of manslaughter. Any other possible issues will remain. If in any case the view is possible that the intent necessary to constitute the crime of murder was lacking then that matter would be left to the jury."

APPEAL DISMISSED.

R. v. McINNES

[1971] 3 All E.R. 295

(1) *There is no rule of law that, for a plea of self-defence to succeed in answer to a charge of murder or any lesser offence against the person, the accused must retreat as far as he can;* (2) *there is no rule of law that, on a charge of murder, the jury must be directed to return a verdict of manslaughter if they think that, though the occasion warranted action in self-defence, the accused used excessive force.*

Facts.

McInnes was charged with murder by stabbing. His defence was that the deceased met his death by running against a knife which the accused was carrying. In addition to directing the jury with regard to accident, the trial judge also directed them on self-defence. The accused was convicted and unsuccessfully appealed to the Court of Appeal.

Extracts from the Judgment of the Court of Appeal.

EDMUND DAVIES, J.—

" The first criticism of the learned judge's treatment of self-defence is that he misdirected the jury in relation to the question of whether an attacked person must do all he reasonably can to retreat before he turns on his attacker. The direction given was in these terms:

' In our law if two men fight and one of them after a while endeavours to avoid any further struggle and retreats as far as he can, and then when he can go no further turns and kills his assailant to avoid being killed himself, that homicide is excusable, but notice that to show that homicide arising from a fight was committed in self-defence it must be shown that the party killing had retreated as far as he could, or as far as the fierceness of the assault would permit him.'

One does not have to seek far for the source of this direction.

It was clearly quoted from *Archbold*,[1] which is in turn based on a passage in *Hale's Pleas of the Crown*.[2] In our judgment, the direction was expressed in too inflexible terms and might, in certain circumstances, be regarded as significantly misleading. We prefer the view expressed by the High Court of Australia[3] that a failure to retreat is only an element in the considerations on which the reasonableness of an accused's conduct is to be judged (see *Palmer* v. *R.*[4]), or, as it is put in *Smith and Hogan's Criminal Law*.[5]

'. . . simply a factor to be taken into account in deciding whether it was necessary to use force, and whether the force used was reasonable.'

The modern law on the topic was, in our respectful view, accurately set out in *R.* v. *Julien*[6] by WIDGERY, L.J., in the following terms:

'It is not, as we understand it, the law that a person threatened must take to his heels and run in the dramatic way suggested by counsel for the appellant; but what is necessary is that he should demonstrate by his actions that he does not want to fight. He must demonstrate that he is prepared to temporise and disengage and perhaps to make some physical withdrawal; and to the extent that that is necessary as a feature of the justification of self-defence, it is true, in our opinion, whether the charge is a homicide charge or something less serious.'

In the light of the foregoing, how stands the direction given in the present case? Viewed in isolation, that is to say, without regard to the evidence adduced, it was expressed in too rigid terms. But the opportunity to retreat remains, as the trial judge said, ' an important consideration ', and, when regard is had to the evidence as to the circumstances which prevailed, in our view it emerges with clarity that the appellant could have avoided this fatal incident with ease by simply walking or running away—as, indeed, he promptly did as soon as the deceased had been stabbed . . .

The final criticism levelled against the summing-up is that the learned judge wrongly failed to direct the jury that, if death resulted from the use of excessive force by the

---

[1] *Archbold's Criminal Pleading, Evidence and Practice*, 1969, 37th Edn., para. 2495.

[2] (1800) vol. I, pp. 481, 483.

[3] In *R.* v. *Howe* (1958), 100 C.L.R. 448 at pp. 462, 464, 469.

[4] [1971] 1 All E.R. 1077, at p. 1085; [1971] 2 W.L.R. 831, at p. 840.

[5] 1969, 2nd Edn., p. 231.

[6] [1969] 2 All E.R. 856, at p. 858; [1969] 1 W.L.R. 839, at p. 843.

appellant in defending himself against the aggressiveness of the deceased, the proper verdict was one not of guilty of murder but guilty of manslaughter . . .

Section 3(1) of the Criminal Law Act, 1967 provides: ' A person may use such force as is reasonable in the circumstances in the prevention of crime . . .', and in our judgment the degree of force permissible in self-defence is similarly limited. Deliberate stabbing was so totally unreasonable in the circumstances of this case, even on the appellant's version, that self-defence justifying a complete acquittal was not relied on before us, and rightly so. Despite the high esteem in which we hold our Australian brethren, we respectfully reject as far as this country is concerned the refinement sought to be introduced that, if the accused, in defending himself during a fisticuffs encounter, drew out against his opponent (who he had no reason to think was armed) the deadly weapon which he had earlier unsheathed and then ' let him have it ', the jury should have been directed that, even on those facts, it was open to them to convict of manslaughter. They are, in our view, the facts of this case. It follows that in our judgment no such direction was called for."

APPEAL DISMISSED.

Comment on R. v. Rose, Palmer v. R. and R. v. McInnes.

According to the above three cases negligence may be a partial basis of liability in murder, for Rose would, according to LOPES, J., have been guilty of that offence if he had lacked reasonable grounds for believing that his mother's life was in danger, while Palmer and McInnes were held guilty of murder although they may have believed, albeit without reasonable grounds, that the force to which they resorted was necessary for their protection. It is true that each accused intended to kill or at least to cause grievous bodily harm, and it is proper for the law to require the utmost caution to be taken before effect is given to such intentions; but verdicts of manslaughter would appear to be more consonant with modern ideas.

The cases illustrate the " all or nothing " approach of the common law. The defences of prevention of crime or self-defence must either succeed or fail, there is no half-way house. A similar approach was adopted to the defence of necessity in *R.* v. *Dudley* and *Stephens*[1], and the difficulties occasioned in the civil law by the all or nothing approach to defences such as contributory negligence are notorious.

[1] P. 109, *supra*.

It is of some interest to recall that, in the case of theft, the accused's belief, however unreasonable it may be, that he has the legal right to deprive his victim of his property is a defence; while, in the case of blackmail, the accused has to be judged entirely on his own beliefs concerning the propriety of his actions. The distinction between these offences and murder can of course be justified on the basis of the sanctity of human life, but even the sanctity of human life hardly justifies the rejection of the half-way house of a finding of manslaughter.

R. v. SALISBURY

(1553), 1 Plowd. 100

If a person kills a stranger in mistake for the person he intends to kill or to whom he intends grievous bodily harm, he is guilty of murder.

Facts.

Five persons were indicted for the murder of the servant of a Doctor Ellis. It appeared that four of them had lain in wait for Doctor Ellis on the highway with the intention of attacking him, and that a fight had ensued in the course of which the servant was killed. It also appeared that one John Vane Salisbury had not lain in wait for the Doctor, although he had participated in the struggle.

Extracts from the observations of the Court.

> And *note* that the Court said thus to the jury; you, jurors, have heard the evidence which has been given to prove the prisoners guilty of the murder whereof they are impeached, which evidence proves that the conspiracy was to kill Doctor Ellis, and the malice prepense was against him, and not particularly against his servant who is killed, and therefore perhaps you will imagine that the evidence does not maintain the indictment, because no malice was against the servant, whom the prisoners perhaps did not know, nor ever heard of him before; and we think it proper to tell you what the law is in this point, to the intent that you may not err in it. And, Sirs, we take the law to be, that the killing of him is murder in the prisoners, if they killed him upon the malice which they had against the master, so that

if you shall find that they had malice against the doctor, that malice does in the eye of the law make the killing of him that was killed, who was the doctor's servant, and in his company, to be murder.

VERDICT, GUILTY OF MURDER SO FAR AS THREE OF THE ACCUSED WERE CONCERNED, GUILTY OF MANSLAUGHTER SO FAR AS JOHN VANE SALISBURY WAS CONCERNED[1], WHILE THE FIFTH WAS ACQUITTED ON THE FACTS.

R. v. GORE

(1611), 9 Co. Rep. 81a

If A. puts poison in medicine intending that B. should consume it and die, and C. dies in consequence of consuming the medicine without being aware of its contents, A. is guilty of C.'s murder.

Facts.

Medicine was prepared for Gore by an apothecary named Martin at the instance of a Doctor Gray. Gore's wife Agnes put ratsbane in the medicine intending that Gore should consume it and die. The medicine was consumed by Gore, Roper his father-in-law and one C. All three of them were taken ill but they recovered. Three days later, Roper took what remained of the medicine to Dr. Gray and complained. Gray summoned Martin who said he would take the medicine himself in order to show that he had put nothing wrong in it. Martin stirred the medicine, consumed it and died a day later.

The question for all the judges was whether Agnes Gore was guilty of murder having regard to the fact that Martin consumed the medicine " of his own head ", and increased the probability of its having fatal effects by stirring it.

---

[1] So far as the modern law is concerned John Vane Salisbury's liability would have to be considered in the light of *R.* v. *Anderson and Morris*, p. 132 *supra*. He would not even be guilty of manslaughter if he was unaware of the intentions of the others and the killing was due to their action.

Extracts from the Opinion of the Judges.

"And it was resolved by all the judges that the said Agnes was guilty of the murder of the said Martin, for the law conjoins the murderous intention of Agnes in putting the poison into the electuary to kill her husband, with the event which thence ensued; *sc.*, the death of the said Martin; for the putting of the poison into the said electuary is the occasion and cause; and the poisoning and death of the said Martin is the event, *quia eventus est qui ex causa sequitur, et dicuntur eventus quia ex causis eveniunt,* and the stirring of the electuary by Martin with his knife without the putting in of the poison by Agnes could not have been the cause of his death.

And it was also resolved, that if A. puts poison into a pot of wine, etc. to the intent to poison B. and sets it in a place where he supposes B. will come and drink of it, and by accident C. (to whom A. has no malice) comes, and of his own head takes the pot and drinks of it, of which poison he dies, it is murder in A. for the law couples the event with the intention, and the end with the cause . . ."[1]

R. v. SERNÉ AND GOLDFINCH

(1887), 16 Cox C. C. 311

It is murder to kill another by an act known to be dangerous to life but the mere fact that the act was done in the course of a felony might not of itself have been sufficient even before the Homicide Act, 1957, *came into force.*[2]

Facts.

The accused were charged with the murder of a boy,

---

[1] There is a dearth of modern authority on transferred malice in murder, and the courts have not been confronted with serious problems involving the time element on facts such as those with which Gore's case was concerned. For example, if Roper had taken the medicine to Dr. Gray six months after Agnes Gore had put the poison into it by which time she was reconciled with her husband, would she still have been guilty of Martin's murder? Similar problems can arise without there being any question of transferred malice. For example, if A. put poison into a bottle of wine, intending that B. should drink it and die, and B. does not drink it as intended but some six months later by which time A. has ceased to have any intention of killing B., and indeed was endeavouring to trace the bottle, would A. be guilty of B.'s murder?

[2] The felony probably had to be a felony of violence. See *Beard's* case, p. 87, *supra.*

the invalid and mentally defective son of Serné. The evidence was that the accused were short of money, that the premises in which Serné lived with his family, together with their contents, were insured, and that inflammable material had been placed in and near them by the accused shortly before they caught fire. The deceased met his death in the course of the ensuing conflagration from which the other members of Serné's family escaped.

There was also evidence that the life of the deceased had been insured by Serné who was in circumstances of pecuniary embarrassment.

Extracts from the summing-up to the jury by:—

STEPHEN, J.—

" . . . It is necessary that I should explain to you, to a certain extent, the law of England with regard to the crime of wilful murder inasmuch as you have heard something said about constructive murder. Now that phrase, gentlemen, has no legal meaning whatever[1]. There was wilful murder according to the plain meaning of the term, or there was no murder at all in the present case. The definition of murder is unlawful homicide with malice aforethought; and the words malice aforethought are technical. You must not, therefore, construe them or suppose that they can be construed by ordinary rules of language. The words have to be construed according to a long series of decided cases, which have given them meanings different from those which might be supposed. One of those meanings is, the killing of another person by an act done with an intent to commit a felony. Another meaning is, an act done with the knowledge that the act will probably cause the death of some person. Now it is such an act as the last which is alleged to have been done in this case; and if you think that either or both of these men in the dock killed this boy, either by an act done with intent to commit a felony, that is to say, the setting of the house on fire in order to cheat the insurance company, or by conduct which, to their knowledge, was likely to cause death, and was therefore eminently dangerous in itself—in either of these cases the prisoners are guilty of wilful murder in the plain meaning of the word. I will say a word or two upon one part of this definition, because it is capable of being

[1] Neither has the phrase " wilful murder " got a legal meaning so far as English Law is concerned.

applied very harshly in certain cases, and also because, though I take the law as I find it, I very much doubt whether the definition which I have given, although it is the common definition, is not somewhat too wide. Now when it is said that murder means killing a man by an act done in the commission of a felony, the mere words cover a case like this, that is to say, a case where a man gives another a push with an intention of stealing his watch, and the person so pushed, having a weak heart, or some other internal disorder, dies. To take another very old illustration, it was said that if a man shot at a fowl with intent to steal it, and accidentally killed a man, he was to be accounted guilty of murder, because the act was done in the commission of a felony. I very much doubt, however, whether that is really the law, or whether the court for the Consideration of Crown Cases Reserved would hold it to be so. The present case, however, is not such as I have cited, nor anything like them. In my opinion the definition of the law which makes it murder to kill by an act done in the commission of a felony might and ought to be narrowed, whilst that part of the law under which the Crown in this case claim to have proved a case of murder is maintained. I think that, instead of saying that any act done with intent to commit a felony and which causes death amounts to murder, it would be reasonable to say that any act known to be dangerous to life, and likely in itself to cause death done for the purpose of committing a felony which caused death, should be murder. As an illustration of this, suppose that a man, intending to commit a rape upon a woman but without the least wish to kill her, squeezed her by the throat to overpower her, and in so doing killed her, that would be murder. I think that everyone would say in a case like that, that when a person began doing wicked acts for his own base purposes, he risked his own life as well as that of others. That kind of crime does not differ in any serious degree from one committed by using a deadly weapon, such as a bludgeon, a pistol, or a knife. If a man once begins attacking the human body in such a way, he must take the consequences if he goes further than he intended when he began. That I take to be the true meaning of the law on the subject. In the present case, gentlemen, you have a man, sleeping in a house with his wife, his two daughters, his two sons, and a servant, and you are asked to believe that this man, with all these people under his protection, deliberately set fire to the house in three or four different places, and thereby burnt two of them to death.

It is alleged that he arranged matters in such a way that any person of the most common intelligence must have known perfectly well that he was placing all those people in deadly risk. It appears to me that if that were really done, it matters very little indeed whether the prisoners hoped the people would escape or whether they did not. If a person chose, for some wicked purpose of his own to sink a boat at sea, and thereby caused the deaths of the occupants, it matters nothing whether at the time of committing the act he hoped that the people would be picked up by a passing vessel. He is as much guilty of murder, if the people are drowned, as if he had flung every person into the water with his own hand.

. . . There was a case tried in this court which you will no doubt remember, and which will illustrate my meaning. It was the Clerkenwell explosion case in 1868 when a man named Barrett was charged with causing the death of several persons by an explosion which was intended to release one or two men from custody; and I am sure that no one can say truly that Barrett was not justly hanged."

VERDICT, NOT GUILTY.

R. v. VICKERS

[1957] 2 Q. B. 664

An intention to do grievous bodily harm is implied malice aforethought, and implied malice aforethought has not been affected by s. 1 *of the Homicide Act,* 1957.[1]

Facts.

Vickers was charged with capital murder in the course of theft. He had entered a shop with the intention of stealing from it. He had been detected by an old lady and he struck her several blows which killed her. There was no suggestion that Vickers intended to kill the deceased, but the trial judge directed the jury that the accused was guilty of murder if he intended to cause grievous bodily harm to the deceased.

---

[1] The marginal note to s. 1 of the Homicide Act, 1957, reads "Abolition of 'constructive malice'". S. 1 (1) reads as follows: "Where a person kills another in the course or furtherance of some other offence, the killing shall not amount to murder unless done with the same malice aforethought (express or implied) as is required for a killing to amount to murder when not done in the course or furtherance of another offence."

Vickers was convicted and unsuccessfully appealed to the Court of Criminal Appeal on the ground that causing grievous bodily harm with intent to do so was " another offence " within the meaning of s. 1 of the Homicide Act, 1957 and that an intent to cause grievous bodily harm was no longer sufficient malice aforethought.

Extracts from the Judgment of the Court of Criminal Appeal.

LORD GODDARD, C.J.—

" Murder is, of course, killing with malice aforethought, but ' malice aforethought ' is a term of art. It has always been defined in English law as, either an express intention to kill, as could be inferred when a person, having uttered threats against another, produced a lethal weapon and used it on a victim, or implied, where, by a voluntary act, the accused intended to cause grievous bodily harm to the victim and the victim died as the result. If a person does an act which amounts to the infliction of grievous bodily harm he cannot say that he only intended to cause a certain degree of harm. It is called *malum in se* in the old cases and he must take the consequences. If he intends to inflict grievous bodily harm and that person dies, that has always been held in English law, and was at the time this Act was passed, sufficient to imply the malice aforethought which is a necessary constituent of murder.

It will be observed that the section preserves implied malice as well as express malice, and the words ' Where a person kills another in the course or furtherance of some other offence ' cannot, in our opinion, be referred to the infliction of the grievous bodily harm if the case which is made against the accused is that he killed a person by having assaulted the person with intent to do grievous bodily harm, and from the bodily harm he inflicted that person dies. The ' furtherance of some other offence ' must refer to the offence he was committing or endeavouring to commit other than the killing, otherwise there would be no sense in it. It was always the English law, as I have said, that if death was caused by a person in the course of committing a felony involving violence that was murder. Therefore, in the present case it is perfectly clear that the words ' Where a person kills another in the course or furtherance of some other offence ' must be attributed to the burglary he was committing. The killing was in the course or furtherance of that burglary. He killed that person in the course of the burglary because he realised that the victim recognised him and he therefore inflicted grievous bodily harm on her, perhaps only intending to render her unconscious, but he did intend to inflict grievous bodily harm by the blows he inflicted upon her and by kicking her in the face, of which there was evidence. The section then goes on: 'the killing shall not amount to murder unless done with the same malice aforethought (express or implied) as is required for a killing to amount to murder when not done in the course or furtherance of another offence.' It would seem clear, therefore, that the legislature is providing that where one has a killing committed in the course or furtherance of another offence, that other offence must be ignored. What have to be considered are the circumstances of the killing, and if the killing would amount to murder by reason of the express or implied malice, then that person is guilty of capital murder. It is not enough to say he killed in the course of the felony unless the killing is done in a manner which would amount to murder ignoring the commission of felony."

APPEAL DISMISSED.

DIRECTOR OF PUBLIC PROSECUTIONS v. SMITH

[1961] A. C. 290

(1) *An intention to do an unlawful act aimed at another person is malice aforethought provided the act was of such a kind that the ordinary responsible man would, in all the circumstances of the case, have contemplated death or grievous bodily harm as the natural and probable result.* (2) *"Grievous bodily harm" means really serious bodily harm both in the context of the law of murder and in that of* s. 18 *of the Offences against the Person Act,* 1861.[1] (3) *Implied malice aforethought constituted by an intention to do grievous bodily harm has not been affected by* s. 1 *of the Homicide Act,* 1957.

Facts.

Smith was charged with the capital murder of Police Constable Meehan who was acting in the course of his duties.

[1] Section 18 punishes unlawfully and maliciously wounding or causing grievous bodily harm with intent to do so.

A car driven by Smith and containing stolen goods had been stopped by an officer on point duty when Meehan questioned Smith about its contents and requested him to draw into the curb. Instead of doing so, Smith drove away at an increasing speed and on an erratic course with Meehan clinging to the car. Meehan was thrown off Smith's car and killed by being run over by another car. It was not suggested that Smith intended to kill Meehan, but he was convicted of capital murder after a summing-up which contained the following passage: " If you are satisfied that . . . he must as a reasonable man have contemplated that grievous bodily harm was likely to result to that officer . . . and that such harm did happen and the officer died in consequence the accused is guilty of capital murder." Smith appealed to the Court of Criminal Appeal and that Court substituted a verdict of manslaughter on the ground that the basic question for the jury to determine was whether Smith personally contemplated grievous bodily harm to Meehan as the probable result of his conduct. The Prosecution successfully appealed.

Extracts from the speeches of the House of Lords.

VISCOUNT KILMUIR, L.C.—

" Putting aside for a moment the distinction which the Court of Criminal Appeal were seeking to draw between results which were ' certain ' and those which were ' likely ', they were saying that it was for the jury to decide whether, having regard to the panic in which he said he was, the respondent in fact at the time contemplated that grievous bodily harm would result from his actions or, indeed, whether he contemplated anything at all. Unless the jury were satisfied that he in fact had such contemplation, the necessary intent to constitute malice would not, in their view, have been proved. This purely subjective approach involves this, that if an accused said that he did not in fact think of the consequences, and the jury considered that that might well be true, he would be entitled to be acquitted of murder.[1]

My Lords, the proposition has only to be stated thus to make one realise what a departure it is from that upon which the courts have always acted. The jury must, of

---

[1] But see the criticism of this kind of argument in the citation in *R.* v. *Gould,* p. 36, *supra,* from the judgment of DIXON, J., in *Thomas* v. *R* (1937), 59 C.L.R. 279 at p. 309.

course, in such a case as the present make up their minds on the evidence whether the accused was unlawfully and voluntarily doing something to someone. The unlawful and voluntary act must clearly be aimed at someone in order to eliminate cases of negligence or of careless or dangerous driving. Once, however, the jury are satisfied as to that, it matters not what the accused in fact contemplated as the probable result or whether he ever contemplated at all, provided he was in law responsible and accountable for his actions, that is, was a man capable of forming an intent, not insane within the M'Naghten Rules and not suffering from diminished responsibility. On the assumption that he is so accountable for his actions, the sole question is whether the unlawful and voluntary act was of such a kind that grievous bodily harm was the natural and probable result. The only test available for this is what the ordinary responsible man would, in all the circumstances of the case, have contemplated as the natural and probable result. That, indeed, has always been the law . . .

Strong reliance was, however, placed on the case of *R.* v. *Steane*,[1] in which Lord GODDARD, C.J., said: 'No doubt, if the prosecution prove an act the natural consequence of which would be a certain result and no evidence or explanation is given, then a jury may, on a proper direction, find that the prisoner is guilty of doing the act with the intent alleged, but if on the totality of the evidence there is room for more than one view as to the intent of the prisoner, the jury should be directed that it is for the prosecution to prove the intent to the jury's satisfaction, and if, on a review of the whole evidence, they either think that the intent did not exist or they are left in doubt as to the intent, the prisoner is entitled to be acquitted.' That, however, was a very special case. The appellant had been charged and convicted of doing acts likely to assist the enemy, with intent to assist the enemy. His case was that while he might have done acts likely to assist the enemy he had only done so out of duress and in order to save his wife and children. Accordingly, this was a case where over and above the presumed intent there had to be proved an actual intent or, it might be said, a desire by the appellant to assist the enemy.

The last criticism of the summing-up which was

---

[1] [1947] K. B. 997, at p. 1004; [1947] 1 All E. R. 813, C. C. A.; p. 3, *supra*.

raised before your Lordships was in regard to the meaning which the learned judge directed the jury was to be given to the words 'grievous bodily harm'. The passages of which complaint is made are the following: 'When one speaks of an intent to inflict grievous bodily harm upon a person, the expression grievous bodily harm does not mean for that purpose some harm which is permanent or even dangerous. It simply means some harm which is sufficiently seriously to interfere with the victim's health or comfort.'

'In murder the killer intends to kill, or to inflict some harm which will seriously interfere for a time with health or comfort.'

'If the accused intended to do the officer some harm which would seriously interfere at least for a time with his health and comfort, and thus perhaps enable the accused to make good his escape for the time being at least, but that unfortunately the officer died instead, that would be murder too.'

The direction in these passages was clearly based on the well known direction of WILLES, J., in *R.* v. *Ashman*[1] and on the words used by GRAHAM, B., in *R.* v. *Cox.*[2] Indeed, this is a direction which is commonly given by judges in trials for the statutory offence under section 18 of the Offences against the Person Act, 1861, and has on occasions been given in murder trials: cf. *R.* v. *Vickers.*[3]

My Lords, I confess that whether one is considering the crime of murder or the statutory offence, I can find no warrant for giving the words 'grievous bodily harm' a meaning other than that which the words convey in their ordinary and natural meaning. 'Bodily harm' needs no explanation, and 'grievous' means no more and no less than 'really serious'. In this connection your Lordships were referred to the judgment of the Supreme Court of Victoria in the case of *R.* v. *Miller.*[4] In giving the judgment of the court, MARTIN, J., having expressed the view that the direction of WILLES, J., could only be justified, if at all, in the case of the statutory offence, said: 'It is not a question of statutory construction but a question of the intent required at common law to constitute the crime of murder. And there does not appear to be any justification for treating

[1] (1858), 1 F. & F. 88.

[2] (1818), Russ. & Ry. 362.

[3] [1957] 2 Q.B. 664; [1957] 2 All E.R. 741, C.C.A.; p. 187, *supra*, where such a direction was given.

[4] [1951] V. L. R. 346, at p. 357.

the expression " grievous bodily harm " or the other similar expressions used in the authorities upon this common law question which are cited above as bearing any other than their ordinary and natural meaning.' In my opinion, the view of the law thus expressed by MARTIN, J., is correct, and I would only add that I can see no ground for giving the words a wider meaning when considering the statutory offence.

It was, however, contended before your Lordships on behalf of the respondent that the words ought to be given a more restricted meaning in considering the intent necessary to establish malice in a murder case. It was said that the intent must be to do an act ' obviously dangerous to life ' or ' likely to kill '. It is true that in many of the cases the likelihood of death resulting has been incorporated into the definition of grievous bodily harm, but this was done, no doubt, merely to emphasise that the bodily harm must be really serious, and it is unnecessary, and I would add inadvisable, to add anything to the expression ' grievous bodily harm ' in its ordinary and natural meaning.

To return to the summing-up in the present case, it is true that in the two passages cited the learned judge referred to ' grievous bodily harm ' in the terms used by WILLES, J., in *R.* v. *Ashman*,[1] but in no less than four further passages, and in particular in the vital direction given just before the jury retired, he referred to ' serious hurt ' or ' serious harm '. Read as a whole, it is, I think, clear that there was no misdirection. Further, on the facts of this case it is quite impossible to say that the harm which the respondent must be taken to have contemplated could be anything but of a very serious nature coming well within the term ' grievous bodily harm '.

Before leaving this appeal I should refer to a further contention which was but faintly adumbrated, namely, that section 1 (1) of the Homicide Act, 1957, had abolished malice constituted by a proved intention to do grievous bodily harm, and that, accordingly, *R.* v. *Vickers*,[2] which held the contrary, was wrongly decided. As to this it is sufficient to say that in my opinion the Act does not in any way abolish such malice. The words in parenthesis in section 1 (1) of

[1] (1858), 1 F. & F. 88.
[2] [1957] 2 Q. B. 664; [1957] 2 All E. R. 741, p. 187, *supra*.

the Act and a reference to section 5 (2) make this clear beyond doubt."

APPEAL ALLOWED.[1]

Comment on Director of Public Prosecutions v. Smith

It is only after much hesitation that we decided to retain this case in this edition. It is arguable that the first proposition stated in our headnote is no longer law, thanks to s. 8 of the Criminal Justice Act, 1967, and it is virtually certain that summings-up in murder cases will in future be in subjective terms. However, there is room for an academic argument that the first proposition in our headnote does still represent the law, and *Smith's* case is of some importance as authority for the remaining two propositions stated in our headnote, and so we decided to retain it.

Section 8 of the Criminal Justice Act, 1967 reads as follows: "A court or jury in determining whether a person has committed an offence (a) shall not be bound in law to infer that he intended or foresaw the result of his actions by reason only of its being a natural and probable consequence of those actions but (b) shall decide whether he did intend or foresee that result by reference to all the evidence drawing such inferences from the evidence as appear proper in the circumstances."

This was the first of three proposals by the Law Commission, and the Commission no doubt intended that it should be enacted simultaneously with the other two in which case there could have been no doubt that the doctrine of *Smith's* case had ceased to be applicable, even to murder; but it is just arguable that it retains its validity in the case of murder, although the doctrine has plainly ceased to be of general application. The doctrine retains its validity for murder, in strict theory, if it is one of substantive law not, thanks to s. 8, if it is a proposition of the law of evidence.

The remaining proposals of the Law Commission which have not yet reached the statute book read as follows:

(1) "Where a person kills another, the killing shall not amount to murder unless done with an intent to kill." (2) "A person has an intent to kill if he means his actions to kill or if he is willing for his actions, though meant for another purpose, to kill in accomplishing that purpose." It is anybody's guess whether *R.* v. *Serné* (p. 184 *supra*) or the *Clerkenwell* explosion case (p. 187 *supra*) would be held to fall within the second of the above provisions should it ever become law.

---

[1] Smith was reprieved, the intention to advise Her Majesty to do so having been announced before the hearing of the appeal to the House of Lords.

MANCINI v. DIRECTOR OF PUBLIC PROSECUTIONS

[1942] A. C. 1

(1) *If a person who kills another with a deadly weapon in the course of a fight alleges that he acted in self-defence, it is not always necessary for the judge to direct the jury that they must return a verdict of manslaughter if they believe that the accused acted under provocation.*

(2) *The test to be applied in determining whether there is sufficient provocation to justify a verdict of manslaughter is the effect of the provocation on a reasonable man.*

Facts.

Mancini was charged with the murder of one Distleman. The evidence which he gave at the trial was that he had been attacked by Distleman and one Fletcher in a club, and that Distleman had an open pocket-knife in his hand. Mancini stated that he struck out blindly with a dagger in self-defence, and that the dagger struck and killed Distleman.

MACNAGHTEN, J., who was the trial judge, directed the jury fully on the question of self-defence, and he also told them that, if they were satisfied that Mancini struck the fatal blow in the heat of the fight without any premeditation, they might return a verdict of manslaughter. Apart from this, he did not allude to the question of provocation.

The jury found Mancini guilty of murder, and he unsuccessfully appealed to the Court of Criminal Appeal on the ground that the jury had not been adequately directed on the question of provocation. He unsuccessfully appealed to the House of Lords on the same ground.

Extracts from the Judgments of the House of Lords.

LORD SIMON, L.C.—

" . . . The main case set up on behalf of the appellant at the trial was self-defence, and the learned judge devoted the first portion of a very careful summing-up to this question. The appellant's counsel found no fault with this part of the judge's charge at all. It was in fact, if anything, too favourable to the appellant, for MACNAGHTEN, J., did not invite the jury to consider whether, even if it were true that the appellant was menaced with the penknife, that would justify the use of the appellant's terrible weapon so as to constitute a case of necessary self-defence, nor did the learned judge make any observations on the question whether the appellant could not have escaped from the threatened danger by retreating from the club. . . .

The fact that a defending counsel does not stress an alternative case before the jury (which he may well feel it difficult to do without prejudicing the main defence) does not relieve the judge from the duty of directing the jury to consider the alternative, if there is material before the jury which would justify a direction that they should consider it. Thus, in *R.* v. *Hopper*,[1] at a trial for murder the prisoner's counsel relied substantially on the defence that the killing was accidental, but Lord READING, C.J., in delivering the judgment of the Court of Criminal Appeal, said[2]: 'We do not assent to the suggestion that as the defence throughout the trial was accident, the judge was justified in not putting the question as to manslaughter. Whatever the line of defence adopted by counsel at the trial of a prisoner, we are of opinion that it is for the judge to put such questions as appear to him properly to arise upon the evidence, even although counsel may not have raised some question himself. In this case it may be that the difficulty of presenting the alternative defences of accident and manslaughter may have actuated counsel in saying very little about manslaughter, but if we come to the conclusion, as we do, that there was some evidence—we say no more than that—upon which a question ought to have been left to the jury as to the crime being manslaughter only, we think that this verdict of murder cannot stand.'

To avoid all possible misunderstanding, I would add that this is far from saying that in every trial for murder, where the accused pleads not guilty, the judge must include in his summing-up to the jury observations on the subject of manslaughter. The possibility of a verdict of manslaughter instead of murder only arises when the evidence given before the jury is such as might satisfy them as the judges of fact that the elements were present which would

---

[1] [1915] 2 K. B. 431.
[2] *Ibid.*, at p. 435.

reduce the crime to manslaughter, or, at any rate, might induce a reasonable doubt whether this was, or was not, the case. . . .

It is not all provocation that will reduce the crime ofmurder to manslaughter. Provocation, to have that result, must be such as temporarily deprives the person provoked of the power of self-control, as the result of which he commits the unlawful act which causes death. 'In deciding the question whether this was or was not the case, regard must be had to the nature of the act by which the offender causes death, to the time which elapsed between the provocation and the act which caused death, to the offender's conduct during that interval, and to all other circumstances tending to show the state of his mind': Stephen's *Digest of the Criminal Law*, Art. 317. The test to be applied is that of the effect of the provocation on a reasonable man, as was laid down by the Court of Criminal Appeal in *R.* v. *Lesbini*[1], so that an unusually excitable or pugnacious individual is not entitled to rely on provocation which would not have led an ordinary person to act as he did. In applying the test, it is of particular importance (*a*) to consider whether a sufficient interval has elapsed since the provocation to allow a reasonable man time to cool, and (*b*) to take into account the instrument with which the homicide was effected, for to retort, in the heat of passion induced by provocation, by a simple blow, is a very different thing from making use of a deadly instrument like a concealed dagger. In short, the mode of resentment must bear a reasonable relationship to the provocation if the offence is to be reduced to manslaughter . . .

The learned judge, indeed, in his summing-up never uses the word 'provocation' as the ground on which a verdict of manslaughter might be based. The passage complained of in the summing up runs as follows: 'If you think that there was such a disturbance going on, unprovoked by him—he was not justified, of course, in using the dagger; assuming you reject the plea of self-defence, that cannot be justified—but if in the whole of the circumstances, as far as you know them, having regard to the character of the people there, and the sort of conduct which was going on in such a place, you think that the blow may have been struck without any premeditation and in the excitement of the disturbance, whatever it was, it seems to me you might be justified in returning the verdict of manslaughter.' It

[1] [1914] 3 K.B. 1116.

seems probable that the judge in this passage was not referring to the defence of provocation, but rather had in mind the excuse which in the old books went by the name of 'chance-medley '[1]: see, for example, Blackstone, Bk. IV, p. 184. But, however the defence may be classified, the verdict should not, in my opinion, be upset on the ground of the above extract from the judge's charge. . . . .

As regards the more general question with which the Attorney-General asks the House to deal, I would formulate the following propositions:—

(1) *Woolmington's* case[2] is concerned with explaining and reinforcing the rule that the prosecution must prove the charge it makes beyond reasonable doubt, and, consequently, that if, on the material before the jury, there is a reasonable doubt, the prisoner should have the benefit of it. The rule is of general application in all charges under the criminal law. The only exceptions arise, as explained in *Woolmington*'s case,[2] in the defence of insanity and in offences where onus of proof is specially dealt with by statute. Thus, when a prisoner is charged with murder and felonious homicide is proved against him, if the jury, when considering the evidence as a whole at the conclusion of the case, are left in reasonable doubt whether the homicide proved is not manslaughter, the jury should return a verdict of manslaughter. *Woolmington's* case[2] was one in which the defence to the charge of murder was that of pure accident in circumstances not alleged to amount to criminal negligence. The prisoner gave evidence to that effect and my noble and learned friend, Lord SANKEY, lays it down that 'if the jury are either satisfied with his explanation or, upon a review of all the evidence, are left in reasonable doubt whether, even if his explanation be not accepted, the act was unintentional . . . the prisoner is entitled to be acquitted. A proposition to the same effect, but in different language, had been laid down by Lord READING, C.J., in connection with a charge of receiving recently stolen goods, in *R.* v. *Abramovitch*,[3] and was approved in the *Woolmington* decision. The law on this subject is thus finally established and is, I think, perfectly clear.

(2) The language employed by Lord SANKEY does not

[1] Since held to have no place in the modern law of homicide (*R.* v. *Semini*, [1949] 1 K. B. 405; [1949] 1 All E. R. 233).

[2] [1935] A. C. 462, at p. 482; p. 1, *supra*.

[3] (1914), 11 Cr. App. Rep. 45, at p. 49.

assert and does not imply that in every charge of murder, whatever the circumstances, the judge ought to devote part of his summing up to directing the jury on the question of manslaughter or the jury ought to consider it. If the evidence before the jury at the end of the case does not contain material on which a reasonable man could find a verdict of manslaughter instead of murder, it is no defect in the summing up that manslaughter is not dealt with. Taking, for example, a case in which no evidence has been given which would raise the issue of provocation, it is not the duty of the judge to invite the jury to speculate as to provocative incidents, of which there is no evidence and which cannot be reasonably inferred from the evidence. The duty of the jury to give the accused the benefit of the doubt is a duty which they should discharge having regard to the material before them, for it is on the evidence, and the evidence alone, that the prisoner is being tried, and it would only lead to confusion and possible injustice if either judge or jury went outside it.

(3) There is no prescribed formula for summing up in a trial for murder, but the essential rules on this particular matter are as above stated. A good example of the proper direction is, as this House in *Woolmington's* case[1] pointed out, that of FINLAY, J. (as he then was) at the abortive trial.

(4) Our attention was called to the recent decision of the Court of Criminal Appeal in *R.* v. *Prince*[2] where the court reduced the jury's verdict of murder to manslaughter on the ground that the trial judge did not give a direction to the jury in accordance with the decision in *Woolmington's* case.[1] *Prince's* case[2] was one in which the defence pleaded that there was provocation sufficient to reduce the charge to manslaughter. The Court of Criminal Appeal must have proceeded on the view that the jury were not adequately directed that reasonable doubt whether such provocation existed, as opposed to confident assurance that it did, was sufficient to require the milder view to be taken. There is no reason to repeat to the jury the warning as to reasonable doubt again and again, provided that the direction is plainly given.

(5) In *Woolmington's* case,[1] the sentence already quoted, which ends ' the prisoner is entitled to be acquitted,' should, of course, be understood as meaning ' the prisoner

---

[1] [1935] A. C. 462, at p. 467 (in the course of the argument).
[2] [1941] 3 All E. R. 37.

is entitled to the benefit of the doubt.' If the jury are left in reasonable doubt whether the act was 'unintentional,' *i.e.*, a pure accident without criminal negligence, the verdict should be not guilty. If they are left in reasonable doubt whether the act was 'provoked,' *i.e.*, perpetrated under the impulse of provocation as above defined, the prisoner should be found guilty of manslaughter. . . ."

APPEAL DISMISSED.

LEE CHUN-CHUEN v. R.

[1963] 1 All E.R. 73

It is wrong for a trial judge to direct the jury that the existence of an intention to kill or cause grievous bodily harm precludes a verdict of manslaughter on a charge of murder.

Facts.

Lee Chun-Chuen was charged with murder of his father-in-law. It was not disputed that he had killed the deceased, but there was evidence to raise the issue of provocation having regard to the bad terms subsisting between the parties and to the possibility that the deceased had thrown stones at the accused. However, the trial judge directed the jury that they could not return a verdict of manslaughter if they thought that the accused intended to kill or cause grievous bodily harm. Lee Chun-Chuen was convicted of murder. He appealed to the Supreme Court of Hong Kong in its appellate jurisdiction, and that court was of opinion that the trial judge had misdirected the jury, but they dismissed the appeal under the equivalent to the proviso to s. 2(1) of the Criminal Appeal Act, 1968 on the ground that there had been no miscarriage of justice. Lee Chun-Chuen appealed to the Judicial Committee of the Privy Council which affirmed the decision of the Supreme Court on both points.

Extracts from the Advice of the Privy Council.

LORD DEVLIN.—

"Before the Board the Crown has not contended that there was not a misdirection. Nevertheless their Lordships think that they should state what in their opinion is the law on the point since, as was noted in the judgment of the

Supreme Court, there is at present some uncertainty owing to an apparent conflict of authority.

The learned judge directed the jury that, if the provocation caused in the mind of the accused an actual intention to kill or cause grievous bodily harm, then the killing would be murder. The judge may well have had in mind the passage in *Archbold's Criminal Pleading, Evidence and Practice,* 34th Edn., 1959, para. 2503, to that effect which is supported by a dictum in a speech of Viscount SIMON in *Holmes* v. *Director of Public Prosecutions.*[1] The decision of the House of Lords in that case was that on the facts the trial judge was right in withholding from the jury the issue of provocation since the only material put forward by the defence consisted of provocative words[2]. In the course of his speech Viscount SIMON laid down the law about the constituents of provocation and the functions of judge and jury in relation to it in terms that have been widely adopted . . . He included[3] the following passage:

The whole doctrine relating to provocation depends on the fact that it causes, or may cause a sudden and temporary loss of self-control whereby malice, which is the formation of an intention to kill or to inflict grievous bodily harm, is negatived. Consequently, where the provocation inspires an actual intention to kill (such as Holmes admitted in the present case), or to inflict grievous bodily harm, the doctrine that provocation may reduce murder to manslaughter seldom applies.

It is plain that Viscount SIMON must have meant the word " actual " to have a limiting effect and that he had in mind some particular category of intention. He cannot have meant that any sort of intention to kill or cause grievous bodily harm was generally incompatible with manslaughter because that would eliminate provocation as a line of defence. In the present case, for example, earlier in his summing-up the judge properly directed the jury that they could not find murder unless there was an intent to kill or cause grievous bodily harm. By telling them that if that intent was present, they could not find manslaughter, he was telling them that they must find murder or nothing and so in effect excluding the issue of provocation."

APPEAL DISMISSED.

---

[1] [1946] A.C. 588, at p. 598.
[2] But see now Homicide Act, 1957, s. 3.
[3] P. 593.

R. v. McCARTHY

[1954] 2 Q. B. 105

In determining whether a plea of provocation should succeed, the jury are not entitled to take account of the fact that the accused was the worse for drink, the question always being whether a reasonable man, in consequence of the provocation received, could be driven through transport of passion and loss of self-control, to the degree, method and continuance of the violence which caused death.

Facts.

McCarthy was charged with murder and pleaded provocation. He had killed the deceased by knocking him down and banging his head many times on the road. McCarthy's evidence was that he had been drinking, that the deceased had made indecent overtures to him, and that, in consequence of these overtures he lost control of himself and acted as he did. The trial judge directed the jury to take no account of the fact that the accused had been drinking, and McCarthy was convicted of murder. He unsuccessfully appealed to the Court of Criminal Appeal on the ground that the jury had been misdirected.

Extracts from the Judgment of the Court of Criminal Appeal.

LORD GODDARD, C.J.—

" We see no distinction between a person who by temperament is unusually excitable or pugnacious and one who is temporarily made excitable or pugnacious by self-induced intoxication. It may be that an excitable pugnacious or intoxicated person may be more easily provoked than a man of quiet or phlegmatic disposition, but the former cannot rely upon his excitable state of mind if the violence used is beyond that which a reasonable, or as we may perhaps say, an average person would use to repel an act which can in law be regarded as provocation. No court has ever given, nor do we think ever can give, a definition of what constitutes a reasonable or an average man. That must be left to the collective good sense of the jury, and what no doubt would govern their opinion would be the nature of the retaliation used by the provoked person. If a man who is provoked retaliates with a blow from his fist on another grown man a jury may well consider, and probably would, that there was nothing excessive in the retaliation even though the blow might cause the man to fall and fracture his skull, for the provocation might well merit a blow with the fist. It would be quite another thing, however, if the person provoked not only struck the man, but continued to rain blows upon him or to beat his head on the ground, as happened in the present case and as the accused apparently did in the case of *R.* v. *Thomas*[1] . . . It is in our opinion now settled that apart from a man being in such a complete and absolute state of intoxication as to make him incapable of forming the intent charged, drunkenness which may lead a man to attack another in a manner which no reasonable sober man would do cannot be pleaded as an excuse reducing the crime to manslaughter if death results."

APPEAL DISMISSED.

BEDDER v. DIRECTOR OF PUBLIC PROSECUTIONS

[1954] 2 All E. R. 801

In determining whether provocation was sufficient to cause a reasonable man to do what the accused did, the jury are not entitled to take account of the physical peculiarities of the accused.

Facts.

Bedder was charged with the murder of a prostitute by stabbing. He pleaded provocation. He was sexually impotent and had attempted to have intercourse with the deceased. His evidence was that she taunted him with his impotence and kicked him, thus causing him to lose control of himself and stab her twice with a knife he was carrying. In the course of his summing-up, the trial judge told the jury that an unusually excitable or pugnacious individual, a drunken one or a man who is sexually impotent is not entitled to rely on provocation which would not have led an ordinary person to act as the accused did. Bedder was

---

[1] (1837), 7 Car. & P. 817.

convicted of murder and unsuccessfully appealed to the Court of Criminal Appeal and thence to the House of Lords.

Extracts from the speeches in the House of Lords.

LORD SIMONDS, L.C.—

" My Lords, no other conclusion was open to the Court of Criminal Appeal, nor is any other conclusion open to your Lordships in view of the recent cases in this House of *Mancini*[1] and *Holmes*.[2] The relevant part of the former decision is accurately stated in the headnote in these words: ' The test to be applied is that of the effect of the provocation on a reasonable man, so that an unusually excitable or pugnacious person is not entitled to rely on provocation which would not have led an ordinary person to act as he did.' And Viscount SIMON, L.C., in a speech in which all their Lordships concurred, referred ([1941] 3 All E. R. 272, at p. 277) with approval to the decision of the Court of Criminal Appeal in *R.* v. *Lesbini*.[3] It is worth recalling that, in that case, the court said ([1914] 3 K. B. 1116, at p. 1120): ' We agree with the judgment of DARLING, J., in *R.* v. *Alexander*[4] and with the principles enunciated in *R.* v. *Welsh*,[5] where it is said that " there must exist such an amount of provocation as would be excited by the circumstances in the mind of a reasonable man, and so as to lead the jury to ascribe the act to the influence of that passion " '.

Finally, in *Holmes*' case,[6] Viscount SIMON, in a speech in which my noble and learned friend, Lord PORTER and I, as well as Lord MACMILLAN and Lord DU PARCQ, concurred, after a prolonged hearing and an exhaustive examination of the relevant law used these words: ' If, on the other hand, the case is one in which the view might fairly be taken (a) that a reasonable person, in consequence of the provocation received, might be so rendered subject to passion or loss of control as to be led to use the violence with fatal results, and (b) that the accused was in fact acting under the stress of such provocation, then it is for the jury to determine whether on its view of the facts manslaughter or murder is the appropriate verdict.'

---

[1] [1942] A. C. 1; [1941] 3 All E. R. 272; p. 195, *supra*.

[2] *Holmes* v. *Director of Public Prosecutions*, [1946] A. C. 588; [1946] 2 All E. R. 124.

[3] [1914] 3 K. B. 1116.

[4] (1913), 109 L. T. 745.

[5] (1869), 11 Cox C. C. 336.

[6] [1946] A. C. 588; [1946] 2 All E. R. 124.

My Lords, in the face of this authority, I am at a loss to know what other direction than that which he gave could properly have been given by the learned judge to the jury in this case. The argument, as I understood it, for the appellant was that the jury, in considering the reaction of the hypothetical reasonable man to the acts of provocation, must not only place him in the circumstances in which the accused was placed, but must also invest him with the personal physical peculiarities of the accused. Learned counsel, who argued the case for the appellant with great ability, did not, I think, venture to say that he should be invested with mental or temperamental qualities which distinguished him from the reasonable man: for this would have been directly in conflict with the passage from the recent decision of this House in *Mancini's* case[1] which I have cited. But he urged that the reasonable man should be invested with the peculiar physical qualities of the accused, as in the present case with the characteristic of impotence, and the question should be asked: what would be the reaction of the impotent reasonable man in the circumstances? For that proposition I know of no authority: nor can I see any reason in it. It would be plainly illogical not to recognise an unusually excitable or pugnacious temperament in the accused as a matter to be taken into account but yet to recognise for that purpose some unusual physical characteristic, be it impotence or another. Moreover, the proposed distinction appears to me to ignore the fundamental fact that the temper of a man which leads him to react in such and such a way to provocation, is, or may be, itself conditioned by some physical defect. It is too subtle a refinement for my mind or, I think, for that of a jury to grasp that the temper may be ignored but the physical defect taken into account.

It was urged on your Lordships that the hypothetical reasonable man must be confronted with all the same circumstances as the accused, and that this could not be fairly done unless he was also invested with the peculiar characteristics of the accused. But this makes nonsense of the test. Its purpose is to invite the jury to consider the act of the accused by reference to a certain standard or norm of conduct and with this object the 'reasonable' or the 'average' or the 'normal' man is invoked. If the reasonable man is then deprived in whole or in part of his reason, or the normal man endowed with abnormal characteristics, the

[1] [1942] A. C. 1; [1941] 3 All E. R. 272; p. 195, *supra*.

test ceases to have any value. This is precisely the consideration which led this House in *Mancini's* case to say that an unusually excitable or pugnacious person is not entitled to rely on provocation which would not have led an ordinary person to act as he did. In my opinion, then, the Court of Criminal Appeal was right in approving the direction given to the jury by the learned judge and this appeal must fail. . . ."

APPEAL DISMISSED.

PHILLIPS v. R.

[1969] 2 A.C. 130

The effect of s. 3 *of the Homicide Act,* 1957[1] *is that the jury has to consider three questions when provocation is pleaded in answer to a charge of murder:* (1) *was the accused in fact provoked*? (2) *Would the provocation have made a reasonable man lose his self control*? (3) *Would a reasonable man, having lost his self-control, have retaliated as the accused did*?

Facts.

Phillips was charged with the murder of his mistress. He alleged that she had provoked him by spitting at his mother and reduced him to a state of automatism by hitting him on the side of the head whereupon he killed her with a machete which he found in his mother's bag. Although the main defence was automatism, the Jamaican judge directed the jury with regard to provocation with reference to a Jamaican statute phrased in identical terms with those of s. 3 of the Homicide Act, 1957. Phillips was convicted and unsuccessfully appealed to the Court of Appeal of Jamaica and to the Privy Council.

---

[1] " Where on a charge of murder there is evidence on which the jury can find that the person charged was provoked (whether by things done or by things said or by both together) to lose his self-control the question whether the provocation was enough to make a reasonable man do as he did shall be left to be determined by the jury; and in determining that question the jury shall take into account everything both done and said according to the effect, which, in their opinion, it would have on a reasonable man."

Extracts from the Advice of the Privy Council.

LORD DIPLOCK.—

"In their Lordships' view it is beyond question that at common law by which the matter was regulated both in Jamaica and in England until the legislation cited above, the relationship between the degree of retaliation and the nature of the provocation was a relevant factor in determining whether the offence proved was manslaughter and not murder. It is sufficient to refer to the words of Viscount SIMON, L.C., in the House of Lords in *Mancini* v. *Director of Public Prosecutions*[1] with whose speech the rest of the House agreed. ' In short,' he said at p. 9, ' the mode of resentment must bear a reasonable relationship to the provocation if the offence is to be reduced to manslaughter.' This is an elliptic way of saying that the reaction of the defendant to the provocation must not exceed what would have been the reaction of a reasonable man.

In their Lordships' view the only changes in the common law doctrine of provocation which were effected by section 3c of the Offences against the Person (Amendment) Law (Jamaica), No. 43 of 1958 were (1) to abolish the common law rule that words unaccompanied by acts could not amount to provocation, and (2) to leave exclusively to the jury the function of deciding whether or not a reasonable man would have reacted to the provocation in the way in which the defendant did. These two changes are inter-related.

The test of provocation in the law of homicide is two-fold. The first, which has always been a question of fact for the jury assuming that there is any evidence upon which they can so find, is ' Was the defendant provoked into losing his self-control? ' The second, which is one not of fact but of opinion, ' Would a reasonable man have reacted to the same provocation in the same way as the defendant did? '

In *Holmes* v. *Director of Public Prosecutions*[2], the case which finally decided that even a sudden confession of adultery could not amount to provocation at common law, it was laid down that although the second question was also one for the jury it was nevertheless the function of the judge to make a preliminary ruling as to whether or not the provocation was such as *could* provoke a reasonable man to react to it in the way in which the defendant did. It was this

---

1 [1942] A.C. 1; [1941] 3 All E.R. 272; p. 195, *supra*.
2 [1946] A.C. 588; [1946] 2 All E.R. 124.

decision, not that in *Mancini* v. *Director of Public Prosecutions*[1] which was reversed by the English legislation of 1957 and the Jamaican legislation of 1958.

In their Lordships' view section 3c of Law No. 43 of 1958, in referring to the question to be left to be determined by the jury as being 'whether the provocation was enough to make a reasonable man do as he [*sc.*, the person charged] did' explicitly recognises that what the jury have to consider, once they have reached the conclusion that the person charged was in fact provoked to lose his self-control is not merely whether in their opinion the provocation would have made a reasonable man lose his self-control but also whether, having lost his self-control, he would have retaliated in the same way as the person charged in fact did.

Before their Lordships, counsel for the appellant contended, not as a matter of construction but as one of logic, that once a reasonable man had lost his self-control his actions ceased to be those of a reasonable man and that accordingly he was no longer fully responsible in law for them whatever he did. This argument is based on the premise that loss of self-control is not a matter of degree but is absolute; there is no intermediate stage between icy detachment and going berserk. This premise, unless the argument is purely semantic, must be based upon human experience and is, in their Lordships' view, false. The average man reacts to provocation according to its degree with angry words, with a blow of the hand, possibly if the provocation is gross and there is a dangerous weapon to hand, with that weapon . . .

Since the passing of the legislation it may be prudent to avoid the use of the precise words of Viscount SIMON in *Mancini* v. *Director of Public Prosecutions*[1] 'the mode of resentment must bear a reasonable relationship to the provocation' unless they are used in a context which makes it clear to the jury that this is not a rule of law which they are bound to follow, but merely a consideration which may or may not commend itself to them. But their Lordships would repeat, it is the effect of the summing-up as a whole that matters and not any stated verbal formula used in the course of it."

APPEAL DISMISSED

---

[1] [1942] A.C. 1; [1941] 3 All E.R. 272; p. 195, *supra*.
[2] [1942] A.C. 1; [1941] 3 All E.R. 272; p. 195, *supra*.

Comment on Phillips v. R.

This case has been followed by the Court of Appeal in *R.* v. *Brown*[1], the Court expressing the opinion that Parliament, when using the simple and straight-forward language in s. 3 of the Homicide Act, 1957, was laying down a precise test which the jury should apply. It followed that the proportionality of the mode of retaliation to the provocation was simply a test to assist the jury in determining whether the provocation was such as to cause a reasonable man to do as the accused did.

In spite of the statement in *Phillips's* case that the only changes made by s. 3 were (1) the abolition of the common law rule that words unaccompanied by acts could not amount to provocation, and (2) the introduction of the requirement that it is exclusively for the jury to determine whether a reasonable man would have reacted to the provocation as the accused did, the following further points should be noted:

(1) were the facts of *Mancini's* case[2] to recur, the issue of provocation would have to be left to the jury;

(2) it is now clear that the detection of a financée or mistress in the act of intercourse, or even a confession of intercourse by such a person may amount to provocation, whereas some of the older cases suggest that this type of provocation was confined to the detection of a spouse in adultery[3];

(3) whatever the position may have been before the Homicide Act, 1957, came into force, it is now clear that the spectacle of an attack upon a third person such as a parent or child may support a plea of provocation[4].

R. v. LARKIN

[1943] 1 All E. R. 217

Manslaughter is committed if death accidentally results from an unlawful act which is likely to injure someone.

Facts.

The accused was charged with murder and convicted of manslaughter. It was not disputed that the deceased, a woman with whom he had been living, was mortally wounded in the throat by a razor which he held. At the trial the accused said that he produced the razor at a house where

---

[1] [1972] 2 Q.B. 229; [1972] 2 All E.R. 1328.

[2] P. 195, *supra*.

[3] *R.* v. *Palmer*, [1913] 2 K.B. 29; *R.* v. *Greening*, [1913] 3 K.B. 846. But see *R.* v. *Larkin*, p. 209, *infra*

[4] *R.* v. *Porritt*, [1961] 3 All E.R. 463.

the deceased was drinking with another man with whom she had been associating, in order to frighten him after a suggestion had been made that further sexual intercourse should take place with the deceased. He also said that the woman, who was groggy with drink, blundered against the razor. The judge directed the jury that if they believed the accused's evidence they must nevertheless return a verdict of manslaughter because he was acting unlawfully. The accused had previously made statements suggesting that he killed the deceased intentionally when under the influence of provocation. After the jury had given their verdict the judge asked the foreman whether they came to their decision because the deceased blundered against the razor or on account of the provocation he received. In dismissing the appeal, the Court of Criminal Appeal disapproved of such a practice.[1]

Extracts from the Judgment of the Court of Criminal Appeal.

HUMPHREYS, J.—

" Perhaps it is as well that once more the proposition of law should be stated which has been stated for generations by judges and, so far as we are aware, never disputed or doubted. If a person is engaged in doing a lawful act, and in the course of doing that lawful act behaves so negligently as to cause the death of some other person, then it is for the jury to say, upon a consideration of the whole of the facts of the case, whether the negligence proved against the accused person amounts to manslaughter, and it is the duty of the presiding judge to tell them that it will not amount to manslaughter unless the negligence is of a very high degree; the expression most commonly used is unless it shows the accused to have been reckless as to the consequences of the act. That is where the act is lawful. Where the act which a person is engaged in performing is unlawful, then, if at the same time it is a dangerous act, that is, an act which is likely to injure another person, and quite inadvertently he causes the death of that other person by that act, then he is guilty of manslaughter.

In this case, in our opinion, it was perfectly right for OLIVER, J., not to leave to the jury any question of acquittal, but to tell the jury, as he did, on the facts of the case,

---

[1] But see *R.* v. *Doherty*, p. 85, *supra* and *R.* v. *Matheson*, [1958] 2 All E. R. 87.

accepting the evidence of the accused man to the highest extent, that it was not open to them to return a verdict of not guilty. . . .

OLIVER, J., as he said a little later, for his own purposes, no doubt to assist him upon the question of sentence, asked the jury in effect what was the ground upon which they had reduced the crime from murder to manslaughter. It might have been on one of two grounds. This was a case in which it was alleged there was great provocation, and there was evidence of provocation, and no one could be surprised if the jury found a verdict of manslaughter upon the ground of provocation,[1] which may, and often does, reduce the crime of murder to manslaughter, but which, incidentally, can never be a ground for acquittal. The other was that the jury had accepted the evidence of the accused, and in that event OLIVER, J., had told them in terms that, if they accepted that, it would be right that they should find a verdict of manslaughter, because there was no deliberate voluntary act on the part of the accused intending to do injury to anybody. . . .

If the verdict appears to be inconsistent, proper questions may be put by a judge to invite the jury to explain what they mean, but where a verdict has been returned which is perfectly plain and unambiguous, it is most undesirable that the jury should be asked any further questions about it at all."

CONVICTION AFFIRMED.

R. v. CONNER

(1835), 7 C. & P. 438

Causing death in the course of improper chastisement of a child is manslaughter, although there was only an intention to frighten the child, and although the person killed is not the child at whom the chastisement was directed.

Facts.

Mrs. Conner was charged with manslaughter. The evidence was that one of her children had behaved improperly and that, as this child was leaving the room, she threw a bar of iron which she had taken up to frighten it towards the

[1] But the deceased was not the accused's wife and there was no evidence of physical violence against the accused, so it might have been argued that the case did not come within the then law of provocation.

door. She did not intend to hit the child in question. Another child of hers came in through the door, and was struck and killed by the iron.

The jury were directed that they must convict of manslaughter on such evidence.

Extracts from the Summing-Up to the Jury of :—

PARKE, B.—

"The law of the land as touching such a case as this is perfectly clear and satisfactory. The prisoner is charged with manslaughter on a coroner's inquisition. I am not surprised at hearing that the grand jury have thrown out the bill in this case, because without the assistance and advice of a person who has spent his life in the study of the law they might think there were strong circumstances of mitigation. No doubt this poor woman had no more intention of injuring this particular child than I have; but that makes no difference in law. When a blow intended for A lights upon B, being given in a sudden transport of passion, if, supposing A had been struck and had died, it would have amounted to manslaughter, it is no less manslaughter if it causes the death of B. If a blow is aimed at an individual unlawfully—and this was undoubtedly unlawful, as an improper mode of correction—and strikes another and kills him, it is manslaughter; and there is no doubt if the child at whom the blow was aimed had been struck and died, it would have been manslaughter, and so it is under the present circumstances. Undoubtedly, that is the law of the land. But there are strong circumstances of mitigation, which are for the consideration of the judge. The prisoner tells the woman at the hospital that she only intended to frighten him; but it is a very bad mode of frightening, and it is clear that she threw the poker towards the door not knowing whom it would hit; and this the law will not tolerate. She did not intend to kill this particular child nor to do bodily harm—ultimate bodily harm—to the other; but she intended to correct him, and in a way that was unlawful.[1]"

VERDICT, GUILTY.

---

[1] If the child at whom the accused aimed had been killed, the case would have been one of accidental death caused by the performance of an unlawful act calculated to injure someone in the sense of causing them alarm. It would have been manslaughter and not murder because there was no intention to kill or cause grievous bodily harm to the deceased (*c.f. R.* v. *Grey* (1666), Kel. 64, where there was an intention to cause grievous bodily harm where a blacksmith struck his apprentice with an iron bar).

R. v. FRANKLIN

(1883), 15 Cox C. C. 163

The mere fact that he killed another while committing a tort against a third party does not render a person guilty of manslaughter.

Facts.

The accused was charged with manslaughter of a man who was bathing off Brighton pier in the morning. The evidence was that the accused took a box from a stall on the pier, and threw it out to sea with the result that it struck and killed the deceased. It was contended for the prosecution that, quite apart from any question of criminal negligence, the accused was guilty of manslaughter because he killed the deceased in the course of an unlawful act, but FIELD, J. insisted that the case should go to the jury on the question of criminal negligence.

Extracts from the statement of law by:—

FIELD, J.—

"I am of opinion that the case must go to the jury upon the broad ground of negligence and not upon the narrow ground proposed by the learned counsel, because it seems to me—and I may say that in this view my brother MATHEW agrees—that the mere fact of a civil wrong committed by one person against another ought not to be used as an incident which is a necessary step in a criminal case. I have great abhorrence of constructive crime. We do not think the case cited by the counsel for the prosecution is binding upon us in the facts of this case, and, therefore, the civil wrong against the refreshment-stall keeper is immaterial to this charge of manslaughter. I do not think that the facts of this case bring it clearly within the principle laid down by TINDAL, C.J. in *R.* v. *Fenton*[1]. . . ."

VERDICT, GUILTY.

---

[1] (1830), 1 Lew. C. C. 179. In this case the accused who was convicted of manslaughter was unlawfully throwing stones down a mine when he struck a lift and killed one of its occupants. TINDALL, C.J., used words suggesting that it is manslaughter to cause death by means of any unlawful act. This is no longer the law and *Franklin's* case is basically irreconcilable with *Fenton's*.

R. v. CHURCH

[1965] 2 All E.R. 72

(1) *Where the accused's acts can be treated as part of one transaction the fact that he believed his victim to be dead when he threw her into a river does not in law render him innocent of murder.* (2) *In order to support a conviction for manslaughter based on an intention to do an unlawful act, the act must be one which would, in the eyes of reasonable people, involve a risk of some bodily harm.* (3) *The court will not, when considering sentence, take account of the possibility that a person sentenced to imprisonment for life may be released after nine or ten years.*

Facts.

Church was charged with the murder of a woman. He admitted that he had had a fight with her and rendered her unconscious. He also admitted that he threw her unconscious body into a river but said that he believed that she was dead. The trial judge directed the jury that they could not convict of murder if they came to the conclusion that the accused believed the deceased to have been dead when he threw her into the river. He also directed them that such belief was irrelevant in the case of a charge of manslaughter. The jury convicted of manslaughter. Church unsuccessfully appealed to the Court of Criminal Appeal, that court being of opinion that, although the direction was defective with regard to manslaughter by an unlawful act, the case was a proper one for the application of the proviso to s. 4(1) of the Criminal Appeal Act, 1907.[1]

Extracts from the Judgment of the Court of Criminal Appeal.

EDMUND DAVIES, J.—

" The jury were thus told in plain terms that they could not convict of murder unless it had been proved that the appellant knew that Mrs. Nott was still alive when he threw her into the river or (at least) that he did not then believe that she was dead. We venture to express the view that such a direction was unduly benevolent to the appellant, and that the jury should have been told that it was still open to them to

---

[1] See now proviso to the Criminal Appeal Act, 1968.

convict of murder, notwithstanding that the appellant may have thought his blows and attempt at strangulation had actually produced death when he threw the body in the river, if they regarded the appellant's behaviour from the moment he first struck her to the moment when he threw her into the river as a series of acts designed to cause death or grievous bodily harm: see *Thabo Meli* v. *R.*[1]

. . . Against the background of the basic direction regarding the nature of the Crown's burden of proof as to murder, it seems to this court that at least three possible bases of the manslaughter verdict call for consideration: (a) Criminal negligence. A grosser case of criminal negligence it would be difficult to imagine. . . . In the judgment of this court, the facts in the present case were such as to render an elaborate direction unnecessary. Utter recklessness was the standard which the jury were told had to be applied, and the evidence amply justified a verdict that it had been established. . . . (c)[2] An unlawful act causing death. Two passages in the summing-up are here material. They are these: (i)—

'If by an unlawful act of violence done deliberately to the person of another, that other is killed, the killing is manslaughter even though the accused never intended either death or grievous bodily harm to result. If (the deceased) was alive, as she was, when he threw her in the river, what he did was a deliberate act of throwing a living body into the river. That is an unlawful killing and it does not matter whether he believed she was dead, or not, and that is my direction to you,'

and (ii)—

'I would suggest to you, though, of course, it is for you to approach your task as you think fit, that a convenient way of approaching it would be to say: What do we think about this defence that he honestly believed the (deceased) to be dead? If you think that it is true, why then, as I have told you, your proper verdict would be one of manslaughter, not murder.' Such a direction is not lacking in authority; see, for example, *Shoukatallie* v. *R.*,[3] in Lord DENNING's opinion, and Dr. Glanville Williams' *Criminal Law* (2nd Edn.) at p. 173. Nevertheless, in the judgment of this court it was a misdirection. It amounted to telling the jury that, whenever any unlawful act is committed in relation to a human being which resulted in death there must be, at least, a conviction

---

[1] [1954] 1 All E. R. 373; p. 174 *supra*.
[2] Ground (b) was provocation of which there was only flimsy evidence.
[3] [1962] A. C. 81; [1961] 3 All E. R. 996.

for manslaughter. This might at one time have been regarded as good law: see, for example, *R.* v. *Fenton.*[1] It appears to this court, however, that the passage of years has achieved a transformation in this branch of the law and, even in relation to manslaughter, a degree of *mens rea* has become recognised as essential. To define it is a difficult task, and in *Andrews* v. *Director of Public Prosecutions*[2] Lord ATKIN spoke of ' the element of " unlawfulness " which is the elusive factor'. Stressing that we are here leaving entirely out of account those ingredients of homicide which might justify a verdict of manslaughter on the grounds of (a) criminal negligence, or (b) provocation or (c) diminished responsibility, the conclusion of this court is that an unlawful act causing the death of another cannot, simply because it is an unlawful act, render a manslaughter verdict inevitable. For such a verdict inexorably to follow, the unlawful act must be such as all sober and reasonable people would inevitably recognise must subject the other person to, at least, the risk of some harm resulting therefrom, albeit not serious harm[3]. See, for example, *R.* v. *Franklin,*[4] *R.* v. *Senior,*[5] *R.* v. *Larkin*[6] in HUMPHREY, J.'s judgment, *R.* v. *Buck and Buck*[7] and *R.* v. *Hall.*[8] . . . 'As to sentence,' the trial judge said: ' I think this is the worst case of manslaughter I have ever heard of.' It was unquestionably a terrible case, and, young though the appellant was (being merely twenty-one at the time of the crime) and minor though his previous convictions were, this court cannot say that sentence of fifteen years, while undoubtedly severe, was wrong in principle. We have been urged to hold that, as it appears to have been said in another place that a life sentence involves incarceration of up to ten years, it was wrong in principle that the appellant, convicted of manslaughter, should be called on to remain in prison at least as long as, and possibly longer, than he would have been had the jury convicted him of murder. This court

---

[1] (1830), 1 Lew. C. C. 179; p. 213 n. 1 *supra.*

[2] [1937] A.C. 576, at p. 581, [1937] 2 All E. R. 552, at p. 555; p. 224, *infra.*

[3] Contrast recent Australian cases where it is said that the act must be one which anyone in the accused's situation would realise would expose the deceased " to an appreciable danger of some really serious injury " *R.* v. *Haywood,* [1971] V.R. 755).

[4] (1883), 15 Cox C. C. 163; p. 213 *supra.*

[5] [1899] 1 Q. B. 283.

[6] [1943] 1 K. B. 174; [1943] 1 All E. R. 217; p. 209 *supra.*

[7] (1960), 44 Cr. App. Rep. 213, at p. 218; see p. 229, *infra.*

[8] (1961), 45 Cr. App. Rep. 366, at pp. 370, 373.

cannot have regard to that consideration. As this court said in *R.* v. *Assa Singh*:[1]

'. . . the court has in mind that " life sentence " means a sentence for life, and that any remission as a result of which a prisoner is released is a matter entirely for the Home Secretary.' "

APPEAL DISMISSED.

R. v. LAMB

[1967] 2 All E.R. 1282

(1) *The unlawful act necessary to render a person guilty of manslaughter on the ground that he intended to do an unlawful act must involve an assault.* (2) *In determining whether he was guilty of criminal negligence, the jury must be told to take into account the accused's beliefs with regard to material facts although, in some circumstances, such beliefs may have been formed in circumstances amounting to criminal negligence.*

Facts.

Lamb was charged with manslaughter. He was inexperienced in the use of firearms. He had a revolver and, acting in jest to the knowledge of his victim, he pointed it at the deceased, his best friend. The accused pulled the trigger and the deceased was shot and killed. The accused knew that there were two bullets in the revolver, but he did not know that pulling the trigger would cause the cylinder to rotate with the result that one of the bullets would be brought under the firing pin. The trial judge in effect directed the jury that the accused had done an unlawful and dangerous act, and his direction with regard to criminal negligence contained no reference to the accused's belief that the pulling of the trigger would have no effect on the position of the bullets. Lamb was convicted of manslaughter, but successfully appealed to the Court of Appeal.

Extracts from the Judgment of the Court of Appeal, Criminal Division

SACHS, L.J.—

" The trial judge took the view that the pointing of the revolver and the pulling of the trigger was something which

---

[1] [1965] 2 Q. B. 312, at pp. 319, 320; [1965] 1 All E. R. 938, at p. 940.

could of itself be unlawful, even if there were no attempt to alarm or intent to injure. This view is exemplified in a passage in his judgment which will be cited later. It was no doubt on this basis that he had before commencing his summing-up stated that he was not going to:

'involve the jury in any consideration of the niceties of the question whether or not the (action of the appellant) did constitute or did not constitute an assault';

and thus he did not refer to the defence of accident or the need for the prosecution to disprove accident before coming to a conclusion that the act was unlawful. Counsel for the Crown, however, had at all times put forward the correct view that for the act to be unlawful it must constitute at least what he then termed 'a technical assault'. In this court, moreover, he rightly conceded that there was no evidence to go to the jury of any assault of any kind. Nor did he feel able to submit that the acts of the appellant were on any other ground unlawful in the criminal sense of the word. Indeed no such submission could in law be made: if, for instance, the pulling of the trigger had had no effect because the striking mechanism or the ammunition had been defective no offence would have been committed by the appellant. Another way of putting it is that *mens rea* being now an essential ingredient in manslaughter (compare *Andrews* v. *Director of Public Prosecutions*[1] and *R.* v. *Church*[2]) this could not in the present case be established in relation to the first ground except by proving that element of intent without which there can be no assault.[3] It is perhaps as well to mention that when using the phrase 'unlawful in the criminal sense of that word' the court has in mind that it is long settled that it is not in point to consider whether an act is unlawful merely from the angle of civil liabilities. That was first made clear in *R.* v. *Franklin*.[4] The relevant extracts from this and from later judgments are collected in *Russell on Crime* (11th Edn. 1958), pp. 651–658. The whole of that part of the summing-up which concerned the first ground was thus vitiated by misdirections based on an erroneous concept of the law; . . . When the gravamen of a charge is criminal negligence—often referred to as recklessness—of an accused, the jury have to consider amongst other matters the state of his mind, and that

[1] [1937] 2 All E. R. 552, at pp. 555, 556; see p. 224 *infra*.
[2] [1965] 2 All E. R. 72, at p. 76; see p. 214 *supra*.
[3] But see *R.* v. *Lipman*, p. 99, *supra*.
[4] (1883), 15 Cox C. C. 163; see p. 213 *supra*.

includes the question of whether or not he thought that that which he was doing was safe. In the present case it would, of course, have been fully open to a jury, if properly directed, to find the accused guilty because they considered his view as to there being no danger was formed in a criminally negligent way. But he was entitled to a direction that the jury should take into account the fact that he had indisputably formed this view and that there was expert evidence as to this being an understandable view. Strong though the evidence of criminal negligence was, the appellant was entitled as of right to have his defence considered but he was not accorded this right and the jury was left without a direction on an essential matter."

APPEAL ALLOWED.

R. v. INSTAN[1]
[1893] 1 Q. B. 450

If a person dies in consequence of another person's failure to perform a duty recognised by the criminal law, such other person will be guilty of manslaughter.

Facts.

The accused lived with her aunt aged 73. The evidence was that the aunt was suffering from a disease and that, during the last ten days of her life, she was not supplied with food or medical attendance by the accused, and that her death had thereby been accelerated. The accused was convicted of manslaughter, but a case was stated for the opinion of the Court for Crown Cases Reserved who were of opinion that the conviction was correct.

Extract from the Judgments of the Court for Crown Cases Reserved.

LORD COLERIDGE, C.J.—

" . . . It would not be correct to say that every moral obligation involves a legal duty; but every legal duty is founded on a moral obligation. A legal common law duty is nothing else than the enforcing by law of that which is a moral obligation without legal enforcement. There can be

---

[1] See *R.* v. *Lowe*, [1973] 1 All E.R. 805, which may go to the House of Lords.

no question in this case that it was the clear duty of the prisoner to impart to the deceased so much as was necessary to sustain life of the food which she from time to time took in, and which was paid for by the deceased's own money for the purpose of the maintenance of herself and the prisoner; it was only through the instrumentality of the prisoner that the deceased could get the food. There was, therefore, a common law duty imposed upon the prisoner which she did not discharge.

Nor can there be any question that the failure of the prisoner to discharge her legal duty at least accelerated the death of the deceased, if it did not actually cause it. There is no case directly in point; but it would be a slur upon and a discredit to the administration of justice in this country if there were any doubt as to the legal principle, or as to the present case being within it. The prisoner was under a moral obligation to the deceased from which arose a legal duty towards her; that legal duty the prisoner has wilfully and deliberately left unperformed, with the consequence that there has been an acceleration of the death of the deceased owing to the non-performance of that legal duty. It is unnecessary to say more than that upon the evidence this conviction was most properly arrived at."

CONVICTION AFFIRMED.

R. v. FINNEY

(1874), 12 Cox C. C. 625

Negligence must be gross in order to render a person guilty of manslaughter on this basis.

Facts.

The accused was an attendant at a lunatic asylum at which the deceased was a patient. After he had bathed the deceased, the accused told him to get out, and there was evidence that the deceased was capable of understanding and obeying such an instruction. While the accused's attention was diverted by a new attendant, the accused turned on the hot tap in the bath in which the deceased had been washed, and the deceased, who had not got out of the bath, was scalded to death. The accused said that he believed that the deceased had got out of the bath, and, in any event, he intended to turn on the cold tap.

Extract from the Direction to the Jury.

LUSH, J.—

"To render a person liable for neglect of duty there must be such a degree of culpability as to amount to gross negligence on his part. . . . It is not every little trip or mistake that will make a man so liable. It was the duty of the attendant not to let water into the bath while the patient was therein. According to the prisoner's own account, he did not believe that he was letting the water in while the deceased remained there. . . . If the prisoner, seeing that the man was in the bath, had knowingly turned on the tap and turned on the hot instead of the cold water, I should have said there was gross negligence, for he ought to have looked to see; but from his own account he had told the deceased to get out and thought he had got out. If you think that indicates gross carelessness, then you should find the prisoner guilty of manslaughter; but if you think it inadvertence not amounting to culpability, or what is properly termed an accident, then the prisoner is not liable."

VERDICT, NOT GUILTY.

R. v. JONES

(1874), 12 Cox C. C. 628

Pointing a gun at a person without looking to see whether it is loaded is negligence sufficient to found a conviction for manslaughter.

Facts.

The accused was charged with manslaughter of a child. While the child was out of the room, he picked up a gun and held it pointed at the door. He did not examine the gun, and believed it to be unloaded. When the child came in through the door, the gun went off and killed him.

Extract from the Summing-Up to the Jury.

LUSH, J.—

"No doubt the prisoner did not intend to discharge the gun at the child What he did was either an accident or was negligence on his part. The charge is that he so carelessly handled the gun as to occasion the death of the deceased. If a person points a gun without examining whether it is loaded or not, and it happens to be loaded and death results, he is guilty of negligence and manslaughter. Can you come to any other conclusion than that the prisoner did either in joke or otherwise point the gun at the boy? If he held the gun pointed at the boy, and so held it until the child came out of the pantry, and it went off, what can that be but so improperly and carelessly handling the gun as to be negligence, and therefore manslaughter?"

VERDICT, GUILTY.

R. v. BATEMAN
(1925), 133 L. T. 730

In order that a person may be convicted of manslaughter by criminal negligence, the jury must be satisfied that he showed such a disregard for the life of others as to amount to a crime against the state.

Facts.

Bateman was a doctor who was charged and convicted of manslaughter. The evidence was that he had attended the deceased upon her giving birth to a dead child. The accouchement was a difficult one, and the mother died some days after the birth. The prosecution gave evidence of negligence against the accused under three heads. Two of them depended on medical technique and the third was that he had not caused the deceased to be removed to hospital as soon as he should.

Bateman successfully appealed to the Court of Criminal Appeal on the ground that the trial judge had not adequately directed the jury on the difference between civil and criminal negligence.

Extracts from the Judgment of the Court of Criminal Appeal read by:

LORD HEWART, C.J.—

" . . . In expounding the law to juries on the trial of indictments for manslaughter by negligence the judges have often referred to the distinction between civil and criminal liability for death by negligence. The law of criminal liability for negligence is conveniently explained in that way. If A has caused the death of B by alleged negligence, then, in order to establish civil liability, the plaintiff must prove (in addition to pecuniary loss caused by the death) that A owed a duty to B to take care, that that duty was not discharged, and that such default caused the death of B. To convict A of manslaughter, the prosecution must prove the three things above mentioned and must satisfy the jury, in addition, that A's negligence amounted to a crime. In the civil action, if it is proved that A fell short of the standard of reasonable care required by law, it matters not how far he fell short of that standard. The extent of his liability depends not on the degree of negligence, but on the amount of damage done. In the criminal court, on the contrary, the amount and degree of negligence are the determining question. There must be *mens rea* . . .

In explaining to juries the test which they should apply to determine whether the negligence, in the particular case, amounted or did not amount to a crime, the judges have used many epithets, such as 'culpable,' 'criminal,' 'gross,' 'wicked,' 'clear,' 'complete.' But, whatever epithet be used and whether an epithet be used or not, in order to establish criminal liability the facts must be such that, in the opinion of the jury, the negligence of the accused went beyond a mere matter of compensation between subjects and showed such disregard for the life and safety of others as to amount to a crime against the State and conduct deserving punishment. . . .

To support an indictment for manslaughter the prosecution must prove the matters necessary to establish civil liability (except pecuniary loss), and, in addition, must satisfy the jury that the negligence or incompetence of the accused went beyond a mere matter of compensation and showed such disregard for the life and safety of others as to amount to a crime against the State and conduct deserving punishment. . .

It is, nevertheless, most desirable that in trials for manslaughter by negligence, it should be impressed on the jury that the issue is not negligence or no negligence, but felony or no felony. It is desirable that, as far as possible, the explanation of criminal negligence to a jury should not be a mere question of epithets. It is, in a sense, a question of degree, and it is for the jury to draw the line, but there is a difference in kind between the negligence which gives a right to compensation and the negligence which is a crime."

CONVICTION QUASHED.

ANDREWS v. DIRECTOR OF PUBLIC PROSECUTIONS

[1937] A. C. 576

The driver of a motor vehicle may be guilty of an offence under s. 11 *of the Road Traffic Act,* 1930,[1] *although he is not guilty of manslaughter if he causes death by his dangerous driving. When a person is charged with manslaughter and with an offence under* s. 11 *of the Road Traffic Act, the judge should first direct the jury on the general law of criminal negligence, and then direct them on what must be proved in order to establish the commission of the statutory offence.*

Facts.

Andrews was charged and convicted of manslaughter by running someone down while driving a car. He unsuccessfully appealed to the Court of Criminal Appeal and thence to the House of Lords on the ground of misdirection to the jury by the trial judge.

He had also been charged with an offence under s. 11 of the Road Traffic Act, 1930. In the course of his summing up the trial judge told the jury that a person was guilty of manslaughter if he caused death in the performance of an unlawful act. The House of Lords did not regard this as a correct direction in such a case but they were satisfied that, taking the summing up as a whole, the jury had been properly directed.

Extracts from the Judgments of the House of Lords.

LORD ATKIN.—

" . . . of all crimes manslaughter appears to afford most difficulties of definition, for it concerns homicide in so many and so varying conditions. From the early days when any homicide involved penalty the law has gradually evolved ' through successive differentiations and integrations' until it recognises murder on the one hand, based mainly, though not exclusively, on an intention to kill and manslaughter on the other hand, based mainly, though not

[1] Re-enacted by s. 2 of the Road Traffic Act, 1972. Note there is now a separate offence of causing death by dangerous driving (Road Traffic Act, 1972, s. 1).

exclusively, on the absence of intention to kill, but with the presence of an element of 'unlawfulness' which is the elusive factor. In the present case it is only necessary to consider manslaughter from the point of view of an unintentional killing caused by negligence, *i.e.*, the omission of a duty to take care. I do not propose to discuss the development of this branch of the subject as treated in the successive treatises of Coke, Hale, Foster and East and in the judgments of the Courts to be found either in directions of juries by individual judges or in the more considered pronouncements of the body of judges which preceded the formal Court of Crown Cases Reserved. Expressions will be found which indicate that to cause death by any lack of due care will amount to manslaughter; but as manners softened and the law became more humane a narrower criterion appeared. After all, manslaughter is a felony, and was capital, and men shrank from attaching the serious consequences of a conviction for felony to results produced by mere inadvertence. The stricter view became apparent in prosecutions of medical men or men who professed medical or surgical skill for manslaughter by reason of negligence. . . .

The principle to be observed is that cases of manslaughter in driving motor-cars are but instances of a general rule applicable to all charges of homicide by negligence. Simple lack of care such as will constitute civil liability is not enough: for purposes of the criminal law there are degrees of negligence: and a very high degree of negligence is required to be proved before the felony is established. Probably of all the epithets that can be applied 'reckless' most nearly covers the case. It is difficult to visualise a case of death caused by reckless driving in the connotation of that term in ordinary speech[1] which would not justify a conviction for manslaughter: but it is probably not all-embracing, for 'reckless' suggests an indifference to risk whereas the accused may have appreciated the risk and intended to avoid it and yet shown such a high degree of negligence in the means adopted to avoid the risk as would justify a conviction. If the principle of *Bateman's* case[2] is

[1] The difficulty is that there is no judicial agreement with regard to the ordinary meaning of the word " reckless ". Does it connote foresight coupled with a disregard of consequences or mere failure to comply with a low standard of care which does not necessarily involve foresight of consequences? The answer appears to vary according to the branch of law which is under consideration. On the whole " recklessness " appears to be used in an objective sense in the law of manslaughter.

[2] (1925), 19 Cr. App. Rep. 8; p. 222, *supra*.

observed it will appear that the law of manslaughter has not changed by the introduction of motor vehicles on the road. Death caused by their negligent driving, though unhappily much more frequent, is to be treated in law as death caused by any other form of negligence: and juries should be directed accordingly. . .

I entertain no doubt that the statutory offence of dangerous driving may be committed, though the negligence is not of such a degree as would amount to manslaughter if death ensued. As an instance, in the course of argument it was suggested that a man might execute the dangerous manoeuvre of drawing out to pass a vehicle in front with another vehicle meeting him, and be able to show that he would have succeeded in his calculated intention but for some increase of speed in the vehicles in front: a case very doubtfully of manslaughter but very probably of dangerous driving. . . . It therefore would appear that in directing the jury in a case of manslaughter the judge should in the first instance charge them substantially in accordance with the general law, that is, requiring the high degree of negligence indicated in *Bateman's* case[1] and then explain that such degree of negligence is not necessarily the same as that which is required for the offence of dangerous driving, and then indicate to them the conditions under which they might acquit of manslaughter and convict of dangerous driving. A direction that all they had to consider was whether death was caused by dangerous driving within s. 11 of the Road Traffic Act, 1930, and no more, would in my opinion be a misdirection.

In dealing with the summing-up in the present case I feel bound to say with every respect to the learned and very careful judge that there are passages which are open to criticism. In particular at the beginning of his charge to the jury he began with the statement that if a man kills another in the course of doing an unlawful act he is guilty of manslaughter, and then proceeded to ascertain what the unlawful act was by considering s. 11 of the Road Traffic Act, 1930. If the summing-up rested there, there would have been misdirection. There is an obvious difference in the law of manslaughter between doing an unlawful act and doing a lawful act with a degree of carelessness which the Legislature makes criminal. If it were otherwise a man who killed another while driving without due care and attention would *ex*

[1] (1925), 19 Cr.App. Rep. 8; p. 222, *supra*.

necessitate commit manslaughter. But as the summing-up proceeded the learned judge reverted to, and I think rested the case on, the principles which have been just stated. . . . "

APPEAL DISMISSED.

GRAY v. BARR

[1971] 2 All E.R. 949

Mens rea *is necessary in the case of all forms of manslaughter.*

Facts.

Mrs. Gray claimed damages under the Fatal Accidents Acts from Mr. Barr for loss of dependency due to the death of her husband caused by Mr. Barr. The principal issue in the case was whether the Prudential Assurance Co., joined as a third party, was liable to indemnify Mr. Barr under a policy, taken out by his wife for the benefit of herself and members of her household, against liability for damages for personal injuries caused by " accidents ".

Mistakenly believing that Mrs. Barr had gone to Mr. Gray's house in order to resume an " affair ", Mr. Barr went there with a gun. He forced his way upstairs, fired a shot in the air, and, on being grappled by Mr. Gray, fell downstairs, firing the fatal shot involuntarily. Mr. Barr had been charged with the murder of Mr. Gray but was acquitted of both murder and manslaughter.

The Court of Appeal (Civil Division) held that the Prudential Assurance Co. was not liable to indemnify Mr. Barr, firstly because Mr. Gray's death was not an accident within the meaning of the policy, and secondly because, notwithstanding his acquittal, Mr. Barr's conduct amounted to manslaughter by the intentional use of unlawful violence and it would be contrary to public policy to allow recovery.

Extracts from the Judgments of the Court of Appeal.

LORD DENNING, M.R.—

" There is no doubt, to my mind, that Mr. Barr was guilty of manslaughter. I know that at the criminal trial he was acquitted altogether. But that was a merciful verdict:

and in this civil action we must, when called upon, give the true decision according to law. During the argument we had much discussion on the issue of manslaughter, such as 'motor manslaughter' when a high degree of negligence is said to suffice: see *Andrews* v. *Director of Public Prosecutions*;[1] and 'weapon manslaughter' when an unlawful and dangerous act has been said to be enough: see *R.* v. *Larkin*.[2] But I do not think it necessary to go into the matter at length. I would only say this: in manslaughter of every kind there must be a guilty mind. Without it, the accused must be acquitted: see *R.* v. *Lamb*.[3] In the category of manslaughter relating to an unlawful act, the accused must do a dangerous act with the *intention* of frightening or harming someone, or with the *realisation* that it is likely to frighten or harm someone, and nevertheless he goes on and does it, regardless of the consequences. If his act does thereafter, in unbroken sequence, cause the death of another, he is guilty of manslaughter. Thus a seaman Larkin brandished an open razor so as to frighten his woman's lover, but in the ensuing dialogue he cut the woman's throat. According to him it was an accident because she swayed against him when the razor was in his hand. The judge directed the jury that, even accepting his own evidence, it was manslaughter; and they could not in law find him not guilty. The Court of Criminal Appeal upheld this direction: see *R.* v. *Larkin*.[2] Next, Sapper Cashmore took a rifle from the armoury, loaded it with live rounds, and went about with it, holding people up, intending to rob them. His officer tried to get him to put the rifle down. In the course of it all, the rifle went off and the officer fell dead. According to Cashmore it was an accident. The Court of Criminal Appeal held that, even if the gun did go off accidentally, 'he is still guilty of manslaughter and there is no escape from it . . . no court-martial properly directed could reach any conclusion but that this was manslaughter at the very least . . .'

In the category of manslaughter which is called 'motor manslaughter', it is settled beyond question that the insured is entitled to recover: see *Tinline* v. *White Cross Insurance Association, Ltd.*;[4] *James* v. *British General Insurance Co., Ltd.*[5] But, in the category which is here in question, it is different. If his conduct is wilful and culpable, he is not

---

[1] [1937] A.C. 576; [1937] 2 All E.R. 552; p. 224, *supra*.
[2] [1943] K.B. 174; [1943] 1 All E.R. 217; p. 209, *supra*.
[3] [1967] 2 Q.B. 981; [1967] 2 All E.R. 1282; p. 217, *supra*.
[4] [1921] 3 K.B. 327.
[5] [1927] 2 K.B. 311; [1927] All E.R. Rep. 442.

entitled to recover: see *Hardy* v. *Motor Insurers' Bureau*[1]. I agree with the judge when he said:[2]

'The logical test, in my judgment, is whether the person seeking the indemnity was guilty of deliberate, intentional and unlawful violence or threats of violence. If he was, and death resulted therefrom, then, however unintended the final death of the victim may have been, the court should not entertain a claim for indemnity.' "

APPEAL DISMISSED.[3]

R. v. BUCK AND BUCK

(1960), 44 Cr. App. Rep. 213

(1) *To kill someone in consequence of an unlawful abortion is at least manslaughter although there is no evidence of criminal negligence.* (2) *Someone who procures the commission of an unlawful abortion which proves fatal may be convicted as an accessory before the fact to involuntary manslaughter.*

Facts.

The accused woman was charged with manslaughter and the accused man was charged with being an accessory before the fact. The deceased had met her death in consequence of an abortion performed by the woman in relation to which the man had acted as go-between. It was submitted on behalf of the accused that it is no longer manslaughter to kill someone by an unlawful act, whatever its nature, in the absence of proof of criminal negligence, and that there cannot be an accessory before the fact to involuntary manslaughter. These submissions were overruled by the trial judge.

Extracts from the judgment.

EDMUND DAVIES, J.—

" I read *Andrews* (p. 224, *supra*) as a case which turned on its facts, the pre-eminent fact being that death had arisen from an act of negligence. Mr. Chapman [counsel for the accused] says that *Andrews* (*supra*) decides that the mere

---

[1] [1964] 2 Q.B. 745; [1964] 2 All E.R. 742.

[2] [1970] 2 Q.B. at p. 640; [1970] 2 All E.R. at p. 710.

[3] The dicto of Lord DENNING with regard to the necessity of *mens rea* in all cases of manslaughter are, of course, quite inconsistent with the judgment of the Court of Appeal (Criminal Division) in the earlier case of *R.* v. *Lipman*, p. 99, *supra*.

fact that death resulted from an unlawful act no longer necessitates a verdict of manslaughter. I think that the answer to that is that one has to have regard to what is the nature of the unlawful act charged. In this case the unlawful act, which for the purpose of the present submission one assumes is proved against the female defendant, is criminal abortion. Can it be said that, if criminal abortion is shown to have been committed and, furthermore, death is shown to have resulted therefrom, the abortionist is not guilty, at the very least, of manslaughter? If a negative answer is demanded since *Andrews* (*supra*) to that question, one is radically departing from the law as it has been established in this country for many years and frequently applied to cases such as the present. I refer in particular to the well-known decision of AVORY, J., in *Lumley* (1912) 76 J. P. 208. The facts were that a physician who had been struck off the medical register was indicted for the murder of a woman on whom he had performed an illegal operation, in consequence of which she died. In his summing up to the jury, which has been frequently regarded as authoritative on this branch of the law and which has since been repeatedly cited, that great judge said: 'If the evidence satisfies you beyond reasonable doubt that the prisoner did, in fact, use either an instrument or other means for the purpose and with the intention of procuring abortion, and death resulted from that act, then you must ask yourselves the further question: when he did that, did he contemplate or must he as a reasonable man have contemplated that death is likely to result, or must he as a reasonable man have contemplated that grievous bodily harm was likely to result? If, in your opinion, he must as a reasonable man have contemplated either of those consequences, then your duty is to find him guilty of murder. If you are of the opinion, and are driven to the conclusion by the evidence, that he did the act which is charged against him, but that he had not at any time any contemplation, and would not as a reasonable man have contemplated, that either death or grievous bodily harm would result, but thought that by his own skill as a medical man he could perform this operation without any risk of either death or grievous bodily harm, then you would be justified in convicting him of manslaughter.' There is not a hint in that summing up and direction to the jury that there could conceivably be an acquittal; but if *Andrews* (*supra*) has, indeed, altered the law applicable to such cases as the present one, then *Lumley* (*supra*) would no longer be an authority to be followed.

Mr. Chapman [counsel for the accused] referred further to *R.* v. *Franklin* (1883), 15 Cox C.C. 163 (p. 213, *supra*). The headnote, for the present purposes, sufficiently conveys what was there decided. It reads: ' The mere fact of a civil wrong committed by one person against another ought not to be used as an incident which is a necessary step in a criminal case, apart from the question of criminal negligence. Therefore, the mere fact of a person wrongfully taking up a box from a refreshment stall on a sea pier and wantonly throwing it into the sea, and thereby unintentionally causing the death of another bathing in the sea, is not *per se* and apart from the question of negligence sufficient to constitute the offence of manslaughter.' That, of course, was a case decided on facts wholly different from those of the present case and although, as Mr. Chapman pointed out, it may be that there was material there on which not merely a civil wrong, but larceny of the box, could have been relied upon, it is noteworthy that the case treats the abstraction of the box merely as a civil wrong.

The offence of manslaughter is unlawful killing without malice aforethought. *Russell on Crime,* 11th ed., Vol. I, p. 622, says that it is a killing which the killer neither intended nor foresaw as likely to happen. It is an accidental, albeit blameworthy and felonious, killing. In my judgment, where death flows directly from a felony of the kind here charged the offence must, at the very least, be manslaughter. In circumstances of a kind which nobody for one moment suggests existed in the present case, it might even be murder. It is an offence which involves a considerable risk to the person, no matter with what care it may be committed.

The second submission, I recall, was that there cannot be any accessory before the fact to involuntary manslaughter and that, despite the fact that I have overruled the first submission, the male defendant therefore ought not to be convicted of being accessory before the fact to manslaughter by criminal abortion. Mr. Chapman submitted that procuring a manslaughter is impossible in law. Procuring an abortion there may be, but even though death results from that criminal abortion, nevertheless there cannot be procuring of manslaughter. The authorities on the matter are not many.

In *R.* v. *Gaylor* (1857), Deane & B. 288, the prisoner was convicted of manslaughter and I quote from the short headnote: ' It appeared that the prisoner procured sulphate of potash and gave it to his wife intending her to take it for the purpose of procuring abortion; and that she, believing herself to be pregnant, although in reality she was not, took the sulphate of potash in the absence of the prisoner, and died from its effects.' It was held that the conviction of the husband for manslaughter was right. Mr. Chapman has criticised this report and particularly the intervention of ERLE, J., at page 293 as affording, perhaps, unreliable guidance to the courts in those days; but I note that that great judge BRAMWELL, B. at page 291 said this: 'Suppose a man, for mischief, gives another a strong dose of medicine, not intending any further injury than causing him to be sick and uncomfortable, and death ensues, would not that be manslaughter? Suppose, then, another had counselled him to do it, would not he who counselled be an accessory before the fact?' Obviously, the learned Baron took the answers to both those questions to be clearly in the affirmative.

I hold that, where criminal abortion is proved to have taken place and death is proved to have resulted from that criminal abortion there must, at least, be a conviction of manslaughter. In my judgment, further, there can be an accessory before the fact to involuntary manslaughter or, to bring the matter more directly to bear on the present case, a man or woman who procures another person to commit a criminal abortion is guilty of being an accessory before the fact to manslaughter if death results from that abortion."

SUBMISSIONS OVERRULED.

Comment on R. v. Buck and Buck.

This decision has been affirmed by the Court of Criminal Appeal in *R.* v. *Creamer*[1] where the appellant's conviction of being an accessory before the fact to manslaughter was affirmed when the deceased's death was caused by an abortion arranged by the appellant. In the course of his judgment Lord PARKER, C.J., said:

"It is the accident of death resulting which makes him guilty of manslaughter as opposed to some lesser offence, such as assault or, in the present case, abortion. This can no doubt be said to be illogical, since the culpability is the same, but, nevertheless, it is an illogicality which runs throughout the whole of our law, both the common law and the statute law. A comparatively recent example is clearly that of dangerous driving and causing death by dangerous driving."

---

[1] [1966] 1 Q. B. 72; [1965] 3 All E. R. 257.

SECTION 5

ASSAULTS AND WOUNDING

FAGAN v. METROPOLITAN POLICE COMMISSIONER

[1968] 3 All E.R. 442

It is an assault for someone who has driven his car inadvertently or negligently on to another's foot deliberately to allow the car to remain there.

Facts.

Fagan was reversing his car on to a pedestrian crossing when he was asked by a constable to pull into the side of the road to produce some documents. He drove his car on to the constable's foot, but the Magistrates were not satisfied that he did so deliberately. When asked by the constable to remove his car, Fagan refused to do so for some little time and the constable's foot was slightly injured. Fagan was charged with assaulting the constable in the execution of his duty, and the magistrates convicted him. He unsuccessfully appealed to Quarter Sessions who stated a case for the opinion of a Divisional Court which affirmed the conviction by a majority.

Extracts from the Judgments of the Divisional Court.

JAMES, J.—

" In our judgment, the question arising, which has been argued on general principles, falls to be decided on the facts of the particular case. An assault is any act which intentionally—or possibly recklessly—causes another person to apprehend immediate and unlawful personal violence. Although ' assault ' is an independent crime and is to be treated as such, for practical purposes today ' assault ' is generally synonymous with the term ' battery ', and is a term used to mean the actual intended use of unlawful force to another person without his consent. On the facts of the present case, the 'assault' alleged involved a 'battery'. Where an assault involved a battery, it matters not, in our judgment, whether the battery is inflicted directly by the body of the offender or through the medium of some weapon or instrument controlled by the action of the offender. An assault may be committed by the laying of a hand on another, and the action does not cease to be an assault if it is a stick held in the hand and not the hand itself which is laid on the person of the victim. So, for our part, we see no difference in principle between the action of stepping on to a person's toe and maintaining that position and the action of driving a car on to a person's foot and sitting in the car while its position on the foot is maintained . . .

For our part, we think that the crucial question is whether, in this case, the act of the appellant can be said to be complete and spent at the moment of time when the car wheel came to rest on the foot, or whether his act is to be regarded as a continuing act operating until the wheel was removed. In our judgment, a distinction is to be drawn between acts which are complete—though results may continue to flow—and those acts which are continuing. Once the act is complete, it cannot thereafter be said to be a threat to inflict unlawful force on the victim. If the act, as distinct from the results thereof, is a continuing act, there is a continuing threat to inflict unlawful force. If the assault involves a battery and that battery continues, there is a continuing act of assault. For an assault to be committed, both the elements of *actus reus* and *mens rea* must be present at the same time. The '*actus reus*' is the action causing the effect on the victim's mind: see the observations of PARKE, B., in *R.* v. *St. George.*[1] The '*mens rea*' is the intention to cause that effect. It is not necessary that *mens rea* should be present at the inception of the *actus reus*; it can be superimposed on an existing act. On the other hand, the subsequent inception of *mens rea* cannot convert an act which has been completed without *mens rea* into an assault."

BRIDGE, J., (dissenting).—

". . . I have been unable to find any way of regarding the facts which satisfied me that they amounted to the crime of assault. This has not been for want of trying; but at every attempt I have encountered the inescapable question: after the wheel of the appellant's car had accidentally come to rest on the constable's foot, what was it that the appellant *did*

[1] (1840), 9 C. & P. 483 at pp. 490, 493.

which constituted the act of assault? However the question is approached, the answer which I feel obliged to give is: precisely nothing."

CONVICTION AFFIRMED.

STEPHENS v. MYERS

(1830), 4 C. & P. 349

A person may be guilty of an assault although he is prevented from touching his victim.

Facts.

This was a civil action in which the plaintiff claimed damages for assault from the defendant. The plaintiff was chairman at a meeting where he sat at the same table as the defendant, but was separated from him by six or seven other people. The plaintiff ordered the defendant to leave the meeting on account of his disorderly behaviour, whereupon the defendant advanced toward the plaintiff with his fists clenched saying that he would remove him from the chair. Other people intervened before he was near enough to the plaintiff to have hit him.

Extract from the Summing-Up to the Jury.

TINDALL, C.J.—

"It is not every threat, when there is no actual personal violence, that constitutes an assault, there must, in all cases, be the means of carrying the threat into effect.[1] The question I shall leave to you will be, whether the defendant was advancing at the time, in a threatening attitude, to strike the chairman, so that his blow would almost immediately have reached the chairman, if he had not been stopped; then, though he was not near enough at the time to have struck him, yet if he was advancing with that intent, I think it amounts to an assault in law. If he was so advancing, that, within a second or two of time, he would have reached the plaintiff, it seems to me it is an assault in law. If you think he was not advancing to strike the plaintiff, then only can you find your verdict for the defendant; otherwise you must find it for the plaintiff, and give him such damages as you think the nature of the case requires."

VERDICT FOR THE PLAINTIFF.

---

[1] *Sed quaere*; see next Case.

R. v. ST. GEORGE[1]

(1840), 9 C. & P. 483

Pointing an unloaded gun at another person amounts to a common assault if the person at whom it is pointed does not know that it is unloaded.

Facts.

St. George was charged under a statute which has since been repealed with feloniously attempting to discharge loaded firearms by drawing the trigger. The evidence was that he had pointed a gun at the prosecutor, and the jury found that it was loaded. He was restrained from drawing the trigger. The judge expressed the view that a person could only be convicted of an assault under the particular section of the statute in question if the assault was connected with the presentation of loaded firearms, but he also expressed the view that the pointing of an unloaded gun at a person might amount to a common assault.

Extracts from the Observations and Summing-Up to the Jury of :—

PARKE, B.—

" . . . My idea is, that the prisoner can only be found guilty under this act of Parliament for that assault which was involved in, and connected with, the presentation of a loaded pistol. Suppose there was a common assault committed in the course of a dispute between the prisoner and the prosecutor, I do not think that the prisoner could be found guilty of that assault on an indictment charging him with felony. . . .

My idea is, that it is an assault to present a pistol at all, whether loaded or not. If you threw the powder out of the pan, or took the percussion cap off, and said to the party, 'this is an empty pistol,' then that would be no assault; for there the party must see that it was not possible that he should be injured; but if a person presents a pistol which has the appearance of being loaded, and puts the party into fear and alarm, that is what it is the object of the law to prevent. I

---

[1] For a discussion of this case in relation to that of *R.* v. *James* (1844), 1 Car. & Kir. 530, see *Modern Approach to Criminal Law*, pp. 352–355.

think that if, in this case, it should be proved that the prisoner presented a pistol purporting to be a loaded pistol, and the jury are satisfied that it was so near as to produce danger to life if the pistol had gone off, that that would be an assault in point of law, and that the prisoner might be convicted of that assault upon this indictment."

VERDICT, GUILTY.

FAIRCLOUGH v. WHIPP

[1951] 2 All E. R. 834

The accused is not guilty of an indecent assault if he invites a young girl to touch him in circumstances amounting to gross indecency.

Facts.

The accused was charged with an indecent assault upon a girl of nine. While making water on the bank of a river he said to the girl as she was passing " touch it " and she did so. The accused was acquitted, and the magistrates stated a case for the opinion of the Divisional Court who were of opinion that the accused was not guilty of the offence charged.

Extracts from the Judgments of the Divisional Court.

LORD GODDARD, C.J.—

" An assault can be constituted, without there being battery, for instance, by a threatening gesture or a threat to use violence against a person, but I do not know any authority which says that where one person invites another person to touch him that can be said to be an assault. The question of consent or non-consent only arises if there is something which can be called an assault and, without consent, would be an assault. If that which was done to this child was of an indecent nature and would have been an assault if done against her will, it would also be an assault if it was done with her consent because she could not consent to an indecent assault. Before we decide whether there has been an indecent assault we must decide whether there has been an assault, and I cannot hold that an invitation to somebody to touch the invitor can amount to an assault on the invitee."

APPEAL DISMISSED.

Comment on Fairclough v. Whipp

(1) Although it is still the case that conduct such as that of the accused in *Fairclough* v. *Whipp* does not constitute an assault, such conduct would now amount to a crime under the Indecency with Children Act, 1959, for s. 1 punishes the committing or inciting of gross indecency with a child of either sex under 14 with a maximum of two years' imprisonment.

(2) It is commonly said that mere words can never constitute an assault, but the authority for this proposition is very slight, and there is now a dictum of Lord GODDARD in *Fairclough's* case which supports the contrary view, for it is clear that he considered that a threat to use violence may constitute an assault.

R. v. DONOVAN

[1934] 2 K. B. 498

(1) *Where the use of force by one person against another is only criminal if done without the consent of such other person, the onus of proving its absence rests upon the prosecution.* (2) *Consent is no defence to a charge of doing an act which is likely, or intended to do serious bodily harm.*

Facts.

Donovan was charged and convicted of an indecent assault upon a girl of seventeen for the purposes of sexual gratification. His defence was that the girl had consented to being caned, and he appealed to the Court of Criminal Appeal on the ground that the jury had been misdirected on the question of consent.

The Court of Criminal Appeal quashed his conviction on this ground, holding that the onus of proving the absence of consent rested upon the prosecution, but the Court was also of opinion that, before any question of consent was put to them, the jury should have been asked whether the blows were likely or intended to cause an unlawful degree of bodily harm.

Extracts from the Judgment of the Court of Criminal Appeal read by:

SWIFT, J.—

" . . . First, it was of importance that the jury should be left in no doubt as to the incidence of the burden of proof in relation to consent. In *R.* v. *May*[1] the principle applicable to cases of this kind was laid down by this Court in these words: 'The Court is of opinion that if the facts proved in evidence are such that the jury can reasonably find consent, there ought to be a direction by the judge on that question, both as to the onus of negativing consent being on the prosecution and as to the evidence in the particular case bearing on the question.'

We have no doubt that the facts proved in the present case were such that the jury might reasonably have found consent; it is, indeed, difficult to reconcile some of the admitted facts with absence of consent. It was therefore of importance (if consent was in issue) that there should be no possibility of doubt in the minds of the jury upon the question whether it was for the Crown to negative consent, or for the defence to prove it. A second observation which may fairly be made is that consent, being a state of mind, is to be proved or negatived only after a full and careful review of the behaviour of the person who is alleged to have consented. Unless a jury is satisfied beyond reasonable doubt that the conduct of the person has been such that, viewed as a whole, it shows that she did not consent, then the prisoner is entitled to be acquitted. . . .

. . . the learned counsel for the Crown relied in this Court upon the submission which he had unsuccessfully made at the trial, and argued that, this being a case in which it was unnecessary for the Crown to prove absence of consent, this Court ought not to quash the conviction.

We have given careful consideration to the question of law which this submission raises. The learned counsel on both sides referred us to passages in the judgments in the case of *R.* v. *Coney*.[2] The subject-matter of that case was very different from that of the present case, but the judgments undoubtedly contain statements of the law which are of great value for the present purpose. Much reliance was placed, on behalf of the Crown, upon the following passage from the judgment of CAVE, J.: 'The true view is, I think, that a blow struck in anger, or which is likely or intended to do corporal hurt, is an assault, but that a blow struck in sport, and not likely, nor intended to cause bodily harm, is not an assault, and that, an assault being a breach of the peace and unlawful, the consent of the person struck is

---

[1] [1912] 3 K. B. 572, at p. 575.
[2] (1882), 8 Q. B. D. 534, at p. 539; p. 140, *supra*.

immaterial.' We have considered the authorities upon which this view of the learned judge was founded, and we think it of importance that we should state our opinion as to the law applicable in this case. If an act is unlawful in the sense of being in itself a criminal act, it is plain that it cannot be rendered lawful because the person to whose detriment it is done consents to it. No person can license another to commit a crime. So far as the criminal law is concerned, therefore, where the act charged is in itself unlawful, it can never be necessary to prove absence of consent on the part of the person wronged in order to obtain the conviction of the wrongdoer. There are, however, many acts in themselves harmless and lawful which become unlawful only if they are done without the consent of the person affected. What is, in one case, an innocent act of familiarity or affection, may, in another, be an assault, for no other reason than that, in the one case there is consent, and in the other consent is absent. As a general rule, although it is a rule to which there are well established exceptions, it is an unlawful act to beat another person with such a degree of violence that the infliction of bodily harm is a probable consequence, and when such an act is proved, consent is immaterial. We are aware that the existence of this rule has not always been clearly recognised. In his *Digest of the Criminal Law* (6th edition), Art. 227, Sir James FitzJames Stephen enunciates the proposition that 'every one has a right to consent to the infliction upon himself of bodily harm not amounting to a maim.' This may have been true in early times when the law of this country showed remarkable leniency towards crimes of personal violence, but it is a statement which now needs considerable qualification. It is to be observed, indeed, that in Art. 230 of his Digest, the learned author says: 'It is uncertain to what extent any person has a right to consent to his being put in danger of death or bodily harm by the act of another.'

In early works of authority, such as Foster's *Crown Law* and East's *Pleas of the Crown*, much learning upon the distinction between lawful and unlawful acts is to be found in the chapters dealing with homicide. At p. 259 of the former work (third edition), Sir Michael Foster gives his reason for the proposition that a man who beats another 'in anger or from preconceived malice' is responsible if fatal consequences ensue, in the following words: 'What he did was *malum in se*, and he must be answerable for the consequence of it. He certainly beat him with an intention of doing him some bodily harm, he had no other intent, he could have no other; he is therefore answerable for all the harm he did.' If an act is *malum in se* in the sense in which Sir Michael Foster used the words, that is to say, is, in itself, unlawful, we take it to be plain that consent cannot convert it into an innocent act.

There are, as we have said, well established exceptions to the general rule that an act likely or intended to cause bodily harm is an unlawful act. One of them is dealt with by Sir Michael Foster in the chapter just cited, where he refers to the case of persons who in perfect friendship engage by mutual consent in contests, such as 'cudgels, foils, or wrestling,' which are capable of causing bodily harm. The learned author emphasizes two points about such contests: (1) that bodily harm is not the motive on either side, and (2) that they are 'manly diversions, they intend to give strength, skill and activity, and may fit people for defence, public as well as personal, in time of need.' For these reasons, he says that he cannot call these exercises unlawful.

Another exception to the general rule, or, rather, another branch of the same class of exceptions, is to be found in cases of rough and undisciplined sport or play, where there is no anger and no intention to cause bodily harm. An example of this kind may be found in *R.* v. *Bruce.*[1] In such cases the act is not in itself unlawful, and it becomes unlawful only if the person affected by it is not a consenting party. It is not necessary to deal in this judgment with other exceptions to the rule which are wholly remote from the present case, such as the reasonable chastisement of a child by a parent or by a person *in loco parentis*. In the present case it was not in dispute that the motive of the appellant was to gratify his own perverted desires. If, in the course of so doing, he acted so as to cause bodily harm, he cannot plead his corrupt motive as an excuse, and it may truly be said of him in Sir Michael Foster's words that 'he certainly beat him with an intention of doing him some bodily harm, he had no other intent,' and that what he did was *malum in se*. Nothing could be more absurd or more repellent to the ordinary intelligence than to regard his conduct as comparable with that of a participant in one of those 'manly diversions' of which Sir Michael Foster wrote. Nor is his act to be compared with the rough but innocent horse-play in *R.* v. *Bruce*[1]. Always supposing, therefore, that the blows which

[1] (1847), 2 Cox C. C. 262, at p. 263.

he struck were likely or intended to do bodily harm, we are of opinion that he was doing an unlawful act, no evidence having been given of facts which would bring the case within any of the exceptions to the general rule. In our view, on the evidence given at the trial, the jury should have been directed that, if they were satisfied that the blows struck by the prisoner were likely or intended to do bodily harm to the prosecutrix, they ought to convict him, and that it was only if they were not so satisfied, that it became necessary to consider the further question whether the prosecution had negatived consent. For this purpose we think that 'bodily harm' has its ordinary meaning and includes any hurt or injury calculated to interfere with the health or comfort of the prosecutor.[1] Such hurt or injury need not be permanent, but must, no doubt, be more than merely transient and trifling.

This being our view of the law, we considered the question whether, in all the circumstances, it would be right to quash the conviction. The whole case was conducted, in so far as it was conducted in the presence of the jury, upon the footing that the issue of consent was the 'vital question in the case'. It is not too much to say that, in all probability, the only question which the jury felt called upon to decide, as the case was left to them, was the question whether in fact the prosecutrix was shown to have consented. We may summarize the position by saying that, of the two questions which should have been left to the jury, the first was not left at all, while the second was left to them with an inadequate and misleading direction. It may well be that, if the first question had been left to the jury, they would have answered it by saying that the appellant intended to cause and inflicted blows likely to cause bodily harm to the prosecutrix, so that the second question would not have arisen. But, although we think it probable that this would have been the jury's view, it is, in our opinion, impossible to say that they must inevitably have so found. There are many gradations between a slight tap and a severe blow, and the question whether particular blows were likely or intended to cause bodily harm is one eminently fitted for the decision of a jury upon evidence which they have heard. We may have little doubt what that decision would have been in this case, but we cannot, consistently with the

---

[1] This definition may require reconsideration in the light of the new definition of "grievous bodily harm" as "really serious bodily harm" in *D.P.P.* v. *Smith*, p. 194, *supra*. The reference to comfort may be superfluous.

practice of this Court, substitute ourselves for the jury and decide a question of fact which was never left to them. . . . "

CONVICTION QUASHED.

Extracts from the Offences Against the Person Act, 1861.

Reference is made to the following two sections of the Offences Against the Person Act, 1861 in several cases given below.

Section 18. " Whosoever shall unlawfully and maliciously by any means whatsoever wound or cause any grievous bodily harm to any person, . . . with intent, . . . to do some . . . grievous bodily harm to any person, or with intent to resist the lawful apprehension or detainer of any person shall be liable . . . to imprisonment for life."[1]

Section 20. " Whosoever shall unlawfully and maliciously wound or inflict any grievous bodily harm upon any other person, either with or without any weapon or instrument, . . . shall be liable to imprisonment for not more than five years."

R. v. CLARENCE

(1888), 22 Q. B. D. 23

(1) *It is neither an infliction of grievous bodily harm nor an assault for a man to infect his wife with gonorrhoea by having sexual intercourse with her, even though he was aware of his condition and she ignorant of it, and even though she would not have had intercourse with him had she known of his condition.*

(2) *Fraud only avoids consent to intercourse if it is as to the nature of the act itself or the identity of the party who does the act.*

Facts.

The accused was charged with unlawfully and maliciously causing grievous bodily harm to his wife contrary to s. 20 of the Offences against the Person Act, 1861, and with an assault causing her actual bodily harm contrary to s. 47. He had had intercourse with his wife when he knew

[1] The omissions show amendments by the Criminal Law Act, 1967.

that he was suffering from gonorrhoea. His wife was unaware of his condition and would not have consented to intercourse had she known of it. The accused was convicted on both counts, but a case was reserved for the opinion of the Court for Crown Cases Reserved and that court was of opinion by a majority of nine to four that the convictions should be quashed.

Extracts from the Judgments of the Court for Crown Cases Reserved.

STEPHEN, J.—

"Indeed though the word assault is not used in the section,[1] I think the words imply an assault and battery of which a wound or grievous bodily harm is the manifest immediate and obvious result. This is supported by *R.* v. *Taylor*[2] in 1869, in which it was held that a prisoner could upon an indictment under that section be convicted of a common assault, because each offence 'wounding' and 'grievous bodily harm' 'necessarily includes an assault', though the word does not occur in the section.

Infection by the application of an animal poison appears to me to be of a different character from an assault. The administration of poison is dealt with by s. 24, which would be superfluous if poisoning were an 'infliction of grievous bodily harm either with or without a weapon or instrument'. The one act differs from the other in the immediate and necessary connection between a cut or a blow and the wound or harm inflicted, and the uncertain and delayed operation of the act by which infection is communicated. If a man by a grasp of the hand infects another with small-pox, it is impossible to trace out in detail the connection between the act and the disease, and it would, I think, be an unnatural use of language to say that a man by such an act 'inflicted' small-pox on another.

In *R.* v. *Hanson*,[3] in 1849, VAUGHAN WILLIAMS, J., after consulting CRESSWELL, J., held that the administration of cantharides was neither a common assault nor a common law misdemeanour; and *R.* v. *Walkden*[4] was a decision to the same effect by PARKE, B. Upon these grounds I am of opinion that s. 20 does not apply to the case.

---

[1] P. 243, *supra*.
[2] (1869) L.R. 1 C. C. R. 194.
[3] (1849), 2 Car. & Kir. 912.
[4] (1845), 6 L. T. O. S. 194.

Is the case, then, within s. 47, as 'an assault occasioning actual bodily harm'? The question here is whether there is an assault. It is said there is none, because the woman consented, and to this it is replied that fraud vitiates consent, and that the prisoner's silence was a fraud. Apart altogether from this question, I think that the act of infection is not an assault at all, for the reasons already given. Infection is a kind of poisoning. It is the application of an animal poison, and poisoning, as already shewn, is not an assault. Apart, however, from this, is the man's concealment of the fact that he was infected such a fraud as vitiated the wife's consent to his exercise of marital rights, and converted the act of connection into an assault? It seems to me that the proposition that fraud vitiates consent in criminal matters is not true if taken to apply in the fullest sense of the word, and without qualification. It is too short to be true, as a mathematical formula is true. If we apply it in that sense to the present case, it is difficult to say that the prisoner was not guilty of rape, for the definition of rape is having connection with a woman without her consent; and if fraud vitiates consent, every case in which a man infects a woman or commits bigamy, the second wife being ignorant of the first marriage, is also a case of rape. Many seductions would be rapes, and so might acts of prostitution procured by fraud, as for instance by promises not intended to be fulfilled. These illustrations appear to shew clearly that the maxim that fraud vitiates consent is too general to be applied to these matters as if it were absolutely true. I do not at all deny that in some cases it applies, though it is often used with reference to cases which do not fall within it. For instance, it has nothing to do with such cases as assaults on young children. A young child who submits to an indecent act no more consents to it than a sleeping or unconscious woman. The child merely submits without consenting. The only cases in which fraud indisputably vitiates consent in these matters are cases of fraud as to the nature of the act done. As to fraud as to the identity of the person by whom it is done, the law is not quite clear. In *R.* v. *Flattery*,[1] in which consent was obtained by representing the act as a surgical operation, the prisoner was held to be guilty of rape. In the case where consent was obtained by the personation of a husband, there was before the passing of the Criminal Law Amendment Act of 1885 a conflict of authority. The last decision in

[1] (1877), 2 Q. B. D. 410.

England, *R.* v. *Barrow*,[1] decided that the act was not rape, and *R.* v. *Dee*,[2] decided in Ireland in 1884, decided that it was. The Criminal Law Amendment Act of 1885 'declared and enacted' that thenceforth it should be deemed to be rape, thus favouring the view taken in *R.* v. *Dee*.[2] I do not propose to examine in detail the controversies connected with these cases. The judgments in the case of *R.* v. *Dee*[2] examine all of them minutely, and I think they justify the observation that the only sorts of fraud which so far destroy the effect of a woman's consent as to convert a connection consented to in fact into a rape are frauds as to the nature of the act itself, or as to the identity of the person who does the act."

CONVICTIONS QUASHED.

R. v. LATIMER

(1886), 17 Q. B. D. 359

On a charge of unlawful and malicious wounding, it is only necessary for the prosecution to prove that the accused intended to do physical harm to someone, provided the other ingredients of the offence are present.

Facts.

Latimer was charged with unlawfully and maliciously wounding a barmaid by a blow with a belt. The evidence was that he had become involved in a quarrel with one Chapple in a public house, and that, after going into the yard for a short time, he returned to the room in which Chapple was sitting, and aimed a blow at him with a belt which he had in his hand as he passed the place where Chapple was sitting. The belt struck and cut the face of the barmaid.

The jury found that he hit the barmaid accidentally. A verdict of guilty was entered, but a case was stated for the opinion of the Court for Crown Cases Reserved who were of opinion that the conviction was correct.

---

[1] (1868), L. R. 1 C. C. R. 156.
[2] (1884), 14 L. R. Ir. 468.

Extracts from the Judgments of the Court for Crown Cases Reserved.

LORD COLERIDGE, C.J.—

" We are of opinion that this conviction must be sustained. It is common knowledge that a man who has an unlawful and malicious intent against another, and, in attempting to carry it out, injures a third person, is guilty of what the law deems malice against the person injured, because the offender is doing an unlawful act, and has that which the judges call general malice, and that is enough. Such would be the case if the matter were *res integra*; but it is not so, for *R.* v. *Hunt*[1] is an express authority on the point. There a man intended to injure A, and said so, and, in the course of doing it, stabbed the wrong man, and had clearly malice in fact, but no intention of injuring the man who was stabbed. . . . So, but for *R.* v. *Pembliton*,[2] there would not have been the slightest difficulty. Does that case make any difference ? I think not, and on consideration, that it was quite rightly decided. But it is clearly distinguishable, because the indictment in *R.* v. *Pembliton*[2] was on the Act making unlawful and malicious injury to property a statutory offence punishable in a certain way, and the jury expressly negatived, and the facts expressly negatived, any intention to do injury to property, and the Court held that under the Act making it an offence to injure any property there must be an intent to injure property. *R.* v. *Pembliton*,[2] therefore, does not govern the present case and on no other ground is there anything to be said for the prisoner."

CONVICTION AFFIRMED.

R. v. CUNNINGHAM

[1957] 2 Q. B. 396

For the purpose of a statutory offence malice connotes foresight of the prohibited consequence.

Facts.

Cunningham was charged with larceny and with unlawfully and maliciously causing W. to take coal gas so as

---

[1] (1825), 1 Mood. C. C. 93.

[2] (1974), L.R. 2 C.C.R. 119; where a stone aimed at another person smashed a window.

thereby to endanger her life contrary to s. 23 of the Offences against the Person Act, 1861. He had torn a gas meter away from the wall and taken its contents. The effect of his conduct was to cause a quantity of gas to escape into the adjoining house in which W. was sleeping and thereby to cause her bodily harm. Cunningham pleaded guilty to larceny and, so far as the other charge was concerned, the trial judge directed the jury that the accused was acting maliciously if he was doing something which he knew he had no business to do. The accused was convicted and successfully appealed to the Court of Criminal Appeal on the ground that the jury had been misdirected with regard to the meaning of the word " maliciously ".

Extracts from the Judgment of the Court of Criminal Appeal.

BYRNE, J.—

" Section 23 provides: ' Whosoever shall unlawfully and maliciously administer to or cause to be administered to or taken by any other person any poison or other destructive or noxious thing, so as thereby to endanger the life of such person, or so as thereby to inflict upon such person any grievous bodily harm, shall be guilty of felony. . .

Mr. Brodie cited the following cases: *R.* v. *Pembliton,*[1] *R.* v. *Latimer*[2] and *R.* v. *Faulkner.*[3] In reply, Mr. Snowden, on behalf of the Crown, cited *R.* v. *Martin.*[4]

We have considered those cases, and we have also considered, in the light of those cases, the following principle which was propounded by the late Professor C. S. Kenny in the first edition of his *Outlines of Criminal Law* published in 1902 and repeated at p. 186 of the 16th edition edited by Mr. J. W. Cecil Turner and published in 1952: ' . . . in any statutory definition of a crime, " malice " must be taken not in the old vague sense of " wickedness " in general but as requiring either (1) an actual intention to do the particular *kind* of harm that in fact was done; or (2) recklessness as to whether such harm should occur or not (*i.e.*, the accused has foreseen that the particular kind of harm might be done and yet has gone on to take the risk of it). It is neither limited to, nor does it indeed require, any ill will towards the person injured.'

[1] (1874), L.R. 2 C.C.R. 119.
[2] (1886), 17 Q.B.D. 359; p. 246, *supra*.
[3] (1877), I.R. 11 C.L. 8.
[4] (1881), 8 Q.B.D. 54; p. 252, *infra*.

We think that this is an accurate statement of the law. It derives some support from the judgments of Lord COLERIDGE, C.J., and BLACKBURN, J., in *Pembliton's* case.[1] In our opinion the word ' maliciously ' in a statutory crime postulates foresight of consequence."

APPEAL ALLOWED ON THE COUNT UNDER S. 23 OF THE OFFENCES AGAINST THE PERSON ACT.

R. v. MOWATT

[1967] 3 All E.R. 47

Where, on a charge under s. 20 *of the Offences against the Person Act,* 1861, *the only issue is whether the accused did the acts complained of or whether he was acting in self-defence, it is unnecessary to direct the jury on the meaning of "maliciously". When a direction on the meaning of that word is necessary, the jury should be directed that the accused was acting maliciously if he foresaw any kind of physical harm to the person he attacked.*

Facts.

Mowatt was charged with wounding with intent contrary to s. 18 of the Offences against the Person Act, 1861. He alleged that he was acting in self-defence when he assaulted the prosecutor. The jury returned a verdict of guilty under s. 20 of the Act, and Mowatt unsuccessfully appealed to the Court of Appeal on the ground that the judge had failed to direct the jury on the meaning of " maliciously " in s. 20.

Extracts from the Judgment of the Court of Appeal, Criminal Division.

DIPLOCK, L.J.—

" ' Unlawfully and maliciously ' was a fashionable phrase of parliamentary draftsmen in 1861. It runs as a theme with minor variations throughout the Malicious Damage Act, 1861, and the Offences against the Person Act, 1861.

R. v. *Cunningham*[2] was a case under s. 23 of the Offences against the Person Act, 1861, . . .

---

[1] (1874), L. R. 2 C. C. R. 119, at p. 122.
[2] [1957] 2 Q. B. 396; [1957] 2 All E. R. 412; p. 247 *supra*.

In the words of the court ' " maliciously " in a statutory crime postulates foresight of consequence ', and on this proposition we do not wish to cast any doubt. But the court in that case also expressed approval obiter of a more general statement by Professor C. Kenny, which runs as follows:[1]

' . . . In any statutory definition of a crime, " malice " must be taken not in the old vague sense of " wickedness " in general but as requiring either (i) an actual intention to do the particular kind of harm that in fact was done, or (ii) recklessness as to whether such harm should occur or not (i.e., the accused has foreseen that the particular kind of harm might be done, and yet has gone on to take the risk of it). It is neither limited to, nor does it indeed require, any ill-will towards the person injured.'

This generalisation is not, in our view, appropriate to the specific alternative statutory offences described in s. 18 and s. 20 of the Offences against the Person Act, 1861, and s. 5 of the Prevention of Offences Act, 1851, and if used in that form in the summing-up is liable to bemuse the jury. In s. 18 the word ' maliciously ' adds nothing. The intent expressly required by that section is more specific than such element of foresight of consequences as is implicit in the word ' maliciously ' and in directing a jury about an offence under this section the word ' maliciously ' is best ignored. In the offence under s. 20 and in the alternative verdict which may be given on a charge under s. 18—for neither of which is any specific intent required—the word ' maliciously ' does import on the part of the person who unlawfully inflicts the wound or other grievous bodily harm an awareness that his act may have the consequence of causing some physical harm to some other person. That is what is meant by ' the particular kind of harm ' in the citation from Professor Kenny's *Outlines of Criminal Law*. It is quite unnecessary that the accused should have foreseen that his unlawful act might cause physical harm of the gravity described in the section, i.e., a wound or serious physical injury. It is enough that he should have foreseen that some physical harm to some person, albeit of a minor character, might result.

In many cases in instructing the jury on a charge under s. 20 of the Act of 1861, or on the alternative verdict which

---

[1] See Kenny's *Outlines of Criminal Law* (1st Edn., 1902); the passage is repeated in the 18th Edn. of that work in 1962 by J. W. Cecil Turner (see para. 158a). The passage in the 16th Edn. was cited in *R.* v. *Cunningham;* see [1957] 2 All E. R. at p. 414.

may be given under that section when the accused is charged under s. 18 it may be unnecessary to refer specifically to the word 'maliciously.' The function of a summing-up is not to give the jury a general dissertation on some aspect of the criminal law, but to tell them what are the issues of fact on which they must make up their minds in order to determine whether the accused is guilty of a particular offence. There may, of course, be cases where the accused's awareness of the possible consequences of his act is genuinely in issue. *R.* v. *Cunningham* is a good example. But where the evidence for the prosecution, if accepted, shows that the physical act of the accused which caused the injury to another person was a direct assault which any ordinary person would be bound to realise was likely to cause some physical harm to the other person (as, for instance, an assault with a weapon or the boot or violence with the hands) and the defence put forward on behalf of the accused is not that the assault was accidental or that he did not realise that it might cause some physical harm to the victim, but is some other defence such as that he did not do the alleged act or that he did it in self-defence, it is unnecessary to deal specifically in the summing-up with what is meant by the word 'maliciously' in the section. It can only confuse the jury to invite them in the summing-up to consider an improbability not previously put forward and to which no evidence has been directed, to wit—that the accused did not realise what any ordinary person would have realised was a likely consequence of his act, and to tell the jury that the onus lies, not on the accused to establish, but on the prosecution to negative, that improbability, and to go on to talk about presumptions. To a jury who are not jurisprudents that sounds like jargon. In the absence of any evidence that the accused did not realise that it was a possible consequence of his act that some physical harm might be caused to the victim, the prosecution satisfy the relevant onus by proving the commission by the accused of an act which any ordinary person would realise was likely to have that consequence."

APPEAL DISMISSED.

Comment on R. v. Mowatt.

The ruling that a person acts "maliciously" within the meaning of s. 20 of the Offences against the Person Act, 1861 if he foresees that his act may have the consequence of causing some physical harm to some person, although he does not foresee the possibility of harm of the gravity prohibited by the statute (a wound or grievous bodily harm) is a further example of the illogicality referred to by Lord PARKER, C.J., in *R.* v. *Creamer* p. 232 *supra*. Though theoretically objectionable, it is not of great practical importance because an accused who, foreseeing only minimal physical harm, in fact causes considerable physical harm will be liable to the same maximum penalty of five years imprisonment as that for an offence under s. 20 on the ground that he is guilty of an assault causing actual bodily harm contrary to s. 47.

R. v. MARTIN

(1881), 8 Q.B.D. 54

A person may be convicted of unlawfully and maliciously inflicting grievous bodily harm although he was merely acting mischievously.

Facts.

The accused was convicted of unlawfully and maliciously inflicting grievous bodily harm, contrary to s. 20 of the Offences against the Person Act, 1861. Shortly before the end of the performance at a theatre, he turned off the lights and opened the exit from a staircase. A panic ensued in the course of which several people suffered grievous bodily harm. There was no evidence that the accused was motivated by ill will towards anyone, and the trial judge directed the jury that they should convict if satisfied that the accused acted " deliberately and intentionally " and not " out of mere mischief ". A case was stated for the opinion of the Court for Crown Cases Reserved, and that Court was of opinion that the conviction was correct.

Extracts from the Judgments of the Court for Crown Cases Reserved.

LORD COLERIDGE, C.J.—

" . . . The prisoner must be taken to have intended the natural consequences of that which he did. He acted ' unlawfully and maliciously,' not that he had any personal malice against the particular individuals injured, but in the sense of doing an unlawful act calculated to injure, and by which others were in fact injured. Just as in the case of a man who unlawfully fires a gun among a crowd, it is murder if one of the crowd is thereby killed. The prisoner was most properly convicted."

STEPHEN, J.—

". . . I wish to add that the Recorder seems to have put the case too favourably for the prisoner, for he put it to the jury to consider whether the prisoner did the act 'as a mere piece of foolish mischief.' Now, it seems to me, that if the prisoner did that which he did as a mere piece of foolish mischief unlawfully and without excuse, he did it 'wilfully,' that is 'maliciously,' within the meaning of the statute. I think it important to notice this as the word 'malicious' is capable of being misunderstood. LORD BLACKBURN (then Mr. Justice Blackburn) in the cases of *R.* v. *Ward*[1] and *R.* v. *Pembliton*,[2] lays it down that a man acts 'maliciously' when he wilfully and without lawful excuse does that which he knows will injure another."

CONVICTION AFFIRMED[3].

R. v. DRISCOLL

(1841), Car. & M. 214

If one person assaults or threatens another, such other is only entitled to give such blows as may be reasonably necessary in self defence.

Facts.

Driscoll was charged with unlawfully and maliciously wounding the prosecutor. The evidence was that he had become involved in a dispute with the prosecutor in the course of which the prosecutor had advanced towards him with clenched fists. Driscoll's wife thereupon pushed the prosecutor down when Driscoll inflicted the injuries in respect of which he was charged.

---

[1] (1872), L. R. 1 C. C. R. 356, at p. 360.

[2] (1874), L. R. 2 C. C. R. 119, at p. 122;

[3] The question whether Martin was guilty of an assault which, on the authorities, is a prerequisite of liability under s. 20 (see *per* STEPHEN, J., in *R.* v. *Clarence*, p. 243, *supra*) does not appear to have been considered in this case.

Extract from the Summing-Up to the Jury of :—

COLERIDGE, J.—

" If one man strikes another a blow, that other has a right to defend himself, and to strike a blow in his defence, but he has no right to revenge himself: and if, when all the danger is past, he strikes a blow not necessary for his defence, he commits an assault and a battery. It is a common error to suppose, that one person has a right to strike another who has struck him, in order to revenge himself, and it very often influences people's minds ; and I have, therefore, thought it right to state what the law upon the subject really is."

VERDICT, GUILTY.

KENLIN v. GARDINER

[1966] 3 All E. R. 931

The use of reasonable force is permitted in self-defence against an assault by a police officer, however technical the assault may be, and, though the accused's ignorance that the person assaulted by him was a police officer is no defence to a charge of assaulting a police officer in the execution of his duty contrary to s. 51 *of the Police Act,* 1964, *a reasonable belief that the officer was a thug is material on the issue of self-defence.*

Facts.

The accused, two schoolboys, were observed going from house to house by police officers. The boys were checking up on members of their rugby team, but the officers thought that they were engaged on some criminal purpose. When the officers approached the boys, the boys thought that they were thugs, and ran away. In capturing them the officers technically committed assaults on the boys because they were seeking to interrogate, not to arrest them. The boys then committed what, subject to the question of self-defence, would be an assault upon the officers. The justices convicted the boys of offences under s. 51 of the Police Act, 1964, but stated a case for the opinion of the Divisional Court. That Court was of opinion that no offence had been committed.

The questions stated for the opinion of the High Court were as follows. (i) Whether the defence of "self-defence" was open to a defendant in answer to a charge laid under s. 51 (1) of the Act of 1964? (ii) Whether *mens rea* was an element required in proving an assault within the meaning of s. 51 (1) of the Act of the 1964? (iii) Whether a genuine mistake of fact, alone or considered together with the defence of self-defence, amounted to a defence to a charge laid under s. 51 (1) of the Act of 1964?

Extracts from the Opinion of the Divisional Court.

WINN, L.J.—

"In the case of a charge of assault under s. 51 of the Police Act, 1964, as in the case of any charge of assault, the justification of self-defence is available just as it is in the case of any other assault. I prefer calling it a justification, to calling it a defence, because it is for the prosecution to exclude justification and not for the defendant to establish it. That is subject to this, that if the self-defence, in this case self-defence by the appellants against a prior assault such as had been committed, in a technical sense, by the respondents taking hold of an arm of each of the appellants, was self-defence against an assault which was justified in law, as, for instance, a lawful arrest, then in law self-defence cannot afford justification for assault in resistance to justified assault by a police officer. So one comes back to the question in the end, in the ultimate analysis: was the respondent entitled in law to take hold of the first appellant by the arm, was he justified in committing that technical assault by the exercise of any power which he as a police constable possessed in the precise circumstances prevailing at that exact moment? The same question arises in regard to the other respondent and the second appellant a little later on. I regret that I feel myself compelled to answer that question in the negative. . . . The justices have asked certain questions, as Lord PARKER, C.J., said, rather in the nature of an examination paper. It is not necessary to give any detailed answers to them, but I will give the answers in case they themselves want to know them, as they have consulted the court. The answer to question (1) is—yes as to any assault unless the assault resisted was itself justifiable. The answer to questions (2) and (3) is that knowledge that the man attacked is a police officer is unnecessary, but a genuine mistake of fact as to the character of the person concerned, e.g., genuine and reasonable belief that he was a thug and not a police officer, would be highly material in judging the scope of reasonableness and the degree of force falling within the liberty or justification of self-defence."

APPEAL ALLOWED.

R. v. FENNELL

[1970] 3 All E.R. 215

A father's mistaken belief that a police officer was unlawfully detaining his son is no defence to a charge of assaulting the officer in the execution of his duty.

Facts.

Fennell's son was involved in a fight and arrested by the prosecutor, a police officer. Fennell pressed the officer to release his son and he struck the officer who was on the point of taking his son to the police station. Fennell was convicted after the trial judge had directed the jury that, if the officer was acting in the execution of his duty as he was, the accused's mistaken belief that the officer had arrested his son unlawfully was no defence. Fennell unsuccessfully appealed to the Court of Appeal.

Extracts from the Judgment of the Court of Appeal.

WIDGERY, L.J.—

"The law jealously scrutinises all claims to justify the use of force and will not readily recognise new ones. Where a person honestly and reasonably believes that he or his child is in imminent danger of injury, it would be unjust if he were deprived of the right to use reasonable force by way of defence merely because he had made some genuine mistake of fact. On the other hand, if the child is in police custody and not in imminent danger of injury, there is no urgency of the kind which requires an immediate decision, and a father who forcibly releases the child does so at his peril. If in fact the arrest proves to be lawful, the father's use of force cannot be justified."

APPEAL DISMISSED.

R. v. CUNNINGHAM

[1959] 1 Q. B. 288

Provocation is no defence to a charge of unlawful and malicious wounding contrary to s. 20 *of the Offences against the Person Act,* 1861.

Facts.

Cunningham was charged with unlawful and malicious wounding. In furtherance of the defence of provocation his counsel put questions to the prosecutor tending to suggest that the prosecutor had made indecent suggestions to the accused in consequence of which the accused attacked the prosecutor. The trial judge held that this cross-examination entitled counsel for the prosecution to put questions to the accused with regard to his criminal record as the nature or conduct of the defence involved an attack upon the prosecutor within the meaning of s. 1(f) of the Criminal Evidence Act, 1898. The accused was convicted and unsuccessfully appealed to the Court of Criminal Appeal who expressed the opinion that the cross-examination of the accused was proper and decided that provocation was no defence to the offence charged.

Extracts from the Judgment of the Court of Criminal Appeal.

LORD PARKER, C.J.—

" The appeal is based on the ground that leave to the prosecution to cross-examine the prisoner as to his previous convictions ought never to have been allowed. If provocation is a proper defence to a charge of this sort, then counsel must, so it is said, be allowed to put that question to the victim without having the prisoner's convictions brought out in court . . . but in this case the court is clearly of opinion that in a case such as malicious wounding, there is no such thing as a defence of provocation. That defence only arises in a case of murder to reduce murder to manslaughter.[1] That, it seems to

---

[1] It has been argued that provocation might negative the intent to do grievous bodily harm on a charge of unlawfully and maliciously wounding with such intent contrary to s. 18 of the Offences against the Person Act, 1861, thus leaving the accused guilty of unlawfully and maliciously wounding contrary to s. 20 (see 75 *Law Quarterly Review* 174 and *R.* v. *Spartels,* [1953] V. L. R. 194). But see *R.* v. *Falla,* [1964] V. R. 78. Under the Queensland Code, provocation is a complete defence even to a charge of assault.

us, is made clear by Viscount SIMON in *Holmes* v. *Director of Public Prosecutions*.[1] It is true that he said:[2] 'The whole doctrine relating to provocation depends on the fact that it causes, or may cause, a sudden and temporary loss of self control whereby malice, which is the formation of an intention to kill or to inflict grievous bodily harm, is negatived.' There it seems to the court clear that Lord SIMON was dealing and dealing only with a defence of provocation in a murder case. The matter is put perfectly clearly by him where, after referring to the fact that provocation may reduce murder to manslaughter, he goes on:[3] 'In the case of lesser crimes, provocation does not alter the nature of the offence at all: but it is allowed for in the sentence.'

Accordingly, in the judgment of this court the defence of provocation was not open to the appellant, and, therefore, there was no defence, and the fact that his convictions were before the jury could have made no difference.

There is yet another difficulty in the way of the appellant, namely, that, even if provocation could be a defence, there is no suggestion that words alone, except in a case under the Homicide Act, 1957, are sufficient to found a defence of provocation."

APPEAL DISMISSED.

---

[1] [1946] A. C. 588; [1946] 2 All E. R. 124.
[2] [1946] A. C. 588, at p. 598; [1946] 2 All E. R. 124.
[3] *Ibid*., at p. 601.

SECTION 6

BIGAMY[1]

Offences against the Person Act, 1861, s. 57

"Whosoever, being married, shall marry any other person, during the life of the former husband or wife, whether the second marriage shall have taken place in England or Ireland or elsewhere shall be guilty of felony . . .[2] Provided that nothing in this section contained shall extend . . . to any person marrying a second time, whose husband or wife shall have been continually absent from such person for the space of seven years then last past, and shall not have been known by such person to be living within that time, or shall extend to any person who, at the time of such second marriage, shall have been divorced from the bond of the first marriage. . . ."

R. v. MORRISON

[1938] 3 All E. R. 787

If a man is prima facie lawfully married to a woman, it is a question of fact for the jury to decide whether the evidence is such as to invalidate the marriage and it is their duty to give the benefit of any doubt to the accused.

Facts.

Mrs. Holman was married in 1919 and went with her husband to live in Canada; she last saw him in Canada in 1928 and subsequently returned to this country. On March 11, 1938, she married Morrison who five days later went through a form of marriage with Florence Ide. In respect of this latter ceremony he was charged with bigamy and

---

[1] Reference should also be made to *R.* v. *Tolson* and *R.* v. *Gould*, pp. 26 and 34, *supra*.

[2] Under s. 12(5)(*a*) of the Criminal Law Act, 1967, "any enactment creating an offence by directing it to be felony shall be read as directing it to be an offence."

convicted. He unsuccessfully appealed to the Court of Criminal Appeal on the ground that the judge should have told the jury that they must acquit unless they were satisfied that Mr. Holman was dead.

Extracts from the Judgment of the Court of Criminal Appeal read by:—

BRANSON, J.—

" . . . the complaint made by the appellant is that the judge failed to direct the jury properly. It is alleged that he should have told them in so many words: 'Unless you are satisfied that Mr. Holman was not (*sic*) dead, you should acquit the defendant Morrison, and should convict only if you are satisfied that Mr. Holman was already dead.' In these circumstances, it is necessary to turn to the summing-up to see what in fact the judge told the jury. He began by telling the jury that the defence had raised this matter, and then he said:

'They say that, although the defendant in this case did go through a ceremony of marriage with Mrs. Holman on Mar. 11, and although he believed at that time that it was a lawful marriage, and although she believed at that time that it was a lawful marriage, it now turns out—and they say that they are able to prove it—that it was not a marriage at all, because she was not free to marry, as she had a husband living.'

The judge then went on to point out that, if the defence could have produced the husband, that would have been an end of the case, because it would then have been established that Mrs. Holman had a husband when she went through a form of marriage with the appellant on March 11. He pointed out that Mr. Holman was not called, and he went on to discuss the question of law. He referred to *R.* v. *Willshire,*[1] . . .

Then he proceeded with a direction to the jury, which I think it right to quote, as it seems to put the matter fairly and clearly to the jury, and to be as favourable to the appellant as it could be. He said:

'The marriage between the defendant and Mrs. Holman being *prima facie* a lawful marriage, do you entertain any doubt about its lawfulness in consequence of the evidence you have heard? If you think it may have been no marriage at all, then the prosecution will not have proved that this man had two wives at the same time, but only one, Mrs. Ide, because the first

[1] (1881), 6 Q. B. D. 366.

woman was not his wife, if that is the view you take of the evidence.'

It seems to us that in that passage the judge told the jury the precise point which they had to consider, and that he told them in perfectly plain language that, if they had any doubt about the first marriage, they had to acquit the accused. . . . In our view, the summing-up adequately put the law before the jury, and the suggestion that this appeal should be allowed upon the ground raised of misdirection fails. . . ."

APPEAL DISMISSED.

R. v. ALLEN

(1872), L. R. 1. C. C. R. 367

Where a person already bound by an existing marriage goes through a form of marriage known to and recognised by the law as capable of producing a valid marriage, he is guilty of bigamy in spite of the fact that the second ceremony would have been void for some reason independent of its bigamous character.

Facts.

In 1853 Allen married Sarah Cunningham who died in 1866 leaving a niece named Harriet Crouch. In 1867 he married Ann Pearson Gutteridge and in 1871, while his wife was still alive and the marriage subsisting, he married Harriet Crouch. As the law then stood marriage to a niece by marriage was void.[1] He was convicted but the question of the correctness of his conviction was reserved for the Court for Crown Cases Reserved who were of opinion that it was correct.

Extract from the Judgment of the Court for Crown Cases Reserved read by:

COCKBURN, C.J.—

" . . . bigamy, in the modern acceptation of the term, namely, that of a second marriage consequent on an abandonment of the first while the latter still subsists, is unfortunately of too frequent occurrence. It takes place, as we all know, more frequently where one of the married

---

[1] Such a marriage is now valid under the Marriage Act, 1949, s. 1.

parties has deserted the other; sometimes where both have voluntarily separated. It is always resorted to by one of the parties in fraud of the law; sometimes by both, in order to give the colour and pretence of marriage where the reality does not exist. Too often it is resorted to for the purpose of villainous fraud. The ground on which such a marriage is very properly made penal is, that it involves an outrage on public decency and morals, and creates a public scandal by the prostitution of a solemn ceremony, which the law allows to be applied only to a legitimate union, to a marriage at best but colourable and fictitious, and which may be made, and too often is made, the means of the most cruel and wicked deception. It is obvious that the outrage and scandal involved in such a proceeding will not be less, because the parties to the second marriage may be under some special incapacity to contract marriage. The deception will not be the less atrocious, because the one party may have induced the other to go through a form of marriage known to be generally binding, but inapplicable to their particular case. Is the scandal or the villainy the less because the man, having represented to the woman, who is his dupe, and to the priest, that he is a Roman Catholic, turns out afterwards to be a Protestant?[1] Such instances as those we have referred to, thus involving public scandal or deception, being plainly within the mischief which we may reasonably assume it must have been the purpose of the legislature to prevent, we are of opinion that we ought not to frustrate the operation of a very salutary statute, by putting so narrow a construction on it as would exclude such a case as the present, if the words are legitimately capable of such a construction as would embrace it. Now the words 'shall marry another person' may well be taken to mean shall 'go through the form and ceremony of marriage with another person.' The words are fully capable of being so construed, without being forced or strained; and as a narrower construction would have the effect of leaving a portion of the mischief untouched, which it must have been the intention of the legislature to provide against, and thereby, as is fully admitted by those who contend for it, of bringing a grave reproach on the law, we think we are warranted in inferring that the words were used in the sense we have referred to, and that we shall best give effect to the

[1] These remarks refer to the Irish case of *R.* v. *Fanning* (1866), 10 Cox C. C. 411, in which the second marriage contravened a statute prohibiting the marriage by a Catholic priest of parties one of whom was a Protestant.

legislative intention by holding such a case as the present to be within their meaning. To assume that the words must have such a construction as would exclude it, because the second marriage must be one which, but for the bigamy, would have been as binding as the first, appears to us to be begging the entire question, and to be running directly counter to the wholesome canon of construction, which prescribes that, where the language will admit of it, a statutory enactment shall be so construed as to make the remedy co-extensive with the mischief it is intended to prevent.

In thus holding it is not at all necessary to say that forms of marriage unknown to the law, as was the case in *Burt* v. *Burt*,[1] would suffice to bring a case within the operation of the statute. We must not be understood to mean that every fantastic form of marriage to which parties might think proper to resort, or that a marriage ceremony performed by an unauthorised person, or in an unauthorised place, would be a marrying within the meaning of the 57th section of 24 & 25 Vict. c. 100. It will be time enough to deal with a case of this description when it arises. It is sufficient for the present purpose to hold, as we do, that where a person already bound by an existing marriage goes through a form of marriage known to and recognised by the law as capable of producing a valid marriage, for the purpose of a pretended and fictitious marriage, the case is not the less within the statute by reason of any special circumstances, which, independently of the bigamous character of the marriage, may constitute a legal disability in the particular parties, or make the form of marriage resorted to specially inapplicable to their individual case. . . ."

CONVICTION AFFIRMED.

R. v. CURGERWEN

(1865), L. R. 1. C. C. R. 1

Where a husband has lived apart from his wife for seven years or more[2] *and he marries again, it is for the prosecution to prove that during that time he was aware of her existence.*

---

[1](1860), 2 Sw. & Tr. 88.

[2] Where there is evidence that this is the case, there can be little doubt that the burden of disproving the fact that the accused has been continually absent from his spouse " for the space of seven years " would be held by an English court to be borne by the prosecution.

Facts.

Curgerwen married in 1852. In January, 1854, he joined a ship at Portsmouth where his wife came to see him off. In July, 1862, he went through a form of marriage with another woman. There was no evidence that between 1854 and 1862 he had ever been near where his wife lived or had seen or heard of her or any member of her family, or known whether she was dead or alive. The prisoner was found guilty but the case was reserved for the Court for Crown Cases Reserved who were of opinion that the conviction should be quashed.

Judgment of the Court for Crown Cases Reserved.

POLLOCK, C.B.—

"This question has arisen more than once before; and we are now asked to settle the law on the subject. The term 'burden of proof' is an inconvenient one, except when a person is called upon to prove an affirmative. Our attention has been called to a note by the editor of *Russell on Crimes*,[1] known as a gentleman of great learning, ability, and research, who appears to have adopted the view that the burden of proof lies on the prisoner. We think, however, that it is contrary to the general spirit of the English law that the prisoner should be called on to prove a negative."

CONVICTION QUASHED.

R. v. TAYLOR

[1950] 2 K. B. 368

For the purposes of s. 57 *of the Offences against the Person Act,* 1861, "*second marriage*" *means the ceremony which forms the subject-matter of the indictment for bigamy.*

Facts.

In 1949 Taylor was charged with having bigamously married Lilian Smithers in 1946 and Olive Briggs in 1948 during the life of Alice Judy Taylor to whom he had been lawfully married in 1925. Alice Judy Taylor was alive at the time of the two ceremonies, but the accused had not

[1] *Russell on Crimes and Misdemeanours*, 4th edition, by Greaves, Vol. I, p. 270, note (1).

heard of her since 1927. In 1927 Taylor had gone through a ceremony of marriage with another woman, and he went through a further ceremony of marriage with yet another woman in 1942. In 1944 he had been charged with bigamy in respect of the ceremony of 1942 during the life of the woman he had married in 1927, but he had been acquitted on account of the invalidity of the 1927 marriage. Taylor had subsequently been charged with bigamy in respect of the 1927 ceremony, but he had been acquitted because, at that time, the prosecution was unable to prove that Alice Judy Taylor was alive in 1927. On account of the decision in *R.* v. *Treanor*[1] Taylor pleaded guilty to the charges in respect of the ceremonies of 1946 and 1947 but, on the hearing of his appeal against sentence, the Court of Criminal Appeal reserved the question whether he was in fact guilty of the crimes charged for the opinion of a full court. The full court of Criminal Appeal were of opinion that he was not guilty and accordingly quashed his convictions.

Extracts from the Judgment of the Court of Criminal Appeal.

LORD GODDARD, C.J.—

" The short point on which this court can decide this case—and it seems to me to be the true way of deciding it—is this:— When a court is dealing with a count charging bigamy, it is concerned with the allegation that on a particular day a man went through a ceremony of marriage when his lawful wife was alive. It is therefore concerned with two ceremonies of marriage and no more, the lawful marriage and the ceremony, whether bigamous or polygamous, in respect of which the charge is made. Directly the bigamous or polygamous later ceremony is proved, it is open to the defendant to show that at the time of that ceremony—which is the only ' second marriage ' with which the court is concerned—he had not heard of his wife for seven years. It does not seem to this court that it is then open to the prosecution to say: ' There have been other ceremonies of marriage in between '. The offence which is charged is that of going through the particular marriage on the particular day when the lawful wife was alive. Therefore the defendant has a defence if it is shown that, at the time when he went through the marriage which is charged against him as a felony, he had not seen his wife for seven years. Any other construction would lead to very astonishing results. It is quite enough to say that, while we do not differ from the opinion of the court in *R.* v. *Treanor*[1] that the words ' second marriage ' must be strictly construed, the second marriage which has to be considered is the second marriage charged in the indictment and no other."

CONVICTIONS QUASHED.

---

[1] [1939] 1 All E. R. 330.

SECTION 7

OFFENCES AGAINST THE THEFT ACT, 1968

Extracts from the Theft Act, 1968.

The following extracts from the Theft Act, 1968 are simply those which are essential to a proper understanding of the cases given below. They are by no means the only portions of the Act with which the student ought to be familiar.

" *Section* 1.—*Basic definition of theft.*

(1) A person is guilty of theft if he dishonestly[1] appropriates property belonging to another with the intention of permanently depriving the other of it; and ' thief ' and ' steal ' shall be construed accordingly.

Section 2.—' *Dishonestly* '.

(1) A person's appropriation of property belonging to another is not to be regarded as dishonest—

(*a*) if he appropriates the property in the belief that he has in law the right to deprive the other of it, on behalf of himself or of a third person; . . .

Section 3.—' *Appropriates* '.

(1) Any assumption by a person of the rights of an owner amounts to an appropriation, and this includes, where he has come by the property (innocently or not) without stealing it, any later assumption of a right to it by keeping or dealing with it as owner . . .

Section 4.—' *Property* '

(1) ' Property ' includes money and all other property, real or personal, including things in action and other intangible property . . .

Section 5.—' *Belonging to another* '.

(1) Property shall be regarded as belonging to any person having possession or control of it, or having in it any proprietary right or interest (not being an equitable interest arising only from an agreement to transfer or grant an interest).

(3) Where a person receives property from or on account of another, and is under an obligation to the other to retain and deal with that property or its proceeds in a particular way, the property

---

[1] See addendum.

or proceeds shall be regarded (as against him) as belonging to the other.

(4) Where a person gets property by another's mistake, and is under an obligation to make restoration (in whole or in part) of the property or its proceeds or of the value thereof, then to the extent of that obligation the property or proceeds shall be regarded (as against him) as belonging to the person entitled to restoration, and an intention not to make restoration shall be regarded accordingly as an intention to deprive that person of the property or proceeds.

Section 9.—*Burglary.*

(1) A person is guilty of burglary if—

(*a*) he enters any building or part of a building as a trespasser and with intent to commit any such offence as is mentioned in subsection (2) below; . . .

(2) The offences referred to in subsection (1) (*a*) above are offences of stealing anything in the building or part of a building in question, of inflicting on any person therein any grievous bodily harm or raping any woman therein, and of doing unlawful damage to the building or anything therein.

Section 12.—*Taking motor vehicle or other conveyance without authority.*

(1) . . . A person shall be guilty of an offence if, without having the consent of the owner or other lawful authority, he takes any conveyance for his own or another's use . . .

Section 15.—*Obtaining property by deception.*

(1) A person who by any deception dishonestly obtains property belonging to another, with the intention of permanently depriving the other of it, shall on conviction on indictment be liable to imprisonment for a term not exceeding ten years . . .

(4) For purposes of this section ' deception ' means any deception (whether deliberate or reckless) by words or conduct as to fact or as to law, including a deception as to the present intentions of the person using the deception or any other person.

Section 16.—*Obtaining pecuniary advantage by deception.*

(1) A person who by any deception dishonestly obtains for himself or another any pecuniary advantage shall on conviction on indictment be liable to imprisonment for a term not exceeding five years.

(2) The cases in which a pecuniary advantage within the meaning of this section is to be regarded as obtained for a person are cases where—

(*a*) any debt or charge for which he makes himself liable or is or may become liable (including one not legally enforceable) is reduced or in whole or in part evaded or deferred . . ."

R. v. TURNER (No. 2)
[1971] 2 All E.R. 441

The owner of a chattel may be guilty of stealing it by dishonestly taking it out of the possession of another, and the question whether he was acting dishonestly depends on whether he believed that he was entitled to act as he did.

Facts.

Turner had his car repaired by a garage. He told the proprietor of the garage that he would come and pay for the repairs on the following day. In the meantime the proprietor retained possession of the car which he left outside his garage. Turner took the car away without paying for the repairs. He was convicted of theft of the car and unsuccessfully appealed to the Court of Appeal.

Extracts from the Judgment of the Court of Appeal.

LORD PARKER, C.J.—

" It is argued from that, in default of proof of a lien—and the judge in his summing-up directed the jury that they were not concerned with the question of whether there was a lien—that Mr. Brown was merely a bailee at will and accordingly that he had no sufficient possession.

The words ' belonging to another ' are specifically defined in s. 5 of the Act. Section 5(1) provides:

' Property shall be regarded as belonging to any person having possession or control of it, or having in it any proprietary right or interest . . .'

As I have said, the judge directed the jury that they were not concerned in any way with lien and the sole question was whether Mr. Brown had possession or control. This court is quite satisfied that there is no ground whatever for qualifying the words ' possession or control ' in any way. It is sufficient if it is found that the person from whom the property is taken, or to use the words of the Act, appropriated, was at the time in fact in possession or control . . .

The second point that is taken relates to the necessity for proving dishonesty . . .

This court, however, is quite satisfied that there is nothing in this point whatever. The whole test of dishonesty is the mental element of belief. No doubt, although the appellant may for certain purposes be presumed to know the law, he would not at the time have the vaguest idea whether he did have in law a right to take the car back again, and accordingly when one looks at his mental state, one looks at it in the light of what he believed. The jury were properly told that if he believed that he had a right, albeit there was none, he would nevertheless fall to be acquitted."

APPEAL DISMISSED.

R. v. HALL

[1972] 2 All E.R. 1009

A travel agent who receives payments for advance bookings of flights and pays the money received into his firm's general account is not, in the absence of some further arrangement, under an obligation to deal with the money in a particular way so as to bring the case within s. 5(3) *of the Theft Act,* 1968[1].

Facts.

Hall, a travel agent, received payments for flights to be made by seven clients. He paid the money into his firm's general account. None of the flights materialised, and none of the money was repaid. He was charged and convicted of theft of the money but successfully appealed to the Court of Appeal.

Extracts from the Judgment of the Court of Appeal.

EDMUND DAVIES, L.J.

"Two points were presented and persuasively developed by the appellant's counsel: (1) that, while the appellant has testified that all monies received had been used for business purposes, even had he been completely profligate in its expenditure he could not in any of the seven cases be convicted of "theft" as defined by the Theft Act, 1968; . . . (2) that s. 1(1) of the Theft Act, 1968 dealing with a person who 'dishonestly appropriates', it is essential that the Crown establish that the appellant was acting dishonestly at the time he appropriated. . . We dispose of point (2) by simply saying that, although the summing-up could with advantage have made the legal position clearer, we have come to the conclusion that it dealt adequately with this aspect of the offence charged, and had there been no other ground of criticism we should have been constrained to dismiss the appeal . . .

---

[1] P. 267, *supra*.

Point (1) turns on the application of s. 5 (3) of the Theft Act, 1968 . . . Counsel for the appellant . . . referred us to a passage in the Eighth report of the Criminal Law Revision Committee[1] which reads as follows:

'Subsection (3) [of cl. 5 "belonging to another"] provides for the special case where property is transferred to a person to retain and deal with for a particular purpose and he misapplies it or its proceeds. An example would be the treasurer of a holiday fund. The person in question is in law the owner of the property; but the subsection treats the property, as against him, as belonging to the person to whom he owes the duty to retain and deal with the property as agreed. He will therefore be guilty of stealing from them if he misapplies the property . . .'

But, in our judgment, what was not here established was that these clients expected them "to retain and deal with that property or its proceeds in a particular way" and that an "obligation to do so was undertaken by the appellant." We must make clear, however, that each case turns on its own facts. Cases could, we suppose, conceivably arise where by some special arrangement (preferably evidenced by documents), the client could impose on the travel agent an "obligation" falling within s. 5(3). But no such special arrangement was made in any of the seven cases here being considered."

APPEAL ALLOWED.

R. v. EASOM

[1971] 2 All E.R. 945

A conditional appropriation is not sufficient to render the appropriator guilty of theft.

Facts.

Easom picked up a handbag which had been placed by a policewoman in front of the seat in which he was sitting in a cinema. He opened the bag and examined its contents. He then closed the bag and replaced it with its contents intact on the floor of the cinema. He was apprehended and convicted of theft of the bag and its contents. He successfully appealed to the Court of Appeal.

---

[1] Theft and Related Offences, Cmnd. 2977 (1966), p. 127.

Extracts from the Judgment of the Court of Appeal.

EDMUND DAVIES, L.J.—

"In the respectful view of this court, the jury were misdirected. In every case of theft the appropriation must be accompanied by the intention of permanently depriving the owner of his property. What may be loosely described as a 'conditional' appropriation will not do. If the appropriator has it in mind merely to deprive the owner of such of his property as, on examination, proves worth taking and then finding that the booty is to him valueless, leaves it ready to hand to be repossessed by the owner, he has not stolen. If a dishonest postal sorter picks up a pile of letters, intending to steal any which are registered, but, on finding that none of them are, replaces them, he has stolen nothing, and this is so notwithstanding the provisions of s. 6(1) of the Theft Act, 1968. In the present case the jury were never invited to consider the possibility that such was the appellant's state of mind or the legal consequences flowing therefrom. Yet the facts are strongly indicative that this was exactly how his mind was working, for he left the handbag and its contents entirely intact and to hand once he had carried out his exploration. For this reason we hold that conviction of the full offence of theft cannot stand . . .

But does it follow from all this that this appellant (as to whose identity and physical acts the verdict establishes that the jury entertained no doubt) has to go scot-free? Can he not, as the counsel for the Crown originally submitted, be convicted at least of attempted theft? Even though the contents of the handbag, when examined, held no allure for him, why was he not as guilty of attempted theft as would be the pickpocket who finds his victim's pocket empty (see *R.* v. *Ring, Atkins and Jackson*[1])? Does a conditional intention to steal count for nothing? In his *Criminal Law, The General Part*,[2] Professor Glanville Williams wrote:

'A conditional intention is capable of ranking as legal intention for certain purposes. Thus, it is no defence to an apparent burglar that his intention was merely to steal a certain paper if it should happen to be there.'

He then cited the American Model Penal Code, s. 2.02, which provides that:

'When a particular purpose is an element of an offence,

---

[1] (1892), 66 L.T. 300; p. 167, *supra*.

[2] 2nd Edn., 1961, para. 23.

the element is established although such purpose is conditional, unless the condition negatives the harm or evil sought to be prevented by the law defining the offence.'
But as to this, all (or, at least, much) depends on the manner in which the charge is framed. Thus: 'If you indict a man for stealing your watch, you cannot convict him of attempting to steal your umbrella', *per* Sir Alexander COCKBURN, C.J., in *R.* v. *M'Pherson*,[1] unless, of course, the court of trial has duly exercised the wide powers of amendment conferred by s. 5 of the Indictments Act, 1915. In our judgment, this remains the law and it is unaffected by the provisions of s. 6 of the Criminal Law Act, 1967. No amendment was sought or effected in the present case, which accordingly has to be considered in relation to the articles enumerated in the theft charge, and in relation to nothing else. Furthermore, it is implicit in the concept of an attempt that the person acting intends to do the act attempted, so that the *mens rea* of an attempt is essentially that of the complete crime (see Smith and Hogan, *Criminal Law*[2]). That being so, there could be no valid conviction of the appellant of attempted theft on the present indictment unless it were established that he was animated by the same intention permanently to deprive the police officer of the goods enumerated in the particulars of the charge as would be necessary to establish the full offence."

APPEAL ALLOWED.

Comment on R. v. Easom.

It is difficult to make a helpful statement on the relationship between this case and *R.* v. *Ring, Atkins and Jackson*[3] owing to the absence of any reasons for the latter decision. It would be hard to quarrel with the conclusion that Easom could not be convicted of attempting to steal the articles mentioned in the indictment; but the "million dollar" question is whether he could have been convicted of an attempt to steal an article, or, more realistically, money which was not in the policewoman's handbag. In *Ring's* case the relevant[4] charge was of an attempt to steal from the person of a person unknown. For aught that appears from any of the reports the victim's pockets might have been full of string from which Ring jerked his fingers away in disgust. In that event his case would have been on all fours with Easom's and he ought not to have been convicted of attempting to steal

[1] (1857) Dears. & B. 197, at p. 200.
[2] 2nd Edn., 1969, p. 163.
[3] P. 167, *supra*.
[4] There was also a charge of assault with intent to commit a felony.

the contents of the pocket. On the other hand, the victim's pocket in Ring's case might have been empty, in which case it would have been reasonable to charge him with an attempt to steal goods or money which were not in the pocket. The problem does not appear to be affected by any procedural considerations.

LAWRENCE v. METROPOLITAN POLICE COMMISSIONER

[1971] 2 All E.R. 1253

(1) *The words " without the consent of the owner " should not be read into s.* 1 *of the Theft Act,* 1968; (2) *the provisions of s.* 1(1) *and s.* 15(1) *of the Act are not mutually exclusive.*[1]

Facts.

Lawrence was a taxi driver charged with theft of £6. The prosecution case was that, on being approached at Victoria Station by Mr. Occhi, a newly arrived Italian with little knowledge of English who requested to be driven to Ladbroke Grove, he said that the journey would be an expensive one. The lawful fare was in the region of 10s. 6d. Mr. Occhi handed Lawrence a pound together with his open wallet and Lawrence was alleged to have removed six further pounds before driving Occhi to Ladbroke Grove. Lawrence was convicted and appealed unsuccessfully to the Court of Appeal and House of Lords.

Extracts from the Speeches of the House of Lords.

VISCOUNT DILHORNE.—

" Prior to the passage of the Theft Act, 1968, which made radical changes in and greatly simplified the law relating to theft and some other offences, it was necessary to prove that the property alleged to have been stolen was taken ' without the consent of the owner ' (Larceny Act, 1916, s. 1(1)).

These words are not included in s. 1(1) of the Theft Act, 1968, but the appellant contended that the subsection should be construed as if they were, as if they appeared after the word ' appropriates '. Section 1(1) provides:

' A person is guilty of theft if he dishonestly appropriates property belonging to another with the intention of permanently depriving the other of it; and " thief " and " steal " shall be construed accordingly.'

[1] These sections are set out at p. 267 and p. 268, *supra*.

I see no ground for concluding that the omission of the words 'without the consent of the owner' was inadvertent and not deliberate, and to read the subsection as if they were included is, in my opinion, wholly unwarranted. Parliament by the omission of these words has relieved the prosecution of the burden of establishing that the taking was without the owner's consent. That is no longer an ingredient of the offence.

MEGAW, L.J., delivering the judgment of the Court of Appeal,[1] said that the offence created by s. 1(1) involved four elements: '(i) a dishonest (ii) appropriation (iii) of property belonging to another (iv) with the intention of permanently depriving the owner of it.' I agree. That there was appropriation in this case is clear. Section 3(1) states that any assumption by a person of the rights of an owner amounts to an appropriation. Here there was clearly such an assumption. That an appropriation was dishonest may be proved in a number of ways. In this case it was not contended that the appellant had not acted dishonestly. Section 2(1) provides, *inter alia*, that a person's appropriation of property belonging to another is not to be regarded as dishonest if he appropriates the property in the belief that he would have the other's consent if the other knew of the appropriation and the circumstances of it. *A fortiori*, a person is not to be regarded as acting dishonestly if he appropriates another's property believing that with full knowledge of the circumstances that other person has in fact agreed to the appropriation. The appellant, if he believed that Mr. Occhi, knowing that £7 was far in excess of the legal fare, had nevertheless agreed to pay him that sum, could not be said to have acted dishonestly in taking it. When MEGAW L.J., said that if there was true consent, the essential element of dishonesty was not established, I understand him to have meant this. Belief or the absence of belief that the owner had with such knowledge consented to the appropriation is relevant to the issue of dishonesty, not to the question whether or not there has been an appropriation. That may occur even though the owner has permitted or consented to the property being taken. So proof that Mr. Occhi had consented to the appropriation of £6 from his wallet without agreeing to paying a sum in excess of the legal fare does not suffice to show that there was not dishonesty in this case. There was ample evidence that there was.

[1] [1970] 3 All E.R. at p. 935; [1971] 1 Q.B. at p. 376.

I now turn to the third element ' property belonging to another '. Counsel for the appellant contended that if Mr. Occhi consented to the appellant taking the £6, he consented to the property in the money passing from him to the appellant and that the appellant had not, therefore, appropriated property belonging to another. He argued that the old distinction between the offence of false pretences and larceny had been preserved. I am unable to agree with this. The new offence of obtaining property by deception created by s. 15(1) of the Theft Act, 1968 also contains the words ' belonging to another '. ' A person who by any deception dishonestly obtains property belonging to another with the intention of permanently depriving the other of it . . .' commits that offence. ' Belonging to another ' in s. 1(1) and in s. 15(1) in my view signifies no more than that, at the time of the appropriation or the obtaining, the property belonged to another with the words ' belonging to another ' having the extended meaning given by s. 5 . . .

The first question posed in the certificate was:

' Whether section 1(1) of the Theft Act, 1968, is to be construed as though it contained the words " without having the consent of the owner " or words to that effect.'

In my opinion, the answer is clearly No.

The second question was:

' Whether the provisions of section 15(1) and of section 1(1) of the Theft Act, 1968, are mutually exclusive in the sense that if the facts proved would justify a conviction under section 15(1) there cannot lawfully be a conviction under section 1(1) on those facts.'

Again, in my opinion, the answer is No. There is nothing in the Act to suggest that they should be regarded as mutually exclusive and it is by no means uncommon for conduct on the part of an accused to render him liable to conviction for more than one offence. Not infrequently there is some overlapping of offences. In some cases the facts may justify a charge under s. 1(1) and also a charge under s. 15(1). On the other hand, there are cases which only come within s. 1(1) and some which are only within s. 15(1). If in this case the appellant had been charged under s. 15(1), he would, I expect, have contended that there was no deception, that he had simply appropriated the money and that he ought to have been charged under s. 1(1). In my view, he was rightly charged under that section."

APPEAL DISMISSED.

R. v. COLLINS

[1972] 2 All E.R. 1105

In order that a person may be convicted of burglary under s. 9(1)(*a*) *of the Theft Act,* 1968[1]*, he must have known that he was entering the premises in question as a trespasser, or at least have been reckless in that regard.*

Facts.

Collins was charged with and convicted of burglary by entering a girl's bedroom with intent to commit rape. He had climbed up a stepladder and, observing that the girl in question, with whom he had a slight acquaintance, was sleeping naked near the window, he descended, undressed, and then reascended, naked. On awaking and observing a naked male form either just outside or just inside her bedroom window, the girl, mistakenly believing that it was her boy friend with whom she frequently had intercourse, beckoned Collins into bed with her. The parties then had intercourse and, on discovering her mistake, the girl slapped Collins and withdrew from the room. There was some evidence that Collins, on entering the bedroom, intended to have intercourse with the girl, if necessary by force, but it was not clear whether he had entered the room before the girl signified her assent to his presence there.

Collins successfully appealed to the Court of Appeal on the ground that the judge had not directed the jury that they could only convict if satisfied that he did not believe that the girl had assented to his presence when he entered her bedroom.

Extracts from the Judgment of the Court of Appeal.

EDMUND DAVIES, L.J.—

> "Under s. 9 of the Theft Act, 1968, which renders a person guilty of burglary if he enters any building or part of a building as a trespasser and with intent to commit rape, the entry of the appellant into the building must first be proved. Well, there is no doubt about that, for it is common ground that he did enter this girl's bedroom. Secondly, it must be proved that he entered as a trespasser. We will develop that

---

[1] P. 268, *supra*.

point a little later. Thirdly, it must be proved that he entered as a trespasser with intent at the time of entry to commit rape therein.

The second ingredient of the offence—the entry must be as a trespasser—is one which has not, to the best of our knowledge, been previously canvassed in the courts . . . According to the learned editors of *Archbold*:

'Any intentional, negligent or reckless entry into a building will, it would appear, constitute a trespass if the building is in the possession of another person who does not consent to the entry. Nor will it make any difference if the entry was the result of a reasonable mistake on the part of the defendant, so far as trespass is concerned.'

If that be right, then it would be no defence for this man to say (and even were he believed in saying), " Well, I honestly thought that this girl was welcoming me into the room and I therefore entered, fully believing that I had her consent to go in." If *Archbold* is right, he would nevertheless be a trespasser, since the apparent consent of the girl was unreal, she being mistaken as to who was at her window. We disagree. We hold that, for the purpose of s. 9 of the Theft Act, 1968, a person entering a building is not guilty of trespass if he enters without knowledge that he is trespassing or at least without acting recklessly as to whether or not he is unlawfully entering . . .

Having so held, the pivotal point of this appeal is whether the Crown established that the appellant at the moment that he entered the bedroom knew perfectly well that he was not welcome there or, being reckless whether he was welcome or not, was nevertheless determined to enter . . .

How did the learned judge deal with this matter? We have to say regretfully that there was a flaw in his treatment of it."

APPEAL ALLOWED.[1]

---

[1] The prime importance of this case is the point as to the requirement of *mens rea* with regard to the trespass in burglary; but the judgment of the Court of Appeal also makes the following further points: (1) a conditional intent suffices for this type of burglary, *e.g.* an intent to commit rape should it prove necessary in order to have intercourse; (2) the doctrine of trespass *ab initio* under which an originally lawful entry may, on the occurrence of an unlawful act on the premises sometimes be treated as trespassory for the purposes of the civil law, has no application to burglary; (3) for the purposes of the law of burglary, the consent of a licensee in the building will suffice. As to the third point, the girl was technically a licensee for the occupier of the house was her mother.

R. v. PEART

[1970] 2 All E.R. 823

A consent obtained by misrepresentations concerning the purpose for which a conveyance is required is a defence to taking the conveyance contrary to s. 12(1) *of the Theft Act,* 1968.[1]

Facts.

Peart induced Black to lend him his car by falsely representing that he had to go to Alnwick by 2.30 p.m. or else he would lose a contract. Peart was stopped later in the evening after the time at which he had promised to return the car while driving the car in Burnley. He was convicted of taking the car without the consent of the owner contrary to s. 12 of the Theft Act, 1968. He successfully appealed to the Court of Appeal.

Extracts from the Judgment of the Court of Appeal.

SACHS, L.J.—

" So far as any issue relevant to the present case is concerned, this court is of the clear opinion that there are no material differences between the currently operating subsection of the Theft Act 1968 and those of the Road Traffic Acts, 1930 and 1960 which have just been mentioned. It is, of course, well known that s. 28 of the 1930 Act was introduced to provide a simple criminal remedy for the spate of occasions when cars were taken against the wishes of owners from the streets or from a garage without permanently intending to deprive the owner of that vehicle. It was intended in its very nature to deal with takings made without any reference to the owner. Forty years have gone by since the 1930 Act was passed, and this is, so far as this court is aware, the first time that it has been suggested that it should be applied to occasions when consent was obtained by false pretences . . .

Whether fraudulent representations vitiate consent was the subject of considerable discussion in the days when there was a distinction between larceny by a trick and obtaining goods by false pretences. That discussion and the resulting decisions must have been known to those who framed and passed the 1930 Act. The principles applicable to consent in relation to obtaining property—and I use the word ' property ' in its technical sense—thus seem to this court to be in

---

[1] P. 268, *supra.*

general applicable to consent to obtaining possession with licence to take and drive. An example of a fraudulent representation which did not vitiate the consent is to be found in *London Jewellers, Ltd.* v. *Attenborough,*[1] decided after the passing of the 1930 Act. There have been other decisions since, but it is not necessary to cite them. In substance these decisions can be said to establish that there may well be a distinction between fraudulent representations of facts that are regarded as fundamental and of facts that are not; those regarded as fundamental fall within a somewhat narrow category, *e.g.* fraudulent representations as to identity or as to the nature of a transaction. These distinctions are of a kind which it would be unfortunate to introduce into the particular provisions under consideration, which were clearly intended to apply to offences of quite a simple type.

Whilst, however, reserving the point whether, in regard to s. 12(1) of the Theft Act 1968, a fundamental misrepresentation can vitiate consent, this court has today to deal with a false pretence of the most usual category, no different in principle to the false pretences which come before the courts on a very great variety of occasions. If this court acceded to the submission put forward by the Crown, it would have some far reaching consequences which can hardly have been within the intention of the legislature."

APPEAL ALLOWED.

R. v. PHIPPS AND R. v. McGILL

(1970), 54 Cr.App.Rep. 300

An offence under s. 12 *of the Theft Act,* 1968[2], *is committed if a car is borrowed for a particular purpose and used for some other purpose.*

Facts.

McGill was charged and convicted of taking a car without the consent of the owner contrary to s. 12 of the Theft Act, 1968, and Phipps was charged with permitting himself to be carried in a car which had been so taken. McGill had borrowed a car from Larking for the purpose of taking Mrs. McGill to Victoria station, but he continued to drive the car

---

[1] [1934] 2 K.B. 206; [1934] All E.R. Rep. 270.
[2] P. 268, *supra.*

with Phipps as a passenger for another purpose instead of returning it to its owner. Phipps and McGill unsuccessfully appealed to the Court of Appeal.

Extracts from the Judgment of the Court of Appeal.

FENTON ATKINSON, L.J.—

"The point that Miss Pearlman takes on their behalf is that so long as the original taking and driving away was with the consent of the owner, it really does not matter for how long they kept it thereafter, or what they did with it short of actually stealing it, and that if they decided the next day to drive off or to take it to the Continent on a holiday, they could not have been taking and driving away without authority, even though they knew perfectly well that the owner would object strongly to what they were doing.

In our view, that is an impossible submission with respect to Miss Pearlman, who has said everything possible in support of this appeal.

The learned Common Serjeant put it to the jury in this way: 'The allegation against him is that having lawfully borrowed the car with Mr. Larking's consent for a particular purpose and for a particular purpose only, he'—referring here, of course, to McGill—'thereafter did not return the car, and if that is the position, then as from the time he decided not to return the car and drove it off on his own business after having taken his wife to Victoria Station, or rather brought her back again because she had missed the train, as from then, as a matter of law, and common sense, if he did not have Mr. Larking's permission, he took it and drove it away, and it is that subsequent taking and driving that the Crown allege constitutes the offence in this matter . . .'

In our view, the way in which the matter was put by the learned Common Serjeant was perfectly accurate."

APPEALS DISMISSED.[1]

---

[1] It is questionable whether this case is reconcilable with *R.* v. *Peart.* In that case consent was given for the purpose of driving to Alnwick, in *Phipps'* case consent was given for the purpose of driving to the station. The fact that the consent was obtained by fraud in *Pearts'* case whereas it may not have been in *Phipps'* should if anything have led to different results.

HALSTEAD v. PATEL

[1972] 2 All E.R. 147

A person may be guilty of dishonestly obtaining money by deception contrary to s. 15 *of the Theft Act,* 1968[1], *in spite of the fact that he intended to repay the money.*

Facts.

Patel, a post office employee, opened a giro account with the post office. The only sums of money paid into the account were his wages. During a strike of post office workers, he drew cheques on the account although he knew that there were insufficient funds in the account to meet them. Patel was charged with obtaining £50 from the post office by deception. The magistrates acquitted him on the ground that he intended to repay the money as soon as he reasonably could. The Magistrates stated a case for the opinion of a Divisional Court which was of opinion that Patel was guilty of the offence charged.

Extracts from the Judgments of the Divisional Court.

LORD WIDGERY, C.J.—

> "One goes back to authority on the earlier law to remind oneself of what representation is made by someone who presents a cheque for payment at a bank other than the bank or branch on which the cheque is drawn, the representations made by a person who draws a cheque which is to be paid by a third party and not the banker on whom it is drawn. We find that conveniently in the case of *R.* v. *Page,*[2] where the extract from Kenny's *Outlines of Criminal Law,*[3] adopted by the court on that occasion, is set out. The extract is this:
>
> 'Similarly, the familiar act of drawing a cheque (a document which on the face of it is only a command of a future act) has been held to imply at least three statements about the present: (1) that the drawer has an account with that bank; (2) that he has authority to draw on it for that amount; (3) that the cheque, as drawn, is a valid order for

---

[1] P. 268, *supra*.

[2] [1971] 2 Q.B. 330; [1971] 2 All E.R. 870, at p. 874; [1971] 2 W.L.R. 1308, at p. 1312.

[3] 19th Edn., 1966, p. 359, para. 346.

the payment of that amount (*i.e.* that the present state of affairs is such that, in the ordinary course of events, the cheque will on its future presentment be duly honoured).' There was here clearly a deception within the meaning of that definition. When the respondent drew these cheques he knew there was no money in the account; he knew he had no business to draw them, yet he made what on Kenny's interpretation of the law was a false representation to the effect that the cheque would be duly honoured in the ordinary course of events. So much for the deception.

The next question is whether it was done with the intention of permanently depriving the Post Office of the money. It is here, I think, with deference to the justices, that they went wrong. There can be no doubt in this case that the actual notes or coins which were handed over the counter to this respondent were leaving the control of the Post Office for ever. There was no doubt at all of an intention permanently to deprive the Post Office of the actual coins or notes which were transferred. Accordingly, the only remaining feature of the offence which justified consideration is the requirement of dishonesty . . .

When the cheques were presented for payment, the respondent knew that he had no right to overdraw, he knew that he had no funds in the giro to meet these cheques, and he had no sort of prospect of providing such funds before the cheques were presented in the ordinary course. He had at best the pious hope of repaying this money at some uncertain future date when the post office strike was over, and that, . . . although it may be a matter in mitigation, is no defence to this charge."

CASE REMITTED TO MAGISTRATES WITH DIRECTION TO CONVICT.

R. v. WATERFALL

[1969] 3 All E.R. 1048

A person is guilty of dishonestly obtaining a pecuniary advantage by deception if he induces a taxi driver to drive him without intending to pay for the journey, but he is not acting dishonestly if he believes, however unreasonably, that he can obtain money to pay the fare at the end of the journey.

Facts.

Waterfall contracted with a taxi driver to be driven from Southampton to London. On arrival in London he got the driver to take him to various places where he alleged he could obtain money. Having failed to do so, he got the driver to take him back to Southampton and made off without paying the fare. He was charged and convicted of obtaining a pecuniary advantage by deception after the trial judge had directed the jury that he would have been acting dishonestly although he may have believed that he would get the money in London if such a belief were unreasonable. Waterfall successfully appealed to the Court of Appeal.

Extracts from the Judgment of the Court of Appeal.

LORD PARKER, C.J.—

" Looking at the ingredients of this offence it was quite clear that there had been an obtaining of a pecuniary advantage, in that the appellant had made himself liable to a debt which he had evaded. Secondly, it is perfectly clear that he did that by deception; not only was the conduct of taking a taxi in those circumstances such as to convey that he had money to pay, but according to the taxi driver there had been a specific assurance that the appellant had money to pay. True, the appellant denied that, his case being that he believed and honestly believed that the accountant in Harley Street would provide the money.

The sole question as it seems to me in this case revolves round the third ingredient, namely whether what was done was done dishonestly. In regard to that the deputy recorder directed the jury in this way:

' if on reflection and deliberation you came to the conclusion that [the appellant] never did have any genuine belief that [the appellant's accountant] would pay the taxi fare, then you would be entitled to convict him. But if you felt on weighing up all of the evidence you have heard that there was some real doubt in your mind, not fantastic but some real doubt in your mind as to whether or not [the accountant] might have paid then, of course, [the appellant] would be entitled to be acquitted.'

In other words, in that passage the deputy recorder is telling the jury they had got to consider what was in this particular appellant's mind; had he a genuine belief that the accountant would provide the money? That, as it seems to this court, is a perfectly proper direction subject to this, that it would be right to tell the jury that they can use as a test, although not a conclusive test, whether there were any reasonable grounds for that belief. Unfortunately, however, just before the jury retired, in two passages of the transcript, the deputy recorder, as it seems to this court, was saying that one cannot hold that the appellant had a genuine belief unless he had reasonable grounds for that belief."

APPEAL ALLOWED.

R. v. PAGE

[1971] 2 All E.R. 870

A debt is evaded within the meaning of s. 16(2)(a)[1] *of the Theft Act,* 1968, *if payment of the debt is evaded.*

Facts.

Page hired a car, giving bad cheques in payment of the deposit and hiring fee. He was charged and convicted with obtaining a pecuniary advantage by deception, and appealed unsuccessfully to the Court of Appeal.

Extracts from the Judgment of the Court of Appeal.

PHILLIMORE, L. J.

" Counsel for the appellant says that these debts were not evaded at all, they still exist. Quite obviously if that was the meaning of the Act you could never evade the debt. The answer is that it means evading payment, and so the court thinks that there is really nothing in that point."

APPEAL DISMISSED.

R. v. LOCKER

[1971] 2 All E.R. 875

In order that a debt should be deferred within the meaning of s. 16(2)(a) *of the Theft Act,* 1968[2], *there must be an agreement under which the creditor's remedy is suspended.*

Facts.

Locker was in arrears with his rent. He gave his landlord a bad cheque for the arrears and was charged with and

---

[1] P. 268, *supra.*
[2] P. 268, *supra.*

convicted of obtaining a pecuniary advantage by deception. He successfully appealed to the Court of Appeal.

Extracts from the Judgment of the Court of Appeal.

WIDGERY, L.J.—

"Much contention has been raised whether, when applying s. 16, we are concerned to see whether the debt has been deferred, or whether all that has happened has been to defer the payment of the debt. This court considers that the distinction drawn between deferment of the debt and deferment of payment of the debt is a misleading and unsatisfactory one. In the context of a debt, the only feature of the transaction which involves time is the time for performance, the time at which the debt is to be paid. We are unable to assist ourselves in the elucidation of this problem by trying to draw distinctions between deferring a debt as opposed to deferring payment. It is, we think, in the end, a question of whether payment has been deferred to which the section is directed, and to which our decision in turn must apply . . .

An extreme view, as I have said, in favour of the Crown in this case, and one supported by counsel for the Crown in his argument, is that if the result of the giving of this cheque were to suspend the landlord's remedy for recovery of the debt whilst the cheque was in the process of being presented and returned, this would be a sufficient deferment of the debt to justify the conviction in the court below. As I have said, the facts of this case would not have involved the appellant in criminal responsibility before 1968, and this court does not think that the mere fact that the creditor's remedies at law are suspended in the manner and for a period such as is suggested here, can amount to a deferment of payment of the debt, or deferment of the debt, if it comes to that, within the meaning of the section.

In our judgment, dealing with antecedent debts (and I emphasise that we are dealing only with debts antecedent to the alleged deception) we think that the Crown has got to prove two essentials. In reaching this conclusion, we are influenced by the fact that s. 16 is concerned primarily with the advantage obtained by an accused and not with the detriment to the victim. The phraseology of the section makes that perfectly clear, and looking at the section as a whole and confining ourselves to antecedent debts, the two matters in our judgment which the Crown has to prove are these. First they must show that the accused practised a deception with the intention of inducing the creditor to refrain from requiring payment on the due date. The whole basis of the offence is deception and dishonesty. There must therefore be a deception by the accused, and we think that it must be a deception which is intended to induce the creditor to refrain from enforcing the payment of the debt on its due date. Secondly, it must be shown that the deception was effective, in other words it must be shown that the deception has caused the creditor to refrain from requiring payment on the date when the debt was originally due . . .

We find it impossible to say in this case that as a matter of cause and effect the deception caused Mr. Manek to decide to refrain from pressing for payment. Accordingly it seems to us that the second requirement of the offence is not present, and that in the result this conviction must be quashed."

APPEAL ALLOWED.

Comment on R. v. Waterfall, R. v. Page and R. v. Locker.

According to Professor J. C. Smith[1], (1) *R.* v. *Waterfall* was a case in which, in consequence of deception, a debt was deferred rather than evaded and the accused should have been charged accordingly; (2) *R.* v. *Page* and *R.* v. *Locker* are irreconcilable because in each instance the victim accepted a cheque in payment of a present debt. As to (1) it may be argued that, when a person obtains credit without intending to pay, a debt for which he makes himself liable is both evaded and deferred and the accused may be charged under either head; the victim would never have allowed the debt to come into existence had he known of the debtor's state of mind. As to (2) it may perhaps be argued that *R.* v. *Page* was a case in which the cheque was given as a means of obtaining credit so that the payment of a debt for which the accused made himself liable was evaded whereas, in *R.* v. *Locker*, the question was whether the payment of an antecedent debt had been deferred in consequence of the giving of the cheque. An affirmative answer would have meant that everyone who pays a debt for which he is already liable with a " dud " cheque would commit a criminal offence. The case is accordingly of some general academic interest because many would probably have considered such a result to be an undue extension of the sphere of the criminal law, the additional civil remedy acquired by the creditor being sufficient. In *R.* v. *Turner* (1973), *Times,* 30 March the Court of Appeal considered itself bound by Locker and quashed a conviction for giving a worthless cheque in respect of a liability for painting and decorating where the creditor was not induced by deception

[1] *The Law of Theft,* 2nd Edn., paras. 265–6.

to accept the cheque instead of cash, but gave leave to appeal to the House of Lords.

Whatever the outcome arguments about the true construction of s. 16(2) of the Theft Act, 1968, are liable to be rather pedantic on account of the ineptitude of its drafting. Happily they may prove to be comparatively short-lived because the subject was referred to the Criminal Law Revision Committee in August 1972.

R. v. GILKS

[1972] 3 All E.R. 280

A punter who is overpaid winnings in consequence of a bookmaker's mistake of which he is aware is guilty of theft, assuming that he acted dishonestly; but the case does not come within s. 5(4) *of the Theft Act,* 1968[1], *because " obligation " in that subsection means legal obligation.*

Facts.

Gilks placed bets with a firm of bookmakers in a betting shop. On the day in question his winnings amount to £10.62 but the firm's acting manager mistakenly paid him a further £106.63, apparently because he thought that a bet made by Gilks on Fighting Scot, an unplaced horse in one of the day's races, had been made on Fighting Taffy, the winner. Gilks was aware of the overpayment at the time he received it, but refused to repay the money on the ground that bookmakers are a race apart and it was " Ladbrokes' hard lines ".

Gilks was charged with and convicted of theft of £106.63. The trial judge held that the money belonged to the firm of bookmakers under s. 5(1) of the Theft Act at the time Gilks received it, but he also held that, if he was wrong, the case was covered by s. 5(4). On the question of dishonesty, the trial judge told the jury that the test was whether the defendant believed that, when dealing with a bookmaker, " if he makes a mistake you can take the money and keep it, and there is nothing dishonest about it ".

Gilks unsuccessfully appealed to the Court of Appeal.

---

[1] P. 268, *supra*.

Extracts from the Judgment of the Court of Appeal.

CAIRNS, L.J.—

"The subsection [s. 5(4)] introduced a new principle into the law of theft but long before it was enacted it was held in *R.* v. *Middleton*[1], that where a person was paid by mistake (in that case by a post office clerk) a sum in excess of that properly payable, the person who accepted the overpayment with knowledge of the excess was guilty of theft. Counsel for the appellant seeks to distinguish the present case from that one on the basis that in *R.* v. *Middleton*[1] the depositor was entitled to withdraw 10s from his Post Office Savings Bank account and the clerk made a mistake in thinking he was entitled to withdraw more than £8, whereas in the present case there was no mistake about the appellant's rights—whether his horse won or lost he had no legal right to payment. In our view this argument is fallacious. A bookmaker who pays out money in the belief that a certain horse has won, and who certainly would not have made the payment but for that belief, is paying by mistake just as much as the Post Office clerk in *R.* v. *Middleton*[1].

The gap in the law which s. 5(4) was designed to fill was, as the deputy chairman rightly held, that which is illustrated by the case of *Moynes* v. *Coopper*[2]. There a workman received a paypacket containing £7 more than was due to him but did not become aware of the overpayment till he opened the envelope some time later. He then kept the £7. This was held not to be theft because there was no *animus furandi* at the moment of taking, and *R.* v. *Middleton*[1] was distinguished on that ground. It was observed[3] that the law as laid down in *R.* v. *Middleton*[1] was reproduced and enacted in s. 1(2) (i) of the Larceny Act, 1916. It would be strange indeed if s. 5(4) of the 1968 Act, which was designed to bring within the net of theft a type of dishonest behaviour which escaped before, were to be held to have created a loophole for another type of dishonest behaviour which was always within the net.

An alternative ground on which the deputy chairman held that the money should be regarded as belonging to Ladbrokes was that 'obligation' in s. 5(4) meant an obligation whether a legal one or not. In the opinion of this court that was an incorrect ruling. In a criminal statute, where a

---

[1] (1873) L.R. 2 C.C.R. 38.

[2] [1956] 1 Q.B. 439; [1956] 1 All E.R. 450.

[3] [1956] 1 Q.B. at p. 445; [1956] 1 All E.R. at p. 452.

person's criminal liability is made dependent on his having an obligation, it would be quite wrong to construe that word so as to cover a moral or social obligation as distinct from a legal one . . .

On the face of it the appellant's conduct was dishonest; the only possible basis on which the jury could find that the prosecution had not established dishonesty would be if they thought it possible that the appellant did have the belief which he claimed to have . . .

It is contended that the jury may have understood this direction to mean that the appellant would be acting dishonestly unless (a) he believed he had the right to take the money and keep it and (b) he believed there was nothing dishonest about that conduct. It is said that the jury may have thought that the appellant's state of mind was 'I believe that in law I am entitled to take from my bookmaker anything he is foolish enough to pay me, though of course I know that it would be dishonest to do so', and he pointed that under s.1(1) this would entitle him to be acquitted whereas the direction might be taken to mean that he would be guilty.

In our opinion this is too refined an argument. We think it is clear that in the context the word 'and' meant 'and therefore' or 'and so' and the jury would understand it in that way."

APPEAL DISMISSED.

Comment on R. v. Gilks.

To constitute theft at common law and under the Larceny Act, 1916, it was essential that there should have been a taking of possession by the accused without the consent of the owner. If goods or money were delivered by A., the owner, to B., the accused, with the intention that B. should become their owner, B. was not guilty of theft (although he might have been guilty of obtaining by false pretences); but, if A. were mistaken as to the identity of B. (believing him to be C. for example), or as to the identity of the thing transferred (believing peas to be beans for example), it was held, rather artificially, that B.'s reception of the goods amount to a constructive taking.

In *R.* v. *Middleton*[1] it was held in the majority judgment of the Court for Crown Cases Reserved that the post office clerk either made a mistake as to Middleton's identity (believing him to

---

[1] (1873) L.R. 2 C.C.R. 38; cited in the above judgment.

be the depositor who had given notice of withdrawal of the larger sum), or else made a mistake as to the identity of the debt which he was discharging. In *Moynes* v. *Coopper*[1] on the other hand, the wages clerk made no mistake as to identity; his mistake was that a full week's wages was due to Coopper, being unaware of the fact that Coopper had already received the greater part of this sum as an advance payment. Coopper did not become aware of the overpayment for some time after he received it, and the implication of Lord GODDARD'S judgment in the Divisional Court, accepted by the Court of Appeal in *R.* v. *Gilks,* was that Coopper would have been guilty of theft had he been aware of the clerk's mistake on receipt of the pay envelope. It is, however, by no means clear that this would have been so for, there being no mistake as to identity, it is arguable that both ownership and possession of the coins would have passed to Coopper as they certainly would have passed if the clerk's mistake with regard to the advance had been induced by Coopper's false pretence[2]. It is just arguable that the acting manager made a mistake as to the identity of the bet he was paying in Gilks's case, but the artificiality of the argument is such as to make it most unconvincing.

It is regrettable that the over subtle distinctions of the old law of theft should be called in aid in the construction of the Theft Act, 1968. In this context the question is whether B. can be said to have appropriated goods or money belonging to A. when A. hands them to him with the intention that he should become their owner under a mistake as to the amount due, a mistake of which B. was aware at the time of the handing-over. Normally s. 5(4) will enable an affirmative answer to be given; but, even when, as in *Gilks's* case, this subsection is held to be inapplicable, an affirmative answer can be given provided a man can be said to assume the rights of an owner when he dishonestly allows ownership to be transferred to him.

A point about *Gilks's* case which is perhaps only surprising at first sight is that it is authority for the proposition that a person can act dishonestly although he does precisely what the law allows him to do, *viz.,* accept and retain an overpayment on a wagering transaction[3].

R. v. *Gilks* was inserted at the end of this section, instead of being placed among the cases on theft because it was thought possible that an appeal would go to the House of Lords, but, somewhat surprisingly, the House refused leave to appeal. In the end, the true view may prove to be that *Morgan* v. *Ashcroft* was

---

[1] [1956] 1 All E.R. 450; cited in the above judgment.
[2] 72 Law Quarterly Review 181.
[3] *Morgan* v. *Ashcroft,* [1938] 1 K.B. 49; [1937] 3 All E.R. 92.

wrongly decided, in which event s. 5(4) of the Theft Act, 1968 would clearly apply to the facts of *Gilks*'s case.

In *Morgan* v. *Ashcroft* it was held that a bookmaker cannot sue civilly for money paid under a mistake of fact when he has overpaid one of his clients. The underlying principles that the court will not take account of wagering transactions and that, in order to support a claim for money paid under a mistake of fact, the mistake must be such that, had the facts been as supposed, there would have been a legal obligation to make the payment, are certainly ones which should some day be reviewed by the House of Lords.

SECTION 8

PUBLIC ORDER

BEATTY v. GILLBANKS

(1882), 9 Q. B. D. 308

An assembly formed for a lawful purpose does not constitute an unlawful assembly merely because to the knowledge of its organisers it will be opposed.

Facts.

The Salvation Army held regular processions through the streets of Weston-super-Mare. Another body of persons called the Skeleton Army was organised to impede its passage. Clashes took place and breaches of the peace occurred. Warning was given by the police and the magistrates to the leaders of the Salvation Army but they nevertheless held a procession and further breaches of the peace occurred. The leaders were then summoned at petty sessions for holding an unlawful assembly; they were ordered to be bound over and appealed successfully by way of case stated to the Queen's Bench Division.

Extracts from the Judgments of the Divisional Court of the Queen's Bench Division.

FIELD, J.—

"The appellants complain that in consequence of this assembly they have been found guilty of a crime of which there is no reasonable evidence that they have been guilty. The charge against them is, that they unlawfully and tumultuously assembled, with others, to the disturbance of the public peace and against the peace of the Queen. Before they can be convicted it must be shewn that this offence has been committed. There is no doubt that they and with them others assembled together in great numbers, but such an assembly to be unlawful must be tumultuous and against the peace. As far as these appellants are concerned there was nothing in their conduct when they were assembled together which was either tumultuous or against the peace. But it is said, that the conduct pursued by them on this occasion was such, as on several previous occasions, had produced riots and disturbance of the peace and terror to the inhabitants, and that the appellants knowing when they assembled together that such consequences would again arise are liable to this charge.

Now I entirely concede that every one must be taken to intend the natural consequences of his own acts, and it is clear to me that if this disturbance of the peace was the natural consequence of acts of the appellants they would be liable, and the justices would have been right in binding them over. But the evidence set forth in the case does not support this contention; on the contrary, it shews that the disturbances were caused by other people antagonistic to the appellants, and that no acts of violence were committed by them. . . .

What has happened here is that an unlawful organization has assumed to itself the right to prevent the appellants and others from lawfully assembling together, and the finding of the justices amounts to this, that a man may be convicted for doing a lawful act if he knows that his doing it may cause another to do an unlawful act. There is no authority for such a proposition, and the question of the justices whether the facts stated in the case constituted the offence charged in the information must therefore be answered in the negative."

APPEAL ALLOWED.

WISE v. DUNNING

[1902] 1 K. B. 167

One who knowingly uses inflammatory language may be taken to intend the natural consequences of his acts.

Facts.

The appellant was a Protestant lecturer who held meetings in Liverpool. At these meetings he used language and gestures which were insulting to Catholics, and some breaches of the peace occurred. It was the declared intention of the appellant to hold further meetings, and he was brought before the magistrate by the police and bound over to keep the peace. A local Act of Parliament prohibited the use of insulting words in the streets of Liverpool whereby a breach of the peace might be occasioned. The appellant had not broken the peace himself, nor had he incited anyone else to do so, and he appealed by way of case stated to the Divisional Court of the King's Bench Division.

Extract from the Judgment of the King's Bench Divisional Court.

DARLING, J.—

"... Counsel for the appellant contended that the natural consequence must be taken to be the legal acts which are a consequence. I do not think so. The natural consequence of such conduct is illegality. I think that the natural consequence of this 'crusader's' eloquence has been to produce illegal acts, and that from his acts and conduct circumstances have arisen which justified the magistrate in binding him over to keep the peace and be of good behaviour. In the judgment of O'BRIEN, C.J. in *R.* v. *Justices of Londonderry*[1] there is this passage: 'Now I wish to make the ground of my judgment clear, and carefully to guard against being misunderstood. I am perfectly satisfied that the magistrates did not make the order which is impugned by reason of there having been, or there being likely to be, any obstruction of the highway, and that the true view of what took place is that the defendants were bound over in respect of an apprehended breach of the peace; and, in my opinion, there was no evidence to warrant that apprehension.' It is clear that, if there had been evidence to warrant that apprehension, the Chief Justice would have held the magistrates' decision in that case to be right. It is said that *Beatty* v. *Gillbanks*[2] is in conflict with that decision. I am not sure that it is. I am inclined to think that ... the whole question is one of fact and evidence. But I do not hesitate to say that, if there be a conflict between these two cases, I prefer the law as it is laid down in *R.* v. *Justices of Londonderry.*[3] If that be a right statement of the law, as I think it is, the magistrate was perfectly justified in coming to the con-

---

[1] (1891), 28 L. R. Ir. 440, at p. 447.
[2] (1882), 9 Q. B. D. 308; p. 293, *supra*.
[3] (1891), 28 L. R. Ir. 440.

clusion he did come to in this case, even without taking into consideration the question of the local Act of Parliament to which we were referred.

For these reasons I am of opinion that the magistrate's order was right."

CONVICTION AFFIRMED.

DUNCAN v. JONES

[1936] 1 K. B. 218

It is the duty of the police to prevent breaches of the peace and in the discharge of that duty they may forbid the holding of a meeting if they reasonably apprehend a breach of the peace although there may be nothing unlawful in the object of the meeting. A person who nevertheless proceeds with the holding of the meeting is guilty of obstructing the police in the execution of their duty.

Facts.

About thirty people, including Mrs. Duncan, collected near an unemployed training centre with a view to holding a meeting which had been advertised. About two months previously a similar meeting addressed by Mrs. Duncan had been held in the same place and had been followed by a disturbance inside the training centre. It was found as a fact that the police reasonably apprehended a breach of the peace and they forbade Mrs. Duncan to hold the meeting. She said " I'm going to hold it," stepped on to the box and started to address the people, whereupon she was arrested. She was convicted of obstructing P.C. Jones in the execution of his duties[1]; she unsuccessfully appealed to quarter sessions and thence by way of case stated to the King's Bench Division.

---

[1] This offence was created by s. 2 of the Prevention of Crime Act, 1885, which punished those who were guilty of " resisting or wilfully obstructing " peace officers and constables in the execution of their duty. The relevant statute is now s. 51(3) of the Police Act, 1964: " Any person who resists or wilfully obstructs a constable in the execution of his duty " shall be guilty, etc.

Extracts from the judgments of the Divisional Court of the King's Bench Division.

LORD HEWART, C.J.—

"... The right of assembly, as Professor Dicey puts it,[1] is nothing more than a view taken by the Court of the individual liberty of the subject. If I thought that the present case raised a question which has been held in suspense by more than one writer on constitutional law—namely, whether an assembly can properly be held to be unlawful merely because the holding of it is expected to give rise to a breach of the peace on the part of persons opposed to those who are holding the meeting—I should wish to hear much more argument before I expressed an opinion. This case, however, does not even touch that important question. . . .

The case stated which we have before us indicates clearly a causal connection between the meeting of May, 1933, and the disturbance which occurred after it—that the disturbance was not only post the meeting but was also propter the meeting. In my view, the deputy-chairman was entitled to come to the conclusion to which he came on the facts which he found and to hold that the conviction of the appellant for wilfully obstructing the respondent when in the execution of his duty was right. This appeal should, therefore, be dismissed."

HUMPHREYS, J.—

"I agree. I regard this as a plain case. It has nothing to do with the law of unlawful assembly. No charge of that sort was even suggested against the appellant. The sole question raised by the case is whether the respondent, who was admittedly obstructed, was so obstructed when in the execution of his duty.

It does not require authority to emphasize the statement that it is the duty of a police officer to prevent apprehended breaches of the peace. Here it is found as a fact that the respondent reasonably apprehended a breach of the peace. It then, as is rightly expressed in the case, became his duty to prevent anything which in his view would cause that breach of the peace. While he was taking steps so to do he was wilfully obstructed by the appellant. I can conceive no clearer case within the statutes than that."

APPEAL DISMISSED.

---

[1] Dicey's *Law of the Constitution*, 8th ed., p. 499.

THOMAS v. SAWKINS

[1935] 2 K. B. 249

A police officer is entitled to attend and remain at a public meeting held on private premises if he reasonably apprehends that a breach of the peace is likely to occur.

Facts.

The respondent, a police officer, was prosecuted before the justices for a common assault under s. 42 of the Offences against the Person Act, 1861. The appellant, the prosecutor, was the convener of a meeting to protest against the Incitement to Disaffection Bill which was then before Parliament, and to advocate the removal of the chief of the County Constabulary. The meeting was held on private premises, and the public were invited to attend without charge. The respondent attended with another police officer, and they both refused to leave on being requested to do so by the appellant who laid his hand on the other police officer. The respondent removed the appellant's hand, saying that he would not have his superior officer molested. Both officers remained at the meeting where no breach of the peace was committed. The magistrates acquitted the respondent, but stated a case for the Divisional Court who were of opinion that the decision of the Magistrates was correct.

Extracts from the Judgment of the Divisional Court.

LORD HEWART, C.J.—

" . . . It is said . . . in the books no case is to be found which goes the length of deciding, that, where an offence is expected to be committed, as distinct from the case of an offence being or having been committed, there is any right in the police to enter on private premises and to remain there against the will of those who, as hirers or otherwise, are for the time being in possession of the premises. When, however, I look at the passages which have been cited from Blackstone's *Commentaries*, vol. 1, p. 356, and from the judgments in *Humphries* v. *Connor*[1] and *O'Kelly* v. *Harvey*[2] and certain

---

[1] (1864), 17 Ir. C. L. R. 1.
[2] (1883), 14 L. R. Ir. 105.

observations of AVORY, J. in *Lansbury* v. *Riley*,[1] I think that there is quite sufficient ground for the proposition that it is part of the preventive power, and, therefore, part of the preventive duty, of the police, in cases where there are such reasonable grounds of apprehension as the Justices have found here, to enter and remain on private premises. It goes without saying that the powers and duties of the police are directed, not to the interests of the police, but to the protection and welfare of the public.

It was urged in one part of the argument of Sir Stafford Cripps (counsel for the appellant) that what the police did here amounted to a trespass. It seems somewhat remarkable to speak of trespass when members of the public who happen to be police officers attend, after a public invitation, a public meeting which is to discuss as one part of its business the dismissal of the chief constable of the county. It is elementary that a good defence to an action for trespass is to show that the act complained of was done by authority of law, or by leave and licence.

I am not at all prepared to accept the doctrine that it is only where an offence has been, or is being, committed, that the police are entitled to enter and remain on private premises. On the contrary, it seems to me that a police officer has *ex virtute officii* full right so to act when he has reasonable ground for believing that an offence is imminent or is likely to be committed."

APPEAL DISMISSED.

HINCHCLIFFE v. SHELDON

[1955] 3 All E. R. 406

A person is guilty of obstructing the police under s. 2 *of the Prevention of Crime Act*, 1885, *if he makes it more difficult for the police to carry out their duty.*[2]

Facts.

The accused, the son of the licensee of a public house, found the police outside the house after hours. As the police were about to enter, the appellant shouted to his parents that the police were there with the result that the police were not

---

[1] [1914] 3 K. B. 229, at p. 236–7.
[2] Now s. 51 of the Police Act, 1964.

admitted to the house for some little time. When the police entered the house they found no evidence that people had been drinking after hours, but suspected that this had been the case. The accused was convicted of obstructing the police in the course of their duty and the Magistrates stated a case for the opinion of the Divisional Court. That court was of opinion the conviction was correct.

Extract from the Judgment of the Divisional Court.

LORD GODDARD, C.J.—

"... The appellant relies principally on *Bastable* v. *Little*,[1] a case in the early days of motoring, where it was held that it was not an offence for a person to say to motorists: 'Look out, you are just entering a police trap', or words to that effect, because there was no evidence in that case that the motorists were committing an offence, and there was no reason to say, as a matter of definite conclusion, that by the time they got to the police trap they would be committing an offence. That case, however, was followed three years later by *Betts* v. *Stevens*,[2] in which it was decided that directly it was shown that an offence was being committed by a motorist in that he was travelling more than twenty miles an hour when an Automobile Association scout gave him warning, then the scout was interfering with the police. The appellant, accordingly, submitted that he could not be convicted unless it was shown that an offence was being committed, but that is to overlook s. 151 (1) of the Licensing Act, 1953. There is no such provision as that in the Road Traffic Acts. Section 151 (1) gives the police the right to enter licensed premises, whether an offence has been committed or not. They can go in to see whether it is likely that an offence will be committed. If they are detained from going in, that does obstruct them in the execution of their duty, because it gives the licensee, if he is committing an offence, the opportunity to get everything out of the way."

CONVICTION AFFIRMED.

---

[1] [1907] 1 K. B. 59.
[2] [1910] 1 K. B. 1.

RICE v. CONNOLLY

[1966] 2 All E. R. 649

There is in general no legal duty to answer questions by the police, and failure to do so does not constitute wilful obstruction of a police officer in the execution of his duty.

Facts.

A police officer observed Rice in suspicious circumstances in the early hours of the morning in a neighbourhood in which there had been a number of breakings during the night. Rice refused to answer questions or to accompany the police officer to the police station for identification. He said: "If you want me you had better arrest me." He was arrested, but it was not suggested that he was connected with any of the breakings, and he was released.

Rice was charged with obstructing the police officer in the execution of his duty and convicted by the magistrates. He unsuccessfully appealed to Quarter Sessions, and then appealed successfully by way of case stated to the Divisional Court.

Extracts from the Judgment of the Divisional Court.

LORD PARKER, C.J.—

"What the prosecution have to prove is that there was an obstructing of a constable, that the constable was at the time acting in the execution of his duty, and that the person obstructing did so wilfully. To carry the matter a little further, it is in my view clear that to 'obstruct' in s. **51**(3) is to do any act which makes it more difficult for the police to carry out their duty. That description of obstructing I take from the case of *Hinchcliffe* v. *Sheldon*.[1] It is also in my judgment clear that it is part of the obligations and duties of a police constable to take all steps which appear to him necessary for keeping the peace, for preventing crime or for protecting property from criminal injury. There is no exhaustive definition of the powers and obligations of the police, but they are at least those, and they would further include the duty to detect crime and to bring an offender to justice.

---

1 [1955] **3** All E. R. **406**, at p. **408**; p. 299 *supra*.

It is quite clear that the appellant was making it more difficult for the police to carry out their duties, and that the police at the time and throughout were acting in accordance with their duties. The only remaining element of the alleged offence, and the one on which in my judgment this case depends, is whether the obstructing of which the appellant was guilty was a wilful obstruction. " Wilful " in this context in my judgment means not only ' intentional ' but also connotes something which is done without lawful excuse, and that indeed is conceded by counsel who appears for the prosecution in this case. Accordingly, the sole question here is whether the appellant had a lawful excuse for refusing to answer the questions put to him. In my judgment he had. It seems to me quite clear that though every citizen has a moral duty or, if you like, a social duty to assist the police, there is no legal duty to that effect, and indeed the whole basis of the common law is that right of the individual to refuse to answer questions put to him by persons in authority, and a refusal to accompany those in authority to any particular place, short of course, of arrest. Counsel for the respondent has pointed out that it is undoubtedly an obstruction, and has been so held, for a person questioned by the police to tell a ' cock-and-bull ' story, to put the police off by giving them false information, and I think he would say: well, what is the real distinction, it is very little away from giving false information to giving no information at all; if that does in fact make it more difficult for the police to carry out their duties then there is a wilful obstruction. In my judgment there is all the difference in the world between deliberately telling a false story, something which on no view a citizen has a right to do, and preserving silence or refusing to answer, something which he has every right to do."

Appeal Allowed.

INGLETON v. DIBBLE

[1972] 1 All E.R. 275

Where a positive act is alleged to constitute a wilful obstruction of the police contrary to s. 51(3) *of the Police Act,* 1964, *it need not be an act which is unlawful independently of its tendency to obstruct the police.*

Facts.

Dibble was charged with and convicted by the Magistrates of obstructing Police Constable Tully in the execution of his duty. P.C. Tully had stopped Dibble who was driving a car without lights at night. On smelling alcohol, P.C. Tully requested Dibble to take a breath test under the Road Safety Act, 1967. Dibble said that only five minutes had elapsed since he had had his last drink. It was accordingly agreed that a further quarter of an hour had to elapse before the test could be administered. During this time Dibble, when walking with P. C. Tully towards his brother's house, encountered a man who had been a passenger in his car and who was carrying a bottle of whisky. Dibble took the bottle and drank some of the whisky with the intention of rendering a valid breath test impossible.

Dibble appealed to quarter sessions where the Recorder held that there was no case for him to answer. The prosecutor successfully appealed to the Divisional Court.

Extracts from the Judgments of the Divisional Court.

BRIDGE, J.—

> " For my part I would draw a clear distinction between a refusal to act, on the one hand, and the doing of some positive act on the other. In a case, as in *Rice* v. *Connolly*[1], where the obstruction alleged consists of a refusal by the defendant to do the act which the police constable has asked him to do—to give information, it might be, or to give assistance to the police constable—one can see readily the soundness of the principle, if I may say so with respect, applied in *Rice* v. *Connolly*, that such a refusal to act cannot amount to a wilful obstruction under s. 51 unless the law imposes on the person concerned some obligation in the circumstances to act in the manner requested by the police officer.
>
> On the other hand, I can see no basis in principle or in any authority which has been cited for saying that where the obstruction consists of a positive act, it must be unlawful independently of its operation as an obstruction of the police constable under s. 51 (3) of the Police Act, 1964. If the act relied on as an obstruction had to be shown to be an offence independently of its effect as an obstruction, it is difficult to

---

[1] [1966] 2 Q.B. 414; [1966] 2 All E.R. 649, p. 301, *supra*.

see what use there would be in the provisions of s. 51(3) of the 1964 Act.

In my judgment the act of the respondent in drinking the whisky when he did with the object and effect of frustrating the procedure under sections 2 and 3 of the Road Safety Act, 1967, clearly was a wilful obstruction of P.C. Tully."

APPEAL ALLOWED.

R. v. SANDBACH, EX PARTE WILLIAMS

[1935] 2 K. B. 192

Justices have a general discretionary power to bind a person over to keep the peace where there is a reasonable apprehension that he will commit a breach of the peace or that he will do something against the law.

Facts.

Williams was convicted by a metropolitan magistrate of obstructing the police in that he gave warning to a street bookmaker of the approach of the police. Evidence was given of previous convictions and that a fine was no deterrent. The magistrate then ordered him to enter into a recognizance in the sum of £20, with two sureties of £10 each, or in default to go to prison for two months. Williams applied unsuccessfully to the King's Bench Division for a rule for a *certiorari* to quash the order on the ground that there was no jurisdiction to make it.

Extracts from the Judgments of the Divisional Court of the King's Bench Division.

LORD HEWART, C.J.—

" I am clearly of the opinion that this rule ought to be discharged. There is no need to reiterate the facts which have been put before the Court. This case is covered in all material respects by *Lansbury* v. *Riley*,[1] and especially by the judgment of AVORY, J.

Counsel who argued in support of the rule asks, if this action by the magistrate be permissible, in what way can that power be limited? The answer I give is that the matter is discretionary and the limits are to be found in discretion. We should assume that judicial powers, when given, will in all cases be exercised properly, as they have been in this case."

---

[1] [1914] 3 K. B. 229.

HUMPHREYS, J.—

"I also agree. Mr. Comyns Carr has argued that the power of a magistrate to order a person to enter into recognizances to find sureties to be of good behaviour is confined to cases where there is apprehension of a breach of the peace in the sense of violence towards some person. In my view it is quite impossible to accept that argument without differing from and refusing to agree with a very important chapter in Blackstone.

AVORY, J., has referred to some words by that great author in vol. iv, chapter 18. I only desire to read a few more words. After dealing with such matters as the nature of this security, how it may be demanded and how it may be discharged and when it is grantable, on p. 256, vol. iv, the learned author says: 'The other species of recognizance with sureties, is for the *good abearance* or *good behaviour*. This includes security for the peace, and somewhat more; we will therefore examine it in the same manner as the other. First then, the justices are empowered by the statute 34 Edw. III, c. I, to bind over to the good behaviour towards the king and his people, all them *that be not of good fame*, wherever they be found; to the intent that the people be not troubled nor endamaged, nor the peace diminished, nor merchants and others, passing by the highways of the realm, be disturbed nor put in the peril which may happen by such offenders. Under the general words of this expression, *that be not of good fame*, it is holden that a man may be bound to his good behaviour for causes of scandal, *contra bonos mores*, as well as *contra pacem*.'

I cannot think that the expression against the peace or apprehension of a breach of the peace is confined to a breach or apprehension of a breach of that part of the law which provides that persons shall not commit assaults, and I think that the distinction which is there drawn by Blackstone is the distinction between such matters as are contrary to morality (*contra bonos mores*) and such matters as are contrary to law (*contra pacem*). Blackstone says in terms that a magistrate may properly bind over a person in any case where it is apprehended that it is likely he will commit a breach of the peace or that he will do something against the law. That in my judgment is the law, and it is too late, in 1935, to attempt to show that Blackstone was wrong. . . ."

APPLICATION REFUSED.

SHELDON v. BROMFIELD JUSTICES
[1964] 2 All E. R. 131

It is contrary to natural justice for magistrates to bind a witness over without warning or giving him an opportunity to know what was passing in their minds.

Facts.

The appellants gave evidence for the prosecution on a charge of assault which was dismissed. The justices who heard the charge bound the witnesses over to keep the peace without warning or giving them an opportunity to be heard. The appellants successfully appealed to the Divisional Court by way of case stated.

Extracts from the Judgment of the Divisional Court.

LORD PARKER, C.J.—

" It is well known that the justices have power pursuant to their commission or pursuant to the Justices of the Peace Act, 1361, to bind over all persons brought before them. It is a very important jurisdiction and is in the nature of preventive justice. No offence need be proven at all. There has been some argument before this court as to when it can be said that a person is brought before, or is before, justices, whether the jurisdiction can only be invoked if complaint has been made, and matters of that sort. For my part, I do not want to throw any doubt whatsoever on the jurisdiction of justices to bind over not only the defendant but also the complainant, and, indeed, witnesses who are before them. Indeed, as I understand it, the decision of the court in *R.* v. *Wilkins*,[1] which is binding on this court, makes it clear that at any rate a complainant can be bound over. In that case, Lord ALVERSTONE, C.J., said this:

' It is contended on behalf of (the complainant) that the order so far as regards him is bad. It is said in the first place that the justices had no power to order him to be bound over, because no formal charge, and, indeed, no charge of any kind, had been made against him. In my opinion, when a person appears before justices, although his appearance is in the capacity of complainant, and facts are proved to the satisfaction of the justices which would justify them in

---

[1] [1907] 2 K. B. 380.

binding him over to keep the peace, the justices have jurisdiction to make an order to that effect, although no formal proceedings by way of information or otherwise have been instituted against the person.' It may be that in some future case it will be necessary to consider the width of the statement there by Lord ALVERSTONE, C.J., but, as I have said, for my part I do not wish to say anything in the present case which will suggest any limitation on the power of the justices.

What have concerned the court however, are the two findings that the appellants were not accorded the opportunity of being heard in their own defence, and that they had not been warned of what was passing through the court's mind.

... It seems to me to be elementary justice that particularly a mere witness before justices should at any rate be told what is passing through the justices' minds, and should have an opportunity of dealing with it. Indeed, as it seems to me, that was dealt with also by Lord ALVERSTONE, C.J., in *Wilkins'* case in these terms. He goes on after the passage which I have just read:

'Justices have a general power under their commission to bind over any person if it appears that that person has been guilty of violent conduct tending to a breach of peace, even though there is no proof of a threat towards any particular person, provided, of course, that the person bound over has had a reasonable opportunity of knowing the nature of the charge brought against him and of making his answer to it.' ...

In my judgment the respondent justices can be said here to have acted contrary to natural justice, and, accordingly, for my part I would allow this appeal and quash the binding over order."

APPEAL ALLOWED.

FIELD v. METROPOLITAN POLICE RECEIVER

[1907] 2 K. B. 853

A person whose property is damaged in a riot may sue for compensation out of police funds under the Riot (Damages) Act, 1886. *To constitute a riot five elements are necessary;* 1, *a number of persons not less than three*; 2, *a common purpose;* 3, *execution or inception of common purpose;* 4, *intent on the part of the persons engaged to assist each other by force, if necessary;* 5, *force or violence displayed so as to alarm at least one person of reasonable firmness and courage.*

Facts.

A number of youths exceeding three gathered together and behaved rowdily: some of them stood with their backs to a wall while others ran up against it with the result that part of the wall collapsed. The caretaker of the adjoining building came out and the youths dispersed. It was held on appeal from the County Court that there was no evidence of an intention to assist each other by force nor of force or violence displayed so as to alarm any person of reasonable firmness and courage[1] and so there was no riot.

Extracts from the Judgment of the Divisional Court of the King's Bench Division read by:

PHILLIMORE, J.—

" . . . Riot is a crime, a misdemeanour at common law. The writer who appears to require the fewest elements to constitute this crime, and who, therefore, is the strongest authority in favour of the plaintiffs, is Lord Coke. He says that riot is where three or more do any unlawful act, as to beat any man, or to hunt in his park, or take possession of another man's land, or cut or destroy his corn, etc. This would seem to imply that any assault or malicious injury to property done by three or more is a riot. It is to be observed, however, that if this is Lord Coke's meaning, he stands alone; also that the whole chapter, which embraces four or five kinds of crime, is short and sketchy, and that his definition of rout is an illogical one, derived, as we see by reference to Brooke, from the reading of Sergeant Marrow in the Inner Temple on the Statute of Peace, a reading very properly criticized by Brooke. Blackstone follows Coke in his definition of rout—a definition which has been since abandoned by text writers, and he nearly follows Coke in his definition of riot; but he makes it plain that there must always be force or violence to constitute a riot. Hawkins requires that the rioters should have an intent mutually to assist one another against anyone who should oppose them in the execution of their enterprise, and should actually execute the same in a violent and turbulent manner to the terror of the people

[1] But see *R.* v. *Sharp and R.* v. *Johnson*, p. 312, *infra.*

(s. 1). A riot ought to be accompanied, he says, by some offer of violence either to the person of a man or to his possessions, as by beating him or forcing him to quit possession of his land or goods, etc. (s. 4); and there must be at least some such circumstances either of actual force or violence, or at least of an apparent tendency thereto, as are naturally apt to strike terror into the people (s. 5). Stephen says that an unlawful assembly must be (1) with intent to commit a crime by open force, or (2) with intent to carry out any common purpose in such a manner as to give firm and courageous persons reasonable ground to apprehend a breach of the peace, and a riot is an unlawful assembly which has actually begun to execute its purpose by a breach of the peace and to the terror of the public. In *R.* v. *Soley*[1] Lord HOLT, C.J., says: 'If I am writing a letter and three or more come hallooing and jogging me, is this a riot ? No; it ought to be *in terrorem populi.*' In *R.* v. *Langford,*[2] where five persons were indicted for riot for ejecting an old man out of a cottage which they claimed, and then demolishing it, the conviction was supported because such force was used as to terrify the old man. *Drake* v. *Footitt*[3] was the case of a violent election riot, where the only question was whether a felony had been committed. In *R.* v. *Cunninghame Graham*[4] CHARLES, J., largely relying upon the passages in Hawkins, instructed the jury that 'a riot is a disturbance of the peace by three persons at the least, who, with intent to help one another against any person who opposes them in the execution of some enterprise or other, actually execute that enterprise in a violent and turbulent manner to the alarm of the people.'

From these passages we deduce that there are five necessary elements of a riot (1) number of persons, three at least; (2) common purpose; (3) execution or inception of the common purpose; (4) an intent to help one another by force if necessary against any person who may oppose them in the execution of their common purpose; (5) force or violence not merely used in demolishing, but displayed in such a manner as to alarm at least one person of reasonable firmness and courage. In this case element No. 1 was present. As to elements Nos. 2 and 3, there was evidence upon which the learned Judge could have found their existence, though,

[1] (1707), 11 Mod. Rep. 100.
[2] (1842), Car. & M. 602.
[3] (1881), 7 Q. B. D. 201.
[4] (1888), 16 Cox C. C. 420.

as far as we can judge from the notes of the evidence and without seeing the witnesses, we think we should not have found the same way. But as to elements Nos. 4 and 5 there is no evidence. The youths ran away as soon as the single caretaker came forward; there is no reason to suppose that they would have resisted if he had come forward earlier and required them to desist. It is true that the caretaker's wife was frightened by the noise of the falling wall, but no one says that he was alarmed by the youths, though the witnesses may have been frightened by other youths on other occasions. Nor was the conduct of the youths such as would be calculated to alarm persons of reasonable firmness and courage. We cannot hold that there was a riot. The appeal must be allowed, and judgment must be entered for the defendant."

APPEAL ALLOWED.

FORD v. METROPOLITAN POLICE DISTRICT RECEIVER

[1921] 2 K. B. 344

Where there is evidence of at least one person being frightened and all the other elements of a riot as set out in Field's case[1] are present the court may find that there is a riot.

Facts.

On Peace night, 1919, rejoicings took place at Canning Town. A bonfire was lighted and to get fuel the crowd, which was in a good humour, broke into an empty house and stripped its woodwork. An action was brought for compensation under the Riot (Damages) Act, 1886, and a next door neighbour gave evidence that he did not interfere because he feared he would be killed if he did so. It was held that the necessary elements of a riot were present.

Extracts from the Judgment of the King's Bench Division.

BAILHACHE, J.—

The learned judge enumerated the first three elements of riot and continued:

[1] *Supra.*

" . . . Fourthly, an intent on the part of the above persons to help one another, by force if necessary, against any person who may oppose them in the execution of the common purpose. I think again that that is satisfied. These people went there with crowbars and pickaxes, and I think there is no doubt that anybody who had interfered with them would have been subjected to rough usage. Fifthly, there must be force or violence, not merely used in and about the common purpose, but displayed in such a manner as to alarm at least one person of reasonable firmness and courage.[1] The determination of this point has given me some trouble, and it is round this one of the elements necessary to constitute a riot that the discussion has most largely turned. The evidence is that of Mr. Whowell, who said that he saw the people coming and that he was afraid they would break into his premises, and that he went out and begged them not to do so. They did not do so, and I do not think they were ever minded to do so. Mr. Whowell said he did not like to interfere with these people injuring the plaintiff's house, because he thought he would have been killed if he had. This is probably an exaggeration, but at any rate, he was afraid. The question, to my mind, is whether that evidence is sufficient to establish the fifth element above mentioned. I have no reason to doubt that Mr. Whowell is a man of reasonable firmness and courage, and it seems to me that his evidence is sufficient. I do not think the fourth and fifth elements can be said to be absent because the people assembled go about the business in hand quietly if not interfered with. If that were so any number of persons might at any time assemble with the unlawful intent of demolishing another's house, and if nobody interfered with them it would be said that as they never threatened anybody what they did did not constitute a riot. That seems to me an impossible view to take, and it might be true of any riot that ever took place . . ."

JUDGMENT FOR PLAINTIFF.

---

[1] But see *R.* v. *Sharp and R.* v. *Johnson*, p. 312, *infra*.

R. v. SHARP AND R. v. JOHNSON
[1957] 1 Q. B. 552

(1) *In order that persons may be guilty of an affray it is not necessary for someone else to be put in fear.* (2) *Someone who is fighting in order to defend himself is not guilty of an affray.*

Facts.

A fight in the street between the two accused was watched by a large crowd. There was no evidence that anyone was put in fear, and each of the accused alleged that he was fighting in self-defence. The judge directed the jury that, to constitute an affray, it was not necessary that anyone should in fact be put in fear provided reasonable people might be frightened by the fight. The judge also directed the jury that it was unnecessary for them to consider whether either of the accused was fighting in self-defence. The accused were convicted and successfully appealed to the Court of Criminal Appeal who quashed the convictions on account of misdirection with regard to self-defence.

Extracts from the Judgment of the Court of Criminal Appeal.

LORD GODDARD, C.J.—

"... The wearing of unusual or dangerous weapons in public is only one species of affray and in our opinion it is open to a jury to find that the circumstances amount to an affray although no person is actually called to say he was put in terror. Just as the mere wearing of a sword in the days when this was a common accoutrement of the nobility and gentry would be no evidence of an affray while the carrying in public of a studded mace or battle axe might be, so if two lads indulge in a fight with fists no one would dignify that as an affray, whereas if they used broken bottles or knuckle-dusters and drew blood a jury might well find that it was, as a passer-by might be upset and frightened by such conduct. ... Indeed, we should have thought that there could be no doubt on this matter were it not for the decision in *Field* v. *Receiver of Metropolitan Police*,[1] where the Divisional

[1] [1907] 2 K. B. 853; p. 307, *supra*.

Court laid down what were the necessary elements to constitute a riot,[1] one of which [the fifth] was force or violence displayed so as to alarm at least one person of reasonable firmness and courage. From this it is deduced that evidence to that effect must be given, though not necessarily, we think, by calling a person to say: 'I was terrified'. It might be enough for a witness to say that persons appeared to be alarmed. Now it is true that affrays are usually classed along with unlawful assemblies, riots and routs as offences against the public peace, but we have only in this case to deal with an affray. The word 'riot' is a term of art and, contrary to popular belief, a riot may involve no noise or disturbance of the neighbours though there must be some force or violence. For instance, if three persons enter a shop and forcibly or by threats steal goods therein, technically they are guilty not only of larceny or robbery but also of riot: see *London and Lancashire Fire Insurance Co. Ltd.* v. *Bolands, Ltd.*[2] It may be that the fifth element referred to in *Field's* case[3] may require reconsideration at some future time, for if disturbances such as necessitated the passing of the Public Order Act, 1936, should occur again, or if there were a repetition of the Trafalgar Square riots which took place towards the end of the last century when most of the club windows in Pall Mall were smashed by an angry mob, it would seem superfluous if someone had to go into the witness-box and say that he or some passers-by felt or appeared afraid or apprehensive. We need give no final decision on this point so far as riots are concerned, but in our opinion there was in the present case evidence on which the jury could find that the appellants were guilty of an affray, and on that matter the recorder's direction was right. . . .

If two men are found fighting in a street one must be able to say that the other attacked him and that he was only defending himself. If he was only defending himself and not attacking that is not a fight and consequently not an affray. A man may well defend himself and then pass to the attack, which is very likely what happened here, or, in repelling an attack, he may use more than necessary force, and again that may be the case here as a razor was used. But it appears to us inescapable that this raised questions for the jury."

CONVICTIONS QUASHED.

---

[1] *Ibid.* at p. 860.
[2] [1924] A. C. 836.
[3] [1907] 2 K. B. 853.

BUTTON v. DIRECTOR OF PUBLIC PROSECUTIONS

[1965] 3 All E. R. 587

An affray occurs when two people fight to the terror of the Queen's subjects, and it is not necessary that the fight should occur in a public place.

Facts.

Button and others fought in a dance hall and were charged, *inter alia*, with affray. The trial judge directed the jury that an affray must occur in a public place but that they were entitled to treat the dance hall in question as a public place. The accused were convicted and appealed unsuccessfully to the Court of Criminal Appeal who were of opinion that an affray need not occur in a public place. The accused then appealed unsuccessfully to the House of Lords.

Extracts from the Speeches of the House of Lords.

LORD GARDINER, L.C.—

"The essence of the offence is that two or more fight together to the terror of the Queen's subjects. Nowhere in the earlier writings is it suggested that the place where the fight occurs is a decisive matter.

Lambard's Eirenarcha (1610 Edn.), c. 3, p. 125, under the side note 'Affray and assault' said:

'The words affray and assault be indifferently used of most men, and that also in some of our booke cases, but yet (in my opinion) there wanteth not a just difference between them. For affray is derived of the french effrayer which signifieth to terrifie, or bring feare.'

He described it (*ibid.*) as a 'common wrong'. It is true that assault and affray were sometimes spoken of loosely as if they were interchangeable. This is perhaps not surprising since in each case the wrongful act is the same yet the mischief of the act falls on the victim in the offence of assault but on the bystander in the offence of affray.

In 1583 *Fitzherbert's l'Office et Authority de Justices de Peace,* having dealt with affrays on a high street and affrays in the presence of the constable, referred to (1617 Edn. at p. 147) 'an affray which has taken place in a house' and also said (*ibid.*) 'If two men are affraying in a house and the door of the house is shut even if no one is hurt before the entry into the house yet the constable may enter . . .' . . . In 1769, however, *Blackstone* (vol. 4, p. 145) used words which led to subsequent error. Citing *Hawkins* he defined affray as 'the fighting of two or more persons in some public place, to the terror of His Majesty's subjects: for, if the fighting be in private, it is no affray but an assault'. There are two reasons which lead me to think that he cannot have been intending to depart from the views expressed by former writers. First he goes on to cite *Hawkins* as to the power of the constable to break open doors when an affray is in a house, and secondly he could hardly have sought to introduce a novel limitation on the old offence of affray without some discussions and justification of his innovation. I think that he used the words 'public place' loosely (and unfortunately) in order to exclude, as *Hawkins* had done, fighting in a private place where none but the contestants were present. . . . The Court of Criminal Appeal took the view that the offence of affray was a useful part of the criminal law in modern times. I agree with that view.

The most powerful argument for the appellant is that afforded by the lapse of over a century since the error crept into the law. During that period one may assume that prosecutions and trials have been based on the hypothesis that only in respect of acts done in a public place can there be a conviction for affray. But no alteration of the surrounding law has been founded on that hypothesis, nor can it properly be regarded as an intentional development of the law of affray. The only result of it has been that during that period the citizen who has been the victim of affray in a private place had in practice been deprived of the protection of the law. That is not in itself any reason to continue the deprivation. Moreover there is no argument of principle or logic to gild the error. In riot and assault, two kindred offences which legal writers have so often treated in association with affray, there is no requirement that they should be committed in a public place. To distinguish affray in this respect is captious and illogical. There seems therefore no adequate reason to perpetuate the error."

APPEALS DISMISSED.

SECTION 9

PUBLIC MISCHIEF AND CONSPIRACY

R. v. MANLEY

[1933] 1 K. B. 529

It is a public mischief knowingly to make a false allegation that a crime has been committed, the effect of which is to cause police officers to waste their time and to expose innocent people to the risk of suspicion, accusation and arrest.

Facts.

Elizabeth Manley told the police that a man whom she described had attacked and robbed her, with the result that police officers spent a considerable time investigating her allegations. She was convicted of unlawfully effecting a public mischief and appealed unsuccessfully to the Court of Criminal Appeal on the ground that she had committed no offence known to the law.

Judgment of the Court of Criminal Appeal read by:

LORD HEWART, C.J.—

" The appellant in this case was indicted at the Central Criminal Court before the learned Recorder of London for having effected a public mischief. [His Lordship read the counts of the indictment, and continued:] The appellant was convicted, and was bound over to come up for judgment when called upon to do so after this Court had decided the question of law now raised. It was then submitted on her behalf, as it is submitted now, that she had committed no offence; but before that proposition can be assented to it is necessary, as counsel for the prosecution has indicated, to consider two questions.

The first is whether it is true at the present day to say that there is a misdemeanour of committing an act tending to the public mischief. In our opinion that question ought to be answered in the affirmative. We think that the law remains as it was stated to be by LAWRENCE, J., in *R.* v. *Higgins*[1]: ' All offences of a public nature, that is, all such

[1] (1801), 2 East, 5.

acts or attempts as tend to the prejudice of the community, are indictable.'[1] That case was referred to with approval in the case of *R.* v. *Brailsford,*[2] and in the still more recent case of *R.* v. *Porter,*[3] where Lord ALVERSTONE, C.J., in delivering the judgment of the Court, said: 'We are of opinion that it is for the Court to direct the jury as to whether such an act may tend to the public mischief, and that it is not in such a case an issue of fact upon which evidence can be given.'

The second question is whether the appellant did acts which constituted a public mischief. As counsel has said, the facts stated in the indictment are not in dispute, and it is admitted that what is there alleged to have been done by the appellant was done by her. In the opinion of the Court the indictment aptly describes two ingredients of public mischief or prejudice to the community, one of these being that officers of the Metropolitan Police were led to devote their time and services to the investigation of an idle charge, and the other being that members of the public, or at any rate those of them who answered a certain description, were put in peril of suspicion and arrest.

For these reasons the Court is of opinion that the conviction should stand and that the appeal should be dismissed."

APPEAL DISMISSED.[4]

---

1 [1801], 2 East, 21

2 [1905] 2 K. B. 730.

3 [1910] 1 K. B. 369 at p. 372.

4 Section 5(2) of the Criminal Law Act, 1967 now provides that " where a person causes any wasteful employment of the police by knowingly making to any person a false report tending to show that an offence has been committed, or to give rise to apprehension for the safety of any persons or property, or tending to show that he has information material to any police inquiry, he shall be liable on summary conviction to imprisonment for not more than six months or to a fine of not more than two hundred pounds or to both "; but a prosecution on indictment is still a theoretical possibility on the facts of *Manley's* case.

SHAW v. DIRECTOR OF PUBLIC PROSECUTIONS

[1961] 2 All E. R. 446

There is such an offence known to our law as a conspiracy corrupt public morals.

Facts.

Shaw and others produced the *Ladies' Directory* in which prostitutes advertised their services. Shaw was charged with and convicted of, *inter alia*, a conspiracy to corrupt public morals. He unsuccessfully appealed to the Court of Criminal Appeal and thence to the House of Lords.

Extracts from the speeches in the House of Lords.

VISCOUNT SIMONDS.—

"Need I say, my Lords, that I am no advocate of the right of the judges to create new criminal offences? . . . But I am at a loss to understand how it can be said either that the law does not recognize a conspiracy to corrupt public morals or that, though there may not be an exact precedent for such a conspiracy as this case reveals, it does not fall generally within the words by which it is described . . .

In the sphere of criminal law, I entertain no doubt that there remains in the courts of law a residual power to enforce the supreme and fundamental purpose of the law, to conserve not only the safety and order but also the moral welfare of the state, and that it is their duty to guard it against attacks which may be the more insidious because they are novel and unprepared for . . . I will say a final word on an aspect of the case which was urged by counsel. No one doubts—and I have put it in the forefront of this opinion—that certainty is a most desirable attribute of the criminal and civil law alike. Nevertheless, there are matters which must ultimately depend on the opinion of a jury. In the civil law I will take an example which comes, perhaps, nearest to the criminal law—the tort of negligence. It is for a jury to decide not only whether the defendant has committed the act complained of but whether, in doing it, he has fallen short of the standard of care which the circumstances require. Till their verdict is given, it is uncertain what the law requires . . . . . There are still, as has recently been said, 'unravished remnants of the common law'. So, in the case of a charge of conspiracy to corrupt public morals, the uncertainty that necessarily arises from the vagueness of general words can only be resolved by the opinion of twelve chosen men and women. I am content to leave it to them.

The appeal . . . should, in my opinion, be dismissed."

LORD TUCKER.—

" Counsel for the appellant put in the forefront of his address the submission that there is no such offence known to the law as a conspiracy to corrupt public morals. Before turning to authority, I would invite your Lordships to pause to consider for a moment how far-reaching are the consequences of such a proposition if it be correct. It has for long been accepted that there are some conspiracies which are criminal although the acts agreed to be done are not *per se* criminal or tortious[1] if done by individuals. Such conspiracies form a third class in addition to the well-known and more clearly defined conspiracies to do acts which are unlawful, in the sense of criminal or tortious, or to do lawful acts by unlawful means. Assuming that the corruption of public morals by the acts of an individual may not be criminal or tortious, does it follow that a conspiracy by two or more persons to this end is not indictable? The difficulty with regard to this third class of conspiracy has always been to define its limits or give it a label which will include all its manifestations. It was referred to by Viscount SIMON, L.C., in *Crofter Hand Woven Harris Tweed Co., Ltd.* v. *Veitch*[2] as one in which ' the purpose aimed at, though not perhaps specifically illegal, was one which would undermine principles of commercial or moral conduct '. The late Professor Kenny in his *Outlines of Criminal Law* (11th Edn.), at p. 290, in a passage which is repeated in later editions, wrote: ' An unlawful purpose. The term " unlawful " is here used in a sense which is unique; and, unhappily, has never yet been defined precisely. The purposes which it comprises appear to be of the following species: . . . (iv) Agreements to do certain other acts, which (unlike all those hitherto mentioned) are not breaches of law at all, but which nevertheless are outrageously immoral or else are, in some way, extremely injurious to the public.' He gives a number of examples.

An instance in modern times is to be found in *R.* v.

---

[1] See now *R.* v. *Kamara*, [1972] 3 All E.R. 999, which may go on appeal to the House of Lords.

[2] [1942] A. C. 435, at p. 439; [1942] 1 All E. R. at p. 146.

Newland,[1] where the appellants had been convicted of conspiring to effect a public mischief by obtaining and distributing on the home market for eventual retail sale decorated domestic pottery which, by orders made under the Defence (General) Regulations, manufacturers and registered exporters were permitted to supply for export only. The orders did not in terms deal with persons who obtained such goods from a manufacturer representing that they were for export and then having obtained them sold them on the domestic market. It was contended on behalf of the appellants that there was no such offence known to the law as set out in the indictment. In delivering the judgment of the Court of Criminal Appeal, Lord GODDARD, C.J., said:[2] ' It is much too late to object that a conspiracy to effect a public mischief is an offence unknown to the law. There have been at least three reported cases during the present century in which that charge has been made and convictions upheld. We refer to *R.* v. *Brailsford*,[3] *R.* v. *Porter*[4] and *R.* v. *Bassey*[5] ... The court is well aware of the caution with which they should approach the consideration of an offence which is alleged to consist of doing acts which tend to effect public mischief as, if extended, it might enable judges to declare new offences which should be the business of the legislature. The objections to such a course were forcibly pointed out by Sir Fitzjames Stephen, the most prominent institutional writer on the criminal law in the last century, in his *History of the Criminal Law*, Vol. 3, p. 359. We think we may say that the court should approach the subject at least with the same degree of caution as must be exercised when considering a plea in a civil action that something has been done contrary to public policy . . . No one has ever attempted to define what may or may not constitute a public mischief and we have certainly no desire to increase the number of criminal offences by adding to the category of misdemeanours, but there are two points which, in our opinion, do not make it necessary for us to consider whether there is here any attempt to create a new offence. In the first place, it is well known that there may be many acts which, if done by an individual, would not be indictable, or even actionable as a tort, and yet may become both actionable and criminal if done by a

---

[1] [1954] 1 Q. B. 158; [1953] 2 All E. R. 1067.
[2] [1954] 1 Q. B. at p. 165; [1953] 2 All E. R. at p. 1071.
[3] [1905] 2 K. B. 730.
[4] [1910] 1 K. B. 369.
[5] (1931), 47 T. L. R. 222.

combination of persons as the result of a conspiracy, and for this really elementary proposition we need only refer to *Quinn* v. *Leathem*.'[1]

My Lords, I have referred to this case as, in my opinion, the decision of the present and other similar cases does not depend on the label which is to be attached to a particular conspiracy. Can it be doubted that a conspiracy to corrupt public morals is a conspiracy to effect a public mischief? Is it to be said that a conspiracy to sell decorated domestic pottery in the home market by means of devices contrived to evade the object of Board of Trade orders is a criminal conspiracy but an agreement to do acts calculated to corrupt public morals is not? Suppose Parliament tomorrow enacts that homosexual practices between adult consenting males is no longer to be criminal, is it to be said that a conspiracy to further and encourage such practices amongst adult males could not be the subject of a criminal charge fit to be left to a jury? Similarly with regard to a conspiracy to encourage and promote lesbianism today, or incestuous sexual intercourse in the year 1907? My Lords, if these questions are to be answered in the negative, I would expect to find some clear authority during the past centuries which would justify such an answer. I know of none . . .

My Lords, counsel for the Crown supported the conviction and the judgment of the Court of Criminal Appeal on count 1 of the present indictment on two alternative grounds, (i) that conduct calculated and intended to corrupt public morals is indictable as a substantive offence and consequently a conspiracy to this end is indictable as a conspiracy to commit a criminal offence, alternatively (ii) a conspiracy to corrupt morals is indictable as a conspiracy to commit a wrongful act which is calculated to cause public injury. The Court of Criminal Appeal dismissed the appeal on the ground that the case fell well within the first of these propositions. I have, I hope, sufficiently indicated that I prefer to base my decision on the second, but, in so saying, I must not be taken as rejecting the first."

APPEAL DISMISSED[2].

---

[1] [1901] A. C. 495.

[2] Lord REID dissented essentially on the ground that the creation of new heads of public policy is for Parliament.

KNULLER (PUBLISHING, PRINTING AND PROMOTIONS), LTD. v. DIRECTOR OF PUBLIC PROSECUTIONS

[1972] 2 All E.R. 898

(1) *Shaw's case is not an appropriate one for the application of the Practice Statement made by the House of Lords in* 1966 *according to which the House will, in appropriate circumstances, regard itself as free not to follow its previous decisions.*

(2) *Notwithstanding the legalisation by the Sexual Offences Act,* 1967 *of homosexual practices in private between consenting males above the age of* 21, *agreements to encourage such practices continue to be conspiracies to corrupt public morals.*

(3) *There is such an offence as a conspiracy to outrage public decency, although it had not been committeed on the facts of this case.*

Facts.

The accused were concerned in the publication of a magazine which contained advertisements designed to attract readers who were prepared to indulge in homosexual practices with the advertisers. They were charged on an indictment containing two counts; one for a conspiracy to corrupt public morals, and the other for a conspiracy to outrage public decency. The prosecution made no point of the fact that the magazine might be read by males under the age of 21. The accused were convicted on both counts. They appealed unsuccessfully to the Court of Appeal. On their appeal to the House of Lords a Majority of four to one upheld the conviction on the first count, but, though for differing reasons, a majority of three to two was for quashing the conviction on the second count.[1]

Extracts from the Speeches of the House of Lords.

LORD REID.—

"It was decided by this House in *Shaw* v. *Director of Public Prosecutions*[2] that conspiracy to corrupt public morals is a crime known to the law of England. So if the appellants are to succeed on this count, either this House must reverse

---

[1] See note at end of case.

[2] [1962] A.C. 220; [1961] 2 All E.R. 446, p. 318, *supra.*

that decision or there must be sufficient grounds for distinguishing this case. The appellants' main argument is that we should reconsider that decision; alternatively they submit that it can and should be distinguished.

I dissented in *Shaw*'s case[1]. On reconsideration I still think that the decision was wrong and I see no reason to alter anything which I said in my speech. But it does not follow that I should now support a motion to reconsider the decision. I have said more than once in recent cases that our change of practice in no longer regarding previous decisions of this House as absolutely binding does not mean that whenever we think that a previous decision was wrong we should reverse it. In the general interest of certainty in the law we must be sure that there is some very good reason before we so act. We were informed that there had been at least 30 and probably many more convictions of this new crime in the ten years which have elapsed since *Shaw*'s case was decided, and it does not appear that there has been manifest injustice or that any attempt has been made to widen the scope of the new crime. I do not regard our refusal to reconsider *Shaw*'s case as in any way justifying any attempt to widen the scope of the decision and I would oppose any attempt to do so. But I think that however wrong or anomalous the decision may be it must stand and apply to cases reasonably analogous unless or until it is altered by Parliament.

I hold that opinion the more strongly in this case by reason of the nature of the subject-matter we are dealing with. I said in *Shaw*'s case[2] and I repeat that Parliament and Parliament alone is the proper authority to change the law with regard to the punishment of immoral acts. Rightly or wrongly the law was determined by the decision in *Shaw*'s case. Any alteration of the law as so determined must in my view be left to Parliament.

I am not greatly impressed by the argument that Parliament must be held to have approved that decision because in recent years there have been several occasions when Parliament could appropriately have dealt with it if it had disapproved of the decision. Much recent legislation on this subject has all the indications of being in the nature of a compromise and we should, I think, accept and interpret it as such . . .

Although I would not support reconsidering *Shaw*'s

---

[1] [1962] A.C. 220; [1961] 2 All E.R. 446, p. 318, *supra*.
[2] *Ibid*., at p. 457.

case I think that we ought to clarify one or two matters. In the first place conspiracy to corrupt public morals is something of a misnomer. It really means to corrupt the morals of such members of the public as may be influenced by the matter published by the accused.

Next I think that the meaning of the word ' corrupt ' requires some clarification. One of my objections to the *Shaw* decision is that it leaves too much to the jury. I recognise that in the end it must be for the jury to say whether the matter published is likely to lead to corruption. But juries, unlike judges, are not expected to be experts in the use of the English language and I think that they ought to be given some assistance. In *Shaw*'s case a direction was upheld in which the trial judge said:

' And, really, the meaning of debauched and corrupt is again, just as the meaning of the word induce is, essentially a matter for you. After all the arguments, I wonder really whether it means in this case and in this context much more than to lead astray morally.'

I cannot agree that that is right. ' Corrupt ' is a strong word and the jury ought to be reminded of that, as they were in the present case. The Obscene Publications Act, 1959 appears to use the words ' deprave ' and ' corrupt ' as synonymous, as I think they are. We may regret that we live in a permissive society but I doubt whether even the most staunch defender of a better age would maintain that all or even most of those who have at one time or in one way or another been led astray morally have thereby become depraved or corrupt. I think that the jury should be told in one way or another that although in the end the question whether a matter is corrupt is for them, they should keep in mind current standards of ordinary decent people.

I can now turn to the appellants' second argument. They say that homosexual acts between adult males in private are now lawful so it is unreasonable and cannot be the law that other persons are guilty of an offence if they merely put in touch with one another two males who wish to indulge in such acts. There is a material difference between merely exempting certain conduct from criminal penalties and making it lawful in the full sense. Prostitution and gaming afford examples of this difference. So we must examine the provisions of the Sexual Offences Act, 1967 to see just how far it altered the old law. It enables subject to limitation that a homosexual act in private shall not be an offence but goes no further than that. Section 4 shows that procuring is still a serious offence and it would seem that some of the facts in this case might have supported a charge under that section.

I find nothing in the Act to indicate that Parliament thought or intended to lay down that indulgence in these practices is not corrupting. I read the Act as saying that, even though it may be corrupting, if people choose to corrupt themselves in this way that is their affair and the law will not interfere. But no licence is given to others to encourage the practice. So if one accepts *Shaw*'s case as rightly decided it must be left to each jury to decide in the circumstances of each case whether people were likely to be corrupted . . .

The second count is conspiracy to outrage public decency . . .

To my mind questions of public policy of the utmost importance are at stake here.

I think that the objections to the creation of this generalised offence are similar in character to but even greater than the objections to the generalised offence of conspiracy to corrupt public morals. In upholding the decision in *Shaw*'s case we are, in my view, in no way affirming or lending any support to the doctrine that the courts still have some general or residual power either to create new offences or so to widen existing offences as to make punishable conduct of a type hitherto not subject to punishment. Apart from some statutory offences of limited application, there appears to be neither precedent nor authority of any kind for punishing the publication of written or printed matter on the ground that it is indecent as distinct from being obscene."

LORD MORRIS OF BORTH-Y-GEST.—

" If by agreement it was arranged to insert advertisements by married people proclaiming themselves to be such and to be desirous of meeting someone of the opposite sex with a view to clandestine sexual association, would it be a justification to say that adultery is not of itself a criminal offence? A person who, as a result of reading the Ladies' Directory, decided to resort to a prostitute was committing no legal offence; but it was open to a jury to hold that those who conspired to insert the advertisements did so with the intention of corrupting the morals of those who read the advertisements. So in the present case it was open to the jury to hold that there was an intention to corrupt . . .

It was suggested and it has been suggested that there is

an element of uncertainty which attaches to the offence of conspiracy to corrupt public morals. It is said that the rules of law ought to be precise so that a person will know the exact consequences of all his actions and so that he can regulate his conduct with complete assurance. This, however, is not possible under any system of law . . . Those who skate on thin ice can hardly expect to find a sign which will denote the precise spot where they may fall in . . .

It has sometimes been asserted that in his speech in *Shaw's* case[1] Lord SIMONDS was proclaiming that the court has power to extend the sphere of the law by devising new extensions of the operation of the criminal law; his use of the words ' residual power ' is pointed to as a basis of what is asserted. In my view, the sustained reasoning of his speech refutes the assertion . . . He held, in agreement with Lord Tucker, that the offence of conspiracy to corrupt public morals was an offence known to the common law. He then proceeded to demonstrate that if offending acts do reveal a conspiracy to corrupt public morals it is not to be said that no offence has been committed merely because the particular acts are novel or unprepared for or are unprecedented . . .

In regard to count 2 the learned judge at the trial reminded the jury of all that he had said as to the nature of a conspiracy and told them that count 2 alleged an offence quite separate and distinct from that alleged in count 1. He told them that they had to be satisfied that the advertisements were lewd, disgusting and offensive and that the particular accused person was a party to an agreement to outrage public decency. He carefully reminded them that public feeling varies from one generation to another so that what would outrage public decency in one generation would pass unnoticed in the next; so the jury had to be satisfied that the advertisements did outrage public decency and that there was an agreement to outrage public decency. The matter was I think clearly and sufficiently submitted to the jury for their consideration and their decision."

LORD SIMON OF GLAISDALE.—

" It was argued for the Crown that it was immaterial whether or not the alleged outrage to decency took place in public, provided that the sense of decency of the public or a substantial section of the public was outraged. But this seems to me to be contrary to many of the authorities which the Crown itself relied on to establish the generic offence [a

[1] [1962] A.C. 220; [1961] 2 All E.R. 446, p. 318, *supra*.

conspiracy to outrage public decency]. The authorities establish that the word "public" has a different connotation in the respective offences of conspiracy to corrupt public morals and conduct calculated to, or conspiracy to, outrage public decency. In the first it refers to certain fundamental rules regarded as essential social control which yet lacks the force of law, in other words, when applicable to individuals 'public' refers to persons in society. In the latter offences, however, 'public' refers to places in which the offence is committed. This is borne out . . . by what is presumably the purpose of the legal rule—namely, that reasonable people may venture out in public without the risk of outrage to certain minimal accepted standards of decency. On the other hand, I do not think that it would necessarily negative the offence that the act or exhibit is superficially hid from view, if the public is expressly or impliedly invited to penetrate the cover . . .

There are other features of the offence which should, in my view, be brought to the notice of the jury. It should be emphasised that 'outrage', like 'corrupt', is a very strong word. 'Outraging public decency' goes considerably beyond offending the susceptibilities of, or even shocking, reasonable people. Moreover the offence is, in my view, concerned with recognising minimum standards of decency, which are likely to vary from time to time. Finally, notwithstanding that 'public' in the offence is used in a locative sense, public decency must be viewed as a whole; and I think the jury should be invited, where appropriate, to remember that we live in a plural society, with a tradition of tolerance towards minorities, and that this atmosphere of toleration is itself part of public decency.

The Court of Appeal said of the direction on count 2 that it might be that it was not wholly satisfactory. I would myself go further. I regard it as essential that the jury should be carefully directed on the lines that I have ventured to suggest, on the proper approach to the meaning of 'decency' and 'outrage' and the element of publicity required to constitute the offence. The summing-up was generally a careful and fair one, but I think it was defective in these regards; and I therefore do not think it would be safe to allow the conviction on count 2 to stand."

APPEAL ALLOWED IN PART.

Note

Lord DIPLOCK dissented on count 1 on the ground that the House had been mistaken in holding in *Shaw's* case that there was a general offence of conspiracy to corrupt public morals and the mistake should now be corrected. Lord DIPLOCK agreed with Lord REID on count 2 that there is no such general offence as a conspiracy to outrage public decency; but Lords MORRIS, SIMON and KILBRANDON held that there is such an offence, although the two latter held that the jury had been misdirected and accordingly concurred in allowing the appeal on count 2.

The opinion was reiterated in all the speeches that the courts have no general or residual common law power to create new offences.

Lords MORRIS, SIMON and KILBRANDON took the view that Parliament had recognised the existence of the offence of conspiracy to corrupt public morals in s. 2(4) of the Theatres Act, 1968, which provides that no person shall be proceeded against at common law for the offence of conspiring to corrupt public morals in respect of an agreement to present a play.

Reference was made in some of the speeches to an undertaking given in the House of Commons on July 3, 1964 that prosecutions for a conspiracy to corrupt public morals would not be initiated to circumvent the provision of s. 2(4) of the Obscene Publications Act, 1959, which prohibits proceedings at common law where it is of the essence of the offence that an article was obscene, *i.e.* calculated to deprave or corrupt the morals of those likely to read it. The importance of the provision lies in the availability of the defence of public good under s. 4(1) of the 1959 Act in prosecutions thereunder; but Lord KILBRANDON took the view that the conspiracy in the *Knuller* case was to promote homosexual associations rather than to publish pornography.

CHURCHILL v. WALTON

[1967] 1 All E. R. 497

A person can only be guilty of conspiring to commit an absolute statutory offence if, on the facts known to him, he has agreed to do an unlawful act.

Facts.

Churchill was charged with conspiring to sell rebated heavy oil for use in road vehicles contrary to s. 200(2) of the Customs and Excise Act, 1952, a subsection which contained an absolute prohibition. The jury found as a fact that the accused did not know that the oil which he agreed to sell had not borne full tax.

Churchill was convicted and appealed unsuccessfully to the Court of Criminal Appeal. He then appealed successfully to the House of Lords.

Extracts from the Speeches of the House of Lords.

VISCOUNT DILHORNE.—

" . . . the law is, in my opinion, the same for conspiracy as for aiding and abetting, as to which Lord GODDARD, C.J., said in *Johnson* v. *Youden*:[1]

' Before a person can be convicted of aiding and abetting the commission of an offence, he must at least know the essential matters which constitute that offence. He need not actually know that an offence has been committed, because he may not know that the facts constitute an offence and ignorance of the law is not a defence. If a person knows all the facts and is assisting another person to do certain things, and it turns out that the doing of those things constitutes an offence, the person who is assisting is guilty of aiding and abetting that offence, because to allow him to say, " I knew of all those facts but I did not know that an offence was committed ", would be allowing him to set up ignorance of the law as a defence. The reason why, in our opinion, the justices were right in dismissing the informations against the first two defendants is that they found, and found on good grounds, that they did not know of the matters which in fact constituted the offence; and, as they did not know of those matters, it follows that they cannot be guilty of aiding and abetting the commission of the offence.'

In answer to the question posed by the Court of Criminal Appeal in this case, I would say that *mens rea* is only an essential ingredient in conspiracy insofar as there must be an intention to be a party to an agreement to do an unlawful act; knowledge of the facts is only material insofar as such knowledge throws a light on what was agreed. In cases of this kind, it is desirable to avoid the use of the phrase '*mens rea*', which is capable of different meanings, and to concentrate on the terms or effect of the agreement made by the alleged conspirators. The question is ' What did they agree to do?' If what they agreed to do was, on the facts

---

[1] [1950] 1 K. B. 544, at pp. 546, 547.

known to them, an unlawful act, they are guilty of conspiracy and cannot excuse themselves by saying that, owing to their ignorance of the law, they did not realise that such an act was a crime. If, on the facts known to them, what they agreed to do was lawful, they are not rendered artificially guilty by the existence of other facts, not known to them, giving a different and criminal quality to the act agreed on."

APPEAL ALLOWED.

R. v. McDONNELL

[1966] 1 All E. R. 193

The one man responsible for the affairs of a limited company cannot be convicted of conspiring with that company.

Facts.

McDonnell was charged with conspiracy to defraud. The other party to the alleged conspiracy was a limited company for whose affairs McDonnell was in fact solely responsible as director. On a motion to quash the indictment it was held that the charge would not lie.

Extracts from the Judgment at Assizes.

NIELD, J.—

" I turn to the last of these points, which is much the most substantial, namely the submission by counsel for the defendant that in the particular circumstances of this case there can be no conspiracy, for the reason that there are not two persons and two minds involved . . . I have reached the conclusion that I should express the opinion or anticipatory ruling that these charges of conspiracy cannot be sustained on the footing that in the particular circumstances here, where the sole responsible person in the company is the defendant himself, it would not be right to say that there were two persons or two minds. If it were otherwise, I feel that it would offend against the basic concept of a conspiracy, namely an agreement of two or more to do an unlawful act, and I think that it would be artificial to take the view that each of these companies can be regarded as a separate person or a separate mind, in view of the admitted fact that this defendant acts alone so far as these companies are concerned.

It is interesting to observe that in the Canadian case[1] an earlier edition of Mr Glanville Williams' book was referred to. I have been shown the later edition, and the learned author there expresses under the heading: ' Crimes for which a corporation can be convicted ', this opinion:[2]

' Probably (thereby being cautious) a company and its director cannot be convicted of conspiracy when the only human being who broke the law or intended to do so was the one director.' "

MOTION UPHELD.

R. v. THOMSON

(1965), 50 Cr. App. Rep. 1

In order that a person may be convicted of conspiracy he must not only have agreed to carry out an unlawful purpose, but must also have intended to carry it out.

Facts.

Thomson and another were charged with conspiracy. It was possible on the evidence that, with regard to one accused, the jury would find that, though he entered into an agreement to do an unlawful act, he never intended to carry it out. After hearing argument on the law, LAWTON, J., held that, on the view of the evidence which has just been mentioned, the accused who did not intend to carry out the agreement would not have been guilty. Both accused were in fact convicted.

Extracts from the Judgment at Assizes.

LAWTON, J.—

" The problem perhaps can be put in general terms, *viz.*, on a charge of conspiracy, must the prosecution prove not only an agreement between the alleged conspirators to carry out an unlawful purpose, as signified by words or other means of communication between them, but also that they had an intention to carry out the unlawful purpose?

The researches of counsel seem to show that this problem has never been resolved by any English court, but it has been

---

[1] *R.* v. *Electrical Contractors Assocn. of Ontario and Dent,* [1961] O.R 265.

[2] *Glanville Williams on Criminal Law* (2nd Edn., 1961) p. 861.

before the Supreme Court of Canada in *R.* v. *O'Brien*, [1954] S.C.R. 666 and before courts in Texas and Tennessee. The Canadian Supreme Court decided, by a majority of three to two, that the prosecution had to prove in each of the alleged conspirators an intention at the time when the agreement was made to carry out the unlawful purpose. This decision was reached after the court had considered the common law of conspiracy. The Texas and Tennessee courts seem to have reached the same conclusion as the Supreme Court of Canada, but I have no first-hand knowledge of their decisions. I agree with the view of the majority of the Supreme Court of Canada.

It has become a judicial usage to explain to juries the nature of conspiracy in the words used by WILLES, J., when giving the opinion of the judges to the House of Lords in *Mulcahy* v. *R.* (1868), L.R. 3 H.L. 306. In most cases it is necessary to refer only to one sentence in the opinion, which is set out at p. 317, namely: ' a conspiracy consists not merely in the intention of two or more, but in the agreement of two or more to do any unlawful act, or to do a lawful act by unlawful means.' Constant reiteration of that sentence has, so it seems to me, resulted in obscuring what WILLES, J., meant by the word ' agreement ' in this context. The meaning of the word ' agreement ' as used by WILLES, J., can be deduced only from the context in which it appears and from the terms in which the House of Lords accepted the judges' opinions. What WILLES, J., in fact said is this: 'A conspiracy consists not merely in the intention of two or more, but in the agreement of two or more to do an unlawful act, or to do a lawful act by unlawful means. So long as such a design rests in intention only, it is not indictable. When two agree to carry it into effect, the very plot is an act in itself, and the act of each of the parties, promise against promise, *actus contra actum*, capable of being enforced, if lawful, punishable if for a criminal object or for the use of criminal means. And so far as proof goes, conspiracy, as GROSE, J., said in *R.* v. *Brisac* (1803), 4 East 164, at p. 171, is generally a " matter of inference deduced from certain criminal acts of the parties accused, done in pursuance of an apparent criminal purpose in common between them." The number and the compact give weight and cause danger, and this is more especially the case in a conspiracy like those charged in this indictment.'

. . . When a man makes an agreement, he assents with his mind to the offer of the other party and communicates his assent to the other party by words or conduct. For the purposes of the law of contract, the words or conduct by which a man manifests his assent are binding on him and the law does not allow him to say that his mind did not go with his conduct. The criminal law, however, is concerned with punishing wrongdoing; the essential element in any crime, other than in the limited class of absolute offences, is a guilty mind. Evidence that the accused person acted and spoke as if he was making and had made an agreement may provide cogent evidence of a guilty mind; . . .

If the facts show, as the jury might on the evidence in this case infer that they do, that the defendant manifested his assent to a criminal enterprise, but that his mind did not go with his assent, then it seems to me that the element of the guilty mind is missing and, accordingly, on those facts he would be entitled to be acquitted, and I propose to direct the jury accordingly."

VERDICT, GUILTY.

R. v. WHITCHURCH

(1890), 24 Q. B. D. 420

A woman who is not pregnant may be convicted of conspiring with others to procure her own miscarriage contrary to the second part of s. 58 *of the Offences against the Person Act,* 1861.[1]

Facts.

Believing herself to be pregnant, Whitchurch agreed with others that they should use instruments and administer things to her with a view to procuring her miscarriage. Instruments were used and things were administered, but there was no evidence that Whitchurch was pregnant, a fact which would, if proved, have meant that she could be convicted of a crime under the first part of s. 58. Whitchurch

---

[1] Section 58 reads " Every woman, being with child, who with intent to procure her own miscarriage, shall unlawfully . . . use any instrument . . . and whosoever, with intent to procure the miscarriage of any woman, whether she be or be not with child shall unlawfully use any instrument . . . with the like intent shall be guilty of an offence." For a helpful discussion of *Whitchurch's* case see [1962] Crim. L. R. 694.

was nonetheless convicted of conspiracy, and her conviction was affirmed by the Court for Crown Cases Reserved.

Extracts from the Judgments of the Court for Crown Cases Reserved.

HAWKINS, J.—

"... The prisoner is not charged with using instruments, or administering drugs to herself, for the purposes of procuring abortion, but with conspiring with others to procure abortion. It is clear that she could not lawfully call in other persons to do that which when done by them is a crime punishable with penal servitude. What she did was a conspiracy to commit a criminal act."

CONVICTION AFFIRMED.

SECTION 10

FORGERY

R. v. CLOSS

(1857), Dears. & B. 460

A picture is not a document within the law of forgery.

Facts.

The evidence was that the accused obtained a sum of money from the prosecutor as the purchase price of a picture upon which the accused, a picture dealer, had written the name of John Linnell, a contemporary artist of some repute who had not painted the picture in question. The indictment contained three counts. The first alleged an obtaining of money by false pretences, but it failed for want of evidence that the purchaser was induced to part with his money by the signature on the picture. The second count alleged cheating, and the third forgery. A case was reserved for the opinion of the Court for Crown Cases Reserved as to whether, on the evidence, the accused ought to have been convicted on any count, and the court was of opinion that he could not be convicted on any one of the three.

Extract from the Judgments of the Court for Crown Cases Reserved.

COCKBURN, C.J.—

" . . . As to the third count we are all of opinion that there was no forgery. A forgery must be of some document or writing; and this was merely in the nature of a mark put upon the painting with a view of identifying it, and was no more than if the painter put any other arbitary mark as a recognition of the picture being his. . ."

CONVICTION QUASHED.[1]

---

[1] The first two counts failed for want of proof but the name on the picture induced the prosecutor to part with his money.

R. v. SMITH

(1858), Dears. & B. 566

A person can only be convicted of forgery if he has made or uttered a false document or instrument.

Facts.

Smith was charged with forging documents, and uttering them knowing them to be forged. He sold baking powder, and the evidence was that he had caused ten thousand labels which the jury found to be almost identical with those used by Messrs. Borwick for their baking powder to be printed.

He was convicted, but a case was stated for the Court for Crown Cases Reserved who were of opinion that the labels were not " documents ", or not " false documents ", within the meaning of the law as to forgery.

Extracts from the Judgments of the Court for Crown Cases Reserved.

POLLOCK, C.B.—

" We are all of opinion that this conviction is bad. The defendant may have been guilty of obtaining money by false pretences; of that there can be no doubt; but the real offence here was the inclosing the false powder in the false wrapper. The issuing of this wrapper without the stuff within it would be no offence. In the printing of these wrappers there is no forgery, nor could the man who printed them be indicted. The real offence is the issuing them with the fraudulent matter in them. I waited in vain to hear Mr. Huddleston shew that these wrappers came within the principle of documents which might be the subject of forgery at common law. Speaking for myself, I doubt very much whether these papers are within that principle. They are merely wrappers, and in their present shape I doubt whether they are anything like a document or instrument which is the subject of forgery at common law. To say that they belong to that class of instruments seems to me to be confounding things together as alike which are essentially different. It might as well be said, that if one tradesman used brown paper for his wrappers, and another tradesman had his brown paper wrappers made in the same way, he could be accused of forging the brown paper."

BRAMWELL, B.—

" I think that this was not a forgery. Forgery supposes the possibility of a genuine document, and that the false document is not so good as the genuine document, and that the one is not so efficacious for all purposes as the other. In the present case one of these documents is as good as the other—the one asserts what the other does—the one is as true as the other, but one gets improperly used. . . ."

CONVICTION QUASHED.

R. v. RITSON

(1869), L. R. 1 C. C. R. 200

The false dating of a document is a forgery if the date of the document is material.

Facts.

W. Ritson was the owner of land upon the security of which he obtained an advance from the prosecutor. He subsequently executed a deed of assignment for the benefit of his creditors, and, as the amount due to the prosecutor exceeded the value of the land, it was conveyed to the prosecutor by W. Ritson with the consent of the trustee of the deed of assignment. W. Ritson then executed a deed conveying the land in question to his son S. Ritson, but the deed was dated prior to that of the deed of assignment and the conveyance to the prosecutor. S. Ritson claimed the land from the prosecutor.

W. Ritson and S. Ritson were charged with, and convicted of forging the conveyance to S. Ritson with intent to defraud the prosecutor. A case was stated for the opinion of the Court for Crown Cases Reserved, and this Court was of opinion that the conviction was correct.

Extracts from the Judgment of the Court for Crown Cases Reserved.

BLACKBURN, J.—

" . . . By 24 and 25 Vict. c. 98, s. 20,[1] it is felony to

[1] Re-enacted by s. 2 (1) (*b*) of the Forgery Act, 1913.

' forge ' any deed with intent to defraud. The material word in this section is ' forge'. There is no definition of ' forge ' in the statute, and we must therefore inquire what is the meaning of the word. The definition in Comyns (Dig., tit. Forgery, A.I.) is ' forgery is where a man fraudulently writes or publishes a false deed or writing to the prejudice of the right of another '—not making an instrument containing that which is false, which, I agree with Mr. Torr, would not be forgery, but making an instrument which purports to be that which it is not. Bacon's Abr., (tit. Forgery, A.), which, it is well known, was compiled from the MS. of Chief Baron Gilbert, explains forgery thus: ' The notion of forgery doth not so much consist in the counterfeiting of a man's hand and seal . . . but in the endeavouring to give an appearance of truth to a mere deceit and falsity, and either to impose that upon the world as the solemn act of another which he is in no way privy to, or at least to make a man's own act appear to have been done at a time when it was not done, and by force of such a falsity to give it an operation which in truth and justice it ought not to have.' The material words, as applicable to the facts of the present case, are, ' to make a man's own act appear to have been done at a time when it was not done.' When an instrument professes to be executed at a date different from that at which it really was executed, and the false date is material to the operation of the deed, if the false date is inserted knowingly and with a fraudulent intent, it is a forgery at common law.

Ordinarily the date of a deed is not material, but it is here shown by extrinsic evidence that the date of the deed was material. Unless the deed had been executed before the 5th day of May [the date of the conveyance to the prosecutor], it could not have conveyed any estate in the land in question. The date was of the essence of the deed, and as a false date was inserted with a fraudulent intent, the deed was a false deed, within the definition in Bacon's Abridgement. . . ."

CONVICTION AFFIRMED.

R. v. RILEY

[1896] 1 Q. B. 309[1]

The falsification of the time of despatch of a telegram may amount to forgery, and a telegram is an instrument within what is now s. 7 of the Forgery Act, 1913.

Facts.

Riley was convicted of feloniously obtaining money from Messrs. Crompton and Radcliffe, a firm of bookmakers, by means of a forged instrument. He had obtained permission from one Barber to place bets with this firm in his name. Riley was a clerk at the head post office, and he despatched a telegram placing a bet on the winner of a race which had already been run. He falsely indicated that it had been handed in at a branch office prior to the running of the race.

A case was stated for the opinion of the Court for Crown Cases Reserved who were of opinion that the conviction was correct.

Extracts from the Judgments of the Court for Crown Cases Reserved.

HAWKINS, J.—

" . . . By the 24 and 25 Vict. c. 98, s. 38,[2] ' Whosoever with intent to defraud shall demand, receive, or obtain, or cause or procure to be delivered or paid to any person, or endeavour to receive or obtain, or to cause or procure to be delivered or paid to any person, any chattel, money, security for money, or other property whatsoever under, upon, or by virtue of *any forged or altered instrument whatsoever,* knowing the same to be forged or altered,' shall be guilty of felony. . . .

I proceed to discuss the question reserved for our consideration: whether the telegram described in the case constitutes a forged instrument in law; and whether it is such an instrument as is contemplated by s. 38.

---

[1] This decision has been followed since the coming into force of the Forgery Act, 1913, in *R.* v. *Cade*, [1914] 2 K. B. 209.

[2] Re-enacted by s. 7 of the Forgery Act, 1913.

My answer to both these questions is in the affirmative.

In 4 Blackstone's Commentaries, 247, forgery at common law is defined as 'the fraudulent making or alteration of a *writing* to the prejudice of another man's right.' I seek for no other definition for the purposes of the present discussion. That a postal telegram is a writing is to my mind clear. It originates in a written message addressed and signed by the sender, and delivered by him into the post office of despatch for the express purpose that it shall, in the very words in which it is penned, be transmitted by means of an electric wire to another post office, which I will call the arrival office, and that it shall there again on its arrival be committed to writing *verbatim et literatim*, and that such last-mentioned writing shall be handed to the person to whom it is addressed. The writing delivered in at the office of despatch is the authority of the postmaster to transmit the message, and of the postmaster at the arrival office to commit it to writing and to deliver it to the addressee as the sender's written message to him. This message sent out from the arrival office is, in my opinion, as binding upon the sender as though he had written it with his own hand. . . .

Assuming the telegram to be such a writing as I have stated, a bare reading of the contents of it, coupled with the admission of its falsity and of the purpose for which it was made, are overwhelming to establish that it was fraudulently made to the prejudice of another man's right, and thus a forgery at common law. For this I need only cite the judgment of BLACKBURN, J., in *R.* v. *Ritson*[1]. . . .

In this case, unless the telegram was dated and despatched before the race was run, it would have been inoperative. The time of despatch was therefore material: falsely to write the telegram so as to make it appear that it was sent in for despatch before the race was run, when it was not sent in till afterwards, was to make it appear on the face of it to be that which it was not . . .

In my view of the case, the telegram in question is an *instrument of contract*; it is the instrument which completed the wager offered by Crompton and Radcliffe to those who were able and disposed to accept it (see *Carlill* v. *Carbolic Smoke Ball Co., Ltd.*,[2] and the cases there cited), and thenceforth an obligation was imposed upon each party in honour to fulfil it according to the result of the race. I say *in honour*,

---

[1] (1869), L. R. 1 C. C. R. 200, at p. 204; p. 337, *supra*.

[2] [1892] 2 Q. B. 484; *affirmed*, [1893] 1 Q. B. 256

because, though it was clearly not an illegal contract, it could not be enforced by any legal process. In virtue of it, and upon the assumption that the telegram was what it purported to be, Messrs. Crompton and Radcliffe paid the £9.

Assuming the document to be an 'instrument,' I come to the only remaining question, whether it is such within the meaning of s. 38 of the statute. Why should it not be so? It is contended that the section has reference only to such instruments as are mentioned in the earlier sections of the statute, and that s. 38 applies only to those forged instruments which are punishable as felonies.

Such a construction is, I think, erroneous. There is no definition of the word 'instrument' in the statute to fetter us in giving to it the ordinary and general interpretation. It was clearly the intention of the Legislature by s. 38 to create a new offence . . ."

CONVICTION AFFIRMED.

R. v. MARTIN
(1879), 5 Q. B. D. 34

For the purpose of the law of forgery, the document in question must be false in itself, and a person is not guilty of forgery if he gives a cheque as his own although he signs it with a false Christian name.

Facts.

Robert Martin met the prosecutor who knew him well, and purchased a pony and carriage from him. He gave a cheque in payment of the purchase price which he signed in the name of William Martin. He had an account at the bank upon which the cheque was drawn, but it was closed, and the cheque was dishonoured.

Martin was convicted of forgery, but a case was stated for the opinion of the Court for Crown Cases Reserved who were of opinion that the conviction was wrong.

Extracts from the Judgments of the Court for Crown Cases Reserved.

COCKBURN, C.J.—

" The case is concluded by authority. In *Dunn's* case[1] it was agreed by the judges that ' in all forgeries the instrument supposed to be forged must be a false instrument in itself; and that if a person give a note entirely as his own, his subscribing it by a fictitious name will not make it a forgery, the credit there being wholly given to himself, without any regard to the name, or any relation to a third person.' Upon authority, as well as upon principle, it is clear that this conviction should be quashed."

CONVICTION QUASHED.

R. v. DODGE AND HARRIS

[1971] 2 All E.R. 1523

A document is not false within the meaning of the Forgery Act, 1913, *unless it tells a lie about itself.*

Facts.

Harris borrowed money from G., falsely representing that he had been left a legacy of £24,000. When pressed for payment by G., he alleged that Dodge owed him £24,000. Harris then prepared bonds under which Dodge undertook to pay him £10,000. Dodge signed these bonds and Harris handed them to G. Dodge was charged with forgery of the bonds and Harris with uttering them. They were both convicted and both of them successfully appealed to the Court of Appeal.

Extracts from the Judgment of the Court of Appeal.

PHILLIMORE, L.J.—

" Now the words ' making a false document ' of course in plain simple language would be wide enough, I suppose, to cover a document which contains statements which are untrue, but it has always been interpreted in a restricted sense —the phrase that is used is that the document must tell a lie about itself. Section 1(2) provides:

[1] (1765), 1 Leach 57.

'A document is false within the meaning of this Act if the whole or any material part thereof purports to be made by or on behalf or on account of a person who did not make it nor authorise its making. [That clearly is not so here. These two bonds were made by the appellant Harris, but with the authorisation of the appellant Dodge, who then proceeded to sign them]; or if, though made by or on behalf or on account of the person by whom or by whose authority it purports to have been made, the time or place of making, where either is material, or, in the case of a document identified by number or mark, the number or any distinguishing mark identifying the document, is falsely stated therein; and in particular a document is false: (a) if any material alteration, whether by addition, insertion, obliteration, erasure, removal, or otherwise, has been made therein; (b) if the whole or some material part of it purports to be made by or on behalf of a fictitious or deceased person; (c) if, though made in the name of an existing person, it is made by him or by his authority with the intention that it should pass as having been made by some person, real or fictitious, other than the person who made or authorised it.'

Quite clearly none of these descriptions applies to these two bonds.

The way the matter is really put is this. Counsel for the appellant Dodge, who has put his arguments very concisely, says this, that any implication which one can infer from the document that the parties intended to implement it is a lie as to the intention of the parties, but is not a lie as to the document itself. It is a lie about something that is extrinsic."

APPEALS ALLOWED.

R. v. GEACH

(1840), 9 C. & P. 499

A person has an intent to defraud for the purposes of the law of forgery although he intends to make good, and in fact makes good, any loss which may be incurred as a result of his action.

Facts.

Geach forwarded a bill of exchange to his bank for discount by them. He had forged the acceptance thereon, and the bank discounted the bill. Geach subsequently paid off the bill, but, on his being charged with forgery, the jury were directed as a matter of law that this, or his intention to do so at the time the bank discounted the bill, was immaterial.

Extracts from the summing up to the jury of:—

PARKE, B.—

"Upon the questions, whether the acceptance is a forgery, and whether the prisoner knew it to be so, there can be no question, if you believe the evidence of Mr. Edward Williams; and with respect to the intent to defraud, I have no doubt that you will take the law from me, which is this, that a person is guilty of forgery, notwithstanding he may himself intend ultimately to take up the bill, and may suppose that the party whose name is forged will be no loser. If, in the present case, you are satisfied that the prisoner knew this acceptance to be forged, and uttered it as true and believed that the bankers would advance money on it, which they would not otherwise do, that is ample evidence of an intent to defraud, and evidence upon which a jury ought to act. It appears that this bill has since been paid by the prisoner; but that will make no difference, if the offence has been once completed at the time of the uttering."

VERDICT, GUILTY.

WELHAM v. DIRECTOR OF PUBLIC PROSECUTIONS

[1961] A. C. 103

It is unnecessary to prove an intention to cause economic loss in order to establish an intent to defraud within the meaning of the Forgery Act, 1913.

Facts.

The accused was charged with uttering forged documents with intent to defraud contrary to s. 6 of the Forgery Act, 1913. He had witnessed forged hire purchase agreements, the object of which was to enable finance companies to make advances in excess of the permitted amount and thus to evade the credit squeeze legislation. The accused was convicted after a direction which in effect told the jury that it was unnecessary for the prosecution to show that the accused intended to cause economic loss to anyone and that he intended to defraud if he intended to induce officials of the Inland Revenue to abstain from making inquiries about the advances. The accused unsuccessfully appealed to the Court of Criminal Appeal and thence to the House of Lords.

Extracts from the speeches in the House of Lords.

LORD DENNING:—

" At this point it becomes possible to point the contrast in the statute between an ' intent to deceive ' and an ' intent to defraud '. ' To deceive ' here conveys the element of deceit, which induces a state of mind, without the element of fraud, which induces a course of action or inaction. Take the case of a private document. For instance, where a man fabricates a letter so as to puff himself up in the opinion of others. BRAMWELL, B., put the instance: ' If I were to produce a letter purporting to be from the Duke of Wellington inviting me to dine, and say, " See what a respectable person I am " ': *R.* v. *Moah.*[1] There would then be an intent to deceive but it would not be punishable at common law or under the statute, because then it would not be done with intent to defraud. Take next the case of a public document. For instance, a parish register. If a man should falsify it so as to make himself appear to be descended of noble family, for the sake of his own glorification, he would not be guilty of an intent to defraud and would therefore not be punishable at common law (see *R.* v. *Hodgson*[2]), but he would have an intent to deceive and he would be punishable under the present statute, as indeed he was under its predecessors, such as the Forgery Act, 1861, s. 36.

So much for the principal point under discussion. Mr. Gerald Gardiner did make a further point. He said that the intent must be to defraud the particular person to whom the document is first presented or his agent, and that it was insufficient if he intended to defraud somebody else. This is not correct. It has long been ruled that it is no answer to a charge of forgery, to say that there was no intent to defraud any particular person, because a general intent to defraud is sufficient to constitute the crime. So also it is no answer to say that there was no intent to defraud the recipient, if there was intent to defraud somebody else: see *R.* v. *Taylor.*[3]

---

[1] (1858), 7 Cox C. C. 503, at p. 504.
[2] (1856), Dears. & B. 3, at p. 8.
[3] (1779), 1 Leach 214.

In my judgment, section 4 (1) of the Forgery Act, 1913, only restates the requirements of the common law of forgery. The 'intent to defraud' there mentioned is the same intent as was required by the common law. It is satisfactory to find that in the cases subsequent to the Act the courts have been giving it the same meaning as they did before (*R.* v. *Bassey*[1] is particularly in point), and I am glad to find this confirmed by what my noble and learned friend, Lord TUCKER, said in *Board of Trade* v. *Owen*.[2]

Applying this meaning to the present case, it appears that Welham on his own evidence had an intent to defraud, because he uttered the hire-purchase documents for the purpose of fraud and deceit. He intended to practise a fraud on whomsoever might be called upon to investigate the loans made by the finance companies to the motor dealers. Such a person might be prejudiced in his investigation by the fraud. That is enough to show an intent to defraud."

APPEAL DISMISSED.[3]

---

[1] (1931), 47 T. L. R. 222.

[2] [1957] A. C. 602, at p. 622.

[3] The speeches in this case approve in general terms the well-known statement of BUCKLEY, J., in *Re London & Globe Finance Corporation*, [1903] 1 Ch. 728 at p. 732; "To deceive is, I apprehend, to induce a man to believe that a thing is true which is false, and which the person practising the deceit knows or believes to be false. To defraud is to deprive by deceit; it is by deceit to induce a man to act to his injury. More tersely it may be put, that to deceive is by falsehood to induce a state of mind; to defraud is by deceit to induce a course of conduct."

SECTION 11
SENTENCING

Preliminary note

The doctrine that imprisonment should be regarded as the sentencer's last resort is now clearly recognised in s. 13(1) of the Criminal Justice Act, 1972 which reads as follows:

"A court shall not pass sentence of imprisonment on a person who has attained the age of 21[1] and has not previously been sentenced to imprisonment unless the court is of opinion that no other method of dealing with him is appropriate; and for the purpose of determining whether any other method of dealing with any such person is appropriate the court shall obtain and consider information about the circumstances, and shall take into account any information before the court as to his character and his physical and mental condition."

A suspended sentence does not count as a sentence of imprisonment in this context, and that is a possibility which may have to be considered in any case whether or not the offender has previously been to prison but only after the possibilities of non-custodial treatment have been eliminated.

"... Before one gets to a suspended sentence at all, a court must go through the process of eliminating other possible courses such as absolute discharge, conditional discharge, probation order, fine, and then say to itself: this is a case for imprisonment, and the final question, it being a case for imprisonment: is immediate imprisonment required, or can I give a suspended sentence?"[2]

The cases given below illustrate certain points with regard to the practice of the courts in fixing the length of sentences of imprisonment. Dominant considerations are the gravity of the offence and the protection of the public, but allowance is made for circumstances peculiar to the offender. The notion of gravity is complex. It includes premeditation, the harm done, the alarm occasioned by the offence and its prevalence. In spite of the importance attached to the protection of the public, it is often of a

---

[1] For restrictions on the imprisonment of offenders under 21 see Cross and Jones, *Introduction to Criminal Law*, p. 380.

[2] *R.* v. *O'Keefe* [1969] 2 Q.B. 29; (1968), 53 Cr. App. Rep. 91, at pp. 94–95.

somewhat short-term nature for it is recognised that only the gravest instances of a particular crime merit the maximum permissible prison sentence.

"In order that there may be a proper grading of sentences to fit the many degrees of gravity presented by the various cases which fall within the same legal category, it is necessary that the maximum sentence authorised by law should be reserved for the rare offences which are exceptionally heinous, that sentences approaching the legal maximum should be reserved for offences falling within the next degree of gravity, and so on—with the result that for ordinary offences (such as form the great majority of cases coming before the courts) the heaviest sentence which the court feels justified in imposing is usually far below the maximum sentence authorised by law for the category of offence in question."[1]

It has thus come to be recognised that, within the statutory limits, there are ranges of sentence appropriate to different examples of the same offence.

The protection of the public from an offender whose record suggests that the offence is likely to be repeated is a relevant consideration within the range appropriate to the particular offence, but it is only permissible to go above the maximum permitted by that range in the case of an extended sentence. This point is elaborated in *Director of Public Prosecutions* v. *Ottewell*.[2] Although the simple notion of a normal fixed term sentence for each sub-category of offence was rejected by Lord REID, he must not be taken to have rejected the notion of a normal range of sentence with an upper and lower limit within each sub-category. Without it, certain aspects of our sentencing practice would be meaningless.[3]

---

[1] Report of the Committee on Persistent Offenders, Cmnd. 4090 (1932) para. 19.

[2] P. 366, *infra*.

[3] For example, the rule that, whereas a sentence may not be increased on account of a plea of not guilty, it may be reduced on account of a plea of guilty (see *R.* v. *De Haan* and *R.* v. *Harper*, *infra*); and the rule that in cases of dishonesty, the limits of the range appropriate to the offence may not be exceeded for therapeutic reasons (see *R.* v. *Ford* and *R.* v. *Moylan*, *infra*).

VERRIER v. DIRECTOR OF PUBLIC PROSECUTIONS

[1966] 3 All E. R. 568

(1) *Subject to any statutory provision to the contrary, the punishment for a common law misdemeanour is imprisonment at the discretion of the court.* (2) *In exceptional cases it is permissible to award a longer sentence for conspiracy to commit a crime than the maximum permitted by statute for the crime itself.* (3) *The punishment for an attempt should never exceed the maximum permitted for the crime attempted.*[1]

Facts.

Verrier and another were charged and convicted of conspiracy to obtain money from an insurance company by false pretences by alleging and making it appear that a person whose life was insured with the company had been drowned. Verrier played the leading part in the conspiracy, and he was sentenced to seven years' imprisonment although the maximum punishment for obtaining by false pretences was five years. Verrier unsuccessfully appealed against sentence to the Court of Criminal Appeal and the House of Lords.

Extracts from the Speeches of the House of Lords.

LORD PEARSON.—

" In *R.* v. *Castro*[2] the decision, as shortly summarised in the headnote, was that:

'Upon an indictment for misdemeanour containing two counts for distinct offences the defendant may be sentenced to imprisonment or penal servitude for consecutive terms of punishment, although the aggregate of the punishments may exceed the punishment allowed by law for one offence.'

In the course of his judgment BRAMWELL, L.J., said:[3]

' By the provisions of Magna Carta and the Bill of Rights judges are restrained from giving inordinate punishments; but as the common law has not drawn a limit to the punishment which may be inflicted for a misdemeanour, even

---

[1] See now Criminal Law Act 1967, s. 7(2).
[2] (1880), 5 Q. B. D. 490.
[3] *Ibid.* at pp. 509, 510.

according to the proposition urged before us no difficulty arises as to a conviction upon an indictment for misdemeanour at common law; the defendant might be sentenced at common law to seven years' imprisonment and a fine upon the first count, and to seven years' imprisonment with or without a fine upon the second count, to commence at the expiration of the sentence upon the first count.' . . .

Having regard to those authorities, and the absence of any authority on the other side, I have no doubt that, whatever the historical origin may have been, the courts have for hundreds of years had power at common law to sentence to imprisonment for misdemeanours, and the length of the imprisonment has been at large and in the discretion of the court. . . .

It is contended that from about the middle of the nineteenth century onwards there grew up a practice of not imposing imprisonment for any greater term than two years; and that the practice became by long usage so firmly settled as to be unalterable; either it hardened into a rule of law, or it came to govern, and according to the correct view should continue to govern, the exercise of the court's discretion; and therefore any sentence of imprisonment for a greater term than two years except under statute, is either unlawful or an improper exercise of discretion. . . .

Soon there came the case of *R.* v. *Morris,*[1] which was decided in 1950. HALLETT, J., at assizes passed a sentence of imprisonment for four years for the common law misdemeanour of conspiracy. On appeal to the Court of Criminal Appeal the argument for the appellant was that there was no record for over a century of a sentence of imprisonment for a common law misdemeanour exceeding two years, and that limit had become part of the common law by long usage. The Court of Criminal Appeal in a judgment delivered by Lord GODDARD, C.J., rejected this argument, holding that the duration of the term of imprisonment for a common law misdemeanour always was and still is at the discretion of the court. He said:

'Of late years the courts have been very reluctant to impose a penalty more severe than that of two years' imprisonment, but that has been because, until the reforms which took place during the latter part of the nineteenth century, imprisonment was a severe punishment . . . The Penal Servitude Act, 1891, s. 1(2) provided that when a sentence

[1] [1951] 1 K. B. 394; [1950] 2 All E. R. 965.

of penal servitude was prescribed by a statute a sentence of not exceeding two years' imprisonment could be given instead. That is why courts frequently gave sentences of imprisonment for not more than two years for offences for which penal servitude up to fourteen years, or penal servitude for life, could be given, but that did not affect their right to give longer sentences of imprisonment for common law misdemeanours. The law was that such misdemeanours could be punished by terms of imprisonment at the discretion of the courts, and there is no statute which has taken that power from the court.' . . .

In *R.* v. *Boal, R.* v. *Wilson, R.* v. *Field*,[1] LAWTON, J., delivering the judgment of the Court of Criminal Appeal said:

'Even if the object of the conspiracy had been the obstruction of the police, which it was not, in the circumstances of this case the fact of the unlawful combination of these appellants to achieve that end would have changed its character and so enhanced its mischief that the joint act might properly be treated as a different and more serious crime. In putting its reasons in those words, the court has applied to the facts of this case a well-known passage in the *Law of Criminal Conspiracies and Agreements* by R. S. Wright (1873), p. 83 . . . There is in the book another passage at pp. 81, 82, which can be used as indicating factors to be taken into account in deciding whether the conspiracy is a crime different from and more serious than the substantive offence. The passage is this:

'There may be cases in which the agreement or concurrence of several persons in the execution of a criminal design is a proper ground for aggravation of their punishment beyond what would be proper in the case of a sole defendant. Such would be cases in which the cooperation of several persons at different places is likely to facilitate the execution or the concealment of a crime, or in which the presence of several persons together is intended to increase the means of force or to create terror, or cases of fraud in which suspicion and ordinary caution are likely to be disarmed by the increased credibility of a representation made by several persons.' . . .

(iii) I cannot imagine any case in which it would be right to give a greater sentence for an attempt than could be given for the substantive offence. It was held to be

[1] [1965] 1 Q. B. 402; [1964] 3 All E. R. 269; p. 357 *infra*.

wrong in *R.* v. *Pearce*,[1] and I agree with the reasons given in that case."

APPEAL DISMISSED.

R. v. BLAKE

(1961) 45 Cr. App. Rep. 292

Consecutive sentences may be passed for a number of offences even though the total exceeds the maximum permitted for any one of them.

Facts.

Blake pleaded guilty to five offences under the Official Secrets Acts, each of which carried a maximum of fourteen years' imprisonment. In the case of three of them he was sentenced to consecutive periods of fourteen years' imprisonment, and in the case of the other two, to periods of fourteen years' imprisonment to run concurrently with the others. Blake unsuccessfully appealed to the Court of Criminal Appeal against his total of forty-two years' imprisonment.

Extracts from the Judgment of the Court of Criminal Appeal.

HILBERY, J.—

" On his behalf it was expressly stated by Mr. Hutchinson (counsel for the appellant) that his application for leave to appeal against that sentence was not based on any point of law, and the application did not, therefore, involve a question of law. His contention was that the sentence was wrong in principle and, furthermore, in the particular circumstances of this case was manifestly excessive. In support of the argument that the sentence was wrong in principle his contention in the first place was that s. 8(1) of the Official Secrets Act, 1920, provided a maximum sentence of fourteen years for an offence against the Act such as was alleged in each of the counts in this indictment, and that to pass consecutive sentences of fourteen years was to evade the limit in the Act. The answer to this is that there is no settled principle that a judge may not pass consecutive sentences of fourteen years where each offence charged in

---

[1] [1953] 1 Q. B. 30; [1952] 2 All E. R. 718.

each count is separate and distinct. Whether the sentences shall be concurrent in such circumstances or consecutive is a matter for the judge to determine in the exercise of his discretion. This discretion is not limited so as to prevent the judge awarding consecutive sentences which will total more than the maximum permitted for any one of the offences taken by itself.

Mr. Hutchinson pressed upon us evidence given by the Home Office before the Royal Commission on Capital Punishment, which showed that, where a life sentence is now passed, it is usual for the Home Office, in the exercise of the powers given to the Home Secretary under section 27(1)[1] of the Prison Act, 1952, to release on licence any prisoner on whom is passed a sentence of life imprisonment after ten years, and that, as that was so, no court ought by making sentences consecutive to pass a sentence which would be longer than the one which he would in practice serve if sentenced to life imprisonment. One answer to this is that where, as in the case of non-capital murder, the statute enacts that the sentence shall be one of life imprisonment, this court passes that sentence giving the words of the statute their natural and ordinary meaning, and that sentence remains the sentence upon the prisoner, the Home Secretary having no power to alter it. The only power, under s. 27 of the Prison Act, 1952, which the Home Secretary has is power to release the prisoner on licence with power, however, to recall him at any time to serve the rest of his sentence. The sentence remains what it is, one for life. Furthermore, this court, in passing such a sentence, has no regard to the possibilities of the exercise by the Home Secretary of his power to let a prisoner out on licence. It has been laid down by this court that in passing sentence a court should not pay any regard to the fact that nowadays a prisoner serving his sentence by good conduct may earn remission,[2] so that he may in practice be confined to prison for a much shorter time than the length of sentence passed upon him, and there is no logical distinction between taking into consideration the possibility of remission for good conduct and the possibility of remission through the Home Secretary's exercising his discretion to allow out on licence and to shorten the period of the prisoner's confinement."

APPLICATION REFUSED.

---

[1] See now Criminal Justice Act, 1967, s. 61.
[2] See *R.* v. *Maguire* (1956), 40 Cr. App. Rep. 92.

R. v. TURNER

(1966), 51 Cr. App. Rep. 72

Remission may be taken into account when reform or treatment is under consideration.

Facts.

Turner had been convicted of arson and similar offences. He was sentenced to five years' imprisonment on the footing that he required mental treatment for a period of about three years. The sentence was affirmed by the Court of Appeal.

Extracts from the Judgments of the Court of Appeal.

LORD PARKER, C.J.—

"... if he is to have treatment for three years, something which is in his best interests, the sentence of this court, bearing in mind remission under the present rules, must be in the nature of five years. It is no doubt true that when one is considering punishment it is quite wrong for the court to take into consideration matters of remission, but it has long been recognised that when one is considering not punishment but considering reform or mental treatment, something which is in the interests of the prisoner, it would be obviously right for this court to take remission into consideration. In those circumstances, it seems to this court that the approach of the learned judge was entirely correct, and that the sentence that he proposed of five years was in this case the appropriate sentence."

APPEAL DISMISSED.

R. v. BALL

(1951), 35 Cr. App. Rep. 164

It is sometimes proper to differentiate between co-defendants even when the facts of their offences are similar and their records are similar.

Facts.

The appellant pleaded guilty to three charges of burglary and asked for five other offences to be taken into consideration. He was sentenced to five years' imprisonment. He had been charged with another person who was older than he was and had an equally bad record; nonetheless that other person, for special reasons, had been put on probation for three years.

The appellant unsuccessfully appealed against sentence to the Court of Criminal Appeal.

Extracts from the Judgment of the Court of Criminal Appeal.

HILBERY, J.—

" In deciding the appropriate sentence a Court should always be guided by certain considerations. The first and foremost is the public interest. The criminal law is publicly enforced, not only with the object of punishing crime, but also in the hope of preventing it. A proper sentence, passed in public, serves the public interest in two ways. It may deter others who might be tempted to try crime as seeming to offer easy money on the supposition, that if the offender is caught and brought to justice, the punishment will be negligible. Such a sentence may also deter the particular criminal from committing a crime again, or induce him to turn from a criminal to an honest life. The public interest is indeed served, and best served, if the offender is induced to turn from criminal ways to honest living. Our law does not, therefore, fix the sentence for a particular crime, but fixes a maximum sentence and leaves it to the Court to decide what is, within that maximum, the appropriate sentence for each criminal in the particular circumstances of each case. Not only in regard to each crime, but in regard to each criminal, the Court has the right and the duty to decide whether to be lenient or severe.

It is for these reasons, and with these purposes in view, that before passing sentence the Court hears evidence of the antecedents and character of every convicted person. It follows that when two persons are convicted together of a crime or series of crimes in which they have been acting in concert, it may be right, and very often is right, to discriminate between the two and to be lenient to the one and not to the other. The background, antecedents and character of the one and his whole bearing in Court may indicate a chance of reform if leniency is extended, whereas it may seem that only a harsh lesson is likely to make the other stop in his criminal career. The argument that a severe sentence on one prisoner must be unjust because his fellow prisoner, who was convicted of the same crime, received a light sentence or none at all, has neither validity nor force. The differentiation in treatment is justified if the Court, in considering the public interest has regard to the differences in the characters and antecedents of the two convicted men and discriminates between them because of those differences."

APPEAL DISMISSED.

R. v. FORD

[1969] 3 All E.R. 782n

In cases of dishonesty the judge ought not to add a period to that which he considers to be the correct sentence for the offence in the hope that the accused will be cured of alcoholism.

Facts.

Ford, who had a bad record which was partly attributable to alcoholism pleaded guilty to housebreaking and was sentenced to 27 months' imprisonment. His co-accused, who also had a bad record, pleaded guilty to the same housebreaking and to another offence; he received concurrent sentences amounting to 12 months' imprisonment. The Recorder who imposed the sentences was influenced by the consideration that Ford might be cured of his alcoholism by a longer period of imprisonment, although there was evidence that Ford would not be cooperative.

Ford appealed against sentence to the Court of Appeal and his sentence was reduced to twelve months' imprisonment.

Extracts from the Judgment of the Court of Appeal.

SACHS, J.—

" In those circumstances the intention of the learned Recorder that he should receive a cure during his imprisonment obviously cannot be implemented, and this court has simply to deal with the matter on the basis of what is the appropriate sentence. The appropriate sentence is 12 months' imprisonment.

This court only desires to add one further thing. In relation to offences of dishonesty sentences of imprisonment —except where there is an element of protection of the public involved—are normally intended to be the correct sentence for the particular crime, and not to include a curative element. This court wishes to make it clear that what it is now saying has nothing to do with the special cases such as those of possessing dangerous drugs or cases where the protection of the public is involved; but it seems to this court that in the case now under consideration the learned Recorder (with the best of intentions) adopted a wrong principle when approaching the question of sentence."

SENTENCE REDUCED ON APPEAL.[1]

R. v. WILSON

(1964), 48 Cr. App. Rep. 329

(1) *Minor differences between the different offenders can be ignored when the crime is a very serious one.* (2) *Severely deterrent sentences are proper when the crime takes the form of organised banditry against society.*

Facts.

Wilson and others were convicted of robbery and conspiracy to rob. They were participants in the robbery of a mail train from which they procured more than two and a half million pounds. Concurrent sentences of thirty and twenty-five years' imprisonment were imposed by EDMUND DAVIES, J., for the robbery and conspiracy respectively. The following extracts from what was said by EDMUND DAVIES, J., when imposing the sentences are taken from *The Times* of April 17th 1964.

Having given a lesser sentence to one who gave information to the police and confessed his guilt, EDMUND DAVIES, J., said to Wilson:

---

[1] This case was followed in *R.* v. *Moylan,* [1969] 3 All E.R. 783, where WIDGERY, L.J., in delivering the judgment of the Court of Appeal said: " In our judgment, in cases of dishonesty where there is, as it were, a background of alcoholism, in respect of the accused the court must first determine what are the limits of a proper sentence in respect of the offences charged. Within those limits it may be perfectly proper to increase the sentence in order to enable a cure to be undertaken whilst the accused is in prison. But on the authority of *R.* v. *Ford* (*supra*) it is clear that it is not correct to increase the sentence above that within the appropriate range of the offence itself merely in order to provide an opportunity to cure."

"No one has said less than you throughout this long trial. Indeed I doubt if you have spoken a half dozen words. Certainly no word of repentance has been expressed by you. I bear in mind those matters which learned counsel has urged on your behalf. My duty as I conceive it is clear. If you or any of the other accused still to be dealt with, had assisted justice, that would have told strongly in your favour. You have not and the consequence of this outrageous crime is that the vast body of something like £2,500,000 still remains almost entirely unrecovered."

WILSON'S APPEAL TO THE COURT OF CRIMINAL APPEAL AGAINST SENTENCE WAS DISMISSED.

Extracts from the Judgment of the Court of Criminal Appeal.

FENTON ATKINSON, J.—

> "In recent years there have been far too many cases of unarmed and defenceless men in charge of wages or other valuables being brutally attacked and robbed by gangs of armed men. All such robberies are grave crimes and in a number of such cases this court has approved sentences of up to fifteen years' imprisonment, but we have to deal here with an armed robbery of enormous and quite exceptional gravity, differing from the ordinary type of case, not only in degree but also in kind. There is the number of men engaged, the extent of the planning and preparation for the crime and the object of attack. To stop, attack and rob a mail train would have been a crime of immense seriousness even if the money stolen had been a one-hundredth part of what in fact it was. This was, as my brother LAWTON said during the argument, an act of organised banditry directed at a vital public service and it had the character of an act of warfare against the community, touching new depths of lawlessness for which the type of sentence normally imposed for armed robbery is in our view inadequate. In our judgment, severely deterrent sentences were necessary, not only to protect the community against these men for a very long time, but also to demonstrate as clearly as possible to others tempted to follow them into lawlessness on this vast scale that if they are brought to trial and convicted, commensurate punishment will follow, and that being so, for the reasons given recently by this court in the case of *R.* v. *Curbishley* (1964), *Times*, May 14th, minor differences

between these men in age and record become in our view irrelevant. Certainly there was no one of them who could claim any favourable consideration for assisting the course of justice or restoring any of the proceeds of their crime which, if we accept some of the submissions made to us, they will be free to enjoy in some ten years from now. The maximum sentence on count 2 was imprisonment for life and such a sentence might well have been imposed. Certainly, in our view, sentences approximating to the maximum are fully justified, not because those who rob a mail train are necessarily worse men than others who commit certain other types of crime for which lesser penalties are laid down, but because of the grave threat that such crimes as this present to the public as a whole."

APPEAL DISMISSED.

R. v. JONES

(1971), 56 Cr.App.Rep. 212

In fixing the length of a prison sentence the court will have regard to the harm done by an offence and its wickedness even though there is no likelihood of its being repeated.

Facts.

The appellant pleaded guilty to child stealing and was sentenced by the trial judge to three years' imprisonment. She was a single woman of 24 who had had an affair with a man and become pregnant by him. The man had indicated that he did not wish to have anything more to do with her or her child. Having had a spontaneous miscarriage she thought that he might be induced to resume his association with her if she produced a child and said it was hers by him. She took a baby from its pram left outside a chemist's shop in which its mother was shopping. She denied any preconceived intention and looked after the child well while she had possession of it. She took steps to have it registered as hers, and endeavoured to conceal it from the police when they interviewed her. The police ultimately recovered the child after the appellant had had possession of it for five weeks.

While of opinion that the trial judge had not erred in principle, the Court of Appeal reduced the sentence to one of eighteeen months as an act of mercy

Extracts from the Judgment of the Court of Appeal.

LORD WIDGERY, C.J.—

" The Medical Officer says in this report, and repeats in stronger terms in a later report, a factor which is of considerable importance to the public as well as to this appellant, namely that this kind of offence arises from quite a unique combination of circumstances, and that there does not tend to be any tendency to repetition. He puts it a little more strongly in his second report when he says: ' I am quite satisfied that there is no likelihood of her committing any further offences of this nature.' The Court thinks it right to stress those passages, because clearly one factor in deciding on the disposal of this appellant today would be the probability or improbability of other mothers losing their babies in the same way. One can at least take some comfort from the positive view of this experienced Medical Officer that this appellant is not likely to do this kind of thing again, because the motivation for the offence arises from quite unique circumstances.

The Court must then on that material before it do its best to decide what is the proper judgment in this case. If one sought to ensure the punishment of this appellant for the injury which she had done to the child's natural parents, one would hardly think that three years' imprisonment was too long. The great suffering which Mr. and Mrs. Weller must have endured really beggars description. In the same way, if one set out to measure the sentence in relation to the public mischief caused by 200 policemen investigating in 25,000 houses the possible disposition of this child, one cannot but think that three years was hardly too long. Again one must consider how far this was a purely impulsive offence, an offence committed perhaps under an overwhelming impulse almost incapable of resistance. The Court would be very ready to accept that the initial taking of the child was largely, at any rate, dictated by that kind of impulse which perhaps this appellant found it difficult to resist. But, of course, the child was not brought back in twenty-four or forty-eight hours, as might perhaps have followed from an impulsive taking. The child, as the Court has stressed, was kept for five weeks, and throughout that five weeks was kept in circumstances which indicated that its permanent retention was intended and the Court feels driven to the conclusion that however impulsive the original taking was, that impulsive action deteriorated into a measure of wickedness before September 3rd when the child was recovered again. We have considered this matter with care, and we have come to the conclusion that the sentence of three years for this kind of offence, when supported by such deliberate intention to retain the child, is not in principle an excessive sentence. We are not prepared to say that the learned trial judge was wrong in the assessment that he made of this matter. But we are moved by Mr. Comyn's address to us, that this is perhaps a case in which this Court, now that matters have cooled down a little, might show a measure of mercy which the trial judge found it impossible to show. We would not do this if we thought there was the slightest risk of other children being stolen by this woman in the same way. The fact that that is ruled out by the experienced doctor is an extremely important factor in our decision. In the circumstances we do find it possible, as a matter of mercy and nothing else, to reduce this sentence."

SENTENCE REDUCED.

R. v. LUCKHURST

(1971), 56 Cr.App.Rep. 209)

In fixing the length of a prison sentence for burglary, the court has regard to the misery caused by the offence.

Facts.

The appellant was given sentences totalling three years' imprisonment for three burglaries and an assault connected with one of the burglaries; he also asked for eleven other burglaries to be taken into consideration. He only had one previous conviction which was for obtaining property by deception. He was a married man with a good work record, and the crimes were committed in order to get money when he became unemployed. The appeal against sentence was dismissed.

Extracts from the Judgment of the Court of Appeal.

BEAN, J.—

" One of the difficulties of this type of case is that this appellant, from all the Court knows about him from the helpful probation report, is a man of good average intelligence. He was a skilled worker, yet, on virtually the first occasion in a long period of years when he found himself without employment, he resorted to crime. No fewer than fourteen different households in the Sheffield area were the subject of visits from him. On one occasion he used quite serious violence. The accumulated amount of misery that these offences must have caused to the families who were concerned, to their immediate neighbours who live in fear and to relatives and friends who heard about it, needs no exaggeration from this Court. Burglary is too often lightly referred to as 'just another crime' and not sufficient account is given to the misery and subsequent fear that result from it.

This was a short but a grave, considered outburst of crime by this man in order to get money. He refused to face up to his domestic problems and chose rather to seek money illegally. In the judgment of this Court, the sentences imposed by the Recorder were proper in the circumstances and this appeal is dismissed."

APPEAL DISMISSED.

R. v. GUNNELL

(1966), 50 Cr.App.Rep. 242

Even though the case is one in which a hospital order could be made, the court may sentence an offender to imprisonment as a punishment.

Facts.

Gunnell was convicted of two attempted rapes and four rapes all on different women. The crimes were accompanied by threats of great violence. Gunnell had a long record of mental disorder, there was medical evidence to warrant the making of a hospital order under s. 60 of the Mental Health Act, 1959, and a place was available at Rampton, a maximum security mental hospital. Nonetheless the trial judge sentenced Gunnell to imprisonment for life.

Gunnell unsuccessfully appealed to the Court of Criminal Appeal against sentence and that court expressed complete agreement with the following remarks made by the trial judge when passing sentence.

Extract from the Remarks of the Trial Judge.

ROSKILL, J.—

"It has been urged upon me that I should deal with you by making a hospital order and sending you to Rampton, where you would be kept in secure conditions and receive any treatment which you may require. In many cases it is clearly right for a court in discharging its responsibilities to have regard solely or mainly to the needs of the offender, but the present case in my view is one of such magnitude that I cannot only have regard to such needs. It is true that to send you to Rampton would involve you being kept under secure conditions and to that extent would keep the public from you. But there are other matters which I must take into account in the public interest, not the least of which is to make it clear that crimes of this kind committed against ordinary housewives in their ordinary homes doing their everyday business while their menfolk are away at work are such as must when brought home to a particular offender be dealt with in such a way as to make it plain that the law is concerned and ever will be concerned to protect people who suffer as you caused those women to suffer by these quite appalling sexual attacks which you made upon them. Punishment must be an element in this case and that punishment can only be achieved by imprisonment."

APPEAL DISMISSED.

R. v. BAKER AND HAWKINS

(1966), 51 Cr. App. Rep. 74

An exemplary sentence is permissible even though the offenders are young and have a clean record.

Facts.

Baker and Hawkins were convicted of unlawful wounding of police officers at a dance. They had behaved with great violence and brutality. They were sentenced to three years of imprisonment and the sentences were upheld by the Court of Appeal.

Extracts from the Judgment of the Court of Appeal.

LORD PARKER, C.J.—

"Now these are young men—Baker is twenty and Hawkins is nineteen—and the tragedy in many ways is that they are two young men with most excellent work records and in the case of Baker an absolutely clean record and in the case of Hawkins a fine of £10 about a year ago for using threatening behaviour. These are very serious crimes and it must be remembered in times of this sort that the court is not by any means solely or even mainly concerned with the prisoners themselves, but rather their object is to wipe out, stamp out, this sort of offence. The learned judge said: 'The public is sick and tired of people like you, the public is sick and tired of having its entertainment broken up by hooligans, and absolutely appalled at the mentality which produces the bottle and the boot. I do not like making examples of young men, particularly young men who have a good work record, but this particular kind of offence is becoming very common.' The court can do no more than entirely endorse what the learned judge said."

APPEALS DISMISSED.

R. v. DE HAAN

[1967] 3 All E. R. 618

In fixing sentence it is right to give the accused credit for pleading guilty but wrong to add anything to the sentence on account of the fact that he pleaded not guilty.

Facts.

The appellant changed his plea to one of guilty in the course of his trial for housebreaking and larceny. He was sentenced to two and a half years' imprisonment on one count and two years on the other count, the sentences to be concurrent. He successfully appealed against sentence to the Court of Appeal who reduced his total sentences to three years.

Extracts from the Judgment of the Court of Appeal (Criminal Division).

EDMUND DAVIES, L.J.—

"It is undoubtedly right that a confession of guilt should tell in favour of an accused person,[1] for that is clearly in the public interest. We have come to the conclusion that, taking an all-round view of the circumstances of this case, to sentence the appellant, grave though the offences are and bad though his record is, to four and a half years is to give inadequate consideration to that mitigating element."

APPEAL ALLOWED.

---

[1] The fact that an accused pleads not guilty should not tell against him. In *R.* v. *Harper*, [1967] 3 All E.R. 619, n. (C.A.), the appellant, who had been charged on several counts, had pleaded not guilty but had been convicted on one count of receiving stolen goods from youths, who were aged fifteen to eighteen; the appellant had been sentenced to five years' imprisonment. He appealed against sentence. It appeared that he had not instigated the receiving, though he had been receiving stolen goods from at any rate one of the youths for some years. The recorder, before sentencing the appellant said:

"The defence which you instructed your counsel to run involved allegations of perjury by prosecuting witnesses, intimidation, threats and improper behaviour by senior police officers, and allegations that two boys who pleaded guilty and have been punished for breaking into (the house) were telling lies."

The recorder had continued by saying that the appellant's behaviour showed that he had no remorse and was sorry only because he had been caught.

Lord PARKER, C.J., giving judgment on the appeal, referred to the passage quoted above and to the recorder's observation that followed it, and said:

"This court feels that there is a real danger that the appellant was being given what was undoubtedly a serious sentence because he had pleaded not guilty and had run his defence in the way indicated by the recorder. This court feels that it is quite improper to use language which may convey that an accused is being sentenced because he has pleaded not guilty or because he has run his defence in a particular way. It is, however, proper to give an accused a lesser sentence if he has shown genuine remorse, amongst other things by pleading guilty."

The Court of Appeal allowed the appellant's appeal against sentence and reduced the sentence of five years to three years' imprisonment.

DIRECTOR OF PUBLIC PROSECUTIONS v. OTTEWELL

[1968] 3 All E.R. 153

An "extended term of imprisonment" under s. 37(2) *of the Criminal Justice Act,* 1967[1], *means a term extended beyond that which the judge would have imposed were it not for the provisions of s.* 37; *a judge may therefore pass an extended sentence of imprisonment for a term shorter than the maximum permitted for the offence.*

Facts.

Ottewell was convicted of two assaults causing actual bodily harm, offences for which the maximum punishment is five years' imprisonment. The trial judge passed consecutive sentences of two years' imprisonment for each offence certifying his sentence as an extended sentence. Ottewell appealed to the Court of Appeal. The Court of Appeal held that the length of sentence was appropriate for the offences, but discharged the extended sentence certificate on the ground that an extended sentence could only be imposed for a term in excess of the maximum permitted for the offence. The Director of Public Prosecutions appealed to the House of Lords on the question of the construction of s. 37(2) of the Criminal Justice Act, 1967, and the House held that an extended sentence might be passed for a term less than the maximum permitted for the offence.

---

[1] The following are the relevant subsections of s. 37:

"(2) Where an offender is convicted on indictment of an offence punishable with imprisonment for a term of two years or more, and the conditions specified in subsection (4) of this section are satisfied, then, if the court is satisfied, by reason of his previous conduct and of the likelihood of his committing further offences, that it is expedient to protect the public from him for a substantial time, the court may impose an extended term of imprisonment under this section.

(3) The extended term which may be imposed under this section for any offence may exceed the maximum term authorised for the offence apart from this section if the maximum so authorised is less than ten years, but shall not exceed ten years if the maximum so authorised is less than ten years or exceed five years if the maximum so authorised is less than five years."

Extracts from the Speeches of the House of Lords.

LORD REID.—

" The difficulty in interpreting this section is caused by the fact that there is no definition or explanation of what is meant by an extended term. So the question immediately suggests itself—extended beyond what? Three possible answers have been suggested: first, extended beyond the term which the judge would have imposed if s. 37(2) had not been enacted; secondly, extended by virtue of the provisions of s. 37(3) beyond the maximum term otherwise authorised by law; and thirdly, extended beyond the normal sentence for that type of crime.

I reject the last alternative without hesitation. It was rather tentatively suggested by the learned Attorney-General that there is a ' tariff ' for each kind of offence which is varied upwards or downwards according to the circumstances of the offence and the character of the accused. Offences of a particular kind vary so vastly, however, in gravity that there cannot and should not be any ' normal ' sentence, and there is no workable standard by which to judge whether any particular sentence is extended beyond what is ' normal '.

It is more difficult to determine which of the other two suggested meanings is correct. The Court of Appeal (Criminal Division)[1] chose the second, . . . It is only towards the end of their judgment that they deal with what I have called the first meaning. Apparently, the argument for it was not elaborated because they say:[2]

' It is suggested that, to protect the public, a sentencing court might, for example, add twelve months to the sentence which it would otherwise have imposed, and in this way impose an extended term of imprisonment.'

They state their main reasons for rejecting this ' suggestion ' as follows:

' The difficulty in giving effect to this suggestion is that (as has already been stated) courts have for a long time felt themselves entitled to lengthen a sentence for the express purpose of protecting the public, and accordingly on this footing sub-s. (2) confers no new power.'

So it is necessary to enquire to what extent the Court of Appeal (Criminal Division) did permit a sentence to be lengthened for this purpose.

---

[1] [1968] 2 All E.R. 593.
[2] [1968] 2 All E.R. at p. 597.

In *R.* v. *Boardman* and *R.* v. *Powis*[1] the two accused were convicted of stealing. The former who had a clean record was sentenced to twelve months' imprisonment; the latter who had a bad record was sentenced to five years' imprisonment. The court stated that having regard to the disparity of the sentences and to the remarks of the chairman it was quite clear that Powis was sentenced very largely on his past record. That seemed very much like punishing him again for his previous crimes. Boardman because of his record had some claim to a degree of leniency which was absent in the case of Powis; but withholding leniency was one thing and inflicting heavier punishment for a record was another. So the sentence on Powis was reduced to two years' imprisonment.

In *R.* v. *Connolly*[2] the accused had stolen letters worth sixpence; but he was a confirmed thief and a pest to society. He was sentenced to five years' imprisonment, but that was reduced on appeal to eighteen months. The court stated that if preventive detention were not imposed in cases of this sort the sentence must bear some relation to the gravity of the offence.

In *R.* v. *Reid*[3] the accused, a persistent offender, had obtained £2 by false pretences. He was sentenced to five years' imprisonment, but this was reduced on appeal to eighteen months. The court said that it was wrong to increase the sentence for a trivial offence by reference to offences in the past for which a man had already paid the penalty. If quarter sessions had thought that preventive detention was the appropriate sentence then such a sentence should have been passed; if not, they should have passed a sentence commensurate with the gravity of the offence.

These cases show that with regard to imprisonment, unlike preventive detention, the previous power to extend a sentence for the purpose of protecting the public from the persistent offender was severely limited. It was regarded as improper to extend a sentence of imprisonment beyond a term which bore some relation to the gravity of the last offence: anything beyond that was regarded as additional punishment for previous offences, and that of course would be improper. In my judgment, however, s. 37(2) of the Criminal Justice Act, 1967, is designed to remove that limitation and

---

[1] [1958] Crim. L.R. 626.
[2] [1959] Crim. L.R. 530.
[3] [1960] Crim. L.R. 276.

to authorise an extended term, not as punishment for the last offence nor as additional punishment for previous offences, but for the purpose stated in the section, *i.e.* the protection of the public from the persistent offender for a substantial time."

LORD DONOVAN.—

" As ASHWORTH, J., indicated in his judgment, judges have always (and I think rightly) felt themselves entitled to deal with a persistent offender by increasing the sentence which they would have passed if he were not. This is not to punish the offender again for his past crimes. Nor is it always primarily for the protection of the public. It may simply be because in the judge's view the sentences passed for previous offences have proved to be an insufficient deterrent and that the effect of a longer sentence must be tried, perhaps in the offender's own interests; or, it may be that repetition has itself increased the gravity of the offence. Eventually, in some cases, a stage is reached where it becomes clear that progressively increasing sentences are not a deterrent; and the protection of the public against a persistent offender then comes to the forefront of the considerations which the judge must take into account. The Criminal Justice Act, 1948, prescribed preventive detention for some such cases. The Criminal Justice Act, 1967, abolished preventive detention but prescribed the ' extended term of imprisonment '."

APPEAL ALLOWED.

ADDENDUM

R. v. FEELY[1]

The question whether an appropriation is dishonest within the meaning of s. 1(1) *of the Theft Act* 1968[2] *is a question of fact to be determined by a jury when there is one.*

Facts.

Feely was a branch manager of a firm of bookmakers who, like other employees of the firm, had received a circular from his employers forbidding him to borrow their money by taking it from the till. He took about £30 from a safe at his branch in order to give it to his father. When the deficiency was discovered, Feely gave an IOU to his successor as branch manager and said that he intended to repay the sum, taking it out of money due to him from his employers, who in fact owed him about twice that amount.

Feely was charged with theft and convicted after the judge had directed the jury that it is dishonest for an employee to do what he knows his employers are not prepared to tolerate, but had failed to make it plain to the jury that it was for them to decide whether the accused's conduct was in fact dishonest. Feely successfully appealed to the Court of Appeal who quashed his conviction on the ground that the question whether an appropriation was dishonest is one of fact.

Extracts from the Judgment of the Court of Appeal.

LAWTON, L.J.—

"... In s. 1(1) of the Theft Act, 1968 the word 'dishonestly' can only relate to the state of mind of the person who does the act which amounts to appropriation. Whether an accused person has a particular state of mind is a question of fact which has to be decided by the jury when there is a

---

[1] [1973] 1 All E.R. 341.
[2] P. 267, *supra*.

trial on indictment and by the justices when there are summary proceedings. The Crown did not dispute this proposition, but it was submitted that in some cases (and this, it was said, was such a one) it was necessary for the trial judge to define 'dishonestly' and when the facts fell within the definition he had a duty to tell the jury that if there had been an appropriation it must have been dishonestly done. We do not agree that judges should define what 'dishonestly' means.

This word is in common use whereas the word 'fraudulently' which was used in s. 1(1) of the Larceny Act, 1916, had acquired as a result of case law a special meaning. Jurors, when deciding whether an appropriation was dishonest can be reasonably expected to, and should, apply the current standards of ordinary decent people. In their own lives they have to decide what is and what is not dishonest. We can see no reason why, when in a jury box, they should require the help of a judge to tell them what amounts to dishonesty. We are fortified in this opinion by a passage in the speech of Lord REID in *Brutus* v. *Cozens*,[1] a case in which the words 'insulting behaviour' in s. 5 of the Public Order Act, 1936 had to be construed. The Divisional Court[2] had adjudged that the meaning of the word 'insulting' in this statutory context was a matter of law. Lord REID's comment was as follows:

'In my judgment that is not right. The meaning of an ordinary word of the English language is not a question of law. The proper construction of a statute is a question of law. If the context shows that a word is used in an unusual sense the court will determine in other words what that unusual sense is. But there is in my opinion no question of the word 'insulting' being used in any unusual sense . . . It is for the tribunal which decides the case to consider, not as law but as fact, whether in the whole circumstances the words of the statute do or do not as a matter of ordinary usage of the English language cover or apply to the facts which have been proved.'

When this trenchant statement of principle is applied to the word 'dishonestly' in s. 1(1) of the Theft Act, 1968, and to the facts of this case it is clear in our judgment that the jury should have been left to decide whether the appellant's alleged taking of the money had been dishonest. They were not, with the result that a verdict of guilty was returned

---

1 [1972] 2 All E.R. 1297.
2 [1972] 2 All E.R. 1.

without their having given thought to what was probably the most important issue in the case . . .

It is possible to imagine a case of taking by an employee in breach of instructions to which no-one would, or could reasonably, attach moral obloquy; for example, that of a manager of a shop, who having been told that under no circumstances was he to take money from the till for his own purposes, took 40p from it, having no small change himself, to pay for a taxi hired by his wife who had arrived at the shop saying that she only had a £5 note which the cabby could not change. To hold that such a man was a thief and to say that his intention to put the money back in the till when he acquired some change was at the most a matter of mitigation would tend to bring the law into contempt. In our judgment a taking to which no moral obloquy can reasonably attach is not within the concept of stealing either at common law or under the Theft Act, 1968 . . .

If the principle enunciated in *R.* v. *Cockburn*[1] was right there would be a strange divergence between the position of a man who obtains cash by passing a cheque on an account which has no funds to meet it and one who takes money from a till. The man who passes the cheque is deemed in law not to act dishonestly if he genuinely believes on reasonable grounds that when it is presented to the paying bank there will be funds to meet it: see *Halstead* v. *Patel*,[2] *per* Lord WIDGERY, C.J. But, according to the decision in *R.* v. *Cockburn*,[3] the man who takes money from a till intending to put it back and genuinely believing on reasonable grounds that he will be able to do so (see *per* WINN, L.J.) should be convicted of theft. Lawyers may be able to appreciate why one man should be adjudged to be a criminal and the other not; but we doubt whether anyone else would. People who take money from tills and the like without permission are usually thieves; but if they do not admit that they are by pleading guilty, it is for the jury, not the judge, to decide whether they have acted dishonestly."

APPEAL ALLOWED. CONVICTION QUASHED.

Comment on R. v. Feely

This case is included in an addendum because it was reported after the rest of the book was in print. It gets rid of the difficulty

---

[1] [1968] 1 All E.R. 466.
[2] [1972] 2 All E.R. 147 at 152; p. 282 *supra*.
[3] [1968] 1 All E.R. 466.

created by the judgment in *R.* v. *Cockburn,* discussed on p. 193 of Cross and Jones' *Introduction to Criminal Law,* 7th Edn. It would be wrong to treat *Feely*'s case as authority for the proposition that, as a matter of law, a person must have reasonable grounds for his belief that he would be able to repay, in order to prevent an appropriation with the intention of doing so from being dishonest; but the reasonableness of the belief is, of course, of the utmost evidential importance when the existence of a genuine intention to repay is under consideration (*c.f. R.* v. *Waterfall,* p. 283, *supra*).

INDEX

A

B

C

E